They Bo

Wounds of

The Mystery of the
Sacred Stigmata

By Michael Freze, S.F.O.

Our Sunday Visitor Publishing Division
Our Sunday Visitor, Inc.
Huntington, Indiana 46750

Our Sunday Visitor Publishing Division
Our Sunday Visitor, Inc.
200 Noll Plaza
Huntington, Indiana 46750

INTERNATIONAL STANDARD BOOK NUMBER: 0-87973-422-1
LIBRARY OF CONGRESS CATALOG CARD NUMBER: 89-60271

PRINTED IN THE UNITED STATES OF AMERICA

Cover design by Rodney Needler

Dedication

To St. Francis of Assisi, Padre Pio of Pietrelcina and to Therese Neumann of Konnersreuth, who faithfully carried the Cross of our Lord in a true spirit of love and devotion: if I have been able to help promote your cause and your mission, then God has answered my prayers and blessed me enormously. May you all watch over us and grant us God's grace and His peace, under the protective mantle of our Mother Mary, whose love you cherished all through your lives.

To all my Franciscan brothers and sisters, wherever you may be, I wish you the peace of St. Francis and my fraternal love. . .

Contents

Rose of Lima, St. Margaret Mary Alacoque, St. Veronica Giuliani, St. Mary Frances of the Five Wounds • Modern Stigmatists (18th-20th Centuries): Anne Catherine Emmerich, Louise Lateau, St. Gemma Galgani, Josefa Menendez, Mary Rose Ferron, Sr. Faustina Kowalska, Berthe Petit, Alexandrina da Costa, Therese Neumann, Adrienne von Speyr, Padre Pio of Pietrelcina, Marthe Robin • Living Stigmatists: A Special Report

Acknowledgments

I would like to extend my thanks and deep gratitude to Fathers Joseph Martin, O.F.M. Cap. and Alessio Parente, O.F.M. Cap. for their permission to quote anything I deemed important from the writings that have been published out of San Giovanni Rotondo concerning the promotion of Padre Pio. Their kindness to me and their cooperation during my summer 1988 stay in San Giovanni Rotondo is an understatement, to say the least. They provided me with intimate interviews concerning Padre Pio, allowed me to take photos and gave me permission to use other pictures I needed concerning this holy stigmatist of Our Lady of Grace Friary. I thank my two new friends and brothers of my Franciscan Order, without whose help this work would be sorely lacking.

A word of thanks must be given to Ms. Dorothy Gaudiose of Lock Haven, Pennsylvania, for providing me with information about her beloved Padre Pio and Mary Pyle (who lived next to Our Lady of Grace Friary and in whose home Padre Pio's parents spent the last years of their life). Ms. Gaudiose is the author of *Prophet of the People: A Biography of Padre Pio*, and *Mary's House*. She had known both Padre and Mary Pile over the years, and her support for this work is greatly appreciated.

To Mr. William Carrigan of Kensington, Maryland, for sharing personal experiences of Padre Pio during the Second World War.

I thank my dear friend and fellow Franciscan, Father Ulrich Vey, O.F.M. Cap., of St. Konrad Monastery in Altötting, which is toward the southeast corner of Bavaria, West Germany. Father Vey was most gracious to my wife Kathy and me while we spent time with him in Altötting, summer of 1988. Thank you, Father, for over four hours of interviews, the many photos, examination of Therese's blood-stained relics, and the hours of laughs we shared as we formed a close friendship in the time spent together. We hope to be back to see you again one day.

To my dear friend Albert Vogl of San Jose, California, through whom I met Father Ulrich Vey, O.F.M.: thank you deeply for your kindness, and most of all, your friendship, which I will always treasure.

A word of thanks to Father Albert Hebert, S.M., of Paulina, Louisiana, who helped me out with names to contact during my time spent in Italy. Although I was unable to take advantage of all the names he gave me, I still have them for future use. Father Hebert is a well-known author of many fine books, including *Prophecies! The Chastisement and Purification; The Three Days' Darkness*; and *The Tears of Mary and Fatima: Why?* (all available from the author, P.O. Box 309, Paulina, Louisiana 70763). Thank you, Father, for continuing to keep in touch with me.

To Antonio Longo and family, owner of the Hotel California in San Giovanni, Rotondo. Thank you for the hospitality, and thank you, Antonio, for the interview of your experiences with Padre Pio when you once knew him many years ago. Good luck with the hotel: your fine command of the English language was a welcome during our stay!

To Mr. Emmeram H. Ritter of Regensburg, West Germany: thank you for the informative letter of valuable contacts concerning the cause of Therese Neumann. Some I saw, some I missed. Perhaps one day I will use these contacts in future works on Therese.

I would like to thank Father Anton Vogl, pastor of St. Lawrence Parish in Konnersreuth, West Germany (Therese Neumann's home-town church and parish). Father Vogl is currently the Postulator for Therese Neumann's cause for beatification. Although you spoke little English, I thank you for being so kind to me and my wife during our stay in Konnersreuth.

To Father Patrick Patton, Franciscan priest in the Diocese of Helena, Montana, your suggestions throughout the writing of this manuscript were most helpful and inspiring. (Father Patton encouraged me to become a Franciscan, and for the past 12 years has been a dear friend, teacher, theological adviser, and director of my spiritual growth and formation.)

To the various copyright holders, especially TAN Books and Publishers, Inc., Rockford, Illinois 61105, many thanks for permission to use quotations from many works, each cited in the text and bibliography. This book would have suffered without such references.

Scripture texts contained in this work are taken from the *Revised Standard Version Bible, Catholic Edition,* © 1965 and 1966 by the Division of Christian Education of the National Council of the Churches of Christ in the U.S.A., and used by permission of the copyright owner.

Thank you to Mr. Eugene Szynkowski, Detroit, Michigan, who supplied me with many photos and information regarding stigmatist Mary Rose Ferron. Mr. Szynkowski is involved in the cause of this United States stigmatist.

I thank the additional publishers, copyright owners, and authors for their cooperation in this work by letting me use their quotes and some of the pictures I needed. Most of all, I would like to thank my publisher, Mr. Robert Lockwood, at Our Sunday Visitor, Inc., for his kindness, support and encouragement throughout this project, as well as to all of the staff there who contributed to making this book a completed work.

A special thanks to the project editor, Mrs. Kelley Renz, for her comments and suggestions throughout this work. Your kindness and support were a real inspiration to me.

I am deeply grateful to my brothers-in-law and their wives for their enormous help: Mick and Mary Lou Sullivan (Edmonds, Washington); Denny and Katie Sullivan (Seattle, Washington); Jim and Kay O'Sullivan (Olympia, Washington); and Kevin Sullivan (Anaconda, Montana). Thank you for watching our children, providing transportation, and helping with our flight plans and reservations in Europe. Thanks, Kevin, for your inspiration.

Finally, I thank my wife Kathy and my three children, Michael, Matthew and Molly for their patience and support throughout the many hours I spent as a hermit researching and writing this book!

Any of the kind people whom I forgot to thank here, it is certainly an unintended oversight on my part, and I apologize for the omission. You know I am deeply grateful to you all. I ask God's blessings for everyone who has helped to make this book a reality, and I give thanks for all the new and dear Franciscan friends I have come to know.

If any copyrighted materials have been inadvertently used in this book without proper credit being given, please notify Our Sunday Visitor in writing so that future printings of this work may be corrected accordingly.

Preface

While I was doing research for this study on the Sacred Stigmata, my work brought me, among other places, to Germany and Italy in the summer of 1988, through friends and contacts I had made. During my stay in San Giovanni Rotondo, Italy (for fifty years the home of the stigmatist Padre Pio of Pietrelcina), I talked with Father Joseph Martin, O.F.M. Cap. about my intentions for this book. Father Martin, a Franciscan priest from Brooklyn, New York, has been at San Giovanni Rotondo for a quarter of a century. He was Padre Pio's aide for the last three years of his life, and was as close to him as anyone had been those last years between 1965-68. In fact, he had assisted him daily, and was there in Padre's room the day he died.

During our conversations, I talked with Father Martin about my writing apostolate and its value for the Church; I also asked him about my work on the Sacred Stigmata. He told me that the mission of the stigmatist was a gift and a sign for the whole world. The stigmata was not given to Padre Pio for his own benefit, but for the benefit of others. Likewise, Father told me, my mission in writing this book is important to the stigmatist, because I will be helping to promote his cause and inform the faithful about the nature of the stigmata and its meaning for the world today. This work I was undertaking was a serious business, he said, and it would bring God's blessing if done with great care and love. Needless to say, I was overwhelmed by the great responsibility I had in attempting to say the right things to the faithful.

I asked Father Martin if Padre Pio would have approved my doing a work on the stigmata, including my efforts to promote his cause and to help explain his mission for the world. He said that, yes, Padre Pio would have approved my work if it contributed to the advancement of the kingdom, inspired the faithful and informed them about the importance of God's redeeming grace that is still available for the world today. This grace is found in the Cross of Christ, and His mission is still to love and to suffer in order that all might be saved. It is through His redeeming Blood and Sacred Body that we are united to the Cross with Him, and share as a Mystical Body in the mystery of divine love.

The stigmatist represents the Crucified Christ to a world continually in need of a loving sacrifice that atones for our sin. The stigmatist is this loving sacrifice, a living crucifix who helps in the plan of God's redemptive action. There are other Christs among us: signs of God's mercy and love for unbelievers, channels for His grace to those who need healing, renewal and conversion. They are inspiring examples to those who are already deeply faithful, models who show the way to the imitation of Christ. Perhaps above all, they show a Christ who is very much alive today, the same Jesus who lived in our midst some two thousand years ago. It is the loving and compassionate Christ who comes during this time of God's grace for humanity, and it is up to us to respond while we still have this opportunity.

I indicated to Father Martin and to others that I intended on doing a serious study on the mystery of the Sacred Stigmata. I wanted to avoid exaggeration and sensationalism as much as possible by really getting behind the exterior wounds and explore the purpose of these wounds, the people who receive them, and the value they have for the faithful today. I also wanted to explain the mystery of suffering as a prelude to the stigmata, and what value the roles of voluntary sacrifice and atonement play in the mystery of our redemption. In this respect, the Cross becomes the focal point for all of my study; for without the Cross, there is no redemption and there is no meaning for the gift of the Sacred Stigmata.

Father Ulrich Vey, O.F.M. Cap. was also pleased that I approach my study in this manner. Fr. Vey, who lives at St. Konrad Monastery in Altötting, Germany, is currently the Vice-Postulator for the cause of Therese Neumann's beatification. Therese was from Konnersreuth, Germany (1898-1962), and bore the stigmata from 1926 until her death. I felt that I was on the right track after gaining the support of both Father Martin and Father Vey for the way I would approach this study. Their kindness and time shared will always be remembered and greatly appreciated.

I have attempted to use sources for this work that are both reliable and well-respected. Besides Sacred Scripture, I relied upon the wisdom of the Magisterium, the Doctors and great theologians of the Church, and the mystics and saints who have been a big influence on the understanding of the various aspects of mystical theology and the spiritual life.

Once again, I must warn the reader that if he or she is looking for a sensational account of the stigmata, or wants to hear about nothing but the exterior wounds that these victims had, then there will be great disappointment. I do include a lengthy description of the wounds in a later section in the book, but this is not the primary focus of the work. Rather, let us focus on the meaning behind these sacred wounds and the role they play for the lives of the faithful. It is only then that we will come to appreciate them for what they really are, and not as a showpiece for curiosity seekers.

Anytime one seeks to understand the world of the supernatural, words are really inadequate to describe these sublime mysteries of our faith. Because much of the information and experiences in the mystical life are of a private nature and not bound to divine revelation, we must all approach this study with a cautious open-mindedness. It is important to realize that in the realm of the supernatural, anyone — including the stigmatist, seer or mystical theologian — could err in matters pertaining to the faith. This is because of the subjective and intensely personal nature of the experiences of the mystical life. Sometimes a private message or vision could be misinterpreted, and the evil one can often distort the truth in the best of souls.

One unit in this text requires a cautious approach, though I thought it too meaningful to not include it in my study: that on the Holy Shroud of Turin. Because of the recent controversies surrounding the findings of several teams of researchers (who claim the Shroud to be inauthentic on the basis of their examinations), I reserve my final judgment to the wisdom of the Church. Until then, and following the traditional treatment of the Church, I consider this a holy relic and treat it with care and great reverence. As one will see, I happen to favor the opinion that this is indeed the authentic burial cloth of Jesus Christ. I will continue to operate out of this premise until the Church makes Her final pronouncement. If the cloth proves not to be authentic, our study will still shed light on the nature of the sufferings and wounds that our Savior had to endure in the last moments of His life; either way, the study will still prove to be beneficial in the context of this work.

I have included a glossary of mystical terms at the end of my text in order to help the reader to better understand particular terms that are used throughout the course of this work. Therefore, I strongly advise one to read through this glossary carefully before the reading of the main body in the text. This is especially so for those who may not have a great deal of background in the studies of mystical theology. Avoiding this preparatory work before engaging in the main text could cause misunderstandings or confusion throughout most of the chapters. If the reader does have an adequate background in these studies, then the glossary will still prove valuable as a quick reference guide.

Another handy reference tool is provided in the biographical profiles of several dozen stigmatists from the medieval period up through the modern era. This, too, can be found near the end of the work. It will give the reader a brief, overall picture of the lives of the stigmatists, and there is a lot of information packed into these few pages. This author advises a careful reading of this material before the study of the main body of text.

Out of obedience to the decree issued by Pope Urban VIII (among others), I willingly submit final judgments about the nature of these phenomena to the teaching Magisterium of the Church, which represents the authority in all matters pertaining to the faith and morals of the Church, as well as all revelation divinely revealed by God.

Michael Freze, S.F.O.

Introduction

Why the Sacred Stigmata?

Nearly two thousand years have passed since the advent of Christianity, shaping our thoughts and directing the lives of countless millions. With an almost unbelievable wealth of information available through the works of some of history's greatest minds, nothing seems to surprise us, and little has been left unsaid.

Yet, despite the rich deposit that Sacred Tradition has left to us, some mysteries of the faith continue to fascinate and even baffle the best of minds, be they theologians or lay persons. Such is the case with a mystical phenomenon known as the Sacred Stigmata: the imprint of our Lord's wounds upon the bodies of His most chosen souls, who become transformed into living crucifixes by sharing in His Passion for the redemption of the world.

According to the renowned Parisian scholar, Dr. Imbert-Gourbeyre, there have been 321 authentic stigmatists (also known as stigmatics) in Church history. This list was composed in his monumental two-volume work, *La Stigmatization*, in 1894. Doctor Gourbeyre identifies sixty-two of those stigmatists who have been canonized or beatified. Since that time, numerous others — Padre Pio, Therese Neumann and Marthe Robin, etc. — have borne the marks of Jesus crucified, either partially or completely, as invisible or external wounds upon their bodies.

Indeed, the twentieth century might be rightly called the "era of the stigmatist," since more than two dozen cases of stigmatization have been reported and investigated, though few have yet been authenticated by the proper Church authorities. But the number is significant. Unlike in past centuries, we now have thoroughly documented cases of many living and recently deceased stigmatists who have undergone extensive investigations by both medical experts and theologians. We also have significant evidence from the world of photography, anatomy, biology, and chemistry to help substantiate these claims.

Because of this evidence before us, the question of authentic stigmatization is now more than a theological curiosity; it is an observable fact.

Understandably a rare phenomenon (considering that there are 850 million Catholics and over one billion Christians in the world), the Sacred Stigmata is truly one of the greatest miracles that Christendom has ever known: perhaps the greatest visible sign of Christ's presence among us today. It's as though our Lord still shows mercy to the doubting Thomases of our world by allowing them to be witnesses to the reality of God in our midst: "Put your finger here and see my hands, and put out your hand and place it in my side: do not be faithless, but believe" (Jn 20:27).

Yet, we need not see the sacred wounds of our Lord upon the living stigmatists in our midst in order to believe they are real; it is sufficient to believe because Jesus has told us so: "Have you believed because you have seen me? Blessed are those who have not seen and yet believe" (Jn 20:29). Admittedly, the "facts" of authentic stigmatization can never be totally proven by scientific observation alone — there is always an element of the divine presence too overwhelming for mankind to grasp, too mysterious for mere mortal creatures to fathom.

Does this really matter? Probably not. The ways of the Lord are not our own. God manifests His presence in any way He chooses; sometimes we are blessed by unusual and rare displays of His wonders, and sometimes we are not.

Faith is still the primary vessel by which we must be guided through uncertain darkness until we enter the fullness of life. As St. Paul reminds us: "For we walk by faith, not by sight" (2 Cor 5:7). Or "we look not to the things that are seen but to the things that are unseen; for the things that are seen are transient, but the things that are unseen are eternal" (2 Cor 4:18).

Yet, God has gifted us today with a sign of the times — a sign displayed through victim souls known as stigmatists, souls who share in the sufferings of our Lord's Passion to redeem the world. These are extraordinary souls, holy and pure, who by imitating Christ so intensely have been invited to become one with Him. They are His beloved, and He demands much from their example and from their sacrifice.

Is this, then, the only role the authentic stigmatist plays in the modern world — a sign of the times, of God's presence among us? No, not at all. As was mentioned previously, God does not have to display His presence to anyone (though He certainly chooses to do so from time-to-time). If He does choose to do so, it is only of secondary importance. What is of greater importance is the role models these souls can be for all of us on our journey towards perfection and salvation: examples of holiness, faithfulness and the Gospel principles that we must try to live by. These models are an inspiration to us all, a realization of God's enduring love among His faithful ones.

Of equal importance is the role of the stigmatist as victim soul, voluntarily united to our Lord's sufferings for the sake of saving souls; to fill up "what is lacking in Christ's afflictions for the sake of his body, that is, the church" (Col 1:24). The victim usually suffers vicariously for others in order to make expiation or atonement for their sins — by appeasing the divine justice and allowing room for God's mercy to enter the sinner's heart. Herein lies the value of the sacrificial victim: to suffer that we might be saved.

But how does the victim soul share in the mystery of our salvation if Christ is our sole Mediator before the Father? Wasn't the cross at Calvary a sufficient means of saving sinners once and for all? These and many other questions I will attempt to answer in the pages that follow. Although we can never fully grasp the mystery of God's designs, we can at least attempt to move closer to understanding how God works through His people to manifest His most holy will. Some of these very special people He has chosen for the works of His providence are the stigmatists we will encounter in this book.

I ask for the Lord's guidance and blessing as I attempt to journey into the supernatural. I pray that I may do justice to this mystery of mysteries, and serve to instruct and inspire those who will read this work. May the evil one, so cruel and cunning, not affect my judgment in these matters. He will not like what I have done, because he detests with a vengeance the good work these victim souls do for the Body of Christ — they who win back souls from him through prayer, sacrifice and suffering. If the evil spirit is upset, then I know I've done something beneficial. I ask for your grace and protection, Lord, as I only want to please you and serve you. I also ask for your prayers, brothers and sisters in Christ, that good seed will indeed fall on good soil.

May the peace of our Lord Jesus Christ touch your hearts, and may our Mother Mary protect us all as we continue the walk of faith under her Immaculate Heart, together with the Sacred Heart of our Savior.

Judgment of the Church

Authentic stigmatization is such an extraordinary charism usually reserved for those rare souls who have lived heroic lives and have possessed holy attributes beyond the normal way of perfection. Because of this supernatural state of existence, the Church wisely proceeds with great caution when she hears of a stigmatist in her midst.

For every authenticated case of stigmata, there have been "false stigmata" normally associated with a series of possible causes: diabolical origins; mental disease or sickness; hysteria; self-hypnotic suggestion; and nervous conditions that can cause the skin to redden, break and even bleed.

Science and medicine have provided us with knowledge about mind and body that was simply unavailable one hundred years ago. This is one reason why the Church insists on medical and psychiatric evaluations before she will consider the possibility of declaring the authenticity of an alleged stigmatist. The credibility of the Church is partly at stake, for she does not want to take lightly the world of the supernatural without first eliminating all possible natural causes. The divine action is simply too overwhelming; it must be looked upon with awe and respect, with the deepest sense of piety and humility. Moses realized this with the burning bush experience: ". . . God called out to him from the bush, 'Moses! Moses!' And he said, 'Here am I.' Then he said, 'Do not come near; put off your shoes from your feet, for the place on which you are standing is holy ground.' And he said, 'I am the God of your father, the God of Abraham, the God of Isaac, and the God of Jacob.' And Moses hid his face for he was afraid to look at God" (Ex 3:4-6).

Again, the words of St. Paul warn us against being too presumptuous: "Oh, the depths of the riches and the wisdom and the knowledge of God! How unsearchable are his judgments, how inscrutable his ways! For who has known the mind of the Lord, or who has been his counselor?" (Rom 11:33-34).

Because the Sacred Stigmata must be categorized in the realm of the truly miraculous, the Church treats it accordingly. She has this to say about prudence in judging miracles:

> While some private manifestations can occur, claims of these are to be approached with caution. Alleged heavenly messages or miraculous events must be investigated and approved by the local bishop before being given any credence. . . . National Conference of Catholic Bishops, November 14-17, 1977.

Yet the possibility of miracles is not to be doubted either, as the Church plainly states:

> If anyone says that no miracles are possible, or that miracles can never be recognized with certainty, *anathema sit*. . . . First Vatican Council, Third Session, 1870.

13

Clearly, caution must be balanced with pure faith and the willingness to believe that God at times does manifest His presence in extraordinary ways. The Magisterium of the Roman Catholic Church reaffirms this fact after prudent and careful discernment, and only then considers authenticating the alleged supernatural experiences.

Since about twenty percent of all documented stigmatists are eventually canonized or beatified, a brief explanation must be made.

Traditionally, the Church has taken several important steps towards canonizing a chosen soul for sainthood. The process of canonization is conducted by the Sacred Congregation of Rites, and later the subject is confirmed by the Holy Father himself if the process proceeded successfully.

The first step is known as the *Ordinary Process*, a formal inquiry that is begun by the bishop in the diocese where the person has lived. A tribunal of three judges, a notary and a "devil's advocate" investigate the subject's background. If this stage is successfully completed, Rome takes over the process for further investigation.

In the second stage, members of the Sacred Congregation of Rites inquire further into the person's actions and virtues. If things proceed smoothly beyond this point, the official *apostolic process* is confirmed.

As a third step in this process, miracles and the nature of the virtues surrounding the candidate for canonization are rigorously examined. Two fully authentic miracles are required before beatification and two distinctly different miracles must be confirmed before canonization. Clearly, the Church preciously guards her discernment process and authentication. She must, lest false rumors of sanctity lead the innocent faithful astray.

Authentic stigmatists should meet these conditions set down by Holy Mother Church. Even for those stigmatists not yet proclaimed as saints, it is even more imperative that careful and extensive evaluation takes place, for this is an extraordinary grace even beyond the ways of some of our most beloved saints. To declare a soul as a near duplication of our Lord crucified (no one, of course, is an exact duplication) is an awesome thing, indeed! We must be prudent, but not unduly skeptical, either.

Once firmly established, the faithful ought to honor her stigmatists as supreme gifts of God, worthy of our love and our affection . . . as examples to emulate by way of their extraordinary virtues.

In a very real sense, these privileged souls represent Christ to a broken world of unbelief and oppression. More than this, they are second Christs who help to satisfy punishment due for the transgressions of our sins; they are a sign of the times, a sign of hope and love from a God who still lives among His people and loves each one of them as His own.

Michael Freze, S.F.O.

CHAPTER 1

The Mystery of Suffering

The Suffering of Job

Perhaps no book in Sacred Scripture so beautifully describes the role of suffering in the lives of God's chosen ones than the Book of Job. Most scholars believe that this pearl of wisdom literature came to be written in the post-Exilic period, sometime during the reign of the Persians in the Near East. At any rate, Job is without question a masterpiece of literature, an intimate account of one man's struggle with extraordinary trials and sufferings that many of God's holy ones endure out of love for their faith. Let us take a closer look at the saint whose endurance led to the immortalized epitaph that we give to him each time we hear his name: "the sufferings of Job" for the love of God.

Job teaches us a classical doctrine on the relation of suffering to human behavior. Even more so, he describes the meaning of man's relationship to God. The problem of good and evil — how the one battles against the other — is very evident as the story unfolds.

In the prologue (1:1-22), we find that Job was once a wealthy man, and holy in the sight of God and His people. Suddenly his world fell apart, and he was stricken with a terrible illness (perhaps leprosy) that appeared to be fatal. Then misfortune struck again, when Job was stripped of all his goods, putting his entire life in shambles. We are told that a confrontation occurs between God and the evil one, who desperately seeks to destroy Job by insisting upon torturing him through trial after trial. What is remarkable is that in spite of all the devil's assaults through the permission of God, Job does not blame God for all of his misfortunes. He had entered his darkest night, yet a blind faith allowed him to endure.

Our story unfolds with a dialogue between Job and his three friends, Eliphaz, Bildad and Zophar. The drama concerns the meaning of divine justice and the sufferings that Job must endure. Naturally disillusioned at his misfortune, Job demands of God a full explanation if He is really a just God.

In time, a fourth figure appears on the scene: Elihu, who confronts both Job and his friends, reminding them that they must conform to the will of God, even under adverse conditions.

Finally, God himself appears to Job and describes how Job's demands for justice are foolish. God's ways are beyond our understanding, yet always done for our own good. Job is humbled through this dialogue with the Almighty, and only then does God restore Job's life to its former greatness. Humility was certainly a cornerstone for the work of grace in the life of the holy servant Job. But he proved to be faithful as he was tried like gold in the crucible. Job became a model for all of God's suffering servants.

All of God's chosen ones are sooner or later put to the test, whether it comes from the evil spirit, or directly from God himself, who wishes to try a person's faith in the midst of great sufferings. This is true for all who travel the road of perfection, and we are no exception. In fact, there are no exceptions. Eventually, we must all be put to the test. If we are faithful, our reward will one day come: "Blessed is the man who endures trial, for when he has stood the test he will receive the crown of life which God has promised to those who love him" (Jas 1:12).

Job appears to have been placed in the dark night that all mystics must pass through, a night of purification of the senses and spirit that one actively pursues through prayer, sacrifice and penance. In time, God himself purifies the soul, leaving one in a dark night of faith, until that soul is purged of every kind of imperfection, in order that he or she might become worthy of the fullness of God's love (often referred to in mystical terms as the divine union). It is the highest spiritual state one can experience in this life, and is given to the few who are intimately united with God and who seek His will alone. Job was being called to a higher state, a closer relationship with his Maker.

If we look closely at our text, we can see the numerous trials and afflictions that Job was subjected to. He speaks of physical afflictions: "My flesh is clothed with worms and scabs; my skin cracks and festers" (Jb 7:5); "My frame takes no rest by night" (30:17); "My face is inflamed with weeping and there is darkness over my eyes" (16:16-17). Job has experienced physical purgations, but the darkest night was yet to come — that of the spirit, where God purifies to the depths of one's soul: "My inmost being is consumed with longing" (19:26); "I will speak the anguish of my spirit; I will complain in the bitterness of my soul" (7:11).

Job describes the longing for God, who temporarily appears to have abandoned him. He longs for light, but "then came darkness" (30:26). Touchingly he describes his desire for the love of his Creator: "Why dost thou hide thy face, and count me as thy enemy?" (13:24). Or again: "the terrors of God are arrayed against me" (6:4).

Then Job describes what many of the great saint-mystics throughout the ages have attempted to explain: the point where the Lord wounds the soul, leaving it to burn with the divine arrow that consumes, yet at the same time is a blessing to the soul. It is the seal of divine love that God bestows on His favored few. Saints such as Teresa of Avila have described the arrows that shoot forth to wound the soul, and Job (nearly two thousand years earlier!) gives the same account of a similar experience: "He has set me up for a target; his arrows strike me from all directions, He pierces my sides without mercy" (16:12-13); "He pierces me with thrust upon thrust" (16:14); "For the arrows of the Almighty pierce me, and my spirit drinks in their poison" (6:4).

Once again, all of these trials and purifications serve to give Job greater humility. We can see that he has fear for his own sin, lest he fall from grace: "How many are my iniquities and my sins? Make me know my transgression and my sin!" (13:23). Yet Job finds peace and strength in the Lord's chastisement of his soul. In fact, he even looks forward to some of the trials in order to gain God's blessing: "happy is the man whom God reproves;

therefore despise not the chastening of the Almighty. For He wounds, but he binds up; he smites, but His hands heal" (5:17-18).

The evil spirit was not long in picking Job as a target for his diabolical attacks on the body, soul and the mind. Ever ready to gain a soul and to cause it eternal misery, he fights to defeat the holy Job with a force unparalleled. Job himself said that he was tossed "about in the roar of the storm" (30:22). In the darkness of night, he is furiously assaulted, for the devil relentlessly pursues God's holy ones. Job's body took no rest, and he feels that affliction has overtaken him (30:16,27). Padre Pio of Pietrelcina (1887-1968), the saintly friar stigmatist of our era, describes the same diabolical attacks in his letters to his two spiritual directors, Padre Agostino and to Padre Benedetto, of San Marco in Lamis (Italy). I have personally seen the effects of the beatings Padre Pio took on the head from the evil one. A personal pillow of his still bears the blood stains from this encounter in his cell in San Giovanni Rotondo, Italy. My meeting with Father Joseph Martin, O.F.M. Cap. (a close friend of the Padre's) in San Giovanni Rotondo reaffirmed this story and many others of the devil's efforts to destroy him.

Like Padre Pio, Job was not spared the snares of the enemy, who "prowls around like a roaring lion, seeking for someone to devour" (1 Pt 5:8). Yet it is his faith in God that gives him the strength and the grace to face the foe, and he does so courageously by relying upon God to see him through.

Job realized through experience that the way to the Lord is a mixture of thorns and roses. Nothing worth striving for is without its trials and tribulations, especially in the spiritual realm. Jesus reminded us that we must take up our cross if we want to become his true disciples, for in order to find eternal life, one must be willing to lose it (Mt 16:24-25). Like the good Job, we must be "tried . . . as silver is tried" by fire (Ps 66:10); again, "For gold is tested in the fire, and acceptable men in the furnace of humiliation" (Sir 2:5). Sirach tells us that when we come to serve the Lord, we should prepare ourselves for trials (Sir 2:1).

By holding firm to the faith, Job received twice as much as he once had through God's goodness and mercy (42:10). It is significant to note in the epilogue of our story that the Lord blessed Job in his latter days even more than his earlier ones (42:12). Perhaps this indicates that life is a series of continuous trials, and those who hold out to the end receive their eternal reward: "I have fought the good fight, I have finished the race, I have kept the faith. Henceforth there is laid up for me, the crown. . . ." (2 Tim 4:7-8). We must prove our fidelity to God by remaining firm to the end — a firmness dictated by the crosses we bear, the sufferings we endure, all for the love of God. The road is rough and narrow (Mt 7:14), but how happy are they who find it!

Let us all learn from the experiences of Job. Nothing is too difficult to overcome if we are firmly grounded in our faith, for trials make for endurance (Jas 1:3), and he who holds out to the end will surely be saved.

The Sufferings of God's People

From the beginning of human history, mankind has suffered in one way or another, whether it was from illness, poverty or persecution. Why is this so? Could a loving and merciful God allow this to happen to His creation?

In the Book of Genesis, we find that "God created man in his image; in the image of God he created him; male and female he created them" (Gn 1:27). We also see that by creating them, He found it to be "very good" (Gn 1:31). Nothing was lacking; man and woman had everything they needed to live a pure and holy life, free of all sin.

Through the instigation of the evil one, man fell victim to the first sin of pride. It has always been debatable whether Satan really caused humanity to first sin, or whether it was man himself because of his free will to choose right from wrong. Nevertheless, Scripture makes it very clear that the evil spirit "has sinned from the beginning" (1 Jn 3:8), and that through the devil "death entered the world" (Wis 2:24). Jesus himself said that the devil "was a murderer from the beginning," and that "he is a liar and the father of lies" (Jn 8:44).

From the moment man first listened to Satan, the doors were opened for diabolical assault forever. The stain of original sin lay firmly upon him, and the descendants of Adam and Eve (you and me) inherit the effects of their sin and disgrace. God allows this because He has given us the freedom to choose, although He certainly doesn't approve our sin.

The evil spirit was not left unpunished for his interference in human affairs, for God banished him from all of His creatures to fend for himself (Gn 3:14), leaving him the enemy of all creation. In turn, God punished our first human couple for their act of sin; both man and woman must pay the price of original sin their entire lives:

> To the woman he said, "I will greatly multiply your pain in child-bearing; in pain you shall bring forth children, yet your desire shall be for your husband, and he shall rule over you." And to Adam he said, "Because you have listened to the voice of your wife, and have eaten of the tree of which I commanded you, 'You shall not eat of it,' cursed is the ground because of you; in toil you shall eat of it all the days of your life; thorns and thistles it shall bring forth to you; and you shall eat the plants of the field. In the sweat of your face you shall eat bread till you return to the ground, for out of it you were taken; you are dust, and to dust you shall return" (Gn 3:16-19).

Throughout the course of the Old Testament, we have numerous examples of sufferings among God's people. When suffering is endured with love, God always blesses those who remain firm in their faith to the end. Although chastisement can often be the reason why one suffers, it can also be a test from God to see if the faith of those pious souls holds up under adverse conditions. God has always tested those whom He loves, especially His chosen ones. How can one prove his or her faith if they've never been put to the test? How can one discern between good and evil if one has never experienced both the bitter and the sweet?

In the Book of Proverbs, suffering or happiness is equated with the faithfulness or lack of faith one has in God. The righteous will live long, rewarding lives, while the unrighteous die in sin before their time, victims of their own infidelity.

The Book of Sirach places emphasis on the fact that man is responsible for his own sufferings: "All these were created for the wicked, and on their

18

account the flood came" (Sir 40:10). One should read Sirach 40:1-10 for a complete synthesis of the author's viewpoint.

A very similar attitude towards suffering appears in Daniel 8:15-27. God will punish Israel for its sins in the form of calamity and tribulation. Our merciful God is also a just God, lest we forget. Our sins must be accounted for, either in this life or in the next; if in the next, we must be purged of all our imperfections before we can see God as He really is (the doctrine of Purgatory is based upon this fact).

Amos talks about a reciprocal love relationship between God and His people. If one is to be blessed by the Lord, he or she has to act as God would: with love, mercy, and justice (see Am 6:7-15). In order to be worthy of His blessings, our Lord expects a lot from His people. Punishment and suffering can come when one takes the favors and blessings of the Lord lightly. Once favored, we are obligated to treat others as God has treated us.

In the Book of Micah, we readily see that God will not allow the sins of His people to go unpunished (see Mi 1:1-7, 3:12). The Lord is ready to deal with those who turn from His ways: "Then they will cry to the Lord, but he will not answer them; he will hide his face from them at that time, because they have made their deeds evil" (Mi 3:4).

Micah also talks about Israel's exile, and how she must learn the lessons of humility before God will deliver her from her wanderings (Mi 4). It is through a humble and pure heart that we come to know the Lord, obediently accepting the Lord's will in all that we do. Years later, Jesus would fulfill the act of humility in a complete and selfless way: He "emptied himself, taking the form of a servant, being born in the likeness of men. And being found in human form he humbled himself and became obedient unto death, even death on a cross! Therefore God has highly exalted him and bestowed on him the name which is above every name" (Phil 2:7-9). Through Jesus, we learn that suffering in conformity to God's will is a sure road to humility, a way to become exalted in the eyes of the Lord.

As we have seen, suffering can be the result of man's sinful nature, or it can be a way of conformity to the divine will, a conformity that leads one to the Cross of Christ: "Whoever does not bear his own cross and come after me, cannot be my disciple" (Lk 14:27). It is at the foot of the Cross that we learn to love as Jesus has loved. God has reserved this type of suffering for His true followers, those who seek the narrow road that leads to eternal life.

Both types of suffering — as punishment and as an imitation of Christ — are necessary for spiritual perfection: the former to purge ourselves of the imperfections we inherit through our sinful nature, and the latter as a way towards divine union. For it is through our willingness to suffer for God that we learn to love, as Christ has loved us in the sacrifice of the Cross.

Sufferings can also serve to draw us closer to God. Because God is love, our yearnings for Him become a form of suffering when we do not possess Him in times of darkness; we suffer for love, and we find in the end that God is the fullness of love. If He were made to suffer for us through His only begotten Son (1 Jn 4:10), then we in turn are made to suffer for Him. This love, however, is not to be strictly limited to the Father, for we are commanded to love our brothers and sisters as He has loved us: "if God has so loved us, we also ought to love one another" (1 Jn 4:11). We are to love one another precisely because this is how the Lord has shown His love for us: "God so loved the world that he gave his only Son" (Jn 3:16). Notice that He did so because He *loved the world* (and not because He only loved His Son). God loves everyone, and we in turn are expected to do the same. We show our love for Him by not only loving Jesus, but also by loving one another, for God is in every one of us. Jesus is very firm with this point: "This I command you, to love one another" (Jn 15:17).

Why, then, can't we just love one another without having to suffer? Why must we pay a price to love our God freely and unconditionally? Because love has always been a mixture of thorns and roses, of laughter and tears, of the pains and joys of life. Love does not exist in a vacuum; it is not self-serving. Love is a two-way street of give-and-take, of learning from our mistakes. It involves a sharing in the sufferings of others (if we truly love them). We help to mend wounds and heal hurts by taking upon ourselves the sufferings of others, and only then will our love become purified and renewed. Since love needs to be shared, how can it exist apart from the sufferings as well as the joys? It is impossible. To love is to suffer, and to suffer is to love.

The Wisdom of the Prophets

The word "prophet" has been used by many over the years to refer to one who predicts the future or warns of chastisement. Although some authentic prophecy indeed concerns these issues, it is by no means the primary role of a true prophet (especially in the Old Testament sense of the word). When prophecy becomes strictly equated with words of doom or disaster for some future apocalyptic event, then the prophet appears to be a fortune teller, soothsayer or astrologer firmly immersed in the practice of divination, which the Scriptures absolutely forbid (Lv 19:31; 20:6; Dt 18:10-11; 1 Sm 15:23). We must be careful when talking about prophecy, for the primary role of the authentic prophet was not to predict the future.

The word "prophet" comes from the Greek word *prophētes*, or "one who speaks before others." Other words used to describe its meaning (especially from the original Hebrew and Akkadian roots) are "to call," or to "speak aloud." In the Scriptures, a prophet has also been called a seer or visionary (1 Sm 9:9,11,18,19; Am 7:12).

One of the chief functions of the prophet was to explain the revelations of God to His people in the times and circumstances they found themselves in. At times they were called to teach, and at other times to admonish. Most of the prophets were moral leaders, warning the people to amend their ways lest the Lord punish them for their sins. But the prophet did not always speak of chastisement. He frequently praised the goodness and mercy of the Lord, emphasizing how God will deliver the faithful ones who follow His commands — a God who judges, yes, but also a God who saves.

Tradition has recognized different types of Old Testament prophets, and the Church has divided them into two main groups: the major prophets, and the minor prophets. The major prophets are so named because they are the longer books (not because they were more important or because they were the first). These major works consist of the Books of Isaiah, Jeremiah, Ezekiel, and Daniel (Daniel, however, is really more of an inspirational and apocalyptic work). The minor prophets are the shorter works, and consist of the following books: Hosea, Joel, Amos, Obadiah, Jonah, Micah, Nahum, Habakkuk, Zephaniah, Haggai, Zechariah, and Malachi. The minor prophets are sometimes referred to as "The Twelve," perhaps symbolic of the twelve tribes of Israel.

The great prophets of old often spoke about the sufferings of their people. But no matter how far they have strayed from the path, no matter how hardened their hearts, God is always there ready to forgive. He is a merciful and loving God, and this the prophet always assures us is so. A true sorrow for sin brings the sheep back to the fold, and prayers of thanksgiving reflect their endless gratitude.

One of the most beautiful descriptions of suffering in the Old Testament comes from the Book of Isaiah (52:13-53:12). It is the story of the suffering servant, the Christ who was yet to come. Isaiah describes this man of sorrow as the Servant who would be exalted through suffering. The mystery of His person would one day be recognized, for through His humiliation, the people will come to know who He really is (Is 52:13-15).

In verses 4-6, we see that the people come to understand the true meaning of Christ's sufferings. Before, they understood Him to be stricken, smitten, and afflicted by God for His own sins. But soon they were to learn that He really suffered for them instead — taking upon himself the sins of the people to restore them to wholeness once again. This man whom they thought to be misfortuned with suffering became a source of their healing:

> It was not Israel's sins that the Servant was bearing, for according to the initial proclamation of the prophet Israel had suffered more than enough for her own sin. The "overplus" of Israel's suffering was vicarious — for the nations. The nations confess that the Servant's sacrifice was Yahweh's redemptive act for their welfare, their salvation: 'All we like sheep have gone astray; we have turned every one to his own way; and Yahweh has laid on him the iniquity of us all' (Is 53:6). Here is a profound insight into the meaning of suffering, for which there is no parallel elsewhere in the Old Testament. . . . (Bernhard W. Anderson, *Understanding the Old Testament*, Prentice-Hall, Inc., 1957.)

The concept of vicarious suffering was common among the ancient peoples. Vicarious suffering means to sacrifice one's self for the sake of others, to atone for their sins. As in the case of Jesus, it is a voluntary sacrifice, one that is pleasing to the Father.

As was previously mentioned, sometimes mankind suffers because of wrongdoing; we sin, and a just judgment is needed to purge the stains of those sins. The prophet Amos describes the way the Israelites were attacked by their enemies and how natural disasters seemed to follow them relentlessly. Amos feels that Northern Israel had taken God's mercy for granted, for even after all the trials they encountered because of their sin, they persisted in the same state (Am 3:1-8; 4:6-13). God will not remain merciful forever to a hardened heart: "Take away from me the noise of your songs; to the melody of your harps I will not listen. But let justice roll down like waters and righteousness like an ever-flowing stream" (Am 5:23-24). Amos suggests that God might still forgive them if they amended their evil ways, but the possibility looked grim, indeed (see Am 3:9-11, 5:1-3, and 7:2-6). The Lord is slow to judge, but will punish the unrepentant: "For three transgressions of Israel and for four, I will not revoke the punishment" (Am 2:6). From this lesson we learn that stubborness — an unwillingness to change or repent — can cause the wrath of God to satisfy for our wrongdoings. It is a lesson to be on guard, to not take the goodness of our Lord for granted.

The prophet Hosea warns us that infidelity to God and His Law can cause reprimands from our Maker:

> Hear the word of the Lord, O people of Israel; for the Lord has a *controversy* with the inhabitants of the land. There is no faithfulness or kindness, and no knowledge of God in the land; there is swearing, and committing adultery; they break all bounds and murder follows murder. Therefore the land mourns, and all who dwell in it languish, and also the beasts of the field, and the birds of the air; and even the fish of the sea are taken away (Hos 4:1-3).

We must know God — not in an intellectual sense — but in our hearts, where our faith is truly sealed. We cannot love God without knowing Him, and if we fail to love Him, all is in vain. Hosea reveals this plea from our Lord: "I desire steadfast love and not sacrifice, the knowledge of God rather than burnt offerings" (Hos 6:6). Here is a lesson to be learned: although to sacrifice our sufferings for God is good, it is much better to love Him with all our heart, soul and mind. After all, it is the greatest of all the Commandments (Mt 22:36-37). Sacrifice without love is dead. What is needed is a purity of heart, where we can be united to the divine love and see Him as He really is (Mt 5:8).

Hosea teaches us that although God must punish those who fail to keep His commands, nevertheless He does not like to do so. Our Lord is slow to judge, and gives every opportunity for man to change his ways before He must correct him. The words of our Lord make this clear:

> How can I give you up, O Ephraim! How can I hand you over, O Israel! How can I make you like Admah! How can I treat you like Zeboiim! My heart recoils within me, my compassion grows warm and tender. I will not execute my fierce anger, I will not again destroy Ephraim; for I am God and not man, the Holy One in your midst, and I will not come to destroy (Hos 11:8-9).

As we see in the above quotation, God does not like to punish us for our faults, but His rightful justice compels Him to eventually act: 'But the Lord of hosts is exalted in justice and the Holy God shows himself holy in righteousness' (Is 5:16).

According to the great prophet Isaiah, the Lord will also bring punishment to those who mistreat or abuse the poor. Pride is still the enemy of God, and He will spare no one who cannot humble himself: "The haughty looks of man shall be brought low, and the pride of men shall be humbled; and the Lord alone will be exalted in that day. For the Lord of hosts has a day against all that is proud and lofty, against all that is lifted up and high" (Is 2:11-12).

Of course, Jesus taught us later the value of humility when he gave us the Beatitudes: "Blest are the meek; they shall inherit the earth" (Mt 5:5). The lesson is clear: if we do not humble ourselves before the Almighty, we will not be favored in His eyes.

The prophet Jeremiah has many things to say about those sinful things that cause our human condition to suffer before others, and especially before God. Jeremiah condemns idolatry (2:23-24) and the quest for power (17:3-5; 48:7; 49:4-5). He is quick to scorn adultery and fornication (5:7-8), and warns people about oppressing the poor (5:25-31). He continually calls the people back to God, pleading with them for their conversion and repentance (see 3:22; 4:1; 7:3; 8:5; 18:8). Jeremiah warns that if the people don't turn back to God, His punishment will be extremely severe (9:5-8; 15:5-9; 18:13-17; 23:19-24).

We have talked about how our sin can cause us much suffering, especially when the Lord sees fit to correct us. Yet there are many who know the pangs of suffering without being directly at fault. People are oppressed, persecuted and scorned. Some live in absolute poverty, while others feel the burdens of illness or even the death of a loved one. Is there any purpose behind these sufferings? If so, how can we offer them up for the glory of God and for the benefit of our souls? Perhaps we need to address this issue more fully by hearing what the prophets have to tell us.

Isaiah the prophet shares with us a message of hope, of comfort for the afflicted, of freedom for the oppressed. Let's take a look at some of the touching passages that came from his hand, for he truly gives inspiration to those in times of need.

Chapters 40-55 of Isaiah are often called the "Book of Consolation" because the prophet speaks of confidence and hope in a God who is about to end the exile of Israel. God gives us some words of consolation through Isaiah's lips with these passages: ". . . fear not, for I am with you, be not dismayed, for I am your God; I will strengthen you, I will help you, I will uphold you with my victorious right hand" (Is 41:10). What a reassuring feeling! Our God tells us that He is our strength and our fortress when our world comes tumbling down. We may fail Him from time-to-time, but He is always there — the Faithful One. We are further reassured, for then the Lord says, "Fear not, I will help you" (Is 41:13). Even though these passages are about Israel's deliverance from the Exile, nevertheless they speak to us from the heart. We too have felt the pains of exile at one time or another: a dear friend who abandons us; relatives who do not understand us; feelings of loneliness and isolation far away from the security of home; and so on. Listen to the voice of God, for He speaks to us all. In our sufferings, let us be assured of His ever-presence, ready to hear our call.

Another lesson that Isaiah gives us is on patience. We must learn to suffer patiently all the trials and tribulations of life, and we must do so by waiting upon the Lord for His deliverance: "They who wait for the Lord will renew their strength, they will fly like eagles on their wings, They will run and not grow tired, walk and not become faint" (Is 40:31). Patience is a virtue not easily gained, but the Lord asks us to rid ourselves of all uneasiness and haste, and to rest in His love — for it is there that we will be delivered, it is there that we find everlasting peace.

Perhaps a fitting end to our prophet Isaiah would best be summed up in those beautiful words of consolation to the afflicted. Here the words of Christ echo in the synagogue in Nazareth through the lips of the holy Isaiah:

The spirit of the Lord God is upon me, because the Lord has anointed me to bring glad tidings to the afflicted; he has sent me to bind up the brokenhearted, to proclaim liberty to the captives and the opening of the prison to those who are bound; to proclaim the year of the Lord's favor, and the day of vengeance of our God; to comfort all who mourn" (Is 61:1-2).

Although the Wisdom writers were not prophets in the true sense of the word, they also offer some counsel and consolation for those suffering servants of God. It would only be fair to include some of their observations in dealing with our sufferings, for they too were inspired by the word of God. Let us look at some of these pearls of wisdom, words that have kept many a troubled soul from the depths of despair, only to enkindle in them a renewed sense of hope in our Lord.

The wisdom writings of the Old Testament consist of five books: Proverbs, Job, Ecclesiastes (in Hebrew, Qoheleth), Ecclesiasticus (in Hebrew, Jesus ben Sira, or Sirach), and the Wisdom of Solomon. One of the central themes in these writings is the treatment of suffering: the problems of life; why God's people suffer and why the wicked prosper; how to live a good moral life and how to behave towards God.

King Solomon is believed to have been the author of all of the wisdom books with the exception of Sirach. The Jewish legends in the Talmud reaffirm this belief, although it is highly doubtful whether Solomon is responsible for all of this material, since many of the sayings are extremely similar (if not identical with) earlier ancient writings of the Near Eastern civilizations. This is particularly true of many Mesopotamian and Egyptian wisdom sayings that have been preserved and predate the wisdom writings of the Bible.

King David himself was known for his wisdom (2 Sm 14:20), and he is known to have written as many as a thousand song-poems during his life. It is possible that many of his sayings found their way into the wisdom literature as well.

In the Book of Ecclesiastes, we are reminded again of the value of patience in dealing with our sufferings. In the memorable passages that follow, we see that the Lord balances our lives with a mixture of blessings and trials, in order that we may grow in patience and in virtue, lest we take His goodness too much for granted. The ebbs and flows of life build moral character, and provide us with the strength to endure our hardships in the midst of our faith. In this respect, our uncertainty forces us to take each day at a time, for we "do not know what a day may bring forth" (Prv 27:1). It helps keep us humble and entirely reliant upon God, lest we boast of any good-doing on our own. God is the source of all our blessings; perhaps this is why He tempers our confidence with the uncertainties of life.

Let us meditate on these profound statements from the Book of Ecclesiastes, where Solomon teaches about the attitude we must have on our journey through life:

For everything there is a season, and a time for every matter under heaven; a time to be born, and a time to die; a time to plant, and a time to pluck up what is planted; a time to kill, and a time to heal; a time to break down, and a time to build up; a time to weep, and a time to laugh; a time to mourn, and a time to dance; a time to cast away stones, and a time to gather stones together; a time to embrace, and a time to refrain from embracing; a time to seek, and a time to lose; a time to keep, and a time to cast away; a time to rend, and a time to sew; a time to keep silence, and a time to speak; a time to love, and a time to hate; a time for war, and a time for peace. . . (Eccles 3:1-8).

The Book of Wisdom counsels the suffering to remain firm in their faith, for the Lord will not desert them. Here we find that at times God tests us to see how true our faith really is: "Having been disciplined a little, they will receive great good, because God tested them and found them worthy of himself" (Wis 3:5).

The willingness to offer up our sufferings for ourselves and for others is very pleasing to God. When we do so voluntarily and with complete submission to the will of God, we build up merits and help to purify our souls. Our sacrifice of self atones for the many sins we commit, and strengthens the grace the Lord has given us: "Like gold in the furnace, he tried them, and like *sacrificial burnt offerings* he accepted them. In the time of their visitation they shall shine" (Wis 3:6-7). Note that when we offer ourselves up to God — our trials and sufferings — we become living sacrifices, or victims of love, helping to repair for the offenses committed against our God. We can also offer up our sufferings through the spirit of penance and prayer to help atone for the sins of others. If done with a sincere heart, we help others on their way to their heavenly home. To sacrifice for others is a supreme act of charity, one that pleases the Father and proves us worthy to be called His sons and daughters.

We cannot escape these tests from our Lord; they are sure signs of the way of perfection: "My Son, if you come forward to serve the Lord, prepare yourself for temptation" (Sir 2:1). We are tried to keep us humble, lest we should swell with pride: "For gold is tested in the fire, and acceptable men in the furnace of humiliation" (2:5). We must fear the Lord and humble ourselves before Him (2:17), yet the Lord is merciful and saves us in times of trouble (2:11).

Perhaps the greatest test we are put to in this life is that of sickness and of death. We are to trust in the Lord's deliverance from illness, and to pray for our healing: "My son, when you are sick do not be negligent, but pray to the Lord, and he will heal you" (Sir 38:9). Yet we know that God sometimes chooses to keep one in illness for reasons He knows best. Yet it is clear that we are to keep on praying for deliverance, and to trust in His mercy.

Illness can be a tragic experience, and so can death. Sometimes we question the loss of a loved one, especially those in the prime of their lives. Feelings of sorrow and even bitterness can overwhelm the best of us, and frequently we ask our God — why?

Sirach addresses this sensitive issue with a reassuring feeling. He comforts us, telling us that we must mourn for awhile, but then it is time to go on with our lives. In fact, he stresses that it is you and I who are lost in sorrow with the departed, for they are now in the peace of their eternal reward. We ought to be happy that they have reached their heavenly home; to dwell on their departure would only be harmful to us, for the dead are now living. Let us turn to the touching homily of death that Sirach has presented to the faithful:

My son, let your tears fall for the dead, and as one who is suffering grievously begin the lament. Lay out his body with the honor
due him, and do not neglect this burial. Let your weeping be bitter and your wailing fervent; observe the mourning according to
his merit, for one day, or two, to avoid criticism; then be comforted for your sorrow. For sorrow results in death, and sorrow of
heart saps one's strength. In calamity sorrow continues, and the
life of the poor man weighs down his heart. Do not give your
heart to sorrow; drive it away, remembering the end of life. Do
not forget, there is no coming back; you do the dead no good, and
you injure yourself. 'Remember my doom, for yours is like it: yesterday it was mine, and today it is yours.' When the dead is at
rest, let his remembrance cease and be comforted for him when
his spirit has departed (Sir 38:16-23).

Although we have not covered all of the prophets or wisdom writings in
this section, at least we are able to touch upon some memorable words that
these sacred writers have given to us under the guidance of the Holy Spirit. I
encourage you to read these inspiring works more fully, for there is a wealth
of wisdom locked behind each and every page. Nurture each line with a
prayerful meditation, and let God's Spirit enlighten you and bring you
peace in the midst of life's burdens.

Jesus Christ as Victim

No talk of God's suffering servants would be complete without a
discussion pointing to Jesus Christ — the ultimate victim soul and
stigmatist. There has been a tendency in the past to emphasize the victim
soul or stigmatist as a bearer of Christ's Passion without a vision of Christ
being a bearer of our sufferings:

... though he was in the form of God, he did not count equality
with God a thing to be grasped, but emptied himself, taking the
form of a servant, being born in the likeness of men. And being
found in human form he humbled himself and became obedient
unto death, even death on a cross. Therefore God has highly
exalted him and bestowed on him the name which is above every
name, that at the name of Jesus every knee should bow, in
heaven and on earth and under the earth, and every tongue
confess that Jesus Christ is Lord, to the glory of God the Father
(Phil 2:6-11).

This reciprocal relationship is so important in understanding the
mystery of our redemption; it was He who sacrificed himself for us (Ti 2:14),
and we in turn must be crucified with Him (Gal 2:19), in order to live with
Him more fully (Rom 6:6-11).

Our Lord became a victim of love, receiving this vocation out of
obedience to the Father (Heb 5:8). He was tested through His suffering, in
order to help those who in turn are tempted (Heb 2:18). God has sent His
Son as an offering for our sins (1 Jn 4:10), and we in turn are expected to
offer ourselves for one another in order to remain fully united in Him (1 Jn
4:11-16). In other words, our attitude must be that of Christ (Phil 2:5), who

offered himself for the sins of all. Jesus, Victim of all victims, continually needs the offering of our sufferings to complete the mystery of our redemption. He is both God and man. What He suffers, we suffer; and what we suffer, He suffers.

Let us remember what St. Paul beautifully describes about the reciprocal role we have with our Lord in His Passion. It is a call to cooperation with Jesus for the salvation of souls:

> Now I rejoice in my sufferings for your sake, and in my flesh I complete what is lacking in Christ's afflictions for the sake of His body, that is, the church (Col 1:24).

Paul further reminds us that:

> For just as the body is one and has many members, and all the members of the body, though many, are one body, and so it is with Christ. If one member suffers, all suffer together; if one member is honored, all rejoice together (1 Cor 12:12,26).

If one closely examines the life of our Lord, he or she will soon discover that His entire being was continually subjected to trials, sufferings and persecutions. It was love that compelled Him to accept these conditions — foremost, the love of the Father (Jn 14:31), and secondly the love for all mankind (Jn 15:12-13). Jesus encourages us to follow His example. He teaches us that to bear our crosses patiently does not go without its reward: "I have said this to you, that in me you may have peace. In the world you have tribulation; but be of good cheer, I have overcome the world" (Jn 16:33).

The reason Jesus is so worthy to be the Father's Victim for the sake of our redemption is that He and He alone humbled himself and became man for the sake of all humankind: nobody else could ever humble themselves in such a manner, for we cannot become humans — we already are. We have never been more than human, yet Jesus was infinitely so. Our humility never reaches such a profound depth as that of our Lord.

Let us recall the immortal passages from Isaiah the prophet, who tells us well how deserving the Lord is to be our Savior. We take our passages from the suffering and triumph of the servant theme in the fifty-third chapter:

> Behold, my servant shall prosper, he shall be exalted and lifted up, and shall be very high. As many were astonished at him — his appearance was so marred beyond human semblance, and his form beyond that of the sons of men — so shall he startle many nations; kings shall shut their mouths because of him; for that which has not been told them they see, and that which they have not heard they shall understand.

> Who has believed what we have heard? And to whom has the arm of the Lord been revealed? For he grew up before him like a young plant, and like a root out of dry ground; he had no form or comeliness that we should look at him, and no beauty that we should desire him. He was despised and rejected by men; a man

of sorrows, and acquainted with grief; and as one from whom men hide their faces he was despised, and we esteemed him not.

Surely he has borne our griefs and carried our sorrows; yet we esteemed him stricken, smitten by God, and afflicted. But he was wounded for our transgressions, he was bruised for our iniquities; upon him was the chastisement that made us whole, and with his stripes we are healed. All we like sheep have gone astray; we have turned every one to his own way; and the Lord has laid on him the iniquity of us all.

He was oppressed, and he was afflicted, yet he opened not his mouth; like a lamb that is led to the slaughter, and like a sheep that before its shearers is dumb, so he opened not his mouth. By oppression and judgment he was taken away; and as for his generation, who considered that he was cut off out of the land of the living, stricken for the transgression of my people? And they made his grave with the wicked and with a rich man in his death, although he had done no violence, and there was no deceit in his mouth.

Yet it was the will of the Lord to bruise him; he has put him to grief; when he makes himself an offering for sin, he shall see his offspring, he shall prolong his days; the will of the Lord shall prosper in his hand; he shall see the fruit of the travail of his soul and be satisfied; by his knowledge shall the righteous one, my servant, make many to be accounted righteous; and he shall bear their iniquities. Therefore I will divide him a portion and he shall divide the spoil with the strong; because he poured out his soul to death, and was numbered with the transgressors; yet he bore the sin of many, and made intercession for the transgressors (Is 52: 13-15; 53:1-12).

Unlikely there are any words in Sacred Scripture so profound, so moving as these passages from the prophet Isaiah (although the words from Philippians 2:6-11 re-echo this theme and are beautiful themselves). Here we find all we need to know about our Suffering Servant; here we find Jesus as the ultimate Victim for our sins, the Lamb who has been led out to slaughter. It will serve us well if we conclude this unit on Jesus as Victim by addressing the main lessons Isaiah has taught us about our Redeemer.

In chapter 53 (verses 4-5), a description of our Lord as Victim is clear. He voluntarily offered himself up to atone for the sins of others, and God used Him for such. By leading a life of expiation for our sins, the Father gave to Him the sufferings allotted to the people for their sins — sufferings that they themselves would be subjected to from the Almighty for their transgressions, if it weren't for the voluntary intercession of the Sacrificial Lamb (vs. 5-6). Jesus *became* our sin in order to free us from our sin (vs. 10), a total unconditional sacrifice that ultimately led to martyrdom — a consummation of the Cross.

At the end of His brief life, Jesus became a stigmatist — a prototype for all victim souls who would follow His way throughout the history of the Church. He is Precursor to all of God's suffering servants, a model that needs no other. Perhaps it sounds strange to refer to Jesus as a stigmatist. Part of this could be because we are not used to seeing our Lord as the Victim of God's love. The other part is because we can associate others as imitating Christ, but it is rather difficult to understand our Lord's imitation of the Father of all. But does the Father suffer? Can Jesus atone for that? Remember that Jesus is not only our brother; He is also our God. The Father *suffers* through the Son, and only out of love for us — not because of any imperfection on His part. In this sense, the Father and the Son have suffered for us because of their enduring love. We, in turn, suffer because of our separation from the fullness of life, caused by the sins we must atone for. Some of God's holy ones have responded by offering themselves in union with Christ to bridge the gap between God's love and our sin. A few of these holy victims have borne the stigmata to do just that.

The great event in the history of Christianity, the climax to Jesus' suffering, is our Lord's resurrection. Preceding this glorious event was the Passion, the total-embodiment of human suffering, past, present and future. It was not only the climax to Jesus' terrible sufferings throughout His earthly life; it was also the consummation of the mystery of our redemption. In one dramatic moment in history, the fall of man through sin had been restored, if he believed in Jesus Christ as his Savior and repented of his sin. The door was now open to salvation if he accepted the consummation of our Lord on the Cross. Though we continue to sin and fall away from grace, the gift of salvation is available to all through this one momentous act. Our freedom of will allows us to receive the Cross and to embrace it; it is our choice: the choice of salvation or ruin.

The blood of our Lord was spilled for the atonement of all. The Victim of all victims was spent; His life was poured out as a ransom for many, a life that delivered us from eternal darkness. No longer need we cry for salvation — the Lord has removed the chains of sin. Yet sin remains because of our choosing; there is no sin inherent in grace. We create our own sin through separation from God, and through submission to the wiles of the evil one. It is therefore necessary that we remain continually in grace, for apart from grace there is no salvation, and apart from Christ there is no grace. Before the coming of our Lord, the Father graced His people; but now that He has given us His only begotten Son, our grace comes from the Father *through* Jesus Christ.

Jesus is the "true vine," and the Father is the "vinegrower" (Jn 15:1). No one comes to the Father except through our Lord (Jn 14:6), and the Father accomplishes all His works through the Son (Jn 14:10). Properly speaking, no true Christian can believe in the Father without believing in His Son (Jn 5:23;14:7). And in order to believe in the Son, our faith has to point to the Cross.

The Cross has always been at the heart of the Catholic faith, and rightly so. The world too often de-emphasizes the role of unmerited grace as a gift freely given (and not earned). Too often others preach a message of self-righteousness and the power of positive thinking, ignoring the redemptive value of the Cross. Paul reminds us all of the centrality of the Cross in his address to the Galatians: "But far be it from me to glory except in the cross of our Lord Jesus Christ!" (Gal 6:14). Positive thinking is fine, but only at the foot of the Cross, lest we forget the lessons of original sin and the harm that pride and self-esteem have caused us throughout the era of human history. We cannot create our own salvation; it is the Lamb of God who will take away the sins of the world (Jn 1:29), a lamb who was led to the slaughter for the ransom of many.

In the Passion narrative of our Gospel, we find a moving discourse on Jesus' sufferings at the Garden of Gethsemani. Jesus tells us that his soul was "very sorrowful, even to death" (Mt 26:38). At one critical point, he finds the weight of His suffering almost unbearable; yet our Lord still submits to the will of the Father, obedient to the very end: "My Father, if it be possible, let this cup pass from me; nevertheless, not as I will, but as thou wilt" (Mt 26:39). What a supreme lesson in faith our Lord teaches us! What humility and obedience our Savior clings to! It is a lesson for all of us in times of darkness and despair. It is reassuring that even our Lord, in His human condition, shows signs of struggle; yet He does not falter, for turning to the Father in prayer He finds His one true hope, His everlasting peace.

The importance of prayer through our struggles cannot be overemphasized. The power of prayer! The best example of this is from Jesus himself, who always resorts to prayer when in need of consolation, favor, or peace in the heart. We see Him resort to prayer with His anguish at Gethsemani (Mt 26:36-44); He prays to the Father on the Cross (Mt 27:46), and even at the point of His death (Lk 23:46). Even in the midst of all this sorrow, Jesus found time to sing songs of praise with His disciples after the institution of the Last Supper (see Mk 14:22-26). His faith and courage were such as has never been known.

In spite of the trials and tribulations our Lord went through, especially at the close of His earthly life, He is forgiving of others, a sign of true charity toward His brothers and sisters. This, too, is a lesson in suffering: the need for patience with each other in times of distress, and the charitable act of forgiveness that creates in us a new heart.

In the Garden of Gethsemani, when Jesus was being arrested, He scolds a disciple for striking the high priest's servant with a sword, cutting off his ear: " 'No more of this!' And he (Jesus) touched his ear and healed him" (Lk 22:51). When confronted before Herod, Jesus was ridiculed and severely questioned, yet He remained silent, unwilling to retaliate or defend himself: "So he (Herod) questioned him at some length; but he made no answer" (Lk 23:9). What patience and kindness toward those who falsely condemn Him! It is a true lesson in charity, as our Lord has taught us throughout His life: "But love your enemies, and do good" (Lk 6:35); "Be merciful even as your Father is merciful. Judge not, and you will not be judged; condemn not, and you will not be condemned" (Lk 6:36-37); "Love your enemies and pray for those who persecute you" (Mt 5:44). This is a true test of faith when we are suffering, yet it is the command of the Lord for all to follow.

When Jesus appeared to His followers after His Resurrection, all of His messages were ones of faith, hope and love. He gives His disciples these reassuring words in the Gospel of Matthew: ". . . And lo, I am with you always, to the close of the age!" (Mt 28:20). In the Gospel of Luke, Jesus appears to the disciples and reassures their sorrowing hearts: "Peace to you" (Lk 24:36). Even the Gospel of John records the words, "Peace be with you" (Jn 20:19), and says it once again (Jn 20:21). John's Gospel concludes the sayings of Jesus with this comforting passage: "Blessed are those who have not seen and yet believe" (Jn 20:29).

Let us learn from the lessons of our Master and by the examples of His life. Suffering, as we have seen, is a necessary part of living, even for the Son of God. Yet He came to show us the way, the truth and the life (Jn 14:6-7), to comfort us in our sorrow, and to help us overcome the battles of our lives. Though we may falter from time-to-time, we remain firm in our faith through the mercy and grace of our Lord Jesus Christ. Let us come to the foot of the Cross, for it is there that we will find our redemption and salvation.

Mary as Suffering Servant

Much has been written over the course of the centuries describing the role of the Blessed Virgin Mary in God's plan of salvation. Many titles and attributes have been used to explain her privileges and sublime virtues. We will limit our discussion to those characteristics of our Lady that relate to the mystery of suffering and the value it has for the Church in the modern world. In order to understand the present, however, one needs to take a step backward as a matter of perspective.

Although the Gospel says little explicitly about the Virgin Mary's role in our faith, nevertheless what is said is both profound and moving. We simply cannot understand our Lord's Passion and the mystery of our redemption without concern for the one who was most familiar with His life and suffering: the Blessed Virgin Mary.

No one in history was as close to our Lord's suffering as the Madonna; no one has better exemplified the role of obedient servant to God's holy will more than she: " 'Behold, I am the handmaid of the Lord; let it be to me according to your word' " (Lk 1:38). We know that Mary was God's highly favored daughter (Lk 1:28), and she was called blest by both Elizabeth (Lk 1:42) and as a self-proclamation through the impulse of the Spirit (Lk 1:48).

To further emphasize Mary's subliminal role, the Gospel tells us more: she was the Mother of God (Mt 1:23); a virgin most pure (Mt 1:23); great before the Lord (Lk 1:46); humble of heart (Lk 1:48); and trusting in her ways (Lk 1:45). Clearly, she deserves the dignity and honor the Church has rightfully given her throughout the ages. No other person in the Gospels except for Jesus is so highly praised as this humble virgin from Nazareth.

But where does the role of Mary fit in with the meaning of suffering in God's people? How does it all tie in with the roles of those chosen souls called to a life of redemptive suffering?

It's no accident that most known stigmatists in Church history have been women. St. Teresa of Avila (1515-82) once said that the Holy Spirit generally selects the weaker sex for extraordinary graces; they have also been more humble and obedient to God and their superiors. Women are usually more receptive to the impulses of the Spirit. They are generally more sensitive and trusting than their male counterparts. According to Father Charles M. Carty, women outnumber men in many callings where courage and consistency of a higher order are necessary; they usually have a greater capacity for suffering than do most men.

All of this is not meant to undermine the male character. Obviously many great saints and stigmatists have come forth from the male ranks. It is only intended to show that these factors and others previously mentioned point to the Virgin Mary as a likely vehicle for the one chosen to be Co-Redemptrix and Mediatrix of grace, in cooperation with our Lord's mission as sole Mediator before the Father in the plan of our redemption. By her grace and virtue, Mary has earned the privilege to represent us before our Master through prayer and by way of vicarious suffering.

Do we know that Mary truly suffered on our behalf? Does she deserve to be honored as Co-Redemptrix and Mother of our Church? Certainly. The Gospel reveals this as well; it is confirmed by the Magisterium of the Catholic Church. Vatican II has this to say about her role:

> The Blessed Virgin is invoked in the Church under the titles of Advocate, Helper, Benefactress, and Mediatrix. By reason of the gift and role of her divine motherhood, by which she is united with her Son, the Redeemer, and with her unique graces and functions, the Blessed Virgin is also intimately united to the Church. . . . (Vatican II, *Lumen Gentium*, November 21, 1964.)

Or again, from the same document:

> She conceived, brought forth, and nourished Christ, and shared her Son's sufferings as he died on the cross. Mary, in keeping with the divine plan, enduring with her only begotten Son the intensity of His suffering, associated herself with His sacrifice in her mother's heart, and lovingly consenting to the immolation of this victim that was born of her. . . .

These passages clearly reflect upon Mary's role in redemptive suffering (Co-Redemptrix), fully uniting her to her Son, the Redeemer of the human race. She became a victim of divine love, the Church's first victim soul.

Pope Benedict XV stated that on Calvary, our Lady "to such extent . . . immolated Him (Christ), in so far as she could, in order to appease the justice of God, that we may rightfully say that she redeemed the human race together with Christ" (AAS 10, 1918). And according to Pope Pius XII, Mary cooperated in our redemption "in such a way that our salvation flowed from the love of Jesus Christ and His sufferings intimately joined with the love and sorrows of His Mother" (AAS 48, 1956).

What does the Gospel message teach us about Mary's suffering? From the very beginning of our Lord's earthly mission, Mary was a suffering servant: She had a trust crisis with her espoused Joseph (Mt 1:18-25); she was "greatly troubled" by the overwhelming sense of her mission as Mother of God (Lk 1:26-36); she struggled through her time of pregnancy and with the birth of her Child; Mary had to endure threats made upon her Child and subsequent travel to a harsh, foreign land (Mt 2:13-15); and the Virgin was troubled over her Son's disappearance in the Temple at Jerusalem (Lk 2:41-50).

After our Lord's mission became public, Mary certainly was mocked and humiliated by unsympathetic friends and neighbors who failed to understand the calling of her Son. Yet she stood faithfully by Him, even unto death on the Cross (Jn 19:25). To watch as Jesus was scourged and beaten, crowned with thorns, brought to trial, and nailed to a cross is a suffering no one has ever known, then or since. Mary shared in the Passion completely, vicariously suffering the wounds of our Lord. Her heart lay truly pierced, just as the pious Simeon foretold (Lk 2:35). She had watched everything (Lk 23:49), and even helped prepare His cold, battered body for burial (Lk 23:55-56).

Was the Virgin Mary the Church's first authentic stigmatist? This author knows of no such claim in historical records, and the Church has never officially declared her as such. But perhaps she was. Simeon gives us the first indication that this may have been the case: "The child's father and mother were marveling at what was being said about him. Simeon blessed them and said to Mary his mother: " 'Behold, this child is set for the fall and rising of many in Israel, and for a sign that is spoken against (and a sword will pierce through your own soul also), that thoughts out of many hearts may be revealed' " (Lk 2:33-35). Perhaps this prophecy indicates a suffering that would produce an invisible stigmata at least of the heart (this phenomenon will be treated later in this book).

Mary certainly carried the Passion of our Lord in her innermost being, sharing each agonizing moment with her most precious Son; His heart was hers, and her heart was His. It is almost inconceivable that so much suffering could not affect at least the soul (if not the body) by injuring it through the pains of love. After all, Mary "kept all these things pondering them in her heart" (Lk 2:19) when reflecting upon her Son (also see Lk 2:51).

It is quite clear from Scripture that our Lady was pierced in the heart. Although this could very well indicate an emotional wound, it may be evidence for our first victim soul in the Church — an internally stigmatized woman called the Mother of God. If this was the case, then Mary truly became our Co-Redemptrix, as sharer in the Passion of Jesus our Lord.

The history of the Church has a rich tradition regarding devotion to the Immaculate Heart of Mary. St. Anselm (d. 1109), Eadmer (d. 1141), St. Bernard (d. 1153), and Hugh of St. Victor (d. 1140) were only a few of the many who helped promote this devotion.

Other well-known Catholic saints helped bring this veneration of Mary's Immaculate Heart to a rich and fuller dimension: St. Mathilda of Hackeborn (1241-1298), St. Gertrude the Great (1252-1302), St. Bridget of Sweden (1303-1373), and the "Doctor of the Heart of Mary," St. Bernardine of Siena (1380-1444).

In more recent times, Mary allegedly appeared to three peasant children at Fatima in Portugal (1917) and announced that she favored devotion to her Immaculate Heart. As recently as 1987, Pope John Paul II announced a new Marian Year to be honored by all the faithful. In his address to the universal Church, the Holy Father encouraged his flock to honor Mary's heart as an intimate part of our devotion to the Sacred Heart of Jesus. The two hearts of our Savior and our Lady are so intimately connected that they are as of one.

It's interesting to note that practically every image of Mary's Immaculate Heart shows the heart being pierced or having been wounded, even bleeding in many cases. In numerous pilgrimages of Marian statues depicting her Immaculate Heart, the bleeding from the eyes and/or heart has been observed and photographed. Literally dozens of cases have been reported in North American pilgrimages from the mid-1970s through the present time. Father Albert Hebert, S.M., covers these miraculous tears and bleedings in his wonderful book, *The Tears of Mary and Fatima: Why?* (P.O. Box 309, Paulina, LA, 70763).

Berthe Petit, the Belgian lay Franciscan mystic (1870-1943) who reportedly received messages from our Lady concerning devotion to her heart, heard this command from our Lord himself: "The Heart of My Mother has the right to be entitled 'Sorrowful,' and I wish this title to be placed before that of 'Immaculate,' because she has won it herself."

Why is this so? Our Lord explained to Berthe: "She has merited it by her identification with My sorrows, by her sufferings, her sacrifices, her immolation on Calvary endured for the salvation of mankind in perfect correspondence with My Grace."

Father and distinguished scholar R.P. Garrigou-Lagrange, O.P., stated that "by referring to Mary's 'Sorrowful Heart,' we recall all that she has suffered and offered for us, in union with her Son — beginning with the words of the aged prophet Simeon up to the day she stood beneath the Cross on Calvary."

This brings us to the question of Mary's suffering as a means of helping atone for the many sins of humankind. How can this be so if Jesus is the one Mediator before the Father? Was He not the perfect sacrificial Victim? How can the Blessed Virgin Mary be considered a victim soul — a Mediatrix or Co-Redemptrix — for us sinners in light of this fact?

It is by Mary's compassion with the sufferings of her Son that the Mother of God became the Mother of Humanity, the Mother of our Church. Mary, then, loves all those whom Jesus died to save, all of us, His Mystical Body, because she was so intimately connected with His Passion. When Jesus told Mary to "behold thy Son" (John), and John to "behold thy Mother," it was clear that Mary was commissioned by our Lord to continue His love and compassion for the souls He suffered for and died to save. Because she brought forth the Savior of the world, Mary is worthy to return to Him the world of hungry souls in need of expiation of their sins. Her Son will refuse her nothing (what son wouldn't?), because she remained true to God's will.

Mary's sufferings have also been recognized in devotions to her sorrows, formally celebrated as the Feast of Our Lady of Sorrows each September 15. This feast dates back to the fourteenth century, but its roots are firmly entrenched in the Gospels. As Pope Paul VI has stated in his encyclical *Marialus Cultus*: "Mary was intimately associated with the mystery of salvation accomplished by Christ, as Mother of the Suffering Servant of Yahweh."

Devotion to Mary's sorrows begins in the fourteenth century, most notably with the Blessed Henry Suso (1295-1365). Eventually, "five sorrows" of Mary became one part of the Passion meditations accepted by the Church (the others being the "five joys," and later the "seven joys").

In the twentieth century, an increase in the number of Marian apparitions has taken place. Indeed, our era in the Church has often been called the "Marian Age" because of this very reason. This Marian Age really begins with our Lady's appearances and messages to St. Catherine Laboure of the Miraculous Medal, which started in 1830 at the Rue du Bac in Paris.

Some will claim that the Marian Age really began in 1531 at Guadalupe, Mexico, where the peasant Juan Diego was visited numerous times by the Blessed Virgin. There he received messages from our Lady, as well as the now famous imprint of our Lady's image on his old, worn cloak. I prefer the 1830 date as a logical starting point, because between 1531 and 1830 there are few legitimately recognized Marian apparitions. The messages and visits have remained constant ever since St. Catherine's supernatural experiences (although I do not doubt for a moment the authenticity of the apparitions at Guadalupe).

Most of these messages concern the sorrows of Mary, warnings of divine

34

judgment, and tears of suffering shed by the Virgin Mother over a sinful world in need of prayer, sacrifice and repentance. Lourdes, France (1858), Pontmain, France (1871), Knock, Ireland (1879), Fatima, Portugal (1917), Beauraing and Banneux, Belgium (1932-33), and Medjugorje, Yugoslavia (1981-present) have all been recognized by the faithful throughout the world as Marian devotion centers. All but Medjugorje have been officially approved by the Church as authentic apparition sites. (Note: because the alleged visions and messages continue to this day at Medjugorje, the Church cannot yet pronounce judgment. Open-mindedness tempered with caution must be the attitude toward current claims such as in Medjugorje until the Church has spent the necessary time — which could be years — investigating and analyzing the situation surrounding the claims. Prudence is necessary for the proper guidance of the faithful, in case such claims prove to be false and the faithful are deceived. This author has been to Medjugorje, and I must say I have seen nothing negative in the messages and the attitudes of the people. Medjugorge has been a blessing to hundreds of thousands, and I felt the presence of God most powerfully. Still, we must wait out of obedience to the Church.)

Because Medjugorje has been visited by more than eight million people since 1981, and because the total number of apparitions and messages are unparalleled in the history of the Church, we should at least take a brief look at what has been going on there. Remember: until the Church makes an official judgment, we are free to believe in terms of *human faith*, or to not believe. In fact, it is never a dogma of our faith to believe or not to believe in any apparitions anyway; it is always a question of human, not divine, faith. The Church can only advise the faithful what she judges to be credible or not; she doesn't enforce a solemn judgment on private revelation. Yet if she pronounces against a reported apparition, we are wise to heed what she says and why. Still, we are free to believe in our hearts what we choose if there is nothing in the teaching contrary to divine law or the solemn teachings of the Church on issues of faith or morals.

Six young seers in Medjugorje, Yugoslavia, have reported daily apparitions of Mary — messages for themselves, for the Holy Father and for the world. These alleged visions are currently under investigation by Rome and may take some time for evaluation, for well over 2,000 messages and visible appearances from Mary have been claimed by these visionaries, if we believe that they have occurred daily since June 24, 1981. Several of the visionaries no longer receive these messages or see the Madonna on a daily basis (because the visions and daily messages end when a seer receives ten "secrets" from the apparition). Yet several of them still claim to see her daily (Vicka, Jakov, Ivan, and Maria). The other two (Marjana and Ivanka) no longer see the daily apparitions, because they now have all ten secrets. The other four have received nine of the ten.

The messages are significant because they stress what our Lady has always said to the faithful: prayer, fasting, conversion, and penance as the road to peace and the way back to God. The messages also emphasize the importance of the sacraments (especially the Eucharist and Reconciliation), the daily Mass, and the centrality of Jesus in our Faith. Theologically and scripturally, the messages are hard to put down, because they echo the Gospel principles so vividly.

The countless healings, both inner and physical, that have occurred at Medjugorje are truly remarkable. One need only visit Medjugorje to see the sincerity of the people, both the villagers and the pilgrims. Perhaps it is the best evidence to date on God's presence in this corner of the world. Yet some messages need careful discernment from the Church because of their eschatological nature. Such messages indeed need careful evaluation.

Significantly, many hours of film footage have witnessed these seers during the actual Marian visits and provide solid evidence for the evaluation process currently going on. Most experts have believed the visions to be authentic through examining these films, psychological tests on the visionaries, and the sound principles the messages seem to bring forth. One ardent supporter has been the Archbishop of Split, Yugoslavia, Fran Franic. Another avid supporter is the world renowned Marian scholar, Father Rene Laurentin of France. Yet some high authorities in the Church remain skeptical, such as Bishop Pavao Zanić, the ordinary of the Diocese of Mostar, which includes the village of Medjugorje. (In all fairness to Bishop Zanić and to understand the alleged statements of Mary about his opposition, please read up on the current books available about Medjugorje. It is a complicated situation, more so than readily meets the eye. Government opposition, local historical tensions and current Church frictions have made the evaluations less than objective and fair at times.) The human element sometimes mixes unfavorably with the divine.

Why have I dealt with a place like Medjugorje so much in this discussion about the sufferings of Mary? Because a great deal of these messages (and other reported apparitions and messages in our era) are concerned with Mary's sorrow over a world on the brink of disaster, caused by its own sin. She has called us to repentance and conversion, and continues to do so. Who can argue with that? Yet we continue to harden our hearts and ignore the warnings our Mother continues to give to us. This should come as no surprise, for mankind has always been enslaved in its own sin (who can doubt the doctrine of Original Sin?). We are still Adam and Eve; we are still in need of God's mercy and our own conversion (*metanoia*; literally, a "change of heart"). The messages of Mary are the same yesterday as today: convert, convert, convert. It is mainly through prayer, fasting, and reconciliation that we achieve these things. It is obvious why our Mother suffers for her children, lost in the web of their own sin.

The messages are *not* of inevitable doom, as fundamentalist doomsday seekers would like to believe. They are in reality positive messages of hope. We still have a chance to appease the Father's wrath, if we will only change our hearts. We are still living in a period of grace, and there is still the opportunity of salvation for everyone. But the time of grace will not last forever, as we are so often reminded throughout Sacred Scripture. Chastisement will occur for those lost in their sin. Yet the Virgin tells us time and again that there's hope in a merciful God who loves us. But if we do not change, there is also a God of justice who will reveal himself, if necessary. What a shocking revelation *that* God will be to hardened sinners!

If these statements from Medjugorje and others in the past are authentic, then the Virgin has taken upon herself the sorrows of her people. As Mother of our Church, she is a "suffering servant" for all souls on behalf of her Son, Jesus. Although Mary says that her sufferings on our behalf have helped to appease divine justice up to this point, it won't always be this way. Let us look to the Mother of Sorrows for mercy and intercession before Jesus her Son, in order that we might all be saved.

What do all of these visions and messages mean to a twentieth-century

Christian? One thing is certain: the Mother of God still cares for us, and re-assures us by her presence that God still cares as well. She still keeps us under her protective mantle, suffering the Passion of Christ on behalf of her Son for the benefit of all her children. If she loves us such, then how much more the Father and the Son! Mary is a victim of God's enduring love for a sin-filled world, an advocate and protectress for our salvation. She is "full of grace," and continues to share that grace with humanity as Mother and Mediatrix to all who pray for her love and her mercy. Let us not disappoint her and keep her bathed in sorrow over our transgressions. Look to Mary our Mother with the eyes of a child and call upon her help.

The Theology of St. Paul

Although many scholars today question the Pauline origins of several of the epistles (most notably the so-called "deutero-Pauline" letters — 2Thessalonians, Colossians, Ephesians, and the pastoral epistles, 1 and 2Timothy and Titus), most agree that these were transmitted by some disciples who wrote under the authority of the Pauline Tradition. Indeed, many of the non-Pauline epistles may in fact be true to the spirit of the teachings of the great Apostle, just as we believe in the Gospel messages even though they too are products of a second generation removed from the time of Christ. With this in mind, I refer to all quotes here as having a direct link to the Pauline Tradition and therefore authoritative in their own right.

Perhaps no New Testament figure describes so vividly the mystery of suffering as the Apostle Paul. Through his letters, Paul gives us a wealth of theological reflections on the values and merits of suffering for the Kingdom of God. Indeed, we might rightfully call him the "Apostle of suffering," for he knew all too well what it meant to live and feel the pains and trials of the Christian life. Let us look a bit closer at our beloved Apostle's mystical journey, a journey that led him to union with the Lord after a long climb on the narrow road to salvation.

Physically, Paul's sufferings really begin after his great conversion experience. He was temporarily blinded (Acts 9:8) and deprived of food for three days (Acts 9:9). Many mystics in Church history have experienced a blindness ("dark night") and a purification on the way to perfection, initiated by our Lord himself to prepare the soul for union with Him (a passive purification, completely free of our own self-imposed penances or acts of purgation). Paul's lack of food further served to purify his physical self, and served a painful reminder of the one thing he lacked for so long before his conversion: Jesus Christ, the true Bread of Life (Jn 6:27,35).

Through Divine Providence, these traumatic trials further serve to create in Paul an insatiable desire to seek the Lord at any cost, to be transformed into His likeness. As a result, Paul the persecutor becomes the persecuted one for Christ, and soon becomes His most enthusiastic witness (Acts 9:20-22).

Trials continued to visit Paul, however, as the darkness of night fell amidst the light of pure faith. The Jews sought to end his life, and his own fellow disciples were afraid of him (Acts 9:23-26).

Like the great mystics of all ages, Paul is, by the Lord's design, placed in the desert to further purify his soul in the ascent to God. From his conversion to his call to missionary work is a period of approximately ten years.

Paul retreats to Arabia, then visits Damascus and Jerusalem, only to be compelled to take flight from the Jews who want his life. He finally ends up in Antioch, spiritually strengthened by the darkness of the desert experience. From Antioch, the Church is born and continues to spread, with Paul at the helm in the crusade for Christianity.

Yet our beloved Apostle's trials continued. His missionary journeys are not without severe hardships (see 2 Cor 11:24-27). On the first journey (ca. A.D. 47-50), hardships occur that cause even John Mark to return to Jerusalem (Acts 13:13-14). While in Lystra, Jews plotted against Paul, wanting to have him stoned. Back in Jerusalem at the first "council" (Acts 15:6), Paul suffers the opposition of his peers. Perhaps most painful of all, Paul and Peter have a falling out at Antioch in A.D.49 over eating regulations of Jewish and Gentile Christians (see Gal 2:11-16).

On his second journey (ca. 51-54), Paul further struggles through Asia Minor, only to be followed by more ordeals in Europe at Thessalonica, Berea, Athens, and Corinth (see Acts 16-18).

Intensity continued on the third journey (ca. 54-58), bringing Paul to Ephesus, Macedonia and Greece. Paul's health suffered, as he himself indicates (2Cor 2:12-13; 4:10-11; 12:7). After the Jews at Corinth plan to murder him, Paul retreats to Philippi. But this was not all. At Caesarea, Paul was forced to spend two years in prison (58-60), and then again in Rome (61-63). Particularly in Jerusalem and Rome, Paul underwent great trials before the Roman governor Felix (Acts 24:22-23); before Festus the Roman governor (Acts 25:6-12); and so on.

By the age of sixty years, Paul had been for more than ten years engaged in the most harsh missionary works and endured ruthless stonings and beatings from the mobs, all for the sake of following Christ Jesus. Let us listen to Paul's own description of his anguish at this time:

> Five times I have received at the hands of the Jews the forty lashes less one. Three times I have been beaten with rods; once I was stoned. Three times I have been shipwrecked; a night and a day I have been adrift at sea; on frequent journeys, in danger from rivers, danger from robbers, danger from my own people, danger from Gentiles, danger in the city, danger in the wilderness, danger at sea, danger from false brethren; in toil and hardship, through many a sleepless night, in hunger and thirst, often without food, in cold and exposure. And, apart from other things, there is the daily pressure upon me of my anxiety for all the churches. Who is weak, and I am not weak? Who is made to fall, and I am not indignant? If I must boast, I will boast of the things that show my weakness (2Cor 11:24-30).

Paul's body and spirit did not escape the continuous night of darkness; only the light of Christ compelled him onward and upward through a cloud of uncertainty: a cloud of mystical ascent that compels one to union with Christ, the lot of the victim souls He chooses to carry on His mission.

Our beloved Apostle teaches us about suffering from an entirely different level. Paul's teachings lead us to the Cross of Christ: "But far be it from me to glory except in the cross of our Lord Jesus Christ. . ." (Gal 6:14). Or again: "Be imitators of me, as I am of Christ" (1 Cor 10:11). This is the way of divine love, the way of union with the Lord of our lives. As Paul so accurately states: "Christ . . . lives in me" (Gal 2:20). To imitate Christ, we are to "put on the Lord Jesus Christ" (Rom 13:14).

As we can see from his personal accounts, Paul experienced all the stages in the mystical life, from the way of beginners through that of the divine union. Beginning with the active purgation of the flesh and senses, the Apostle speaks from experience: "Though our outer nature is wasting away, our inner nature is being renewed every day" (2 Cor 4:16).

Again we hear the voice of the Apostle:

> . . . but I pommel my body and subdue it, lest after preaching to others I myself should be disqualified (1 Cor 9:27).

> Put to death therefore what is earthly in you: immorality, impurity, passion, evil desire, and covetousness, which is idolatry (Col 3:5).

> In him also you were circumcised with a circumcision made without hands, by putting off the body of flesh in the circumcision of Christ. . . (Col 2:11).

> . . . Let us cleanse ourselves from every defilement of body and spirit (2Cor 7:1).

> And those who belong to Christ Jesus have crucified the flesh with its passions and desires (Gal 5:24).

Yet Paul is positive of the outcome, for "as you share in our sufferings, you will also share in our comfort" (2 Cor 1:7). In fact, Paul calls the present burden of trial a "slight momentary affliction," and it "is preparing for us an eternal weight of glory beyond all comparison" (2 Cor 4:17); we may be "afflicted in every way, but not crushed" (2 Cor 4:8).

Although Paul feels crushed under these various trials, he is assured of victory in Christ. He is so confident of this that he encourages others to hold firm to the faith, knowing that the end leads to divine union, where we are "built into it for a dwelling place of God in the Spirit" (Eph 2:22).

On the road to perfection, the spirits of darkness soon make their presence felt in an attempt to discourage one's journey toward God. With Paul it is no exception: "And to keep me from being too elated by the abundance of revelations, a thorn was given me in the flesh, a messenger of Satan, to harass me, to keep me from being too elated" (2 Cor 12:7). The Apostle further warns us of this inevitable encounter with the evil one and teaches us to prepare for it: "Put on the whole armor of God, that you may be able to stand against the tactics of the devil. For we are not contending against flesh and blood, but against the principalities, against the powers, against the world rulers of this present darkness, against the spiritual hosts of wickedness in the heavenly places" (Eph 6:11-12).

In the course of Paul's mystical journey, he feels an obligation to offer up his sufferings to God to help atone for the sins of his people: to become a victim through the desire to unite himself to the Cross. He does this freely and voluntarily, knowing that his trials and sufferings are not in vain; they have a higher, redemptive purpose in the plan of salvation. The Lord took him at his word and granted his request. Paul became a victim of God's love, and a sharer in His unending Passion. Paul understood his vocation well: "For it has been granted to you that for the sake of Christ you should not only believe in him but also suffer for his sake. . ." (Phil 1:29). He desires to help carry our burdens (Gal 6:2), and does so voluntarily: "I will most gladly spend and be spent for your souls" (2 Cor 12:15). And again we hear of his efforts to appeal to God's mercy for the sake of saving others: "To the weak I became weak, that I might win the weak. I have become all things to all men, that I might by all means save some" (1 Cor 9:22).

In fact, Paul encourages everyone to offer their sufferings to God for the sake of all sinners:

> God comforts us in all our affliction, so that we may be able to comfort those who are in any affliction, with the comfort with which we ourselves are comforted by God (2 Cor 1:4).

> Do not yield your members to sin as instruments of wickedness, but yield yourselves to God as men who have been brought from death to life, and your members to God as instruments of righteousness (Rom 6:13).

> I appeal to you therefore, brethren, by the mercies of God, to present your bodies as a living sacrifice, holy and acceptable to God, which is your spiritual worship (Rom 12:1).

This is based upon Paul's teaching that if one member of Christ's Body suffers, then all the members suffer with it (1 Cor 12:26). In other words, we can all help one another in our trials by offering up to the Lord our sufferings for the sake of our fellow Christians: each of us can help atone for the sins and sufferings of others in a spirit of penance and reparation: "If we are afflicted it is for your comfort and salvation; and if we are comforted, it is for your comfort, which you experience, patiently enduring the same sufferings that we suffer" (2 Cor 1:6).

Paul responds literally to the words of our Lord to take up His cross and follow Him if he is to remain a true disciple. Because he offers himself up voluntarily and unconditionally to atone for sinners, he becomes one specially marked by God to be His victim for others — to help Jesus carry His unending Cross for humanity: "Now I rejoice in my sufferings for your sake, and in my flesh I complete what is lacking in Christ's afflictions for the sake of his body, that is, the church" (Col 1:24). Paul puts "on the Lord Jesus Christ" (Rom 13:14), "conquering evil with good" (Rom 12:21), and does so out of love and compassion for sinners everywhere:

> Even if I am to be poured as a libation upon the sacrificial offering of your faith, I am glad and rejoice with you all (Phil 2:17).

> I appeal to you therefore, brethren, by the mercies of God, to present your bodies as a living sacrifice, holy and acceptable to God, which is your spiritual worship (Rom 12:1).

> Now I rejoice in my sufferings for your sake. . . (Col 1:24).

Our Blessed Lord appears to have rewarded Paul's intense desire for the Cross by making of him a living crucifix, a victim of love who follows in the footsteps of Christ. Paul himself seems to indicate that he has been given the gift of the stigmata: ". . . I bear on my body the marks of Jesus" (Gal 6:17); and again he tells us: "And to keep me from being too elated by the abundance of revelations, a thorn was given me in the flesh. . ." (2 Cor 12:7). Paul is "always carrying in the body the death of Jesus, so that the life of Jesus may also be manifested. . ." (2 Cor 4:10). Certainly we have enough passages here to justify a conclusion that Paul became a stigmatist — the first known visible stigmata in Church history. As we have seen, there are many more verses that relate to this idea and seem to substantiate this claim. Jesus apparently gave Paul the visible stigmata in order to be a sign to unbelievers or to those who are weak in faith (again, see 2 Cor 4:10 quoted above). This explanation has been used time and again from theologians in their feelings about the stigmata — that God gives some souls the visible sign in order to be a sign themselves of Christ's Passion in our midst.

If Paul was truly a victim soul, a living stigmatist, then the question must be raised: why Paul and not the Apostles John or James? Why Paul and not John the Baptist or Simeon? This remains a mystery, for God's ways are not our own: "But by the grace of God I am what I am" (1 Cor 15:10), concludes the Apostle Paul. Perhaps it was because Paul was so intimately associated with the Cross of Christ and with His Passion — a choice he freely made — that God rewarded his fidelity with this most precious grace; perhaps it was because he offered himself up voluntarily to be God's victim for sinners, to help cooperate in the plan of redemption through the Cross of our Lord. More than likely, it was a combination of the two that explains Paul's extraordinary gift. Besides, how many souls in Sacred Scripture so loved the Cross as Paul? How many would offer themselves as living sacrifices as he did?

For Paul and the other victims of God's love, there is always hope and confidence in the future. They all recognize that the sufferings of this life will one day be no more, and for the sake of the Kingdom they endure, storing up treasure for their heavenly reward: "I consider that the sufferings of this present time are not worth comparing with the glory that is to be revealed to us" (Rom 8:18). The present time of darkness will one day turn to light (Eph 5:8), when we shall see God face to face as He really is and live.

God answered Paul's plea to share in the Passion of our Lord Jesus Christ. He wanted to be literally transformed into another Christ crucified, as he himself so clearly states: ". . . that I may know him and the power of his resurrection, and may share his sufferings, becoming like him in his death. . ." (Phil 3:10).

Although we can never prove if St. Paul bore the Sacred Stigmata, the internal evidence from his own pen seems quite strong and convincing. What else could he possibly mean by "I bear on my body the marks of Jesus" (Gal 6:17)? I must conclude privately that this indeed seems to be the case, although the Church has never formally recognized this to be so. (I don't think she's denied it either, for that matter.) I submit to her judgment if she were to decide otherwise.

Vatican II on Suffering

The Council of Vatican II (1962-65) became the twenty-first Ecumenical Council in the history of the Roman Catholic Church. This council became the "voice" of the Magisterium for the teachings of our Faith; more importantly, it is the voice of a renewed expression of our Faith, where traditional teachings and newer ones blended to meet the conditions of our life in the Faith today. The Church responded to a need for updating traditional beliefs and practices without sacrificing her timeless principles. Although the feelings of many traditionalists and conservatives remain mixed, nevertheless most will agree in retrospect that Vatican II was brilliant. Never had the Church gone through such radical changes in the world as at this time, and never has she responded more powerfully and positively as with this council.

Because so much of the Church's contemporary teaching centers around the wisdom of Vatican II and the post-Vatican II declarations, we will briefly examine the Second Vatican Council's documents to see what the titles are and what each document emphasizes. As this book progresses, much of the teachings on the themes in this book, including our present study on suffering, comes from these documents, as well as from numerous post-Conciliar works, declarations and addresses from the Holy Fathers, and from the Code of Canon Law (1983 revision). I will also continue to use Sacred Scripture as a primary source for my material. These make up the official teachings of the Magisterium of the Church. In addition to these sources, we also have the wisdom from our saints, doctors and mystics. These latter sources do *not* represent the official teachings of the Magisterium (although what they teach re-echos the Magisterium's teachings and are often quoted by the Church in her teachings to the faithful).

Vatican II was opened by Pope John XXIII in St. Peter's Basilica, Rome, on October 11, 1962. Pope John announced the coming of the new Council on January 25, 1959, as well as a future revision of the 1917 Code of Canon Law (which was completed in 1983).

Pope John XXIII died on June 3, 1963, and was unable to complete the Second Vatican Council that he had started. His successor, Pope Paul VI, continued the Council, which was completed by December 8, 1965. In all, there were four separate sessions that produced sixteen documents of instruction in the faith: issues of ethics and morality, justice and equality, human rights, and ecumenism dominated the themes of Vatican II. These documents were the result of the combined efforts of hundreds of bishops and theologians the world over. In fact, the number of participants approached 3,000: there were 2,600 bishops from all corners of the globe out of 2,908 eligible to attend the first session. Even numerous Protestant theologians were a part of this great event that would change the course of the Church in the modern world.

Briefly, here are the names of the sixteen documents produced from Vatican II, as well as a short statement of their main themes:

1) **Dogmatic Constitution on the Church** (*Lumen gentium*, **LG**): the Church has the role of making the light of the Gospels shine in all people through all nations.

42

2) **Dogmatic Constitution on Divine Revelation** (*Dei verbum*, **DV**): an assessment of the Church's role in fulfilling the words of St. John: ". . . that which we have seen and heard we proclaim also to you, so that you may have fellowship with us. . ." (1 Jn 1:3).

3) **Constitution on the Sacred Liturgy** (*Sacrosanctum concilium*, **SC**): emphasis on the newer, revised liturgy of the Mass, and an emphasis on everyone's participation in the Sacred Liturgy.

4) **Pastoral Constitution on the Church in the Modern World** (*Gaudium et spes*, **GS**): man's calling within the Church, and separate problems that need addressing.

5) **Decree on the Instruments of Social Communication** (*Inter mirifica*, **IM**): emphasis on the unity of the interior and exterior life, contemplation and action, prayer and the active ministry.

6) **Decree on Ecumenism** (*Unitatis redintegratio*, **UR**): emphasis on Christian unity throughout the world.

7) **Decree on Eastern Catholic Churches** (*Orientalium ecclesiarum*, **OE**): an effort to bring about further unity between the Roman Catholic Church and the Eastern Churches.

8) **Decree on the Bishop's Pastoral Office in the Church** (*Christus Dominus*, **CD**): emphasizes the role of the bishop as an image of the Father and of Christ.

9) **Decree on Priestly Formation** (*Optatam totius*, **OT**): a theology of the priesthood and its relationship to the episcopacy.

10) **Decree on the Appropriate Renewal of the Religious Life** (*Perfectae caritatis*, **PC**): the perfect life of the evangelical counsels through one's Religious profession.

11) **Decree on the Apostolate of the Laity** (*Apostolicam actuositatem*, **AA**): the role of God's plan for all humanity, with special emphasis on the importance of involvement of the laity.

12) **Decree on the Ministry and Life of Priests** (*Presbyterorum ordinis*, **PO**): theology of the role of the priest as an image of Christ for the faithful, and his duties thereof.

13) **Decree on the Church's Missionary Activity** (*Ad gentes divinitus*, **AGD**): missionary work and evangelization is the responsibility of all humankind, in their particular place and state.

14) **Declaration on Christian Education** (*Gravissimum educationis*, **GE**): a pattern of life through Christian values is the dominant theme, even for non-Christians by way of our example and evangelization.

15) **Declaration on the Relationship of the Church to Non-Christian Religious** (*Nostra aetate*, **NA**): emphasis on the total human family and the need for mutual respect for life and for common values.

16) **Declaration of Religious Freedom** (*Dignitatis humanae*, **DH**): talks about the dignity of the individual and of freedom and justice.

These are the documents of Vatican II that will be quoted from through this book. It is necessary to know what the simple two-letter abbreviations of the Latin terms are to understand the quotes taken from them. It is also more convenient to reference these quotes this way than to repeat the entire length of the names for each document.

The numerous post-conciliar documents I quote from will be treated in the same way. To see what each of the shortened letter code abbreviations refer to, please consult the bibliography at the end of this text.

Our discussion on the treatment of suffering will begin with man's fallen nature through the effects of original sin (see Gn 3). The Council has this to say about the nature of our sinful condition, and the cause of its roots:

> Although set by God in a state of rectitude, man, enticed by the evil one, abused his freedom at the very start of history. He lifted himself up against God, and sought to attain his goal apart from him. Although they had known God, they did not glorify him as God, but their senseless hearts were darkened, and they served the creature rather than the creator. What Revelation makes known to us is confirmed by our own experience. For when man looks into his own heart he finds that he is drawn towards what is wrong and sunk in many evils which cannot come from his good creator. Often refusing to acknowledge God as his source, man has also upset the relationship which should link him to his last end; and at the same time he has broken the right order that should reign within himself as well as between himself and other men and all creatures . . . (VCII, GS, no. 13.)

Once again, we see that the evil spirit has been infiltrating man's heart and mind ever since he came to be. No question, the reality of Satan has caused many a soul to fall to the pit, and has disrupted the natural order of God's creation. This is a sobering reflection from the Church, for many today, including respected theologians and theologian-priests, deny the existence of the evil one. Some claim that our sin is exclusively caused by our own human weakness and the misuse of free will. But this argument denies the reality of the spirits of darkness, whom the Scriptures have always acknowledged as real and powerful foes to mankind. Jesus certainly believes in them, as can be seen through His earthly ministry from our Gospel sources.

This, of course, caused us to be tempted, but it was man's decision to give in to the evil one and thus start the road to his ruin. Man set himself up before God, and the first sin that we call pride entered into the human arena. It is perhaps the most dreadful of all sin, for all wrongdoing seems to have its roots in pride: the goal being to seek pleasure before God, to elevate one's self before others and to abuse the undeserved life of grace that only God can give. We are nothing without our Maker, yet we continually try to exist as if we make ourselves into something through our thoughts, words and actions. Even to impress others with our physiques, our intelligence, or our talents undermines the true source of all goodness: God. When we boast of ourselves, we deny the Creator the true source of all goodness. And this can cause us much sorrow and suffering, for we find ourselves separated from the only lasting source of peace we have: that of the Father, and the Son and the Holy Spirit.

The Council continues along the same line:

> Man therefore is divided among himself. As a result, the whole life of men, both individual and social, shows itself to be a struggle, and a dramatic one, between light and darkness. Man

44

finds that he is unable of himself to overcome the assaults of evil successfully, so that everyone feels as though bound by chains. But the Lord himself came to free and strengthen man, renewing him inwardly and casting out the "prince of this world" (Jn 12:31), who held him in the bondage of sin. For sin brought man to a lower state, forcing him away from the completeness that is his to attain. . . (VCII, GS, no. 13.)

Man never seems to learn his lesson, and therefore is bound to his own sin even unto this day. But how long will this suffering continue for his relentless pursuit of self? Is there any hope for our condition? The voice of the Church tells us:

> The whole of man's history has been the story of dour combat with the powers of evil, stretching, so our Lord tells us, from the very dawn of history until the last day. Finding himself in the midst of the battlefield, man has to struggle to do what is right, and it is at great cost to himself, and aided by God's grace, that he succeeds in achieving his own inner integrity. . . (VCII, GS, no. 37.)

Now that we've taken a brief glimpse at the sources of our sufferings from the standpoint of human history, we need to look at the reality of suffering in the world today: a reality that goes much further than a diabolical origin. As human beings, we are subjected to trials from the world, as well as an inner conflict within ourselves. Indeed, "man is his own worse enemy," oftentimes a mere stranger to himself. We have to fight three battles — evil, the world, and ourselves — in order to conquer our sin and to follow the precepts of God. It is easy to see that man is literally surrounded by conditions that lead to suffering. It takes courage to persevere, but above all it requires unconditional faith in a God who loves us, a God of mercy who watches over those who trust in His ways. Jesus appeals to us: "Let not your hearts be troubled; believe in God, believe also in me" (Jn 14:1). Faith will be the one cornerstone that delivers us from our sorrow.

In today's modern world, the transgressions against the commands of God are numerous and often serious. Some of these sinful acts the members of the Vatican Council long ago recognized:

> The varieties of crimes are numerous: all offenses against life itself, such as murder, genocide, abortion, euthanasia and wilful suicide; all violations of the integrity of the human person, such as mutilation, physical and mental torture, undue psychological pressures; all offenses against human dignity, such as subhuman living conditions, arbitrary imprisonment, deportation, slavery, prostitution, the selling of women and children, degrading working conditions where men are treated as mere tools for profit rather than free and responsible persons: all these and the like are criminal: they poison civilization; and they debase the perpetrators more than the victims and mutilate against the honor of the creator. . . (VC, GS, no. 27.)

Over twenty-five years later, we still face the same set of problems; we are as blind as we always were and perhaps more so, for our crimes against

God, man and nature seem to escalate and become more serious as modern man advances intellectually and technologically. All of humankind is on the brink of disaster because in its advancement, it has lost the simplicity to know and to love God: "Blest are the pure in heart for they shall see God" (Mt 5:8). The Beatitude reminds us ever so clearly that we must keep our simplicity; we must also keep our spiritual innocence and purity of heart, in the manner of trusting and loving children: "Let the children come to me . . . for to such belongs the kingdom of heaven" (Mt 19:14), or again: ". . . whoever does not receive the kingdom of God like a child shall not enter it" (Lk 18:17).

Yet it is so hard to be simple! To love with an undivided heart, to have a pure and uncluttered faith — oh, what a difficult task in a world that has lost its innocence and humility. We must work extremely hard these days to find it; it is indeed much more difficult than in any generation past. It is much easier to be complicated than to be simple; it is much easier to love God through our intellect than through our hearts. And it is much simpler and convenient to turn our back on those who cry out in need instead of facing them and offering them our love. To do so steals a part of our time, as well as our hearts. But the Gospel message insists that we do.

Man has become stubborn and self-serving, lost in a narrow vision of his own time and space. He can barely hear words of truth anymore, because he would prefer to hear his own. Christ has warned us long ago: "If you were blind, you would have no guilt; but now that you say, 'We see,' your guilt remains" (Jn 9:41); ". . . seeing they do not see, and hearing they do not hear. . ." (Mt 13:13). Our Lord continues: " 'You shall indeed hear but never understand, and you shall indeed see but never perceive. For this people's heart has grown dull, and their ears are heavy of hearing, and their eyes they have closed, lest they should perceive with their eyes, and hear with their ears, and understand with their heart, and turn for me to heal them" (Mt 13:14-15).

We can run, but there is nowhere left to hide. God's words still echo from the beginning of human history: "Where are you?" (Gn 3:9). Like Adam and Eve, we are continually called to account for our actions, to return to the loving God who saves.

The Church teaches us that we must reach out to our neighbor in need, for this constitutes true charity that is pleasing to the Lord. When others suffer because of injustice, it is our moral duty to respond. Listen to what she has to say about reaching out to others:

> Today there is an inescapable duty to make ourselves the
> neighbor of every man, no matter who he is, and if we meet him,
> to come to his aid in a positive way, whether he is an aged person
> abandoned by all, a foreign worker despised without reason, a
> refugee, an illegitimate child wrongly suffering for a sin he did
> not commit, or a starving human being who awakens our
> conscience by calling to mind the words of Christ: "As you did it
> to one of the least of these my brethren, you did it to me" (25:40)
> . . . (VC, GS, no. 27.)

All of these demeaning conditions need to be equally matched with acts of Christian charity, to "love one another" as our Lord commands us to do (Jn 15:17). Without helping our brother or sister in need, we are merely paying lip service to our faith, instead of living our faith as an act of charity towards God and our neighbor: "For where your treasure is, there will your heart be also" (Lk 12:34).

Listen to the words from the Magisterium:

> Wherever men are to be found who are in want of food and drink, of clothing, housing, medicine, work, education, the means necessary for leading a truly human life, wherever there are men racked by misfortune or illness, men suffering exile or imprisonment, Christian charity should go in search of them and find them out, comfort them with devoted care and give them the helps that will relieve their needs. This obligation binds first and foremost the more affluent individuals and nations . . . (VC, AA, no. 8.)

It is always easy to help others whom we like, be they relatives, friends, family, or neighbor. Although acts of charity towards these are certainly proper and meritorious, nevertheless the true test of our faith in an act of charity includes even those we despise: "For if you love those who love you, what reward have you?" (Mt 5:46). For we all know that God's "sun rise(s) on the evil and on the good," and that God "sends rain on the just and on the unjust" (Mt 5:45). In fact, to prove that we are even sons and daughters of God, we must love our enemies (not merely tolerate them) and pray for them. This is a command of our Lord (Mt 5:44), one that we better not take too lightly, lest the Father who "sees in secret" (Mt 6:4) passes a verdict of judgment against us one day, according to the judgment we have given others (Mt 7:2). The council reaffirms this concern for our neighbor, without exception or favoritism:

> The Council lays stress on respect for the human person: everyone should look upon his neighbor (*without any exception*) as another self, bearing in mind above all his life and the means necessary for living it in a dignified way, lest he follow the example of the rich man who ignored Lazarus, the poor man (Lk 16:19-31) . . . (VC, GS, no. 27.)

Note the words that I intentionally italicized: "without any exception." This is indeed the most difficult obligation, but we are nevertheless to do so according to the teachings of the Church and the teachings of our Lord.

Let us look at one more instruction from Holy Mother Church:

> We must distinguish between the error (which must always be rejected) and the person in error, who never loses his dignity as a person even though he flounders amid false or inadequate religious ideas. God alone is the judge and the searcher of hearts: he forbids us to pass judgment on the inner guilt of others.

> The teaching of Christ even demands that we forgive injury (Mt 5:43-47), and the precept of love, which is the commandment of the New Law, includes all our enemies: "But I say to you, love your enemies, do good to them that hate you; and pray for those who persecute and calumniate you" (Mt 5:43-44).

Here the Church teaches us that although we must love the enemy, we do not need to love his sin. Too often we associate the human person with what he does, thinks or says. Yet these do not in themselves make up the essence of the human person; they are only extensions of his feelings and personality. Behind these external manifestations are found the real self, the self that God so loved that He gave His only begotten Son for (Jn 3:16). Unfortunately the manifestation of self is often misguided and impure. Let us look to help correct the faults of others while keeping a loving eye on the beauty of their souls, where God resides in the depths of their hearts. It is our duty to love them, to forgive their offenses, and to help them overcome their imperfections.

It is so important we forgive our brother; in fact, we are not even to approach God's altar if we intentionally remain embittered with others: "So if you are offering your gift at the altar, and there remember that your brother has something against you, leave your gift there before the altar and go; first be reconciled to your brother, and then come and offer your gift" (Mt 5:23-24). If this stern warning is not enough to convince us of the importance of reconciliation, then perhaps this will: anger alone will make us liable to God's judgment (Mt 5:22), and our bitterness can even cause our damnation (Mt 5:22). This is serious business; we must heed these warnings, no matter the excuse. As difficult as it is to do at times, we must at least keep on trying, keep on forgiving: " 'Lord, how often shall my brother sin against me, and I forgive him? As many as seven times?' Jesus said to him, 'I do not say to you seven times, but seventy times seven' (Mt 18:21-22). Our reconciliation must be a continual process in our earthly lives, a continual renewal with our brothers and sisters in Christ.

We have talked a great deal about other people's sufferings and the need to be charitable towards them all. Now we will address our own sufferings, and how to cope with the trials and tribulations this life has to offer.

How can we accept the sufferings that overcome us in the course of our lives? Is there any hope in the midst of endless grief and turmoil? One way we can better cope with suffering is when we unite our pains and struggles to that of Christ, who offers himself as a victim of our love:

> In a special way, those who are weighed down by poverty, infirmity, sickness and other hardships should realize that they are united to Christ, who suffers for the salvation of the world; let those feel the same who suffer persecution for the sake of justice, those whom the Lord declared blessed in the Gospel and whom "the God of all grace, who has called us to his eternal glory in Christ Jesus, will himself restore, establish, strengthen, and settle" (1 Pt 5:10) . . . (VC, LG, no. 41.)

Because we live in a world saturated with persecutions of one kind or another, it is important to know that our Lord is in our midst, offering us hope against all odds, asking of us to be courageous and firm in the faith throughout our trials; they who do so will not go without their reward:

> Since Jesus, the Son of God, showed His love by laying down His life for us, no one has greater love than he who lays down his life for Him and for his brothers (1 Jn 3:16; Jn 15:13). Some Christians have been called from the beginning, and will always

be called, to give this greatest testimony of love to all, especially to persecutors. Martyrdom makes the disciple like his master, who willingly accepted death for the salvation of the world, and through it he is conformed to Him by the shedding of blood. Therefore the Church considers it the highest gift and supreme test of love. And while it is given to few, all however must be prepared to confess Christ before men and to follow Him along the way of the cross amidst the persecutions which the Church never lacks . . . (VC, LG, no. 42.)

It is the risen Lord who gives us the hope and the courage to remain firm in the faith, sacrificing our lives if necessary out of love for Him and our brethren. For if Christ did not rise from the grave, conquering death once and for all, then our faith is in vain (1 Cor 15:14). If we remain strong, unfaltering in the waves of the storm, the end will not go without eternal reward:

By the power of the risen Lord the Church is given strength to overcome, in patience and in love, her sorrows and her difficulties, both those that are from within and those that are from without, so that she may reveal in the world, faithfully, however darkly, the mystery of her Lord until, in the consummation, it shall be manifested in full light . . . (VC, LG, no. 8.)

It is reaffirming to know that we do not have to fight our struggles alone; there by our side is Mother Church, always interceding before us, always sharing in our sufferings on behalf of Jesus Christ:

The Church encompasses with her love all those who are afflicted by human misery and she recognizes in those who are poor and who suffer, the image of her poor and suffering founder. She does all in her power to relieve their need and in them she strives to serve Christ. Christ, "holy, innocent and undefiled" (Heb 7:26) knew nothing of sin (2 Cor 5:21), but came only to expiate the sins of the people (Heb 2:17). The Church, however, clasping sinners to her bosom, at once holy and always in need of purification, follows constantly the path of penance and renewal . . . (VC, LG, no. 8.)

The Church embraces her sufferings in order to conform to the Cross of Christ, to "proclaim liberty to the captives" (Lk 4:18) in union with her Savior for the sake of the faithful. We are to imitate our Lord, the way of humility and spiritual poverty, in our journey of faith. For it is by identifying with our Savior that we come to know Him, love Him and embrace His way that leads to eternal life:

Just as Christ carried out the work of redemption in poverty and oppression, so the Church is called to follow the same path if she is to communicate the fruits of salvation to men. Christ Jesus, "though he was by nature God . . . emptied himself, taking the nature of a slave" (Phil 2:6-7), and "being rich, became poor" (2

49

Cor 8:9) for our sake. Likewise, the Church, although she needs human resources to carry out her mission, is not set up to seek earthly glory, but to proclaim, and this by by her own example, humility and self-denial. Christ was sent by the Father "to bring good news to the poor . . . to heal the contrite of heart" (Lk 4:18), "to seek and save what was lost" (Lk 19:10) . . . (VC, LG, no. 8.)

This leads us to the last of our trials and sufferings upon this earth: grave illness and even death. How do we cope with the finality to human life that awaits us all from the sting of death? St. Paul reminds us that through faith in our Lord's resurrection, we too look forward to another life of eternal bliss: "Death is swallowed up in victory; O death, where is thy victory? O death, where is thy sting?" (1 Cor 15:54-55). Indeed, if all we have to look forward to in this earthly life is death as an ultimate end, then we share the same feelings of St. Paul: "If for this life only we have hoped in Christ, we are the most pitiable people of all" (1 Cor 15:19). The Church also reaffirms our hope in the resurrection of all the faithful: "When the Lord will come in glory, and all His angels with Him (Mt 25:31), death will be no more and all things will be subject to Him (1 Cor 15:26-27). But at the present time some of His disciples are pilgrims on earth. Others have died and are being purified, while still others are in glory, contemplating in full light God himself triune and one, exactly as He is" (VC, LG, no. 49).

It is in our human nature to quarrel with death, for we all realize that one day our lives as we know them will come to a conclusion. Without Christ in our hearts, we are never consoled, for the only sure way of peace and assurity rests within our firm faith in the Lord:

It is in regard to death that man's condition is most shrouded in doubt. Man is tormented not only by pain and by the gradual breaking-up of his body but also, and even more, by the dread of forever ceasing to be. But a deep instinct leads him rightly to shrink from and to reject the utter ruin and total loss of his personality. Because he bears in himself the seed of eternity, which cannot be reduced to mere matter, he rebels against death. All the aids made available by technology, however useful they may be, cannot set his anguished mind at rest. They may prolong his lifespan; but this does not satisfy his heartfelt longing, one that can never be stifled, for a life to come . . . (VC, GS, no. 18.)

It is by the gift of faith that we come to look forward to another type of existence, a life that will be placed at the eternal bosom of the Father:

Faith, with its solidly based teaching, provides every thoughtful man with an answer to his anxious queries about his future lot. At the same time it makes him able to be united in Christ with his loved ones who have already died, and gives hope that they have found true life with God . . . (VC, GS, no. 18.)

This concludes our treatment of suffering from the teachings of the Second Vatican Council. Although the Church recognizes the oppressive nature of life itself, she has told us that there is meaning in all of our trials: a meaning that finds its fulfillment in union with the Cross of Christ, where true peace can only be found. No matter the cross we bear — whether it be poverty, persecution, illness, or even the oncoming of death — we can always find strength in the ultimate and final Cross of our Lord. On our own part, we make efforts to live out our Christian lives through the sacraments, prayer, conversion of heart, and reconciliation with our Creator and with each other. The most important part, our unending faith, is a gift that God gives to us. We merely have to accept it and claim it as our own.

By seeing our sufferings in the shadow of the Cross, we honor our Lord and comfort His Sacred Heart. It is here at the foot of the Cross that the totality of our faith experiences come together; it is here that we find everlasting reconciliation and forgiveness, because we now live in the fullness of Christ: "put on the Lord Jesus Christ" (Rom 13:14). As Christ has given himself to us, we in turn must live totally for Him. Then and only then can we confidently say with St. Paul: "Christ . . . lives in me" (Gal 2:20).

Words from the Holy Fathers

A treatment of the meaning of suffering could not be complete without a few words of wisdom from the Holy Fathers throughout Church history. Important reflections on this mystery from various Popes have been presented in their dialogues with the faithful, particularly in the form of papal addresses, exhortations and encyclicals. We will only explore a few of these reflections from some of the memorable sources, for to explore them all would go beyond the means of this book.

Often the Pope does not speak alone, but represents the combined efforts of himself and his bishop colleagues when addressing important issues concerning the faith. This is particularly true since the importance of collegiality has taken a firm hold in the Church; it is particularly true of Vatican Councils and statements made in collaboration with the Sacred Congregations of the Vatican (often referred to as Post-Conciliar documents of the Second Vatican Council). Yet his Holiness often writes formal statements alone for the instruction of the faithful. These teachings are usually called "encyclicals," which are directed to all the bishops and to the people of the world for their instruction.

Our statements will come from a variety of these sources, as well as others. These words are not intended to be the definitive statements about everything we need to know about suffering; indeed, we have only begun to understand the meaning behind this mystery in God's plan. But through the grace of the Spirit, these Holy Fathers have provided us with profound insights into the meaning of suffering in humanity, as well as in the redemptive value it possesses for all of God's people.

One such Pope who gives us meaningful views on the reality of suffering is Pius XII (1939-1958). Here he describes the nature of suffering, its origins and how we have been delivered through the mercy of God:

> God, in creating man, had exempted him, through the gift of
> grace, from that natural law of every living and sensitive body,
> and had not designed to include pain and death in his destiny. It
> was sin that brought them upon him. But He, the Father of

mercy, took them into His hands and caused them to pass
through the body, the veins and the heart of His beloved Son,
Who was God like unto himself, made into man to be the Savior
of the world. Thus pain and death have become the means of redemption and sanctification for every man who does not deny
Christ. Thus the path of the human race, which unfolds in its entire length under the Sign of the Cross and under the law of pain
and death, while it matures and purifies the soul here on earth,
leads it to unlimited happiness of a life without end. . . (*The
Pope Speaks*, from the Vatican Archives, Pantheon Books Inc.,
New York NY: 1957.)

Thus we learn that suffering becomes a way or means of redemption in
union with the Cross. Pope Pius XII reminds us again of the central role
that sin plays in the sufferings we must bear, whether physical or spiritual.
But our merciful God does not leave us orphaned, choosing to redeem us
through the most precious blood of His Son, whom He offers for the
salvation of all mankind.

What happens if we do not respond to the forgiving and cleansing value
of the Cross? Can suffering be an eternal reality in light of man's separation
from God? Pope Benedict XII (1334-1342) has this to say:

We define that according to the general disposition of God, the
souls of those who die in actual mortal sin go down to hell
immediately (*mox*) after death and there suffer the pain of hell.
Nevertheless, on the day of judgment all men will appear with
their bodies "before the judgment seat of Christ" to give an
account of their personal deeds, "so that each one may receive
good or evil, according to what he has done in the body" (2 Cor
5:10) . . . (Pope Benedict XII, *Constitution Benedictus Deus*,
1336.)

To further emphasize the gravity of a persistent sinful nature, we have
the following warning from Pope Innocent III:

The punishment for original sin is the loss of the beatific vision,
but the punishment of actual sin is the torture of eternal hell. . .
(Pope Innocent III, *Letter to Humbert*, Archbishop of Arles,
1201.)

Even closer to our own time, Pope John Paul II has solemn words for
the reality of everlasting judgment towards unrepentant sinners (although
he recognizes that some are not lost altogether from their sin):

In fidelity to the New Testament and Tradition, the Church
believes in the happiness of the just who will one day be with
Christ. She also believes that there will be eternal punishment
for the sinner, who will be deprived of the sight of God, and that
this punishment will have a repercussion on the whole being of
the sinner. She believes in the possibility of a purification for the
elect before they see God, a purification altogether different from
the punishment of the damned. This is what the Church means

52

when speaking of Hell and Purgatory. . . (Pope John Paul II, *Doctrine of the Faith on Certain Questions Concerning Eschatology*, May 17, 1979.)

Like the other writers from the Second Vatican Council, the Popes throughout Church history agree with the grim reality of an eternal punishment in the plan of salvation. They are merely re-echoing the voice of Christ, who continually warned us of this fact:

The Son of man will send his angels, and they will gather out of his kingdom all causes of sin and all evil doers, and throw them into the furnace of fire; there men will weep and gnash their teeth (Mt 13:41-42);

But I say to you that everyone who is angry with his brother shall be liable to judgment; whoever insults his brother shall be liable to the council, and whoever says 'You fool!' Shall be liable to the hell of fire (Mt 5:22);

And if your hand causes you to sin, cut it off; it is better for you to enter life maimed than with two hands to go to hell, the unquenchable fire (Mk 9:43);

But I will warn you whom to fear: fear him who, after he has killed, has power to cast into hell; yes, I tell you, fear him (Lk 12:5);

And do not fear those who kill the body but cannot kill the soul; rather, fear him who can destroy both body and soul in hell (Mt 10:28);

You serpents, you brood of vipers, how are you to escape being sentenced to hell? (Mt 23:33);

'Truly, I say to you, as you did it not to one of the least of these, you did it not to me.' And they will go away into eternal punishment, but the righteous into eternal life (Mt 25:45-46).

These are but few of our Lord's words concerning the reality of a heaven and a hell. We ought to pay close mind to them, for our entire salvation rests upon these warnings. But what does all of this have to do with suffering in the here-and-now? It has *everything* to do with it, because what we do now affects the verdict of our judgment one day before the Lord: "They will give account to him who is ready to judge the living and the dead" (1 Pt 4:5); "Why do you despise your brother? For we shall all stand before the judgment seat of God" (Rom 14:10).

This leads us back to charity towards one another, even those who cause us hardship and suffering. We are taught by Christ and it is reaffirmed by the Church that we must bear our crosses if we are to become true disciples of our Lord (Lk 9:23). If we hate our brother or sister yet proclaim to be true followers, we are liars (1 Jn 4:20). Suffering — even in the midst of that which is undeserved — is a true test of our faith; it is also a cleansing process, whereby we are purified of our sin and humbled in our weaknesses. We have also seen how suffering has redemptive value when we voluntarily unite ourselves to the Cross of Christ in order to atone for the sins of humanity. Finally, our trials and tribulations serve to unite us closer to the historical Jesus, who took upon himself the sufferings of the world in order to free us from sin and damnation (Is 53:4-6,10-11). We come to know and love our Lord more intimately when we experience a part of His sufferings as our own; we become one with Him (1 Jn 4:16), as He becomes one with us.

Let us now take a closer look at what Pope John Paul II says about our attitudes towards the Cross and others:

> Unity, which comes from God, is given to us at the Cross. We must not want to avoid the Cross, passing to rapid attempts at harmonizing differences, excluding the question of truth. But neither must we abandon one another, and go our separate ways, because drawing closer calls for the patient and suffering love of Christ crucified. . . . (Pope John Paul II, *Address to the German Episcopal Conference*, Munich, November 17, 1980.)

The Holy Father continues to enlighten us on the role we as Church have towards one another in need, and the unitive value the Cross has in the place of our interrelationships:

> If Christ united himself with each man, the Church lives more profoundly her own nature and mission by penetrating into the depth of this mystery and into its rich universal meaning. It was not without reason that the Apostle spoke about Christ's Body, the Church. If this Mystical Body of Christ is God's people . . . this means that each man who belongs to it is filled with that bread of life that comes from Christ. This means that the Church herself, who is a body, an organism, a social unit, when she turns to man with his real problems, his hopes and sufferings, his achievements and falls, receives the same divine influences, the light and strength of the Spirit that comes from the crucified and risen Christ. . . . (Pope John Paul II, Encyclical Letter *Redemptor Hominis*, 1979.)

Indeed, other Popes of this century have also strongly defended the Church's role in helping others who suffer the burdens of life; they call upon her charitable action toward all brothers and sisters of the human race:

> Numerous bishops from all continents, especially the bishops from the Third World, spoke at the last Synod . . . of peoples . . . engaged with all their energy in the effort and struggle to overcome everything which condemns them to remain on the margin of life: famine, chronic disease, illiteracy, poverty, injustices in international relations and especially commercial exchanges, situations of economic and cultural neo-colonialism, sometimes as cruel as the old political colonialism. The Church . . . has the duty to proclaim the liberation of millions of human

beings — many of whom are her own children — the duty of assisting the birth of this liberation, of giving witness to it, of ensuring that it is complete. This is not foreign to evangelization. . . . (Pope Paul VI, Apostolic Exhortation *Evangelii Nuntiandi*, 1975.)

The same Pope further acknowledges our duty as good Christians to help others improve their quality of life:

The members of mankind share the same basic rights and duties, as well as the same supernatural destiny. Within a country which belongs to each one, all should be equal before the law, find equal admittance to economic, civic, and social life and benefit from a fair sharing of the nation's riches. . . . (Pope Paul VI, Apostolic Letter *Octogesima Adveniens*, 1971.)

Although we can readily see that all of us must help to lessen the sufferings in the world community, what can we do in a practical manner to carry our share of the burden?

One of the ways is through our attitudes about material possessions — our temporal goods. While many of us live in wealth or comfort, just as many (if not more) live on the brink of poverty and starvation. We need to strip ourselves of the material things we do not need, and give to the poor who beg of our mercy.

There are many who choose to take advantage of another's goods, imposing an unnecessary burden when they could help themselves toward a better existence. If we are able to sustain ourselves at a reasonable standard of living, then we need to be careful in how much we impose ourselves on the generosity of others. Our desires have to be distinguished from our needs. What we are talking about here is a spirit of *evangelical poverty*, where we temper our lives with modesty through sacrifice and humility. Jesus himself alluded to this in one of the Beatitudes: "Blessed are the poor in spirit: for theirs is the kingdom of God" (Mt 5:3). He also praised humility of heart, which has its own reward for those who practice it: "Blest are the meek; for they shall inherit the earth" (Mt 5:5). In fact, Jesus even sends His first disciples out with as little material goods as necessary to survive (Mt 10:1-10).

Money can lead to greed, and in this we must be careful. Money in itself is not evil, but it's in the way we use it (or hoard it) that makes us sin against our neighbor:

Riches are not seemly for a stingy man; and of what use is property to an envious man? Whoever accumulates by depriving himself, accumulates for others; and others will live in luxury on his goods. If a man is mean to himself, to whom will he be generous? He will not enjoy his own riches. No one is meaner than the man who is grudging to himself, and this is the retribution for his baseness; even if he does good, he does it unintentionally, and betrays his baseness in the end. Evil is the man with a grudging eye; he averts his face and disregards people. A greedy man's eye is not satisfied with a portion, and mean injustice withers the soul (Sir 14:3-9).

We would do well to internalize the following advice from the same Sirach: "Nevertheless, be patient with a man in humble circumstances, and do not make him wait for your alms. Help a poor man for the commandment's sake, and because of his need do not send him away empty" (Sir 29:8-9). These words remind us of the need for a spirit of evangelical poverty, where our love of neighbor should compel us to share with the less fortunate in time of their need. Let us close this point with the wisdom of Pope Pius XII:

> Our love of God, our love of Christ, must be accompanied by a corresponding charity towards our neighbor. How can we say that we love the divine Redeemer if we hate those He has redeemed with His precious blood to make them members of His mystical Body?. . . Indeed it must be said that our union with God, our union with Christ, will become proportionately closer as we become more and more members one of another (Rom 12:5), more and more mutually careful one for another (1 Cor 12:25); and, similarly, our union with each other by charity will become more intimate as we cleave more ardently to God and our divine Head. . . . (Pope Pius XII, Encyclical *Mystici Corporis*, 1943.)

Why do we equate charity with human suffering? Would there be no suffering if we replaced evil with good, hate with love, unbelief with faith, and apathy with the flame of the living Spirit? Although one could never reasonably argue with the change in our hearts that leads to a fullness of life, nevertheless we cannot escape suffering completely in our lives; this is not the precept of Christ, who teaches us that we must take up our cross, to lose our life in order to save it (Mt 16:24-25); to enter through the narrow door of salvation (Lk 13:22-24), to gain eternal life through dying to one's self (Jn 12:24-25). Indeed, Jesus explicitly commands that in order to serve Him, we must follow Him (Jn 12:26). And in order to follow Him, we are brought full circle back to the Cross: "If any man would come after me, let him *deny* himself and take up his *cross* daily and *follow* me" (Lk 9:23).

Notice that I have italicized the three key words in this last command: deny, cross and follow. If you look at the Scripture reference carefully, you will find exactly who Jesus is referring to with this command. Verse 23 opens with, "And he said to all" (Lk 9:23). That is you and me, not just the disciples who lead the Church (Apostles, presbyters, bishops). In fact, the same verse repeats this point in the very next word, lest anyone excuse themselves of their duty and obligation: "If any man" (Lk 9:23). Luke is talking here about discipleship, not just about Church leadership (of the Twelve and their successors), but of all people who desire to faithfully follow our Lord (see Lk 9:23-27).

It is very important that one understand this verse (Lk 9:23) with a fuller meaning than readily appears on the surface. In fact, this one verse is a most profound statement that embodies the totality of any authentic Christology, past or present. In its mystical dimension, these words are at the heart of our spirituality in union with Christ. Great theologians have written volumes on explaining the mystery of the Cross, and how our Christian faith is centered around our following and imitating that Cross, be it through thought, prayer or action. We have no Christian faith without the centrality of the Cross, as St. Paul so aptly reminds us: "But far be it from me to glory except in the cross of our Lord Jesus Christ!" (Gal 6:14).

Let us not be misled with the notion that suffering for its own sake has any personal or redemptive value! Remember, Jesus said He was sent to bring glad tidings to the poor, to proclaim liberty to the captives (Lk 4:18). Furthermore, He tells us the following: "Come to me, all who labor and are heavy laden, and I will give you rest. Take my yoke upon you, and learn from me; for I am gentle and lowly in heart, and you will find rest for your souls. For my yoke is ready, and my burden is light" (Mt 11:28-30). Jesus came to free us of our oppressions, but notice the words: "Take *my yoke* upon *you*" (emphasis mine). Jesus will comfort us, but not by running away from our crosses. Like Simon the Cyrenean (Lk 23:26; Mt 27:32; Mk 15:21), we in faith help to carry our Lord's Cross by uniting our sufferings to His own. Then and only then can we help ease the sufferings of our Lord, and cling more intimately in faith to His heart; then and only then can our burdens be made light (Mt 11:30) and our spirits renewed in the fullness of life. Such is the wisdom of the Cross, a wisdom shared time and again through the mystics who have been able to offer their sufferings to God with willing and confident hearts. These victims through the ages have understood the meaning of Jesus' words well. We need only read the rich deposits they have left us concerning the mystery of the Cross, and to understand their positive attitudes towards suffering for and in union with Christ.

Prudence in Judgment

I hope this exposition leads one to conclude that the real value of suffering is not for its own sake (which would be a morbid desire, indeed!), but rather for its redemptive value when offered up to God in a spirit of voluntary sacrifice. This offering must serve three purposes: 1) to purify and renew our own souls to make us worthy to share in the eternal life of Christ; 2) to atone for the sins of our brothers and sisters as a supreme act of charity; and 3) to lead us to the way of divine love, that union with God that comes through participating in the Cross of our Lord, in order that we may be one with Him as He is with us (1 Jn 4:12-15). This is the way of the victim soul, and it is the way for all the people of God. Some chosen souls are called to the Cross in a more intense manner, but all of us have a share in it, no matter the trial, no matter the tribulation. We give what we have been given, even if it be in the ordinary way of life. For it is not the quantity of giving in which we please God, but in the quality, the sincerity of our hearts, that we will be rewarded.

Let us not assume that we must therefore look for suffering to live a good Christian life. That would be misleading and missing the point altogether. We need not love our sufferings, we need only embrace them once they are there, acknowledging that we receive what we will from God's good designs, each according to his measure. Remember that God will not let us be tempted beyond our strength (1 Cor 10:13), and that he allows our trials for a very good reason: "In this you rejoice, though now for a little while you may have to suffer various trials, so that the genuineness of your faith, more precious than gold which though perishable is tested by fire, may redound to praise and glory and honor at the revelation of Jesus Christ" (1 Pt 1:6-7).

Why many souls have to suffer more in this life than others is a mystery of God's will. Perhaps some are in more need of chastisement for their sin, if their earthly lives were lived in dark separation from God; some may be especially chosen to help as co-redemptors in the plan of our salvation through union with our Lord and His sufferings; then some may be used by the Master as signs of love and mercy to an unbelieving and unrepentant world. Many are the ways of the Lord, as the Apostle instructs the faithful: "O the depth of the riches and wisdom and knowledge of God! How unsearchable are his judgments, how inscrutable his ways! For who has known the mind of the Lord? Who has been his counselor?" (Rom 11:33-34). We need only trust that whatever the Lord deems best to give us — chastisement or blessings, darkness or light, sickness or health — is given only out of His mercy for the good of our soul, for God loves us and corrects us as our heavenly Father, wishing that all might be saved.

I have talked about the values of atonement for the satisfaction of sin; I have briefly described the role of the victim soul who unites his sufferings (and even offers them up) for the salvation of sinners. This has been done in the context of understanding what role suffering has played in our history, and many reasons why we still suffer in God's merciful but just plan. This first thematic unit on suffering is important as this book progresses in order to understand the mystery of the stigmata and its meaning for us in the world today. Great care must be taken to assure that the reader does not look upon the stigmatist as a mere sensational display of God's wonders among His people. This would only serve to lure the people into a sensationalism that creates a circus-like approach to what is in reality a very sacred and serious mission these victims offer for us. It would also mock God's gift of the stigmata by focusing on the external phenomena as if they were a kind of "show piece" for the world to drool over. This, above all, is what we must avoid at all cost.

Out of necessity in our study of the Sacred Stigmata, I will be investigating the external phenomena as the book unfolds, but only as a theme of secondary importance. The primary focus needs to center around the mystery of suffering, atonement for that suffering and the people behind the stigmata that were found worthy by God to share in Christ's Passion for the salvation of the world. This includes their background, their virtuous lives and the way they came to understand the vocation that God had called them to. Then and only then can we focus more specifically on the wounds of the stigmata and what they represent for each victim soul, as well as (and more importantly) what they mean for the world as a whole.

CHAPTER 2

The Meaning of
Co-Redemption

Victim of Love

Now that we have spent a great deal of time attempting to better understand the mystery of suffering, we will further explore the redemptive values of suffering in the context of atonement, reparation and expiation. In general, those who sacrifice themselves for the sake of sinners are called *victim souls*. These souls help atone for our sin in union with Christ. Not all victim souls become stigmatists, although all stigmatists by the nature of their vocation are victims.

All victims have several things in common: 1) they are chosen by God for this way of life because it is His will for them: "You did not choose me, but I chose you. . ." (Jn 15:16); 2) they are free to reject the role of victim, because God wants the consent of His chosen ones first before He assigns them to this supernatural task. He respects our freedom, and does not force us to do anything against our will. Once the soul consents, however, God is free to do whatever He wills with the person who will be His redemptive helper; 3) sometimes a soul becomes a victim first without realizing his or her lot; usually, however, the chosen ones freely offer their sufferings up to God with the specific intention of making atonement or expiation for their own sin, or for the sins of others. This voluntary offering usually comes through prayer and intense devotions to the Cross and the Passion of our Lord, in union with sacrifices and penances the victim performs. The key point is that the offering is a voluntary and unconditional surrender to God's holy will. With some of these servants, God answers their prayers and offerings and takes them at their word. In even fewer cases, God sometimes chooses to unite them even more intimately with the Son on the Cross; hence, they become stigmatists — true victims of divine love who offer their lives for the ransom of many.

Up to this point in the book, I have intentionally limited my quotes to either the Magisterium of the Church, or to the words from Sacred Scripture. One reason for this was the nature of the topic material covered. The other reason was to treat the important theme of suffering with the weight and authority of the Church and of God's Word. As the book progresses, I will continue to use these same sources, but I will also use sources from the great theologians, saints and mystics throughout Church history. The logic behind this rests with the field of mystical theology itself: so much of what we know about mysticism and the phenomena associated with it springs from the words of these people, ones who have experienced the very things they talk about, and ones who are profoundly gifted in spiritual discernment and the ways toward divine union. At times the Magisterium of the Church (as well as Sacred Scripture) does not treat the mystical world and its phenomena in any in-depth manner, because this subject matter does not lend itself too easily to the intellectual approaches that often define our doctrines and dogmas. In fact, the Magisterium has frequently quoted from the mystic-saints as well as the great mystical theologians for the rich treasure of wisdom they possess on this state that is more experiential than it is intellectual. This is why I choose to do the same, borrowing from the best the Church has to offer in the following material we will encounter.

The first part of our discussion here will be an attempt towards understanding the nature of a *victim soul*. One definition defines a victim as a living being offered as a sacrifice in a religious rite. This definition for our purposes is rather limited, for it tends to imply a cultic offering made upon an altar, similar to Abraham's offering of Isaac (see Gn 22). The victim soul we are talking about is not put to death immediately as a sacrifice to God, but lives his life in a state of suffering for the atonement of sin. Furthermore, our victim offers himself in the privacy of his heart, and God likewise works in the depths of the soul; in other words, it is not a public display or event, although the victim does often suffer for the sins of many in the community or the world.

One early form of atonement that was common from the Old Testament was the sacrifice of animals and grain (see Lv 1-7; Ex 12:1-20; Ex 29; Nm 15:1-31; Dt 21:1-9). As one can readily see in these examples, atonement was made for man's offenses against God through the sacrifice of bulls, lambs, sheep, goats, birds, crops, and the like. These traditional offerings survived into the time of the New Testament, as can be seen from the following examples: Mary and Joseph's sacrifice of the doves (Lk 2:22-24); the "offerings" of the altar (1 Cor 9:13); the sacrifices of the Jewish high priests (Heb 7:26-28; 13:9-11).

It is only when we come to the story of Jesus as the ultimate and eternal high priest that we first learn of a sacrificial offering of self as a means of atonement for sin. Now, instead of an animal or a grain, a man becomes a victim of God's love for the salvation of many: "He has no need, like those high priests, to offer sacrifices daily, first for his own sins and then for those of the people; he did this once for all when he offered up himself" (Heb 7:27). Notice that Jesus voluntarily *offered* himself to God as a victim — a point we addressed that is common to most victim souls throughout history. As I had mentioned earlier in this text, Jesus became our first victim soul and stigmatist for the redemption of all mankind; he was the prototype for all future victim souls to come (see the unit on "Jesus as Victim").

How does the Church define a victim soul? What does she see in the merits of suffering for the sake of others? The Church places the primary emphasis toward understanding the victim's role in the example of Christ as the ultimate victim. Then and only then can we understand the co-redemptive work the victims have undertaken in union with Christ for the sake of saving others from their sin. Let's take a look at some of the Church's wisdom in seeing our Lord as the prototype victim that others have followed:

Christ was himself without sin, yet, in fulfillment of the prophecy of Isaiah He underwent His own passion and came to know human sorrow (Is 53:4-5). Christ still suffers and undergoes torments whenever we his followers suffer. . . . (S.C.D.W., *Hominum dolores*, Dec. 7, 1972.)

Here we see that Christ still suffers for the sins of humanity. He shares our sufferings continually, for love compels Him to do so. A God who does not suffer would not be a God of perfect love, for where there is true love there is suffering, and where there is suffering one can find love.

Christ loved the Church and gave himself up for her, that He might sanctify her. He united her to himself as a spouse. . . . (S.C.D.W., *Misericordiam suam*, Feb. 7, 1974.)

It is interesting to hear the Church speak of her members as spouses to the risen Lord. This idea has a long tradition with the mystics, who often refer to the soul as the "bride" of Christ the "groom." In a later discussion on the various mystical states, we will examine the meaning of the spiritual marriage that our Lord rewards to some of His chosen souls. It is the highest spiritual state possible in this earthly life — the pinnacle of divine union.

Many of the faithful have a hard time believing that our Lord in His risen glory could possibly suffer, especially now that He is at the right hand of the Father in the eternal kingdom we call heaven. I have always felt that in some mysterious way, Jesus continues to suffer His Passion for us because of the sins that we commit. Yes, the Cross was a victory over evil and the act that led to our salvation, but it was not an act that was meant for just one moment in time. The Cross was a moment that continues throughout history until the end of time. Man continues to sin, and therefore is in continual need of conversion, repentance and the ever-present Cross that calls us back to God's love and mercy. Since we continue to sin and fall away from our Lord, He could not help but suffer for those who offend Him; if He were to quit caring, He would not be a God of love, compassion and mercy. But we know through Scripture that He was very much so these things. We also know that He wept for our sin and sweated blood (Lk 22:44). Jesus wept for the people of Jerusalem as well: "O Jerusalem, Jerusalem, killing the prophets and stoning those who are sent to you! How often would I have gathered your children together as a hen gathers her brood under her wings, and you would not" (Mt 23:37). Jesus could not hold back His emotions for His beloved Lazarus when Mary confronted Him (see Jn 11:17-36). Of course, there are many more examples of Jesus' compassionate love for humanity in the Gospels — a love that transcends all time and knows no bounds.

A few other examples from the wisdom of the Church would be appropriate at this point. Let us look at further reaffirmations concerning Christ as our ultimate Victim through the words of the Magisterium:

Christ, holy, innocent and undefiled knew nothing of sin, but came to expiate only the sins of the people. . . . (S.C.D.W., *Misericordiam suam*, Feb. 7, 1974.)

Jesus accepted death for the sake of His brothers and sisters as their Mediator, death being for them the wages of sin. . . . (S.C.C., *Ad normam decreti*, April 11, 1971.)

He who alone 'was made sin' (2 Cor 5:21) for our sake, became sacrifice for our sins. . . . (Eleventh Council of Toledo, *Symbol of Faith*, A.D. 645.)

The plentiful redemption of Christ brought us abundant forgiveness of all our sins. . . . (Pope Pius XI, *Miserentissimus Redemptor*, 1928.)

The Father manifested His mercy by reconciling the world to himself in Christ, making peace by the blood of His cross with all who are in heaven and on earth. The Son of God became man and lived among men so that He might liberate them from slavery to sin and call them out of darkness into His wonderful light. . . . (S.C.D.W., *Misericordiam suam*, Feb. 7, 1974.)

In the sacrifice of the Mass, the passion of Christ is represented. The body which is given for us and the blood which is shed for the remission of sins are offered to God by the Church for the salvation of the whole world. . . . (S.C.D.W., *Misericordiam suam*, Feb. 7, 1974.)

These are but a few of the many statements that Holy Mother Church makes concerning the ever-present and ongoing reality of Christ's redemptive action in the world. In the last statement from *Misericordiam suam* (see above), we see that Jesus as Victim continually offers himself, body and blood, for the sake of sinners everywhere. It is a sacrifice that continues the work of the Cross at Calvary some two thousand years ago. Since Jesus continually offers himself up at the altars each day, He likewise has suffered the pains of His Passion regularly since His death on the Cross. The Cross is a present reality that will not end until the consummation of the world.

Because of the identity with Christ's Passion, the victim soul suffers, to a greater or lesser degree, the same sufferings that consumed our Lord. Normally the victim atones for the sins of another. This is sometimes identified as *vicarious suffering* because the victim suffers in the place of the one he or she is atoning for; in other words, they take on the punishments due for those sinners, even to the point of feeling the pains associated with those punishments. These are given directly from God as the victim's penalty to be paid — as a just appeasement to make up for God's retribution rightfully held against them:

To be a victim necessarily implies immolation, and as a rule atonement for another. Although strictly speaking one can offer oneself as a victim to give God joy and glory by voluntary sacrifice, yet for the most part God leads souls by that path only when He intends them to act as mediators: they have to suffer and expiate for those whom their immolation will be profitable, either by drawing down graces of forgiveness on them, or by

acting as a cloak to cover their sins in the face of divine justice. It stands to reason that no one will on his own initiative take such a role on himself. Divine consent is required before a soul dares to intervene between God and His creature. There would be no value in such an offering if God refused to hear the prayer. . . .
(H. Monier Vinard, S.J., from the Introduction of *The Way of Divine Love*, Tan Books and Publishers, Inc., 1981; reprint.)

Father Vinard has beautifully expressed the nature of the victim who atones for the sins of others. Notice that (as I've said before) it is God who does the choosing; it is He who decides who will be His victims, and the victims must give their consent. It is very much like a two-way agreement or covenant whereby the sacred vocation is established and lived out. If the soul chooses to refuse the invitation for this precious vocation, then God respects their free will and chooses another according to His good designs.

Sometimes victims are chosen to atone for the sins of a particular person, and not for a group of people, a country or the world. When this occurs, the victim suffers the penalties due to the one they sacrifice for. Every trial imaginable may have to be endured, including illnesses, persecution and diabolical assaults.

Above all, the victim is the enemy of the evil one, who abhors the soul who through vicarious suffering takes the place of the sinner once held by his chains. The evil spirit does not like to lose any soul that he has in his grip, especially to God whom he hates with a vengeance. Consequently, these spirits of darkness often torment these victims in order to scare them, fatigue them, or to make them lose faith and abandon their mission. The more the victim resists the evil one, the more holy the soul is, the stronger the attacks become. Harassments, threats and even physical beatings are not uncommon to these chosen ones. Why does God allow such evil to affect the very souls He chooses to save others from the darkness? One of the reasons is so that God's power and majesty may show forth in the midst of the "prince of this world" and his activities; another reason is to show doubters and unbelievers the reality of the evil spirit and the existence of an eternal hell. Once confronted with the dreadful spirit, perhaps many agnostics will come back to the faith. The world continues to have its "doubting Thomases," and many are not satisfied until they can see for themselves a particular reality the Church has always believed in. We also need to be reminded from time to time of the very serious consequences our unbelief and sin can have on the future of our souls. Satan is real, and so are his cohorts. Hell and Purgatory are also very real, and it will be a rude awakening for the many who refuse to believe in them up to their dying day. Yet we know that Heaven is also real, and it is this thought that keeps our faith and hope alive. We know that Jesus promised this to be so, as the Gospel of John tells us:

In my Father's house are many rooms; if it were not so, would I have told you that I go to prepare a place for you? I am indeed going to prepare a place for you. . . . I will come back again and will take you to myself, that where I am you may be also . . . (Jn 14:2-4).

Everyone knows the claim that our Lord made concerning the reality of Heaven for those who believe in the Son:

> I am the living bread which came down from heaven; if any one eats of this bread, he will live for ever; and the bread I shall give for the life of the world is my flesh (Jn 6:51).

Do victim souls really desire to suffer for others? Is there ever desire expressed even before the vocation is given by God? If so, will God respond favorably to those who offer themselves in this way? Not always, but it has happened many times in the past. If the soul is found to be worthy to share in the Cross, if he or she is pure and humble, if the soul is persistent and truly faithful, God has been known to respond to their desires. Padre Pio (1887-1968) was one holy soul that fervently longed to share the Cross with Christ in order to atone for sinners (even himself). We can see from his letter to Padre Benedetto (his spiritual director at the time) that he desired the Cross very much, even ten years before he received the visible stigmata. Here is what he says:

> Patience! It is true that I am suffering, but I am very happy in this state for you have assured me that it does not mean that God has abandoned me but rather shows the delicacy of His exquisite love. I hope that the Lord is pleased to accept my sufferings in satisfaction for the innumerable times I have offended Him. After all, what is my suffering in comparison to what I deserve for my sins?

> However that may be, for me it is sufficient to know that God wills it and then I am quite happy. Now, my dear Father, I want to ask your permission for something. For some time past I have felt the need to offer myself to the Lord as a victim for poor sinners and for the souls in Purgatory.

> This desire has been growing continually in my heart so that it has now become what I would call a strong passion. I in fact have made this offering to the Lord several times, beseeching Him to pour out upon me the punishments prepared for sinners and for the souls in the state of purgation, even increase them a hundredfold for me, as long as He converts and saves sinners and quickly admits to paradise the souls in Purgatory, but I should now like to make this offering to the Lord in obedience to you. It seems to me that Jesus really wants this. . . . (Padre Pio, *Epistolario* [Letters, Vol. I], Nov. 29, 1910.)

Padre Pio's desires for redemptive suffering are not unusual, though he is an extraordinary case, having visibly bore the wounds of our Lord in his body for fifty years (by far the longest of anyone known in history). Notice that he is obedient to his director, and even asks his permission to offer himself up. This obedience to his superior is really an obedience to Christ, who told us to do whatever the Church leaders tell us because He would be guiding them through His Spirit: "As thou didst send me into the world, so I have sent them into the world. And for their sake I consecrate myself, that they also may be consecrated in truth" (Jn 17:18-19).

It is very clear from many of Padre's letters that he desired to suffer in union with Christ for a long time. The following are more examples of this unending desire of the holy priest from the Gargano Mountains:

My heart wants more and more to experience any affliction whatever if it pleases Jesus. . . . (*Epist.*, Vol. I, Aug. 17, 1910.)

While I am impatient to go to Christ, I would rebuke myself if I sought to be left without the Cross even for only one hour. . . . (*Epist.*, Vol. I, Sept. 20, 1912.)

I am suffering and would like to suffer even more. I feel myself consumed and would like to be consumed even more. I wish to live, in order to suffer more and more because Jesus has made me understand that the sure proof of love is only in suffering. . . . (*Epist.*, Vol. I, May 6, 1913.)

I know for certain that I have a burning thirst to suffer a great deal. . . . (*Epist.*, Vol. I, Aug. 15, 1915.)

I accept, O Lord, all this earth's tortures rolled up into one. I desire them as my due. . . . (*Epist.*, Vol. I, Oct. 17, 1915.)

I want to suffer: This is what I long for. . . . (*Epist.*, Vol. I, July 27, 1918.)

As we can see, Padre Pio's entire life was one of unending suffering, yet he willed it that way. Other saints in the Church's history have often done the same. But does God desire victim souls as much as these souls desire to be victims? This is a very important point to consider. If He doesn't, then we are faced with many chosen souls who are only following their own will instead of the Father's. Yet Padre Pio himself tells us that indeed the Lord does desire victims of His love: "He chooses some souls for himself. And among those He has chosen mine in order to be helped in the great negotiation for final salvation" (*Epist.*, Vol. I, Sept. 20, 1912); or again he says: "It is he (Jesus) who comes to beg sufferings and tears from us. He needs them for souls" (*Epist.*, Vol. I, April 2, 1912). But it is not just Padre who tells us of God's will; it is Jesus himself who conveyed this message to him: "I need victims . . . renew the sacrifice of your whole self to me" (*Epist.*, Vol. I, March, 1913).

Another saintly soul, the mystic-victim Sister Mary of the Holy Trinity (1901-42), was known for her private revelations from Jesus, who taught her the way of the victim soul. In these messages, we learn that Jesus wants victims from every walk of life to atone for the sins of the world — not just the religious living a conventual life. Listen to what our Lord has told her: "Yes, I ask for an army of victims, scattered everywhere — for everywhere evil is mingled with good: in the organization of states as in that of communities, in families as in each soul. I ask that those who love me should offer themselves as victims to make reparation by overcoming evil by good in the environment in which they find themselves" (*The Spiritual Legacy*: May 6, 1942, Tan Books and Publishers, Inc., 1981).

What are the necessary conditions for the Lord to accept the offering of the potential victim? Again we look to the words of Sister Mary of the Holy Trinity, as were given to her by our Blessed Lord:

> That they consecrate themselves to that reparation by imitating that which I pursue in My Eucharistic life: by silence; by offering Me on every occasion an act contrary to the evil they have seen; by exacting nothing from others, but from themselves; by obtaining from God the triumph of truth. My little daughter, it is *that* which I desire. . . (May 6, 1942).

We have spent a great deal of time discussing the role of the victim soul, but it is so necessary to understand this vocation in order to appreciate the role of the ultimate victim, the stigmatist. Since all stigmatists were true victims of divine love, they have all experienced the role of victim in a most intimate and intensive manner. Therefore, we will continue a bit more on the nature of the victim soul, and then move on to the specific ways these souls sacrifice for sinners: through atonement, reparation and expiation.

The above given to Sister Mary was a Vow of Victim that our Lord had explained to her. Let us continue with the other things Jesus taught us about this vow through Sister Mary:

> I desire an army of apostolic souls consecrated to Me by the Vow of Victim, not to expiate the sins of others by extraordinary trials; no, that is not what I desire. I desire a great army of victim souls who will join me in the apostolate of My Eucharistic Life, who will bind themselves by the Vow of Victim to choose the methods which I chose. . . (no. 363).

> I desire these victims to be everywhere: in the world and in the cloisters; in every occupation, in every station of life, in the fields and in the factories, in schools and in stores, in families and in convents, in business and in the arts, everywhere. . . (no. 363).

> I ask four things of the souls who bind themselves more closely to Me by the Vow of Victim:
> 1) to listen to me more than to speak to me;
> 2) to strive to reproduce My actions, My way of acting rather than My words;
> 3) to be before men as they are before God in a state of poverty that begs, not in a state of spiritual wealth that gives alms of its superfluity. Victim souls will beg more than they will give;
> 4) to confine their efforts to spreading My Spirit, My gentleness and My kindness which does not dwell on evil, but overcomes evil by good. . . (no. 366).

> The state of victim is to bear without defending oneself, as I did in My Passion, insults, slander, mockery, brutality — to allow yourself to be stripped, yes, even to nakedness. You will never have all that; but accept the acts of self-stripping that solicit your generosity. . . (no. 457).

I desire your soul to be immolated, in imitation of My
Eucharistic Life, in silence, in neglect, in the gift of yourself in
Me — by ceaseless intercession, by welcoming every occasion for
expiation, in joy. . . (no. 634).

What I ask of you, what I expect of you, is that you act not by
becoming irritated or by speaking, but according to My way of
acting, by imitating My Eucharistic Life. That is the Vow of
Victim that I have asked of you. . . (no. 661).

I want souls to know that by the Vow of Victim they enter into a
life of union with Me. They must know that I ardently desire this
Vow of Victim. It is thus that society will be reconstituted. I
desire that there be some of them everywhere, in every state of
life; I greatly desire this Vow of Victim, wherever there are
generous souls. . . (no. 666).

This Poor Clare of Jerusalem has given us through our Lord a
summation of a victim soul's life, her duties and obligations, with a depth
and beauty that few have ever done. Although we are to be cautious towards
private revelations of any sort, we nevertheless can hear what they have to
say and reflect on them in light of the Gospel message. Since so much of our
knowledge, let alone experience, in the mystical life comes from these
revelations and supernatural experiences of the great mystics, it would
serve us well to take them seriously as God's chosen messengers who are
vessels of His unending grace.

What we do need to be extremely cautious about regarding these
messages is the attitude we might have toward the nature of these gifts.
Although we are all called to be victims through God's desire and our
voluntary cooperation (according to Sr. Mary), we are *not* all called to be
heroic, extraordinary victims. Most of us are called to the ordinary ways of
perfection, and it is in this realm that we offer up what we are able to,
according to what God has given us and how much strength we have for our
sufferings. It would be a mistake to suffer more than our Lord has designed
for us; this would even go against His most holy will. We should not go
further than we are called until the voice of the Lord takes us beyond that
place where we are. This, of course, requires careful spiritual discernment
from one's director, as well as listening to God's silent voice in the depths of
our heart. Above all, let no one think that everyone is called to bear the
stigmata of our Lord, just because we are all called to offer our sufferings up
for sinners! Needless to say, this would be very presumptuous on our part
and a cause for deception among a great many people.

On the other hand, it is not impossible that the Lord would choose
someone from among our midst to live the life of victim, or even to bear His
most precious wounds. He has done this time and again over the centuries.
But let us understand that these gifts — these vocations — are truly
extraordinary and supernatural, reserved for a very few who are placed in
God's plans for such a mission. The purity and holiness of these chosen ones
are extraordinary in themselves, for few have ever lived so closely the life of
the suffering Christ as they have. Although no one is worthy to share our
Lord's Passion and to help redeem the world, nevertheless these souls come
as close to being worthy as one could possibly get in this earthly life.

Atonement

In the Christological sense, the term "atonement" refers to Jesus' reconciliation of a sinful world with the Father through His suffering, death and resurrection. It is through Christ that we are graced and have salvation (2 Cor 5:18-21).

Atonement for a victim soul in the general sense refers to a reparation for an offense. In order to be effective, this atonement must be voluntary and from the heart; it stems from the seeds of charity, where Christian love recognizes the responsibility and moral duty to help those who are in need of conversion and renewal. If one attempts to repair offenses against God by and for himself, then it is atonement in the sense of personal sacrifice and self-denial; if one attempts to atone for the sins of another person, then we understand this to be what we call *vicarious suffering* — literally, the suffering of one on behalf of another.

The central value of atonement for the one who sacrifices appears to be the supreme act of charity that one displays for his brother or sister in need. Indeed, St. Paul says that love fulfills the law (Rom 13:8,10). Love is the pinnacle of our faith; it makes our joy complete (Jn 15:11-12). Love is the commandment given to us by Christ (Jn 15:17), and it is the greatest of all things (1 Cor 13:13). To atone for others, then, is really to love them and care for them, to lead them back to the embrace of the Father in the spirit of reconciliation.

The Church has described atonement in the same context as our love for neighbor. Pope Paul VI says it well:

> Every Christian will have to live for his brethren, completing 'in
> his flesh that which is lacking in the sufferings of Christ . . . for
> the benefit of His body, which is the Church' (Col 1:24). . . .
> (Pope Paul VI, *Paenitemini*, Feb. 17, 1966.)

Here the Holy Father re-echoes the teaching of Christ, who not only said that we must live for our brethren with the same love we show for Him (1 Jn 4:19-21), but that we must be prepared, if necessary, to even sacrifice our lives for our brothers and sisters who are in danger of losing their own (Jn 15:13).

As we have seen, atonement implies a voluntary effort on one's part to pay for the debts of others. Pope Paul VI connects this offering to the community-at-large, not for a self-seeking satisfaction:

> We find among the just ones of the Old Testament those who
> offered themselves to satisfy with their own personal penitence
> for the sins of the community. . . . (Pope Paul VI, *Paenitemini*,
> Feb. 17, 1966.)

The Holy Father addresses the fact that atonement is usually beneficial for the whole Body of Christ, and not for a favored few (however, many times the Lord will ask of a victim soul to atone for a single person's sin). General atonement for peace in the world, the local community, the Church as a whole, or the poor souls in Purgatory are the most common needs the victim responds to. Once again, this is not always true, but it does appear to be the norm in God's plans. The reason for this is that we are a body — the Mystical Body of Christ — and what affects one person usually has ramifications for all: "The body is *one* and has many members, and all the members of the body, though many are *one body*" (1 Cor 12:12); St. Paul explains this further: "God has so adjusted the body, giving the greater honor to the interior part, that there may be no discord in the body, but that the members may have the same care for *one another*" (1 Cor 12:24-25).

I have intentionally emphasized the word "one" in order to stress the importance Paul placed in the unity of all Christians. Our faith is community; no one is an island unto himself. Even the great contemplatives and hermits do not retreat from the world, but enter the world through loving sacrifices and prayers for it. In silence and solitude they find the time to gaze upon our Savior and seek His mercy for all souls in need of redemption.

Pope Paul VI once again emphasizes the need of atonement for our brethren in the same address to the faithful. He beautifully describes the way in which suffering can be offered up as atonement, even that which we possess as our own; in other words, we don't always have to take upon ourselves the sufferings of others. We can also offer up the trials we already have for the benefit of our brethren by uniting them to the sufferings of Christ. This alone is beneficial for the faithful, and very pleasing to our Lord:

> Those members of the Church who are stricken by infirmities, illnesses, poverty or misfortunes, or who are persecuted for the love of justice, are invited to unite their sorrows to the sufferings of Christ in such a way that they not only satisfy more thorough-ly the precept of penance but also obtain for their brethren a life of grace and for themselves that beatitude which is promised in the Gospel to those who suffer. . . . (Pope Paul VI, *Paenitemini*, Feb. 17, 1966.)

Reparation

The Latin word from which reparation comes is *reparare*, which means to make new, to restore, to make amends. It is an attempt to right what is wrong; in the spiritual sense, the soul desires to help renew a sinful world with its own cooperation in the mystery of our redemption. The soul who makes reparation for sin is really making an attempt to appease the divine justice — to plead with our Lord to delay His wrath as he or she appeals to His divine mercy. In order to do so, the victim must share in the ongoing plan of redemption through the agony of the Cross. Those who make reparation, in a sense, "bargain with the Lord" in order to hold back His chastisement — to buy as much time as possible so that more sinners might be saved through the prayers and sacrifices they offer for them.

The acts of atonement and reparation are very similar in nature. It is not easy to separate them in terms of defining them, for often they are both found working simultaneously in the victim soul. One distinction that might be considered is this: whereas atonement means to take upon the sufferings of others in order to save their souls before God, one who offers reparation is more concerned with appealing to God's mercy to forgive the sinner by means of prayer and sacrifice. Reparation seeks to undo the damage already done from past sin (to "repare" a past wrong). More often than not, a victim soul who makes reparation for past transgressions will also be concerned about atonement for others in the present time or in the future; thus, it is difficult to see them as separate modes used for the conquest of sin.

Reparation is a close ally of the Sacrament of Reconciliation. A victim of reparation longs for the soul to make an act of contrition for their sin, to be truly sorry from the depths of their hearts, and to confess their wrongdoings in order to be converted and reconciled with the Savior of all mankind. In order for this change of heart to occur, the victim takes upon himself the acts of penance that actually belong to the sinner alone. This is done out of deep love for the sinner, as well as out of great confidence in a God of mercy who saves.

Atonement is really a part of reparation in the sense that it is itself a reparation for an offense through a voluntary act that compensates for the injustice against God.

A victim soul who had much to say about reparation was Sister Josefa Menendez (1890-1923), a Coadjutrix Sister of the Society of the Sacred Heart of Jesus. She had been blessed with many visions and revelations of our Lord during her short earthly life, and one of the main themes she encountered in the Lord's teachings was that of reparation. Let us hear the words that she heard from our Lord, with a hope that we might better understand this sublime vocation that serves to make due for our sin:

> One faithful soul can repair and obtain mercy for many ungrateful ones. . .

> One single act of love in the loneliness in which I leave you repairs for many of the acts of ingratitude of which I am the object. . .

> The obstinacy of a guilty soul wounds My Heart deeply, but the tender affection of one who loves Me not only heals the wound, but turns away the effects of My Father's Justice. . . .

In these words from our Lord to Josefa Menendez, we see that acts of love help to erase the effects of sin. Jesus made this point in the Gospel:

> I tell you, her sins, which are many, are forgiven, for she loved much; but he who is forgiven little, loves little (Lk 7:47).

In this example, Jesus was referring to the penitent woman who anointed his feet with perfume.

Josefa indicates that the Father's chastisement upon the sinful world is already due, but because of the reparation being made by His chosen ones, the punishment has been temporarily averted. Listen to what the Lord has said to her:

> The sins committed are so many and so grave that the wrath of the Father would overflow were it not for the reparation and love of My consecrated brides. . . . How many souls are lost!. . .

What sobering words from our Lord! We have already tested the Father's patience beyond His limits. Because He is a just God, we will one day have to account for our sin. Yet victims of reparation seem to help make amends for some of the sin through their own efforts to pay the penalty due for just retribution from God. They appeal to the Lord's mercy by showing so much love, mercy and forgiveness themselves that the Lord is pleased with their example.

The Lord must have approved of Josefa's efforts, for later in her short but heroic life He blessed her with the gift of the Sacred Stigmata, which she bore until her death in 1923. We will be seeing more of Josefa later on in this work.

What are some of the ways we can make reparation for the sinners of the world? What do the victim souls say about this? Returning to the thoughts of Sister Mary of the Holy Trinity, we have these words of wisdom:

> I have need of acts of generosity that make reparation for the infidelities of those who are Mine. I have need of sacrifices, of hidden charity, that make reparation for destructive selfishness. I have need of acts of courage, of humble and true obedience that make reparation for falsehood, rebellion, the errors of pride. . . .

> Pray for the wicked, suffer and expiate for them. Ah, yes, make smooth the ways of the Lord!

Here we have a list of ways to make amends to our Lord for the offenses committed against His Heart. Obedience, sacrifice, suffering, and prayer in a spirit of humility and love are the ways of reparation. Now let us turn to the third way of the victim soul: that of expiation.

Expiation

Expiation is taken from the Latin word *expiare*, which means to atone for fully. Expiation involves making reparation, suffering the penalty due to someone else and their sin, and performing works of penance. It is very similar to atonement in that the victim takes upon him or herself the punishments of another to please the divine justice. One form of expiation is the unity of one's sufferings with the Cross of Christ. Yet it is not one's own sufferings that is unified with the Cross, but that which is really another's; the victim has voluntarily taken them as their own, a suffering that would not have been deserved or needed in their own natural state which is pure and most holy. One needs to be as pure as snow, as innocent as a dove, in the image of the Maker himself. How few there are!

Although similar to atonement in its purpose, expiation even more so than atonement or reparation involves identity with the Cross, a total immersion into the Passion of our Lord. When one expiates for sin, they are acting on our Lord's behalf as co-Redemptors, sharing in the mission of the Son for the salvation of the whole world. Some victims who make expiation are rewarded with the wounds of Jesus himself, in the form of the invisible or visible stigmata. These expiatory victims become partners with the Crucified Lord, at times even spilling their blood for the offenses of others. Expiation embodies all of the atonement and reparation the victim can give for the love of Jesus and the love for humanity. The expiatory victim is nailed to the Cross of Christ, and lives perpetually in a state of suffering for the sole purpose of helping in our redemption.

Who is called to expiate for sinners? Is this vocation only reserved for a chosen few? Pope Paul VI says that "all are called upon to participate in the work of Christ and therefore to participate also in His expiation" (*Paenitemini*, Feb. 17, 1966). Note how he associates expiation with the work of Christ. Jesus' entire ministry was a work of redemption that culminated in the Cross. He gave His life as an offering for sin (Is 53:10), and justified many through His life-long sufferings (Is 53:11). The expiatory victim is called to do the same. Yet Pope Paul VI recognizes that as our lives contain a series of trials and tribulations, we too can live the life of our Lord's sufferings until we are crucified with Him into the newness of life: "whoever would save his life will lose it, and whoever loses his life for my sake will find it" (Mt 16:25).

Indeed, our Lord's sufferings are completed in our own, as Pope Pius XI once exclaimed: "Christ's expiatory suffering is renewed and in a way continued and completed in His Mystical Body, which is the Church" (*Miserentissimus Redemptor*, 1928). We must all continue the work of expiation for the sufferings that continue to plague our Lord over hardened sinners, even though Jesus was the perfect Victim. All are called to eat at His supper (Lk 22:14-20), all are chosen to share in the bloody sacrifice of the Savior. Some, however, are chosen in a special way to continue His sacrifice more intensely. The great St. Augustine (A.D. 354-430) had this to say about the continual sacrifice our Lord makes in union with His people: "Christ suffered all that He should have suffered; there is now nothing lacking in the measure of His sufferings. His sufferings as Head, then, were completed; yet for Christ in His Body sufferings still remained" (*Enarrationes in Psalmos*, Ps. 86.5). Because our sufferings continue to oppress us, expiation is needed to satisfy the causes of what makes us continually suffer, especially where it pertains to sin, our separation from God.

Why would Christ — the sole Mediator before the Father — need expiatory victims to help in the plan of salvation? Why are some of us involved with all of this? Pope Pius XI explains the reason very well:

> It is entirely proper that Christ who is still suffering in His Mystical Body should want to have us as His companions in the work of expiation. This is required of us also by our close union with Him, since we are 'the Body of Christ and individual members of it' (1 Cor 12:27), and all the members 'ought to suffer with the Head anything that the Head suffers' (1 Cor 12:26). . . . (Pope Pius XI, *Miserentissimus Redemptor*, 1928.)

The Holy Father points out that we must "crucify our flesh" by participating in the mystical crucifixion that obligates us all to expiate for sin according to our measure and our state of life:

> We shall reap a more abundant harvest of mercy and forgiveness for ourselves and for others to the extent that our own offering and sacrifice corresponds more perfectly to the sacrifice of our

Lord; in other words, to the extent that we immolate our self-love and our passions and crucify our flesh with that mystical crucifixion of which the Apostle speaks. . . . (Pope Pius XI, *Miserentissimus Redemptor*, 1928.)

Many of God's chosen servants have offered themselves as expiatory victims because of the immense love that flows out of their hearts for all humanity. But it is a selfless love that imbues their spirit: "Self-love is a poison that ruins everything. Self must die, and it dies only through sufferings, humiliations, and by being buried in oblivion" (Fr. James J. Doyle, S.J.). Father Doyle states that there is a mysterious but delightful connection between love and suffering, especially a selfless love given up for the salvation of others:

Christ's love led Him to choose suffering and humiliation as means for man's redemption. To love Him, then, is to love as He loved. There is a mysterious, mystical connection between love and suffering. It is almost as if one's sufferings are really Christ's when taken in the spirit of love. German stigmatist Anne Catherine Emmerich (1774-1824), whom we will encounter later in this book, described these feelings: 'It is not I who suffer; it is my Lord Jesus who suffers in me!' she said while continually offering herself as a victim of expiation. . . . (*The Life of Anne Catherine Emmerich: Vol. I*, p. 151; TAN Books and Publishers, Inc., reprint 1976).

Love has been the prime motivator in most of the lives of the victim souls and stigmatists who have offered their lives as a holocaust to God for His people. In another example, we find these words from the victim Mother Louise Margaret Claret de la Touche (1868-1915),to whom the Lord taught His way of divine love:

I must make it my aim that these three words: union, love and suffering, be the resume of my life. I must love our Lord as my only and dear Spouse, to love Him as my greatest Benefactor, as my Principle, my End and my only Happiness; to love my neighbor as the loved object of my Beloved; to love souls as the most perfect works of my Creator; to suffer for God, in soul and body, as sacrifice and as holocaust; to suffer for myself, as expiation and necessary consequence of the faults of the past; to suffer for my neighbor, as reparation, offering, propitiation, and as means of union between God and souls. . . (*Intimate Notes*, Oct. 31, 1892.)

Mother Louise goes on to describe her selfless love for others and her willingness, even eagerness, to suffer more out of love for God and for sinners:

I give myself to Thee for the salvation and conversion of souls; I give myself to Thee, undivided and without restriction, ready to suffer in my soul, in my body and in my heart, in order to expiate, and to merit the salvation of sinners. If by suffering and toiling on earth, I can obtain the salvation of some poor souls,

that is enough for me, O my Lord. I give myself entirely to Thee
for souls, I give myself entirely for Thee and for souls; I give
myself entirely to souls with Thee; I wish for nothing but Thee
for my soul, nothing but my soul alone for Thee. . . (*Intimate
Notes*, Oct., 1892.)

Although there are many such saintly souls in the history of the Church
who offer themselves in love for the salvation of the world, I felt it
appropriate to show one example — that of Mother Louise — and how these
fervent souls on fire with the love of God could offer themselves
unconditionally as victims to expiate for our sin. We owe them more than
we can possibly repay, for their mission was that of Jesus Christ, so united
were they to His love and His Cross. They literally became transformed into
a new image of Christ, brought about by the God of love who abides in each
of us: "God is love, and he who abides in love abides in God, and God abides
in him" (1 Jn 4:16). It is we who respond to this love, but it is God who is the
source of all love: "We love, because he first loved us" (1 Jn 4:19).

The love that is directed to the spiritual welfare of our neighbor is the
best (St. Alphonsus Liguori). And according to St. Bernard, one soul is
worth more than the whole world. Again in the words of St. Alphonsus
Liguori: "If you truly love yourself, you will make every possible effort to
win souls to God, for he who converts a sinner saves not only the sinner, but
himself." How can we save ourselves by helping to save others? Because
when we help others, we are really helping Christ, who dwells in the recesses
of every heart: "Then the righteous will answer him, 'Lord, when did we see
thee hungry and feed thee, or when did we see thee a stranger and welcome
thee, or naked and clothe thee? And when did we see thee sick or in prison
and visit thee?' And the king will answer them, 'Truly, I say to you, as you
did it to one of the least of these my brethren, you did it to me' " (Mt
25:37-40).

Thus concludes our treatment of the meaning of victim soul and the
values of atonement, reparation and expiation. We will now look a bit
further into the ways Christ has called us to unite our sufferings with His
Cross from the examples in Sacred Scripture. Later, we will explore how
victim souls in general and how stigmatists in particular relive the Passion
of our Lord through the mystical state of ecstasy, how they bleed from the
wounds the Lord has given them, and how they suffer physically and
spiritually for the transgressions of all sinners.

The Synoptic Gospels

The call to be a victim soul — those who share the Cross of Christ to satisfy
for the sins of the world — is admittedly rare. We have seen how these pious
souls take upon themselves the chastisements intended for others in order
to save them from eternal separation from God. This, we have noted, is
caused by their sinful nature.

Divine justice is required, and it is satisfied in three ways: through
atonement, reparation and expiation. Sometimes a victim is chosen to
sacrifice his or her entire life at the foot of the Cross, being consumed by the
penalties of sin that God in His wisdom reaps upon them. Of course, this is
always done with the permission of the victim, or as a voluntary offering
that they themselves make. Never does God impose upon a soul without

letting them choose otherwise; for He is a respecter of free will and individual constitutions. Once they accept the offering to become victim, or once they voluntarily offer themselves to be consumed for the sake of sinners, then the Lord is free to impose upon them in whatever manner He so chooses, often showering relentless trials and sufferings upon them to the very limits of their endurance, for God does not try us beyond our means (1 Cor 10:13).

Again, we are not talking about the ordinary way of the faithful; these are extraordinary souls specially chosen by God to help redeem the world in union with His Son. A choice few, such as the stigmatists we will soon encounter, have the rare capacity to endure the greatest of pains, sufferings and trials. They have been found worthy to sacrifice their blood on the Cross of our Lord. Because they are chosen to atone for sins, they must be extraordinarily pure: "You are all fair, my love; there is no flaw in you" (Sg 4:7). Indeed, our Lord claims them as His own, and "seals them in His heart," the Sacred Heart that consumes but does not destroy (Sg 8:6).

As we have understood from the previous chapters, everyone is called to share in the redemptive works of the Cross; this we do through the daily crosses we must bear (Lk 9:23), and according to the state our Lord has placed us in. Some are called to carry heavier crosses, but every cross offered up to our Lord — no matter how small — helps the Mystical Body in the plan of salvation, if done voluntarily with a selfless love and a pure heart.

We will now examine the Synoptic Gospels (Matthew, Mark and Luke) to see how Jesus invites us to share His Cross by bearing our own. Later we will do the same with the "mystical Gospel" of John. Then we will move to the wisdom of the Apostles (excluding Paul, whom we dealt with in a separate chapter).

One cross that our Lord teaches us to bear is the many temptations we encounter in our everyday lives, be they from the devil, the world or ourselves. In the Gospel of Matthew, Jesus is led to the wilderness to be tempted by the evil spirit (Mt 4:1). Yet it is more than the devil that becomes a temptation to Him. The entire episode shows us the three means of temptation we are subjected to, the very ones St. John of the Cross alludes to in his work, "The Precautions" (see *The Collected Works of St. John of the Cross*, ICS Publications, pp. 656-61). Again, these are from the devil, the world and ourselves, where we must continually battle our pride, our lusts and our temperaments.

Firstly, the devil tempts Jesus in the ways of the flesh, a test against fasting, which is a form of bodily mortification: "The tempter came and said to him, 'If you are the Son of God, command these stones to turn into bread' " (Mt 4:3). Jesus teaches us that by sacrifice and mortification, one opens himself to God's presence and fills himself with His Spirit; in other words, he empties himself to let the God of life in: "But he answered, 'It is written, Man shall not live by bread alone, but by every word that proceeds from the mouth of God' " (Mt 4:4). When we are tested with sacrifice or self-denial, we can rely upon the Word of God, Who is the true Bread that will sustain us (Jn 6:33).

The next temptation Jesus experienced was pride in the form of presumption. When the devil placed our Lord upon the temple, he said: "If you are the Son of God, throw yourself down; for it is written, 'He will give his angels charge of you;' and 'On their hands they will bear up lest you strike your foot against a stone' " (Mt 4:6). Sometimes our secret pride assumes that we can manipulate God's merciful actions in our lives, forgetful of the fact that God is the Master of our destiny, the supplier of all goodness that we receive. We are not to be too presumptuous, lest we fall away from the unmerited gifts we receive from His bounty. Jesus taught us this lesson in His response to the evil one: "Again it is written, 'You shall not tempt the Lord your God' " (Mt 4:7). We need to forever balance our confidence in the Lord with a holy fear that we are undeserving of all that He gives us. This attitude will keep us humble and fearful of our own actions that do not rely upon the Source of all grace which we might receive. Then and only then will the Lord be pleased to grant us graces beyond whatever we might dream of receiving.

The last trial in the desert shows how the devil can use the world to tempt us, even against our very faith. The evil spirit offers Jesus "all the kingdoms of the world" if He would only come worship him instead of the Father. Here we can see that the devil knows there are many who make material things their God, sacrificing the love of God for an abuse of power. This form of temptation should come as no surprise to us, for the evil one used this tactic even at the beginning of time. In Genesis, the serpent uses the lust for knowledge (which is a form of power) to turn man away from God (see Gn 3:1-5). How does Jesus respond to all of this? He tells the devil: "You shall worship the Lord your God and him alone shall you serve" (Mt 4:10). Here we are taught the importance of following the first Commandment, which is a direct opposition to idolatry in the form of love for other gods, self, money, or any material possessions. Our God is a jealous God; He expects us to love Him more than anything, even to the point of wanting us to see Him as the very Source of our being. The devil will do all in his power to win pious souls over to his side. He is very capable of doing so, as he confirms himself: "To you I will give all this authority and their glory; for it has been delivered to me, and I will give it to whom I will" (Lk 4:6). Jesus also reaffirmed the devil's power over the world (see Jn 12:31), although we know that it is only temporary and will one day be completely crushed through the Cross of our Lord — a victory already achieved for those who remain firm in their faith: "The devil has come down to you in great wrath because he knows his time is short" (Rv 12:12).

What do all of these temptations have to do with how we bear our crosses in daily life? For one thing, Jesus shows us the weapons we have to fight off the diabolical, worldly, and self-centered evils that attempt to rob us of our union with God. We can defeat these enemies of our soul through two main sources: the eternal Word of God that we know to be unfailing, and by our faith and confidence in a God Who truly loves us and will not let us down if we center our lives around Him. The above examples are real temptations we must all face on a daily basis, and they signify continuous crosses that we must bear in order to follow the Cross of our Lord. We know this is so, for He had been subjected to the very same things throughout His earthly life. Why should it be any different for His followers?

Before we examine the ways our Lord invites us to help carry His Cross, let us reflect on the priorities of life, according to the words from the Holy Gospel:

No servant can serve two masters; for either he will hate the one and love the other, or be devoted to the one and despise the other. You cannot serve God and mammon (Lk 16:13).

For where your treasure is, there will your heart be also (Lk 12:34).

Take heed, and beware of all covetousness; for a man's life does not consist in the abundance of his possessions (Lk 12:15).

You lack one thing; go, sell what you have, and give to the poor, and you will have treasure in heaven; and, come, follow me (Mk 10:21).

Blessed are the poor in spirit, for theirs is the kingdom of heaven (Mt 5:3).

It is very evident from the many lessons quoted above that one of the greatest temptations against our faith lies in the greed for more wealth or material possessions. Man has become accustomed to the pleasures of the world, which lure him into a false sense of accomplishment and security. The danger lies in substituting these wordly pleasures for the lasting fulfillment that can only come through Jesus Christ. We must be constantly on our guard, resisting the temptations of the world for the poverty of Christ. This must be done through self-denial and self-detachment, in a true spirit of the poverty our Lord speaks of in the beatitude. If we are blessed with fortune, let us not allow it to become the master of our lives. It does not matter the amount we have, for we can become attached to anything, no mater how insignificant it might seem. Rather, we must look at all as transitory in light of what we possess in God. It is in this context that Jesus gave us these words: "So therefore, whoever of you does not renounce all that he has cannot be my disciple" (Lk 14:33). Jesus does not mean that we may not possess things; rather, we are not to cling to them or to put them first before acts of charity or the love of God. We renounce our possessions by not being attached to them, and by being able to give them up for the sake of the kingdom.

Another way in which man is tempted is in the lusts and passions of the heart. Sexual impurity is a very serious sin, one that the Lord has condemned in no uncertain terms. We know that spirit and flesh continue to battle one another throughout our earthly lives (see Rom 8). Yet it is our moral duty and obligation to subdue our carnal desires and to keep our heart and our thoughts pure, for we are living temples of the Holy Spirit, and to destroy this temple is to destroy ourselves and our relationship with our God (1 Cor 4:16-17).

Let us look briefly at a few of the warnings Jesus gave us in terms of temptations of the flesh, and the consequences for succumbing to them:

"And if your eye causes you to sin, pluck it out and throw it from you: it is better to enter life with one eye than with two eyes to be thrown into the hell of fire" (Mt 18:9).

"Do not commit adultery. . ." (Mk 10:19).

"You have heard that it was said, 'You shall not commit adultery! But I say to you that every one who looks at a woman lustfully has already committed adultery with her in his heart" (Mt 5:27-28).

Another temptation that man is subjected to is that against charity. How difficult it is to love our enemies! How trying it is to show patience and concern for those who wrong us in some way! Jesus has this to say about the way we treat our brother and sister, whether we are tempted to retaliate against them, or even when we choose to be apathetic towards them:

But I say to you that everyone who is angry with his brother shall be liable to judgment; whoever insults his brother shall be liable to the council, and whoever says, 'You fool' shall be liable to the hell of fire (Mt 5:21-22).

So if you are offering your gift at the altar, and there recall that your brother has something against you, leave your gift there before the altar and go; first be reconciled to your brother, and then come and offer your gift (Mt 5:23-24).

But I say to you, love your enemies and pray for those who persecute you so that you may be sons of your Father who is in heaven, for he makes his sun rise on the evil and on the good, and sends rains on the just and the unjust (Mt 5:44-45).

You have heard the command, 'An eye for an eye, a tooth for a tooth.' But I say to you, Do not resist one who is evil. But if anyone strikes you on the right cheek, turn to him the other also, and if anyone would sue you and take your coat, let him have your cloak as well; and if anyone forces you to go one mile, go with him two miles (Mt 5:38-41).

. . . to love one's neighbor as oneself, is much more than all burnt offerings and sacrifices (Mk 12:33).

Obviously, the list goes on and on. The central point here is that we must show compassion to others who may not do the same for us; we must be willing to embrace the trials of our broken relationships, just as Jesus reconciled us to His broken-ness through the sufferings He endured out of love for all of His people. Since God is love (1 Jn 4:8), we must have love and compassion for others in order to be united to Him in faith. For it is only through love for others that we prove our love for Him.

Of course, there are many other temptations we must face as we go through life, and numerous other examples that Jesus has left us in the Synoptic Gospels. Numerous trials are brought about by the spirits of darkness (more of which we will discuss in a later section in this book). A host of temptations are further caused by our own human weaknesses that involve our physical, emotional and psychological chemistries. Finally, we mustn't forget the lures of the world, a world so often filled with violence, crime and immorality that to live a good Christian life becomes a very difficult thing to do.

We have briefly discussed some of the ways we are tempted as human beings in our journey through life. Now we will explore some of the ways our Lord has asked us to bear our daily crosses in order to imitate more closely His way of perfection. We are reminded that when we bear our crosses patiently and with a true spirit of love, we associate ourselves more intimately with the living Cross of our Redeemer, and move closer to union with Him through the sacrifices we make.

In each of the Synoptic Gospels, Jesus welcomes us to not only bear our daily crosses, but to share in His Cross and participate in the plan of redemption. Because we are all a community of God — a Body of Christ — we cannot suffer for ourselves alone, but as a Body we must be united to each other through the God Who resides in us all: "In that day you will know that I am in my Father, and you in me, and I in you" (Jn 14:20). Let us take a closer look at what these Synoptic Gospels tell us about participation in the Cross through the words of our Lord:

> If a man would come after me, let him deny himself and take up his cross and follow me. For whoever would save his life will lose it; and whoever loses his life for my sake and the gospel's will save it (Mk 8:34-35).

Note how the Lord tells us that we must follow Him. These very important words emphasize that it is not enough to merely bear our daily crosses; we are to follow Him most intimately by uniting our sufferings to His. This is the only way we can really follow in His footsteps, to make His life our own. This does not always mean we have to be wounded upon the Cross (which the stigmatist is called to do), but rather to unite whatever crosses our Lord deems best to give us, be they physical, emotional or spiritual.

> . . . he who does not take his cross and follow me is not worthy of me (Mt 10:38).

Once again we see that it is not enough just to take up our cross. We are called to go a step further — to follow Him in a spirit of sacrifice and reparation, united to our Lord in the fullness of His love.

> Whoever does not bear his own cross and come after me, cannot be my disciple (Lk 14:27).

Not only are we not worthy of Jesus if we aren't prepared to follow His precious Cross, we aren't even worthy to be His disciples. *Disciple* (literally, "one who follows") implies a commitment to the one followed and a belief in his or her ideals. Because the Lord is committed to the plan of salvation, so we too must be devoted to the cause of saving souls, our own and others. God has designed that this take place through the Cross of our Lord by way of suffering for the offenses of others. This means to be consumed by love, in whatever capacity God has chosen for us.

Did Jesus promise us that our crosses would be easy? One thing He said about our burdens can be found in Matthew's Gospel: "Come to me, all who labor and are heavy laden, and I will give you rest. Take my yoke upon you, and learn from me; for I am gentle and lowly in heart, and you will find rest for your souls. For my yoke is easy, and my burden light" (Mt 11:28-30). But Jesus does not mean that we will not be burdened by our crosses that we are called to bear. He tells us that when we offer our trials and sufferings up in a spirit of love, the crosses will be lighter because we will recognize that they have a redemptive value that our Lord invites us to share with Him. Indeed, we can come to cherish our sufferings if we truly recognized that we are sharing them with Christ himself; by doing so, we become intimately involved with the life of our Lord, to the point of being almost one with Him. It is in this sense that our burdens will be lightened, and it is the attitude we all must achieve in order to welcome our crosses with complete confidence and surrender to the Lord who loves us all.

Jesus did indicate that our crosses would not always be easy or free of pain. Let us look at a few of His teachings from the Gospel:

> Enter by the narrow gate; for the gate is wide and the way is easy, that leads to destruction, and those who enter by it are many. For the gate is narrow and the way is hard, that leads to life, and those who find it are few (Mt 7:13-14).

> I came to cast fire upon the earth; and would that it were already kindled. . . . Do you think that I have come to give peace on earth? No, I tell you, but rather division. . . (Lk 12:49,51).

> Everyone to whom much is given of him will much be required; and of him to whom men commit much they will demand the more (Lk 12:48).

Nor must we become too presumptuous about our salvation or the good effects of our intentions. Jesus warns us to be humble of heart, lest we lose our own soul while trying to sacrifice our sufferings for others:

> Take heed then how you hear; for him who has, more will be given, and from him who has not, even what he thinks he has will be taken away (Lk 8:18).

> . . . for he is kind to the ungrateful and the selfish (Lk 6:35).

> But if that wicked servant says to himself, 'My master is delayed, and begins to beat his fellow servants, and eats and drinks with the drunken, the master of that servant will come on a day when he does not expect him and at an hour he does not know, and will punish him, and put him with the hypocrites; there men will weep and gnash their teeth (Mt 24:48-51).

We need not overemphasize the fear of the Lord, but we must balance our self-confidence with a humble attitude that realizes by grace alone through God's mercy are any of us saved. This is a pious fear that is wholesome to the soul and pleasing to the Lord.

We are instructed to be forever on the alert, cautiously guarding our thoughts and actions so that we do not fall from the grace that God has given us. This is also a lesson on how to bear our crosses that He deems to send us:

Take heed, watch and pray; you do not know when the time will come (Mk 13:33).

But take heed; I have told you all things beforehand (Mk 13:23).

Take heed that no one leads you astray (Mk 13:5).

Watch therefore, for you do not know on what day the Lord is coming (Mt 24:42).

Watch therefore, for you know neither the day or the hour (Mt 25:13).

In order to please our Lord, there are many sacrifices and sufferings that He accepts from us if done with a true spirit of charity. Our intentions are very important, for a sincere heart will win the favor of our God: "Beware of practicing your piety before men in order to be seen by them. . . . But when you give alms, do not let your left hand know what your right hand is doing, so that your alms may be in secret; and your Father who sees in secret will reward you" (Mt 6:1,3-4); "You are those who justify yourselves before men, but God knows your hearts; for what is exalted among men is an abomination in the sight of God" (Lk 16:15).

In order for us to bear our crosses in ways that are pleasing to God, we must strive to follow His will for us and for those we sacrifice for. To sacrifice only what we choose or in the manner we choose is to put our own will before God's. Following His most holy will is frequently stressed by Jesus in the Gospel:

Not every one who says to me, 'Lord, Lord,' shall enter the kingdom of heaven, but he who does the will of my Father who is in heaven (Mt 7:21).

But seek first his kingdom and his righteousness, and all these things shall be yours as well (Mt 6:33).

But it is easier for heaven and earth to pass away, than for one dot of the law to become void (Lk 16:17).

How can we strive to be more humble before the Lord? What attitude must we have in order to make our sacrifices more meaningful? Jesus once told His disciples: "If anyone would be first, he must be last of all and servant of all" (Mk 9:35). This same theme is addressed in the Gospel of Matthew: "whoever exalts himself will be humbled, and whoever humbles himself will be exalted" (Mt 23:12); "the last will be first, and the first last" (Mt 20:16); "whoever would be first among you must be your slave" (Mt 20:27).

To be humble is to serve each other and to care for each other's needs. It is to live the way Christ taught us to live, by way of His earthly example: "even as the Son of Man came not to be served, but to serve, and to give his life as a ransom for many" (Mt 20:28). Everyone on the path to perfection must serve each other (Mk 10:43), for in doing so we are really serving the

Lord: "Truly I say to you, as you did it to one of the least of these my brethren, you did it to me" (Mt 25:40).

There are many ways our Lord teaches us to perform acts of penance and sacrifice for the sake of the kingdom. The main concern is that we do so from the depths of our hearts, and not as a showpiece for public praise and admiration. Jesus teaches us this very lesson with regards to fasting (Mt 6:16-18) and almsgiving (Mt 6:2-3). He even tells us to pray from the silence of our heart, and not to draw attention to our prayers through public displays of frenzied exhibitionism (Mt 6:5-8). These lessons should serve to warn us that God takes great care to read the sincerity of our hearts. He is not very interested in prayers or sacrifices that are only motivated by public displays of aggression and emotionalism: "Be still, and know that I am God" (Ps 46:11). When we listen to God more than talk to Him, God communicates His will for us through the silence of our soul: "Speak, Lord, for thy servant hears" (1 Sm 3:9).

Jesus has taught us the way to bear our persecutions that is acceptable to the Father, especially through the strength and guidance of the Holy Spirit (see Mt 10:18-20; Mk 13:11-13; Lk 12:11); He has shown us how to live in a spirit of poverty and how to resist the temptations toward greed and materialism (see Mt 19:21; Mt 6:19-21; Mk 10:17,20-25). We need only look into the Scriptures to find a wealth of wisdom that shows us the way to bear our crosses. Jesus shows us that true discipleship involves unity with His Cross, a unity that comes with a loving acceptance of all the daily crosses we endure for Him and for each other. This is the way of redemptive sacrifice, and it is the way towards our salvation.

The Gospel of John

The Gospel of John was written sometime between A.D. 90 and A.D. 100. It is attributed to the "beloved" disciple of Jesus, traditionally thought to be John, the son of Zebedee (Mt 10:2). The Gospel itself refers to the term "beloved disciple" twice (Jn 21:20 and Jn 13:23), and the author himself claims to be the Apostle who witnessed all that he wrote about concerning Jesus and His ministry (Jn 21:24). Many scholars do not think that the author of this Gospel is the same author of Revelation because the language, style and messages are very different. For our purposes, we will follow the traditional view that the Gospel of John is the product of the Apostle whom Jesus loved.

What becomes immediately apparent is that this Gospel is so different from the Synoptic Gospels. It has often been referred to as the "mystical Gospel," for the author is heavily influenced by spiritual themes in his work, as well as describing Christ in His risen majesty much more so than the other Gospels, which tend to emphasize Jesus' humanity more than His divinity. It is from this vantage point — the risen Christ — that we must understand the main messages and themes of our sacred text.

Even though the divinity of Christ is emphasized more than His humanity, there is still a wealth of information concerning the human way in which we can offer up our crosses in unity with the Cross of our Lord, thus contributing to the role of redemption and salvation that the Redeemer has planned for us all.

The Gospel of John tells us about taking up our cross for the love of our

Lord and each other. Let us look at the various passages we encounter that deal with this theme:

> I am the good shepherd; I know my own and my own know me, as the Father knows me and I know the Father; and I lay down my life for the sheep. And I have other sheep, that are not of this fold; I must bring them also, and they will heed my voice. So there shall be one flock, one shepherd. For this reason the Father loves me, because I lay down my life, that I may take it again (Jn 10:14-17).

Although Jesus doesn't directly call us to share in His Cross in these passages, He does seem to imply that we must do so; to "know" the Good Shepherd means to hear His voice and to follow Him. If we decide to follow Him, then we must ask: what has He done that we must imitate ourselves? What will draw us closer to the Son and the Father, and what will allow us to help the "other sheep" that Jesus refers to? The answer is found in the last line of this quote: "For this reason the Father loves me, because I lay down my life, that I may take it up again." We in turn must be willing to sacrifice our lives for the sake of the Body of Christ, and the way we are able to do this is by the crosses we bear and offer in our particular state of life and circumstances.

We certainly cannot have the Cross that Jesus has. Nobody can ever equal what He has done for our salvation. Yet, we can *share* in that Cross by the co-redemptive values our sufferings and sacrifices allow us if voluntarily offered to God, and if it be God's will to accept it as such. Normally, the Lord does hear our prayer and accepts our offerings. But He gives us a share of His Cross according to His own mysterious designs — some, such as the stigmatists, receive the fullest share of the Cross possible in this earthly life; others, who are called to be victims of divine love, are called for a lifetime of sacrifice as well (some victims have become stigmatists); finally, all others who follow the ordinary ways of the Christian life are called to offer whatever crosses the Lord sends them. No particular person's sacrifices are better than another's (perhaps only more intense and all-consuming). We all contribute, for every member of Christ's Body is affected by every other member (see 1 Cor 12). Thus, each of us in his or her own way influences all the members, and each of us can be closely united to Jesus our Lord; He invites us all to partake in the mystery of our salvation, but only as instruments of His plan, for we very well know that He alone is our sole Mediator before the Father; He and He alone is "*the source* of eternal salvation" (Heb 5:9); He is the shepherd, we are the sheep (Jn 10:14); He is the vine, whereas we are merely branches (Jn 15:5).

What else does the Gospel say about taking up the Cross? John has recorded these interesting lines:

> If anyone serves me, he must follow me; and where I am, there shall my servant be. . . (Jn 12:26).

These words reaffirm the fact that it is not enough to just believe in our Lord; we must both serve and follow Him if we are to be His true disciples. In Jn 12:25, we see that to "love our life is to lose it," and to lose our life really implies a commitment to sacrifice that finds its ultimate fulfillment in the Cross. To follow Jesus is really to sacrifice for Him. This sacrificial offering is unity with the Cross, for Jesus himself was the perfect sacrificial model for all to follow (see Heb 10:12). Although St. Paul speaks of good deeds and generosity as pleasing sacrifices to God (Heb 13:16), he also indicates that it is important to suffer for Him (Phil 1:29), to offer our sacrifices to Him (Rom 12:1), to know the Lord better by sharing in His sufferings (Phil 3:10) and to carry His Cross within us so that we might reveal Him to the world (2 Cor 4:10).

John reveals another interesting way that we are invited to share the redemptive life with Christ. It is in this Gospel that Jesus invites us to full union with the sacrificial offering of himself through His institution of the Eucharist. Jesus offers us full participation in the perpetual sacrifice of the Cross by partaking in His Body and Blood, thereby uniting himself with each member of the Mystical Body that is His:

> I am the bread of life; he who comes to me shall not hunger and
> he who believes in me shall never thirst (Jn 6:35).

> Do not labor for the food which perishes, but for the food which
> endures to eternal life, which the Son of man will give to you; for
> on him has God the Father set his seal (Jn 6:27).

> Truly, truly I say to you, unless you eat the flesh of the Son of
> man and drink his blood, you have no life in you; he who eats
> my flesh and drinks my blood has eternal life, and I will raise
> him up at the last day. For my flesh is indeed food and my blood
> drink indeed. He who eats my flesh and drinks my blood abides
> in me, and I in him (Jn 6:52-56).

Jesus makes it very clear that the most important way to find unity with His Cross is to partake in the holy Eucharist. He also makes it strikingly clear that the bread and wine we perpetually share in the sacred Mass are His real Body and Blood, and not mere symbolic representations of them (as so many misguided souls are led to believe). There is simply no room to doubt that He instituted this most precious sacrament himself (see Mt 26:26-28; Lk 22:17-20; Mk 14:22-24). From the text quoted above in John's Gospel, Jesus is even more forceful in His desire that we participate in this holy Sacrifice. In fact, it is such a holy obligation that He tells us if we don't receive this offering, we will have no life in us at all! It is not my intention to offend those denominations that don't believe in this holy Sacrament, but it is difficult to understand how anyone could misread these clear and concise words from our Lord. We not only have all of this information from all four Gospels, but even St. Paul has given a lengthy discourse on the reality of the Eucharist (1 Cor 11:17-24). It is much too important to compromise as a principle of our faith. Remember: it is a command from our Lord himself.

This Eucharistic life that we lead brings us in union with the sacrifice of our Lord. We are also brought to union with God through the workings of the Holy Spirit. The life in the Spirit opens us to a closer relationship with our Creator. The Spirit helps us to bear our crosses by giving us the gifts we need to do the will of God (1 Cor 12:4-11); it is the Spirit of Christ that gives us the strength we need to attain a newness of life, a better life that is shared with the risen Lord. Jesus talks about this role of the Spirit in John's Gospel. Listen to what He has taught us:

> It is the spirit that gives life, the flesh is of no avail; the words I have spoken to you are spirit and life (Jn 6:63).

> If any one thirst, let him come to me and drink. He who believes in me, as the scripture has said, 'Out of his heart shall flow rivers of living water.' (Here he was referring to the Spirit, whom those that came to believe in Him were to receive) (Jn 7:37-39).

> Nevertheless I tell you the truth: it is to your advantage that I go away, for if I do not go away, the Counselor will not come to you; but if I go, I will send him to you. . . . When the Spirit of truth comes, he will guide you into all the truth. . . (Jn 16:7,13).

We see that the Spirit of Christ is the source of our very life, and it is He who continually invites us to a deeper union with our Lord and Redeemer. The Spirit helps us by interceding for us to the Father when we are in need, and continually guides us to the way, truth and life of our existence, which is found in the life of the Lord (Jn 14:6).

When do we commit ourselves to this fullness of life that is shared with Christ? How can we know when we are called to this higher purpose? Jesus has answered these very questions in a response to His disciples: "My time has not yet come, but your time is always here" (Jn 7:6). Now is the time of salvation, for we know not when our lives will end, nor when the Lord will come to judge the lives we have led (Mt 24:36-42).

If we choose to commit ourselves to a fuller union with Christ, we must be willing to accept the death of our former life in order to be transformed into a new creature in Christ: "Truly, truly, I say to you, unless a grain of wheat falls into the earth and dies, it remains alone; but if it dies, it bears much fruit. He who loves his life loses it, and he who hates his life in this world will keep it for eternal life" (Jn 12:24-25).

Like the Synoptic Gospels, the Gospel of John gives us words of hope for following Jesus in His life of suffering: "Truly, truly, I say to you, you will weep and lament, but the world will rejoice; you will be sorrowful, but your sorrow will turn into joy" (Jn 16:20). Again Jesus reiterates this point: "I have said this to you, that in me you may have peace. In the world you have tribulation; but be of good cheer! I have overcome the world" (Jn 16:33).

The beloved disciple assures us through the words of Christ that it is through service to others that we best express the spirit of our faith. Love involves our sacrifices for each other, not just in terms of prayer or vicarious suffering, but also through positive action that leads to a wholeness of life. This example was taught to us by Jesus himself, who not only suffered for us, but also served others in time of need: "You call me Teacher and Lord; and you are right, for so I am. If I then, your Lord and Teacher, have washed your feet, you also ought to wash one another's feet. For I have given you an example, that you also should do as I have done to you" (Jn 13:13-15). The motive that Jesus gives for service to one another is selfless love. Sacrifice and suffering for others is simply not enough, even if one's vocation is to be a victim soul. Faith without action is dead, as the good St. Paul has reminded us all.

Jesus gave us an interesting statement related to the necessity of doing good works (in contrast to living a life totally in a passive state, oblivious to all that goes on around us). In fact, He goes so far as to say that without visible signs that express one's faith to others — without backing our faith up with action — one's faith life is to be seriously questioned: "If I am not doing the works of my Father, then do not believe me; but if I do them, even though you do not believe me, believe the works, that you may know and understand that the Father is in me and I am in the Father" (Jn 10:37-38). Of course, action must be tempered with contemplation, but we still need to be a light that shines unto the world — a sign of Christ's presence among us.

The Twelve Apostles and Companions

We now come to the last section of Sacred Scripture which we will use to examine the ways our Savior calls us to the Cross and invites us to share in His work of redemption and salvation. We turn to the epistles written by members of the Twelve Apostles and by their close companions: James, 1-2 Peter, 1-3 John, Jude, and Revelation. Acts is also included here, although little is drawn from it since it is used on the unit on St. Paul. Of course, Acts is not an epistle, but rather a companion book to the Gospel of Luke. I have deliberately left out the works of St. Paul, since I treated his material extensively in a separate chapter. Because it is uncertain whether or not the Book of Hebrews is of Pauline origin, I will avoid its use altogether in this section (some of it has been included in the chapter, "The Theology of St. Paul").

The Book of Acts relates how Paul was called to a life of suffering as part of his mission to follow and serve Christ. Indeed, his entire vocation was a call to suffer for others. At the scene of the baptism, the Lord himself tells Ananias about His will for Paul to suffer for his faith: "Go, for he is a chosen instrument of mine to carry my name before the Gentiles and kings and the sons of Israel; for I will show him how much he must suffer for the sake of my name" (Acts 9:15-16). It is important to note that the Lord had chosen Paul to be a victim of His love for the sake of the salvation of His people. This is the normal rule for victims who help the Lord to redeem the world: one must be chosen by God to participate in this life of suffering; it is not something one does without the consent of God. Remember the words that Jesus told His disciples: "You did not choose me, but I chose you. . . ." (Jn 15:16). Here Paul has been invited by the Lord to accept his trials and tribulations for the sake of the people — to help atone for their sin, to consume himself for others as a witness to the new life he was then encountering.

As indicated before in the unit on St. Paul, we find many references in Acts to the sufferings he had endured for the sake of the kingdom. Many others had to endure the same trials as well. One characteristic of these souls is their willingness to forgive others for their sin, even pleading with the Father to have mercy upon them. This itself is a form of reparation on behalf of others — to plead for their salvation through prayer, vicarious sufferings, etc. It is a way of imitating our Lord, who also pleaded for His brothers and sisters to be forgiven in order that they might be saved: "Father, forgive them; they know not what they do" (Lk 23:34). Similarly, we hear the same pleas from the suffering servants who do not want to see any soul lost. The martyr Stephen imitated the Crucified Lord on behalf of his enemies: "And as they were stoning Stephen, he prayed, 'Lord Jesus, receive my spirit.' And he knelt down and cried out with a loud voice, 'Lord, do not hold this sin against them.' And when he had said this, he fell asleep" (Acts 7:59-60). This victim Stephen lived the Cross of our Lord so intimately that he became one with Him in His Passion and in His death. Stephen, like Paul, internalized the words of his Savior: "I in them and thou in me, that they may become perfectly one. . ." (Jn 17:23).

If we choose to follow the Cross that Jesus gives us, it is certain that we will have to bear persecutions from time-to-time, just as Jesus and His close followers had to do. We know that James the brother of John was beheaded for his belief (Acts 12:1-2), and St. Peter was imprisoned (Acts 12:3-5). Furthermore, we also know that Paul and Silas were tortured in a way very similar to our Lord: "The crowd joined in attacking them; and the magistrates tore the garments off them and gave orders to beat them with rods" (Acts 16:22). Once again, so reminiscent of our Savior and His fate: "Then Pilate took Jesus and scourged him" (Jn 19:1). Few of us are ever subjected to such extremes, but it does go to show how heroic these early saints were in taking up their crosses to become one of Jesus' disciples. As we have seen, some did this literally — they not only bore their crosses, but they bore *the* Cross with courage and conviction. Is it any wonder why the Lord chose them to be His worthy servants?

The Scriptures give many inferences to the call of some to be victims of divine love. Peter recognized this, for he told the faithful Christian community: "For it is better to suffer for doing right, if that should be God's will, than for doing wrong" (1 Pt 3:17). This statement implies that it is sometimes God's will to be called in this way. Again St. Peter tells the same people: "Therefore let those who suffer according to God's will do right and entrust their souls to a faithful Creator" (1 Pt 4:19). Here he is more direct about it.

We also know from Sacred Scripture that God desires victim souls who will suffer the penalties due to others who sin and fall from grace. (We will see this desire expressed later in the lives of some of the stigmatists we will encounter.) Although it may appear to be more of a punishment for the victim than a blessing, remember that God purifies and chastises those whom He loves: "Those whom I love, I reprove and chasten" (Rv 3:19).

The Lord does ardently desire our sufferings, if they are voluntarily given with a purity of heart. These sacrifices are meritorious, whether they be everyday crosses we bear, or heavy crosses that challenge our lives from time-to-time. If this is so, then what are the merits that we build up for ourselves and for others? What reward do we receive for offering up the sufferings we bear for others? Let us look at a few of the passages that serve to explain these questions:

Blessed is the man who endures trial, for when he has stood the test he will receive the crown of life which God has promised to those who love him (Jas 1:12).

Be wretched and mourn and weep. Let your laughter be turned to mourning and your joy to dejection. Humble yourselves before the Lord and he will exalt you (Jas 4:9-10).

> As an example of suffering and patience, brethren, take the prophets who spoke in the name of the Lord. Behold, we call those happy who were steadfast. You have heard of the steadfastness of Job, and have seen the purpose of the Lord, how the Lord is compassionate and merciful (Jas 5:10-11).

It is evident from these statements in the Book of James that the reward we merit from our patient suffering is none other than this: eternal life and happiness with our Lord Jesus Christ, who promised this eternal reward for all who remain firm in the faith to the end: "In my Father's house are many rooms; if it were not so, would I have told you that I go to prepare a place for you? And when I go and prepare a place for you, I will come again and will take you to myself, that where I am you may be also" (Jn 14:2-3). What a reassuring promise! What joy awaits those who remain steadfast without faltering! This promise of our Lord should stir the hearts of all of us in hope for a better life to come, spent in the bosom of our Father's heavenly care.

These inspiring words continue in other parts of Scripture:

> In this you rejoice, though now for a little while you may have to suffer various trials, so that the genuineness of your faith, more precious than gold which though perishable is tested by fire, may redound to praise and glory and honor at the revelation of Jesus Christ (1 Pt 1:6-7).

> . . . keep yourselves in the love of God; wait for the mercy of our Lord Jesus Christ unto life eternal (Jude 21).

> Blessed are those who wash their robes, that they may have the right to the tree of life and that they may enter the city by the gates (Rv 22:14).

This last statement from Revelation uses the image of clean robes as a comparison with the state of one's soul before it meets its Creator. Clean, it rejoices, for it is found to be worthy to be in the presence of the Lord; unclean, and it will not rejoice, for nothing defiled can ever fully enter the presence of God and His infinite holiness: "Thou who art of purer eyes than to behold evil and canst not look on wrong. . ." (Hb 1:13).

Thus concludes our treatment on the meaning of suffering in lives of God's people. We have examined how some suffering is caused (and rightfully deserved) by our own inclination toward sin, thus separating us from God's love, mercy and grace. We have seen that the evil spirit is a powerful force, forever meddling in the lives of the just and the unjust alike. Because of this reality, we acknowledge that the Prince of Darkness is the underlying cause of Original Sin. Yet the human spirit continues to sin from other sources as well, including temptations from the world and from the flesh; thus, man is surrounded by an endless barrage of potentially sinful situations.

We know that there is hope, however, in the sanctifying and redeeming presence of Christ, who came to free us of our sin by offering His life as a ransom for many. It is up to each one of us to accept this merciful act of the Cross, to embrace it, and to in turn offer our crosses up in union with His.

We may not be victims of divine love, for the Lord will choose whomever He wills; yet, we are all called to sacrifice and to offer whatever we can for our state of life and in the circumstances we may find ourselves. Sometimes, just bearing our trials and tribulations is all we are asked to do. If so, this in itself is redemptive work for our own souls as well as for others. The Lord who sees in secret awards each of us according to the designs we have in our hearts. Like Mary, it is up to us to give our *fiat* (our "yes" to the Lord) once the Lord has invited us to the task.

We will leave this lengthy discourse on suffering in order to deal more directly with the life of the stigmatist. First we need to explore the world of mysticism, where the greatest heights of spirituality are obtained, and where the most extraordinary charisms are experienced by the stigmatist. Since the stigmata is a product of the mystical experience, it will be appropriate to begin our next study in this area. Then we will move directly into the personal lives of the stigmatists, hopefully with a better understanding of the precious gift he or she bears for the people of God.

CHAPTER 3

Understanding the Sacred Stigmata

The Mystical Life

As we move further in our study of the mystery of the Sacred Stigmata, one thing becomes quite clear: the role that mysticism plays is fundamental in the life of the stigmatist. Because every authentic stigmatist has reached the greatest heights of the mystical world, we need to better understand this spiritual state that every great saint has experienced at some point in his or her life. Some of these pious souls have lived continuous lives in the mystical realm, arriving at the glorious divine union; this union is as close to the beatific vision that one can get in this earthly life. Such is the lot of the stigmatist, who shares the life and death of Jesus Christ so intimately that he or she is transformed into His very likeness.

Let us now look into the mystical life, a spiritual state or dimension that, paradoxically, defies explanation. Words are inadequate to define the nature of this most intimate relationship with the divine. The best of theologians (yes, and even the greatest of mystics!) unanimously agree that we can only get a glimpse of the mystical experience through reason or reflection — words can hardly explain a supernatural state that is experiential in nature and not based upon reason or intellect. I, too, will fall short of effectively describing this spiritual state of life; yet, it is only by peeling away at the surface that we ever hope to move closer to the divine love at the center of our being. A moment of truth, however dim, makes this less-than-perfect effort all worthwhile.

Because the word "mysticism" has been understood in so many different ways, we need to look at a variety of expressions that have come to form our impressions of what this state is all about. Perhaps the reader will paint an overall picture by synthesizing these various ideas from the best of minds in the history of the Church. Remember: one must grasp at least something about the mystical life in order to understand the gift of the Sacred Stigmata, for it is in this arena that the life of the stigmatist is to be found.

Father John G. Arintero, O.P. (1860-1928), a spiritual master whose cause for beatification is being promoted, once described mysticism as such:

> "Mystical" means the same as "hidden." The mystical life is the mysterious life of the grace of Jesus Christ in faithful souls who,

dead to themselves, live hidden with Him in God. More properly it is that interior life which just souls experience when, animated and possessed by the Spirit of Jesus Christ, they receive more and more perfectly, and sometimes clearly perceive, His divine impulses, delightful or painful, whereby they grow in union and conformity with Him who is their Head until they become transformed in Him. By mystical evolution we understand the entire process of the formation, growth, and expansion of that prodigious life until Christ is formed in us, and we are transformed in His divine image . . . (*The Mystical Evolution*, Tan Books and Publishers, Inc., 1978.)

The Venerable Bartholomew once said that mysticism consisted of "lofty contemplation, ardent affection, and transcendent raptures by which we are more easily able to arrive at a knowledge of God than by human studies" (*Compendium mysticae doctrinae*, chpt. 26).

Mysticism involves experiential knowledge of God from an intimate encounter with the divine love, an encounter that ultimately leads to the divine union. It must be stressed that this state is a gift from God. No one can ever achieve a mystical state — let alone an authentic experience — through his or her own efforts; rather, God must invite these souls and gift them with the necessary grace to live a life of spiritual union with Him. It is a gift because not all are called to such a lofty state (although all are called to different degrees of the contemplative state). True, we are all called to perfection (Eph 1:4), but the Lord does call particular people to higher missions (1 Cor 12:4-6). These souls must carry a heavier burden than most, suffering trials and tribulations that the ordinary among the faithful rarely experience. Such is the fate of the mystic and victim, and particularly so for the life of the stigmatist, whose very being is a continual state of martyrdom that is sustained through the power of love.

Two of the Church's best-loved spiritual Doctors, St. Teresa of Avila (1515-82) and St. John of the Cross (1542-91) were contemporaries who knew each other very well. In fact, St. John met Teresa in 1567 and was profoundly influenced by her life and teachings. He went on to become one of the greatest of all mystical theologians. We will hear more from these two extraordinary souls throughout the remainder of this work.

St. Teresa once described the "experience" of mystical theology as "a feeling of the presence of God that comes upon me unexpectedly so that I could in no way doubt He was within me or I totally immersed in Him. The soul is suspended in such a way that it seems to be completely outside itself. The will loves, but the memory, it seems to me, is almost lost" (*Book of Her Life*, Autobiography, chpt. 10). When the soul is suspended and enraptured in this state, then the intellect ceases to work, for the Lord infuses His love and one's knowledge of Him without the aid of the senses or reason. Rather, God communicates and loves directly with the soul, where the mental faculties cannot reach the very essence of His being. This is why the mystical experience is a gift solely from God and not acquired by our own efforts, no matter the sincerity. We humans can only "know" through the ordinary channels of the intellect and the senses. In this state, God bypasses these channels and goes directly to the heart and soul, where He has promised to make His dwelling place for those in the state of sanctifying grace: "If a man loves me, he will keep my word, and my Father will love him, and we will come to him and make our home with him" (Jn 14:23). Although this passage indicates that God lives in all the faithful, He does so much more profoundly and intimately in His chosen souls that seek Him without reserve: "But seek first his kingdom and his righteousness, and all these things shall be yours as well" (Mt 6:33). Note that it is *His* righteousness. Few souls ever completely abandon themselves to only His will. Perhaps that is why there are so few true mystics in the world.

Getting back to the difficulty of describing the mystical state, we can see now why even the best of the mystics have trouble explaining with words the communications they share with the divine, the knowledge they receive, and the intense love unknown in the normal state of life. St. Teresa says that she "doesn't know how to explain how this comes about and what it is, not how to use the proper vocabulary" (*Life*, chpt. 18).

Let us turn to St. John of the Cross for further statements on the almost indescribable state that the mystic finds himself in:

> Not only does a man feel unwilling to give expression to this wisdom, but he finds no adequate means or similitude to signify so sublime an understanding and delicate a spiritual feeling. Even if the soul should desire to convey this experience in words and think up many similitudes, the wisdom would always remain secret and still to be expressed.
>
> Since this interior wisdom is so simple, general and spiritual that in entering the intellect it is not clothed in any sensory species or image, the imaginative faculty cannot form an idea or picture of it in order to speak of it; this wisdom did not enter through these faculties nor did they behold any of its apparel or color. Yet the soul is clearly aware that it understands and tastes that delightful and wondrous wisdom. . . (*The Dark Night*, Book II, chpt. 17: ICS Publications, Washington, D.C., 1979.)

St. John summarizes his feelings in the following statement:

> Since the wisdom of this contemplation is the language of God to the soul, of Pure Spirit to the spirit alone, all that is less than spirit such as the sensory, fails to perceive it. Consequently this wisdom is secret to the senses; they have neither the knowledge nor ability to speak of it, nor do they even desire to do so because it is beyond words. . . (*The Dark Night*, Book II, chpt. 17.)

Sacred Scripture records the inability to convey the divine experience as well (see Jer 1:6 and Ex 4:10). Words are only expressions of a reality, whereas a mystical experience is that reality itself.

Because these divine experiences are not produced by our reason or intellect, we call them *passive* experiences because we do nothing to cause or attain them; God infuses them into the soul independent of all our efforts. As St. Teresa of Avila teaches, this is a *supernatural* experience, and the manifestations are totally supernatural. All we can do if called to this state is to be receptive to God's secret action within the soul. Indeed, this is why we call it a "passive contemplation."

We should further note what St. John of the Cross says about this passive state:

> The Divine Majesty communicates himself to the soul which remains passive, as light is communicated to the mind of him who has his eyes open. It is necessary, therefore, for the soul to assume an almost passive attitude without any thought of acting by herself; but keeping herself in a simple, pure and loving attention, as a person would do who voluntarily opens his eyes to look with love upon another. God is the agent who infuses and touches, whilst the soul is the recipient. . . (*The Ascent of Mount Carmel*, Book II, chpt. 15: ICS Publications, Washington, D.C., 1979.)

The knowledge of God that one receives in the mystical state is *experiential*. No one knows God like those souls who have experienced Him intimately and directly, especially within the union of love. Once, they had only heard about Him; now they know Him because they have felt, tasted and touched His goodness, His tenderness, and His character. The Venerable John of St. Samson describes this as "God ineffably perceived," because it is a mysterious and supernatural experience.

The stigmatist has reached the highest mystical state, the divine union, because of his profound love for God as himself, and not for the favors he receives from Him. He has desired and obtained His Love and Goodness. God rewards the stigmatist with the Cross of His beloved Son, for he suffers to love, and loves in order to suffer for Jesus and humanity.

To love God so intensely is the greatest of all graces: "So faith, hope, love abide, these three; but the greatest of these is love" (1 Cor 13:13). The marks of the Cross signify this divine union in love through the greatest manifestation of love that is known: the sacrificial love of Christ, who redeemed the world through His Passion and His Cross. Like Jesus, the stigmatist is called to empty her heart and spill her blood for the sins of many. This is a mystical love that few ever obtain because the cost is so great: a total consummation of one's life, where the only reward is to suffer for others.

Unlike most souls, some have found the height of love in suffering, and God rewards them with the greatest gift of all: that of His Son, to share in His mission and to adopt the soul as His very own. Hence, we occasionally find a stigmatist in our midst — another Christ to perpetuate the Savior's redeeming mission. He or she becomes a living crucifix for a crucified world, a world lost in a sea of sin and in need of deliverance. They *share* in Christ's Passion, not replace it, by representing His humanity to a people in need of a human Christ-figure that will keep the divine-human Savior ever present in our lives.

When I had the privilege of being in San Giovanni Rotondo, Italy, in the summer of 1988, I asked Father Joseph Martin, O.F.M. about the mission of stigmatists who are in our midst. (Father Martin was a close friend and aid of Padre Pio the last three years of his life.) He had this to say:

> The stigmata is not a gift given for the benefit of the stigmatist;

it is a gift — a sign — for the world. . . (*Interview in San Giovanni Rotondo*, Italy, July, 1988.)

In my further discussions with Father Martin, he explained how stigmatists must be sensitive, open and loving. They must not be afraid to open their hearts to others, to let their feelings show. It is the sensitive and delicate natures of these spiritual souls that allow them to offer themselves as victims for sinners, for love cannot be restrained when one's heart is on fire for God. We will encounter more from Father Martin later in this book.

To conclude our brief introduction to the state of the mystical life, let us hear a few more descriptions of this way of perfection that has permeated the lives of every stigmatist from all eras.

St. Francis de Sales (1567-1622), another holy Doctor of the Church, describes the differences between *speculative theology* (which uses the intellectual and the rational) and *mystical theology*:

> There are three following differences: 1) Speculative theology treats of God as God, while mystical theology speaks of Him as supremely worthy of love. That is, the first regards the divinity of the supreme goodness, and the second regards the supreme goodness of the divinity. 2) Speculative theology treats of God as dealing with men and among men; mystical theology speaks of God with God and in God himself. 3) Speculative theology strives for knowledge of God, and mystical theology for love of God. Therefore, the first makes its students wise and learned men, that is, theologians; but the second makes its students ardent, affectionate lovers of God. . . . (*Love of God*, Book VI, chpt. 1: Tan Books and Publishers, Inc., 1975.)

The key point here is that mysticism "strives for the love of God." It is love that propels the stigmatist (or any victim soul-mystic) toward union with God — his entire being is consumed with a love for Love; that is, for the God Who is Love and Who invites us to be Love. The main difference between the mystic-victim and the stigmatist is that with the latter, this thirst for Love is more intensely found in the redemptive suffering of the Crucified Lord; the Cross and the stigmatist become as one. There are many ways of love in the lives of the mystics and victim souls, but the way of the stigmatist is the most consuming and Christ-like of all who follow the Cross.

Another observation of this mystical love is given by St. Francis de Sales:

> Mystical theology and prayer are the same thing. Mystical theology speaks of God as supremely worthy of love; it regards the supreme goodness of the divinity; it speaks of God with God and in God himself; mystical theology strives for love of God. . . . (*Love of God*, Book VI, chpt. 1.)

St. Francis further explains the intense prayer life of the mystic:

> Prayer is called mystical because its conversation is altogether secret. In it nothing is spoken between God and the soul except

from heart-to-heart, by a communication incommunicable to any others but those who make it. . . (*Love of God*, Book VI, chpt. 1.)

It is here that we now turn in our discourse on the mystical life: that of the intense prayer life that the mystic leads on his way to union with God.

The Ways of Prayer

We now enter the first realm of the mystical life: that of the ways of prayer. Fittingly enough, for prayer is really the beginning of the road towards perfection; it is the way that every mystic and/or victim-stigmatist travels. The reason for this is that a deeper spirituality is necessary in order to know God's will, to love Him and to be receptive to the graces that He is prepared to give us. If God is the Source of our gifts, then prayer is the channel from which all grace grows and is nurtured. In the life of the mystic, prayer is particularly important for spiritual growth, for it is through prayer that one communicates with God and hears the soft whispers of His voice. Prayer is the door through which one enters into the mystical state. It is also the door to the active and the contemplative life, and in fact, to any state of life whereby one earnestly seeks a closer relationship with God. It is here that the mystic begins, and it will be here that we will start our mystical journey.

Prayer means a lot of different things to a lot of different people. Therefore, like in any discussion on the meaning of mysticism, we will explore many thoughts on this theme from a variety of sources, with the intention of gaining some perspective of what prayer and spirituality are all about.

The most common definition for prayer was given by St. John Damascene (c. 675- c.749), a holy Doctor of the Church. He described prayer as the "elevation of the soul to God." Others from the early Church have expressed the same feeling in slightly different ways. Here are a few samplings of what these saints have believed:

Prayer is a conversation with God. . . (Clement of Alexandria, *Stromateis*, 7, 2nd century.)

When prayer is poured forth, sins are covered. . . . (St. Ambrose, *De Interpel. Job*, 2, 8, 4th century.)

He causes his prayers to be of more avail to himself, who offers them also for others. . . . (Pope St. Gregory I, *Morals*, 35, 21, 6th century.)

All the virtues assist the soul to attain to a burning love of God, but, above all, pure prayer. By means of it the soul escapes completely from the midst of creatures, carried to God, as it were, on wings. . . . (St. Maximus the Confessor, *Centuries on Charity*, 1, 2, 7th century.)

Clearly, there is no one standard definition of prayer, as the above examples show. Prayer is many things to different people. One reason is each individual is unique and special, and God treats him or her as such. Because He communicates His will for each one differently, we are going to have a wide diversity of ways in which the life of the spirit is manifested in our faith experience. Each of us has different needs and unusual gifts; we all relate to God in our own special way. Yet one thing all spiritual people have in common is this: a desire for the love of God. Some feel this desire more intensely than others, and they travel on to a higher, deeper spirituality that encounters meditation, contemplation and for some, the mystical life.

Now that we have a general understanding of the importance of prayer in our faith experience, we will look at the four types of prayer that all are familiar with: adoration, thanksgiving, petition and contrition. All ways are important and each has its place. The ordinary person is most likely to petition when he or she prays, wanting something from God that they do not possess. Giving thanks to the Lord is probably the second most common intention in prayer, especially for those who follow the ordinary way. Because we are focusing on the prayer life of the mystic, we must keep in mind that the perception of and the experiences in their prayer life are not necessarily the same as what the ordinary person perceives or experiences. For these holy ones, prayer usually centers around the life of love and of suffering. For the victim, to love is to suffer, and to suffer is to love. All love is ultimately directed to God, Who is the supreme Love of their lives.

Being advanced and matured in the ways of the spirit, these humble souls seek first to love God with all their hearts and souls in the form of adoration (Lk 10:27); secondly, they love their neighbor as themselves (Mt 19:19) and, including themselves, they plead for forgiveness of past sin, begging the Lord to show them His mercy so that none might ever perish (contrition), but instead have eternal life (Jn 3:16). These two types of prayer are selfless and most charitable, for they are only concerned with love and with sacrifice: a sacrifice of the heart, for God and for man.

It is the passion of love that propels the mystic forward; love is the catalyst that moves the soul and carries it to the heights of the interior life. There, in the deepest recesses of the soul, one is consumed by the all-embracing Love that is God. It is here that the Lord gives us His peace (Jn 14:27), and it is here that He nourishes the soul with the living waters of life (Jn 4:14). "Love is the life of the soul" (St. Francis de Sales), the source of its being: "What do you possess if you possess not God?" (St. Augustine).

It is through prayer that one seeks the Beloved, much as the bride seeks after the groom. In mystical language, the bride is the pure and spotless lamb, whereas the Groom is Jesus Christ, Lord and Shepherd of the soul. In this mystical language of love, it is the kiss of love that each mystic seeks, longing to possess and to be possessed by the fire of divine love. St. Margaret Mary Alacoque (1647-90), a victim soul, once said these moving words: "Our heart is made for God. Woe, then, if it be satisfied with less than God, or if it allow itself to burn with any other fire than that of His pure love!"

Most of all, as we have seen in the above examples, the prayers of contrition and adoration adhere to the Gospel message that Jesus gives: love your God, love your neighbor. This is not to say that the prayers of petition and thanksgiving are less important. God forbid! They are every bit as important when used for the proper intentions. The danger that most beginners fall into is praying in a way that becomes too self-centered, too self-serving. It is with petition that this is especially troublesome, although it can be found in thanksgiving as well. If we choose to thank God for only those things that are beneficial to us, we become victims of self-deception. We must also give thanks for the blessings that others have been given, as well as the trials and tribulations that come from the hand of God.

Let us now move to a brief discussion about the prayer of petition in the life of the victim soul. Unlike many of the faithful, the mystic seldom petitions the Lord for personal favors or satisfaction, unless it be for the purification of her own soul or for the spiritual needs of others. When petitions are intended for one's own sanctification or for the spiritual welfare of others, it is the most beneficial and meritorious petition that can be implored. This is especially true for the offering of trials and sufferings in union with the Cross. Here, the petitioning takes on a redemptive nature and is very pleasing to the Lord, Who forever wills that we take up our cross and follow Him (Lk 9:23). The victim soul is especially sensitive to this form of petitioning; in fact, it is at the very core of her vocation that calls for charity towards the brokenness of people in need of spiritual healing.

The stigmatist Adrienne Von Speyr (1902-67) was a woman whose intense love for the Cross moved her to pray for the sufferings of others, asking the Lord to unite their pains with the Cross in order that they might be redeemed. Here is an excerpt from a prayer she composed:

> Lord, bless those who are sick; all those who know or feel that they are sick, all those who are in pain, all those who must soon die. Do not bless them merely so that they are able to endure; bless them also so that they learn to endure for you and to see a grace in suffering. Show them that every suffering has received a meaning through your suffering on the Cross, a meaning which is taken by the Father into the meaning of your own suffering and is used for the redemption of the world. Show them that pain and sickness become fruitful if they are willing to suffer in your name, that you can use them to help others, to ease the burdens of others, to make passable roads which otherwise could not be traveled. Give them not only strength and courage; give them patience. Finally, give them love for the sufferings which are demanded of them, that love which can only spring from your love and which only together with your love can bear fruit, even if these fruits remain hidden from view, even if they do not know exactly where you want to use the grace which springs from their suffering. . . (*First Glance at Adrienne Von Speyr*, Part III, p. 211: Hans Urs Von Balthasar, Ignatius Press, San Francisco, 1981.)

Adrienne's prayer is typical of the prayers that all stigmatists offer up to God for the salvation of souls. These prayers are supreme acts of charity that inflame the hearts and spirits of these generous souls, all for the love of God.

When the stigmatist prays the prayer of thanksgiving, it is very seldom for the material benefits she or he might receive. The primary focus is not even on the good that she has brought to others for the sacrifices she has made on their behalf; rather, it is the thankfulness for God's mercy upon their souls that is the center of this type of prayer. The stigmatist is extraordinarily humble, and is overwhelmed by the thought that God would love them as much as He does. As in all the prayers they offer up, God as

Love saturates their heart and mind: Who is worthy to be so blessed? Who is deserving of such a perfect and pure love? The stigmatist is overcome with gratitude, never for a moment taking the Lord's blessings for granted. She is forever consumed with the desire to share in His Love. Thanksgiving is never far from the heart and lips of these holy and humble souls.

St. Catherine of Siena (1347-80), that great Doctor of Christian spirituality in the Middle Ages, was also a mystic and stigmatist. In her *Dialogue* (a spiritual classic that records her talks with God during ecstasies), she describes the incredible feelings of awe and wonder she experienced each time she thought of the blessings that God had given her. As is typical with the victim soul, Catherine feels unworthy (though infinitely grateful) to share in the divine love that is purer than any love we have ever known from humanity. In her prayer of thanksgiving, we listen to the words that poured from her heart:

> Oh! Supreme and Eternal Goodness of God, who am I, miserable one, that Thou, Supreme and Eternal Father, hast manifested to me Thy Truth, and the hidden deceits of the Devil, and the deceitfulness of personal feeling, so that I, and others in this life of pilgrimage, may know how to avoid being deceived by the Devil or ourselves! What moved Thee to do it? Love, because Thou lovest me, without my having loved Thee. Oh, Fire of Love! Thanks, thanks be to Thee, Eternal Father! I am imperfect and full of darkness, and Thou, Perfection and Light, hast shown to me perfection, and the resplendent way of the doctrine of Thy only-begotten Son. . . (St. Catherine of Siena, *Dialogue: A Treatise of Prayer*, 1370.)

Again, the entire dialogue is filled with prayers of thanksgiving; not for material favors received, but rather for the spiritual favors she had been granted, and, above all, for the grace to be able to share in the Father's love. Such is the way of the victim soul, and in particular it is the way of the stigmatist.

Once a soul has been elevated beyond the way of vocal prayer (the normal way for most of the faithful), he or she usually finds that mental prayer can offer a more intimate relationship with the Lord; for in this state, one comes to appreciate the mysteries of our faith. The practice of mental prayer is usually a prelude to contemplative prayer, although not everyone reaches this noble state.

There are several types of mental prayer, the two most common being the *prayer of quiet* and *meditation*. Meditation is the first step beyond mere vocal prayer, whereas the prayer of quiet is the early stages of the mystical prayer. Let us examine the nature of meditation, as well as the pious thoughts that are associated with this type of prayer.

St. John of the Cross gives us a model to go by, and includes some of the worthy thoughts that these souls meditate upon:

> Meditation is the discursive act built upon forms, figures and images, imagined and fashioned by the senses. For example: the imagining of Christ crucified, or at the column, or in some other scene; or of God seated upon a throne with resplendent majesty; or the imagining and considering of glory as a beautiful light,

etc.; or the picturing of any other human or divine object imaginable. . . (*The Ascent of Mount Carmel*, Book II, chpt. 12.)

The important thing to remember here is that meditation uses *discursive* reasoning to concentrate on an image or thought. It is entirely from one's own doing. In contrast with this, authentic mystical contemplation does not use discursive reasoning, but rather empties itself of all considerations and rests silently in the Lord. The Lord is then free to act as He wills upon the soul, communicating with it through the many impulses that He gives. Strictly speaking, true contemplation is a gift from God; the one who prays need only wait passively for the Lord to visit his soul. It is never achieved through our own efforts, but given to those according to His will.

St. Teresa of Avila says it in another way:

By meditation I mean much discursive reflection with the intellect in the following way: we begin to think about the favor God granted us in giving us His only Son, and we do not stop there, but go on to the mysteries of His whole glorious life; or we take a phase of the Passion, the flight of the apostles, and all the rest; this kind of reflection is an admirable and meritorious prayer. . . . (St. Teresa of Avila, *The Interior Castle*, VI, chpt. 7.)

For Teresa, meditation is not limited to a particular reflection. It can encompass virtually every pious thought that enriches our faith. Yet the intellect is forever working to keep the thought alive: "These souls work almost continually with the intellect, engaging in discursive thought" (*The Interior Castle*, IX, chpt. 1).

Other thoughts can be found on the purposes of meditation:

Meditation considers in detail and as it were piece by piece objects suitable to move us. . . . (St. Francis de Sales, *Love of God*, Book VI, chpt. 5.)

The word "meditation" is often used in Holy Scripture and means simply attentive, repeated thought of such nature as to produce either good or bad affections. All meditation is thought, but not all thought is meditation. . . . (St. Francis de Sales, *Love of God*, Book VI, chpt. 2.)

Meditation is the basis for acquiring all the virtues, and to undertake it is a matter of life and death. . . . (St. Teresa of Avila, *The Way of Perfection*, chpt. 16.)

St. Alphonsus Liguori (1696-1787), a holy Doctor of the Church, believed that there are two principle reasons why we should meditate: 1) to unite ourselves more completely to God; and 2) to obtain from God, by prayer, the graces that are necessary in order to enable us to advance in the way of salvation, to avoid sin and to take the means that will lead us to perfection. St. Alphonsus believed meditation to be so important that he doubted if we could ever live or die in a state of grace without it: "He who does not practice meditation will find the greatest difficulty in persevering in grace till death" (*The Way of Salvation and Perfection*, Part II, chpt. 15).

What are some of the desirable things that one should meditate upon? What sort of things do the mystics lose themselves in? Perhaps foremost of all the considerations is the mystery of the Passion of our Lord. Padre Pio, the stigmatized friar of San Giovanni Rotondo, once remarked about this holy meditation: "Most Divine Spirit, enlighten and inflame me in meditating on the Passion of Jesus, help me to penetrate this mystery of love and suffering of a God, who, clothed with our humanity, suffers, agonizes and dies for the love of the creature! Oh that I could penetrate to the innermost recesses of the Heart of Jesus to read there the essence of His bitterness, which brought Him to the point of death in the Garden; that I could comfort Him in the adandonment by His Father and His own. Oh that I could unite myself with Him in order to expiate with Him" (*The Agony of Jesus: A Meditation on Our Lord's Agony in the Garden*; reprinted by TAN Books and Publishers, Inc., 1974). What a profound intimacy the Padre had with the Lord's sufferings! Is it any wonder that God granted his wish to imitate the Crucified Christ?

Traditionally, one of the most cherished methods of meditating on the Passion of our Lord has been through the *Way of the Cross* (also called the *Stations of the Cross*). This devotional practice incorporates fourteen meditations on the successive mysteries of Christ's Passion, from His agony at Gethsemani to His death on Calvary. The officially approved method is to have fourteen wooden crosses at each station where one meditates on a particular mystery (pictures are not the approved method). In turn, each cross at every station must be blessed by the priest. The devotions to these mysteries have always been highly indulgenced. Father Paul of Moll (1824-96) has given us these reflections: "When making the Way of the Cross, try to have compassion for the sufferings of Christ; for all those who took part in His sorrows became saints as, for example, Simon of Cyrene, Veronica, the good thief, the holy women and so many others."

Our Lord himself has recommended devotion to His Passion. This He has done countless times through the private revelations He has given to saints of the greatest order, including St. Gertrude the Great (1256-1302), Doctor and stigmatist of the medieval Church. Listen to the words she received from Jesus after she feared that she might be spending too much time in devotion to His Cross:

Fear not, My beloved; for this cannot hinder your spirituality, since I alone will occupy you; for I am not a little pleased with those who honor the image of My crucifixion very devoutly; and as it often happens that, when a king has a spouse with whom he cannot always remain, he leaves one who is most dear to him to take charge of her in his absence, and regards all the duties of friendship and affection which she renders to him as if they had been offered to himself, because he knows that this proceeds from her love for him — so I take pleasure in the veneration offered to My cross, when it is offered purely for My love — when the cross is not desired for itself, but that it may serve to renew the memory of the love and fidelity with which I endured the bitterness of My Passion, and when there is an ardent desire to imitate the example of My Passion. . . . (*The Life and Revelations of St. Gertrude*: Christian Classics, Inc., reprint 1983.)

What beautiful words from the lips of uur dear Savior! Jesus desires that we all devote ourselves to the mystery of His Passion; there can never be too much veneration of the Cross, because by piously considering the suffering Christ, we understand Him better, draw closer to His Sacred Heart, and learn to imitate His ways most perfectly.

St. Bernard of Clairvaux (1090-1153), that great Doctor and theologian of the Church, has described the meditations on the Passion with these inspiring words:

> To meditate on the life and sufferings of Jesus Christ I have called wisdom; in these I have placed the perfection of righteousness for me, the fullness of knowledge, the abundance of merits, the riches of salvation. . . (*On the Canticle of Canticles*, 12th century.)

St. Bernard claims that there is nothing greater to meditate on than the Passion of our Lord: "My philosophy is this, and it is the loftiest in the world: to know Jesus and Him crucified." We come to know Jesus through our prayers, meditations, contemplations, by following His Word, and by imitating His earthly life. All of these components draw us closer to our Savior and help us to grow in His grace.

Closely related to meditation is the mental prayer known as the *prayer of quiet*. This name was given by St. Teresa of Avila (*Life*, chpt. 14) to describe a state of prayer whereby one begins to experience the contemplative life. The soul, being infused with divine grace, has begun to shed its intellect and reason, but not yet perfectly so; distractions still occur in the mind which impedes the state of the total contemplative experience.

Along with this entrance into the contemplative state comes the short *prayer of affection* (also known as *ejaculatory prayer*). These are prayers of few words, such as, "Lord, have mercy"; "Jesus, I love you"; or even simply, "Jesus!" Other names for these inspiring prayers are "aspirations" and "invocations." In this state, one truly gazes upon the Lord with purity and simplicity, praising and loving Him with no discursive thought at all. The soul simply acknowledges His Love and His Goodness in one sweeping breath. These, too, have been indulgenced by the Church. In fact, these aspirations do not even have to be said aloud to gain the indulgence. Why is this so? Because God knows the secrets of our hearts, whether we speak them out or not: "God knows your hearts" (Lk 16:15). Prayer does not have to include the benefit of many words; in fact, it does not have to include them at all. This is what we will find in the true contemplative experience. (Although at times the contemplative does use vocal prayer; the state of contemplation is never constant nor permanent, even for those in the highest of states.) All of the stigmatists have generously used the prayer of affection throughout their lives. Consumed by the overwhelming presence of God in their soul, they cry out in joy:

Oh, inestimable Charity! Sweet above all sweetness! Who would not be inflamed by such great love?. . . . (St. Catherine of Siena [1347-80], *Dialogue*.)

O my sweetest Love! May my soul bless Thee, O Lord God, my Creator, from the inmost depths of my heart. . . . (St. Gertrude the Great [1263-1302], *Life and Revelations*.)

Praised be You, my Lord! Most High, all-powerful, good Lord!. . . . (St. Francis of Assisi [1182-1226], *Canticle of the Sun*.)

O most pure Jesus! Bridegroom of virgin souls, I love Thee!. . . . (Josefa Menendez [1890-1923], *The Way of Divine Love*.)

My God! My God! O heaven! O life!. . . . (Padre Pio [1887-1968], *Letter to Padre Benedetto*, June 19, 1918.)

O God of my soul! O Divine Sun! I love you, I bless you, I praise you, I abandon myself completely to you. . . . (Marthe Robin [1902-81], *The Cross and the Joy*.)

O my Jesus! O my Grandeur and Majesty!. . . . (St. Teresa of Avila [1515-82], *Life*.)

Thus we have numerous examples of how affective prayer springs forth from the depths of the victim's heart.

This type of prayer continues on in the mystical-contemplative life, although in the heights of true contemplation it is usually felt or spoken with the heart instead of words. Still, different types of prayer do mingle in any particular state, and the prayers of affection and contemplation are certainly examples of this interchange.

This concludes our focus on meditation. While meditation is the way of beginners in the pre-mystical state, contemplation is for those who are advanced in the ways of the spirit. It is the highest expression of the spiritual life, the narrow road that leads to the fullness of grace (Mt 7:14). Here we will find those victims of love whom God calls in the stillness of the heart; here resides the stigmatist, consumed in the fire of unending love.

Like meditation, contemplation can mean many things to different people. While everyone is called to a contemplative experience from time to time, few are chosen to lead a total contemplative life: "You are not of the world, but I chose you out of the world" (Jn 15:19).

Thomas Merton (1915-68), one of the great mystic-contemplatives of the twentieth century, says that contemplation is an acute awareness of God's presence (*New Seeds of Contemplation*: New Direction Books, N.Y. 1961). I might add to this by saying that it is a deep awareness of God's presence *which is known by love*. Love is the only way we can experience God because God in fact is Love. God loves whether we do or not; it is His very essence to love, being Love itself.

The contemplative sees God by gazing at Him through the windows of the soul. It is not a vision of the senses, but rather a vision of the heart. The mystic in this state comes to know God for what He is, and not for what the mind perceives Him to be, for no one has ever seen God (1 Jn 4:12). Yet it is a vision all the same. When one strips away all preconceived perceptions of God, He is then free to visit the soul and appear as He really is. At this point, any thought of God is futile, for only He can show us a glimpse of what He is through no effort of our own.

Paradoxically, we come to know God by "unknowing," as the anonymous author states in his classical work, *The Cloud of Unknowing* (late fourteenth century). Because the mind is incapable of forming a true impression of God, discursive reasoning once used in vocal prayer and meditation can no longer be of any use to the soul in this state. When the pure God of Light manifests himself to the impure soul, the manifestation leaves him in darkness because he cannot handle the breathless Purity and Love that is God (more about this in the next unit on the "Dark Night").

St. John of the Cross has this to say concerning those just entering the mystical state of contemplation:

> The attitude necessary . . . is to pay no attention to discursive meditation, since this is not the time for it. They should allow the soul to remain in rest and quietude, even though it may seem very obvious to them that they are doing nothing and wasting time, and even though they think this disinclination to think about anything is due to their laxity. Through patience and perseverance in prayer, they will be doing a great deal without activity on their part. All that is required of them here is freedom of soul, that they liberate themselves from the impediment and fatigue of ideas and thoughts and care not about thinking and meditating. They must be content simply with a loving and peaceful attentiveness to God, and live without concern, without effort, and without the desire to taste or feel Him. All these desires disquiet the soul and distract it from the peaceful quiet and sweet idleness of the contemplation which is being communicated to it. . . . (Kieran Kavanaugh, O.C.D. and Ottilio Rodriguez, O.C.D., *The Collected Works of St. John of the Cross*, "Dark Night," Book I, chpt. 10; Institute of Carmelite Studies, Washington, D.C., 1979.)

Before we discuss any particular aspects of the contemplative life that are found in the stigmatist, it is important that we look at a few more statements concerning the meaning of contemplation. We will do this through the eyes of two of the Church's outstanding saints and theologians: St. Francis de Sales (1567-1622) and St. Bernard of Clairvaux (1090-1153), both who have been declared Doctors of the Faith we profess.

> Contemplation takes a completely simple, unified view of the object it loves. It is like one who smells water containing perfume made up of all kinds of flowers. In a single sensation, one takes in all those odors united together. . . . (St. Francis de Sales, *Love of God*, Book VI, chpt. 5.)

In turn, this odor that pours forth from the heavenly Spouse saturates the soul, who becomes inebriated with the divine love. Many of the stigmatists become so absorbed in this divine perfume that they take on what is known as an *odor of sanctity*: a state where a sweet smell like that of perfume issues forth from the victim, especially from his or her wounds. This effect has been noticed by many who have been in the presence of the stigmatist, and many have even claimed to smell this sweet odor of perfume long after the victim has died. This odor is a sign of the soul's intimate union with the divine, and is a most delightful smell. We will talk more about this in a later section that deals with the extraordinary gifts of the stigmatist.

Another characteristic that occurs with the contemplative is the loving "gaze" they give to the Lord. St. Francis describes this singular, loving act as an important part of the contemplative experience:

> In contemplation we consider with one single, steady mental gaze. The simple gaze of contemplation is made in any one of three ways: 1) His infinite goodness, for example, without thinking of His other attributes or virtues; 2) sometimes too we fix our attention on more than one of God's infinite perfections, but still with a simple gaze without making distinctions; 3) at other times we consider neither many of God's perfections nor just one of them, but only a certain divine action or work on which we fasten our attention — an act of mercy, the act of creation, St. Paul's conversion, etc. . . . (*Love of God*, Book VI, chpt. 6.)

Here St. Francis tells us that the contemplative experience usually centers around one particular aspect of God or His loving goodness, and even then without discursive reasoning, but rather with a simple, loving gaze that allows the Lord to manifest himself to the soul.

St. Bernard continues this theme, but further tells us that the state of contemplation is usually reserved for only those who have had a passionate desire for union with God — a desire to be totally immersed in the divine love, to be lost in one's self to all things but the Lord:

> The grace of contemplation is granted only in response to a longing and importunate desire: nevertheless He will not present himself, even in passing, to every soul; but only to that soul which is shown by great devotion, vehement desire, and tender affection, to be His bride, and to be worthy that the Word in all His beauty should visit her as a Bridegroom. . . . (St. Bernard, *On the Canticles of Canticles*, 22,3: 12th century.)

Once again, we see that the gift of contemplation is not for everyone, but only for those whom the Lord deems fit for such a lofty state. It is not a grace that we can earn by our own effort (although one must be worthy of such a grace through the degree of sanctity that is obtained); rather, it is given by God according to His good will to those whom He calls to a higher state of perfection. The stigmatist is required to attain such a state in order to be worthy of sharing the Cross with our Lord; he must totally conform to the image of Christ in body, mind and soul as much as humanly possible in this life. Only then can he hope to suffer for Christ and for the world; only then can he atone for the sins of others, for he must be quite pure himself. God demands only the best from those who dare imitate His ways, for nothing defiled can enter the heavenly kingdom. This is why the stigmata is such a rare and precious gift for the world: few are able to meet the demands of God's justice in order to satisfy for sin. Fewer still are able to carry our Lord's Cross in such a manner that it lightens His suffering and helps Him on the way to Calvary. Such is the lot of the stigmatists who find their way into our midst from time to time in the history of the Church.

In order for the soul to reach the state of the divine union, a person must pass through a series of states or experiences before arriving at this highest degree of perfection. Because the soul is not perfected yet, God will occasionally allow her to experience His sweetness and love through holy inspirations, divine impulses and sensual joys, lest she become discouraged in the long and painful process that is necessary on the road to perfection.

One of the first things required in the ascent to God is the elimination of all sensual appetites, personal desires and imperfections that serve to hinder one's progress toward perfection. In order to do this, one has to embark on an all-out war against the self by purifying all stains of the mind and flesh. This occurs over a period of time through acts of penance, fasting, mortification, etc. It is a very painful process because one is rebelling against the natural tendencies of the flesh: "To set the mind on the flesh is death, but to set the mind on the Spirit is life and peace" (Rom 8:6).

Yet this is nothing compared to the future purifications that await him. At the beginning of this journey, it is the self that purges the soul of its imperfections. Later, God sees fit to purge the soul through the fire of His love, a fire that reaches to the very depths of the soul, cleansing it from all impurities. In this state (called the *dark night of the soul*), it is God Who acts upon the soul without his or her help. One must become passive by letting God become active. This is indeed painful, for it runs contrary to what we think or do as human beings. In fact, most feel that they are doing nothing and are helpless to remedy the situation. In a sense, they are right; we do nothing while God acts, thereby purging the soul of its darkness in order to prepare us for the immense light that will one day follow.

God is pure Light, and all in darkness are blinded by this Light: "God is light and in him is no darkness" (1 Jn 1:5). If there is no darkness in God at all, then the slightest stain of impurity will blind the soul to this Light. That is why it is so painful to feel God's presence in the midst of our souls; if we do experience Him intimately and profoundly, we are overcome by His perfection, holiness and love: to experience God as He really is.

Such is the dark night that St. John of the Cross so profoundly describes. We will explore the night of the senses and spirit in the next chapter.

God in His mercy does not keep the soul in darkness forever. Delights of the Spirit and consolation will occasionally overtake him, in order that the fragile soul remains firm in the faith. But these consolations are fleeting in nature, and only temporarily serve to rejuvenate the wearied soul. This is because the battle with imperfection and temptation is a life-long process, especially where the evil spirit is concerned. He continues to attack the soul destined for unity with God, so the trial remains.

Many souls labor in darkness and in unity with God at the same time; there is both darkness and light, consolation and desolation. This two-fold state of the spirit has been found among many a stigmatist, and the battle is never quite won in this life. Yet some have reached such an intimate union with the Lord that the light far outshines the darkness; in this degree of perfection, the spirits of darkness have less control over the opponent, though they are still able to tempt him and harass him at will.

For a very privileged few who reach the heights of sanctity and perfection, God sometimes transforms them into His very image, drawing them into full unity with His divine love. These souls reach what is known in mystical terms as the *spiritual marriage*, the highest state possible for one to attain while in this life. The bride has been united to her Groom in heavenly splendor, enjoys a share of the beatific vision, and exchanges hearts with her Beloved that is nothing less than becoming one with Him. Some mystic-victims have reached this state of divine union, and most authentic stigmatists have reached this union as well. More will be said about this at a later time.

There are many other things to say about the contemplative life. Volumes of material have been written by the best mystical theologians describing this most wonderful journey of the soul towards God. It is my intention to limit those things that apply to the stigmatist in particular, including the extraordinary charisms they have been gifted with and have become well-known for. Let us now turn to that mysterious state that the stigmatist must undergo on his way toward union with the Cross of Christ: that of the dark night.

Dark Night of the Senses

St. John of the Cross (1542-91) is, perhaps, the greatest authority on mystical theology that the Church has ever known. In particular, his *Dark Night* has been the classical work on the experience of the desert, that night of darkness in which those called to higher states of perfection must endure. Therefore, I will refer to this master of the spiritual life quite frequently, as I have done before. There is simply no better source than St. John in this area, although St. Teresa of Avila runs a close second.

St. John's opening stanza on the dark night reads as follows:

> One dark night, fired with love's urgent longings — Ah, the sheer grace! — I went out unseen, my house being now all stilled. . .

What is this mysterious dark night that so many mystics have tried to explain? Robert C. Broderick has described it this way: "It is a time when the soul seeks God by pure faith and is given no assistance from the senses, when it may be difficult to make acts of prayer, when nature rebels against self-scrutiny and the effort demanded to draw closer to God. This period may be accompanied by actual suffering of the spirit, as though scruples and temptations against faith, or physical suffering in the form of sickness, permitted by God as a trial" (*The Catholic Encyclopedia*, Thomas Nelson Publishers, Nashville, TN, 1976).

This night of the senses comes at the dawn of contemplation, where God increases the trials of the soul in order to purify it and prepare it for the higher, mystical state. As souls are elevated to a higher state, God makes them realize their own nothingness and weakness in order to preserve their humility and to increase their gratefulness. It is a state that works against presumption, lest the soul harbors a secret pride and falls from this moment of grace.

This night of the senses is dark because God must purify their eyes from the impurities of the world, in order that they might come to see the pureness of Light, which is God himself. He blinds them in order that they might see.

This darkness can last briefly, or it may take years to dispel. Some souls (such as Padre Pio of Pietrelcina) encountered the dark night all of their lives, but usually have the Light along with this darkness so that the two operate simultaneously in the soul on his way to divine union. Once again, this is probably designed to keep the extraordinarily privileged soul humble and open to God's mercy and forgiveness. Then the light shines brighter, bringing the soul into the most intense and loving relationship imaginable in this life.

This discourse on the mystical dark night needs special attention and extensive treatment, for every mystic, victim and stigmatist must pass through this crucible in order to be tried and proven by God: "Having been disciplined a little, they will receive great good, because God tested them and found them worthy of himself; like gold in the furnace he tried them. . ." (Wis 3:5-6). This is especially true if one ever hopes to attain the divine union. Stigmatists in particular are prone to the darkest of nights and the severest attacks from the evil one. This is because their vocation calls them to represent Christ to a broken world, and to help win back souls from the clutches of Satan. (More on the spiritual warfare in a later chapter.)

When a soul leaves behind the prayers of beginners (vocal prayer and meditation), God places him into the state of *proficients*; that is, those who have entered or who are well into the mystical and contemplative life. This intermediate step in the spiritual life is a gradual journey toward the way of perfection, which ultimately leads to divine union and, for some, the spiritual marriage.

As one begins to enter the dark night of the senses, he must learn to practice *mortification* and *penance* in order to free the flesh and the senses from imperfections that hinder the spiritual progress of the soul. These mortifications (also known as *purgations*) are divided into two types: *active purgation* and *passive purgation*.

Active purgation is the purifying process by which one voluntarily moves to rid himself of imperfections that impede his spiritual relationship with God. This is done through various acts of penance or self-denial: prayer, contrition, fasting, denials of the senses and appetites, and at times even self-flagellation and other physical disciplines. These are active purgations, whereby God is not the primary purifier of flesh and spirit; it is the person himself who does most of the purging (although God will cooperate to a certain point by giving him or her the discernment necessary to know what needs to be perfected, and the grace necessary to sustain the difficult journey).

We have many examples of these self-imposed purgations of the flesh and of the senses in the lives of the stigmatists. Most continued to discipline themselves severely, even when God took over. The active and passive purgations occur simultaneously in these holy souls.

There is another purifying experience called the *passive purgation*, whereby God does all the acting upon the soul without his or her help. Instead of the flesh or the senses, God now chooses to cleanse the soul itself (which no one can do on his own). It is even more painful than the active purgation because the person inflicted is unable to control the purgings or their intensity. He must simply let God act, oblivious to what is occurring deep within his very being. He or she is helpless for a remedy until God is finished purifying the depths of the soul, stained by Original Sin and the subconscious cause of many an imperfection that needs to be weeded out. Even worse, one isn't always aware of *what* needs purging in the heart of the soul. This, too, becomes a most painful experience; one becomes lost as to cause and effect, helpless to remedy what God must do.

We will leave a more thorough treatment of the passive night of purgation for the next unit on the dark night of the soul, since this state begins this dreadful night that is much more painful than that of the senses, often leading into a feeling of abandonment by God.

Returning to our discussion on penance and mortification, we need to see exactly what these things are, and the importance the Church attaches to them. Let us look at some of the descriptions the saints and the Magisterium have used for these considerations:

> Mortification aims at the liberation of man, who often finds himself, because of his concupiscence, almost chained by his own senses. Through corporal fasting man regains strength and the wound inflicted on the dignity of our nature by intemperance is cured by the medicine of a salutary abstinence. . . . (Pope Paul VI, *Paenitemini*, Feb. 17, 1966.)

Here we see that fasting and abstinence from sensual things are important ways to purify the soul. These two ways need not be strictly related to food or drink; they also apply to self-denial of many conveniences or bodily pleasures that we must moderate or eliminate: pleasures of the senses, sexual gratifications, even desires of the heart that keep us from the vision and will of God. Let us continue with Pope Paul's statement:

> One fasts or applies physical discipline to chastise one's own soul, to humble oneself in the sight of his own God, to turn one's face toward Jehovah, to dispose oneself to prayer, to understand more intimately the things which are divine, or to prepare oneself for the encounter with God. . . . (Pope Paul VI, *Paenitemini*, Feb. 17, 1966.)

We can see that the understanding of fasting or abstinence goes far beyond what we eat or the amount we eat. It encompasses the whole person — body, mind and soul. Food in itself has little to do with the proper attitude or benefits derived from these acts of self-denial. What else can we learn from the wisdom of the Church? Here are other descriptions for the motivation of penance and mortification:

> The duty of doing penance is motivated above all by participation in the sufferings of Christ. . . . (Pope Paul VI, *Paenitemini*, Feb. 17, 1966.)

> The necessity of the mortification of the flesh stands clearly revealed if we consider the fragility of our own nature, in which, since Adam's sin, flesh and spirit have contrasting desires. . . . (Pope Paul VI, *Paenitemini*, Feb. 17, 1966.)

The people of God do penance continually in many and varied ways. Sharing in the sufferings of Christ by their own suffering, performing works of mercy and charity, undergoing a constant conversion to the Gospel of Christ, they become to the world a symbol of conversion to God. . . . (S.C.D.W., *Misericordiam suam*, Feb. 7, 1974.)

Penance affords reconciliation with a man's brothers, who likewise are injured by sin. . . . (S.C.D.W., *Ms*, Feb. 7, 1974.)

The great St. Francis de Sales (1567-1622), mystical Doctor of the Church, has described the motives and needs for penance and mortification beautifully in the following passages:

For us the beginning of good health is to be purged of our sinful tendencies. . . . (*The Devout Life*, Part I.)

The usual purgation and healing, whether of body or of soul, takes place only little by little and by passing from one advance to another with difficulty and patience. . . . (*The Devout Life*, Part I.)

To practice humility it is absolutely necessary for us at times to suffer wounds in the spiritual warfare. The first purgation we must make is that of sin and the way to make it is by the holy sacrament of penance. . . . (*The Devout Life*, Part I.)

The work of purging the soul neither can nor should end except with our life itself. We must not be disturbed at our imperfections, since for us perfection consists in fighting against them. . . . (*The Devout Life*, Part I.)

As I had commented before, the role of purgation continues throughout the life of the victim, because he or she is never totally free from sin, imperfections or temptations while here in this life. Therefore, life will always remain a constant struggle against the forces of self, the world and the evil spirit. The stigmatist — though perhaps free of serious sin and only plagued with imperfections hardly noticeable — nevertheless fights to further cleanse his soul, in order to be as pure as possible for the divine union that beckons him. Grace and struggle will always occur throughout the life of the chosen one, sometimes separately, but usually simultaneously. If nothing else, this serves to keep the holy soul humble, lest he contribute any good to himself or any grace possessed entirely because of his own doing.

Returning to the master, St. John of the Cross gives us a challenging attitude towards this period of self-denial and mortification. As one can see, total abandonment of self in order to conform to the divine image is difficult but always possible. Perhaps this is why few souls pass through the dark night successfully and enter the divine union: it is a journey that requires the greatest display of faith, love and patience that can ever be experienced:

Endeavor to be inclined always: not to the easiest, but to the most difficult; not to the most delightful, but to the harshest; not to the most gratifying, but to the less pleasant; not to what means rest for you, but to hard work; not to the consoling, but to the unconsoling; not to the most, but to the least; not to the highest, but to the lowest; not to want something, but to want nothing; do not go about looking for the best of temporal things, but for the worst; and desire to enter for Christ into complete nudity, emptiness and poverty in everything in the world. . . . (*The Collected Works of St. John of the Cross*, "The Ascent of Mount Carmel," Book I, chpt. 13.)

These words echo the same sentiments traditionally associated with the stigmatist St. Francis of Assisi (1182-1226) in the *Prayer of St. Francis*: "Oh, Master, grant that I may never seek so much to be consoled as to console; to be understood as to understand; to be loved as to love with all my soul," etc.

In the same book, St. John further teaches the importance of self-denial in order to surrender unconditionally to the love of our God: "Try to act with contempt for yourself and desire that all others do likewise; endeavor to speak in contempt of yourself and desire all others to do so; try to think lowly and contemptuously of yourself and desire that all others do the same" (*Collected Works*, "The Ascent," Book I, chpt. 13). Is this not the very message of Jesus? The Gospel is full of references from our Lord that teach of self-denial and humility: "Blessed are the meek, for they shall inherit the earth" (Mt 5:5); "Blessed are the pure in heart, for they shall see God" (Mt 5:8); "Blessed are the poor in spirit, for theirs is the Kingdom of heaven" (Mt 5:3); "For everyone who exalts himself will be humbled, and he who humbles himself will be exalted" (Lk 14:11); "If any man would come after me, let him *deny* himself" (Mk 8:34); and so on. These are messages for all of us, but how few there are who are able to climb the mystical ladder toward God!

John of the Cross describes the seven main imperfections that the soul must battle in order to ascend higher in the spiritual life: pride, spiritual avarice, lust, anger, spiritual gluttony, spiritual envy, and sloth. Before moving on to the experience of the dark night in the stigmatist, let us hear a description of these imperfections by St. John in order to better appreciate the struggles the stigmatists have in their ascent towards heaven.

• **Pride**. These beginners feel so fervent and diligent in their spiritual exercises and undertakings that a certain kind of secret pride is generated in them which begets a complacency with themselves and their accomplishments, despite the fact that holy works do of their very nature cause humility. Then they develop a desire somewhat vain — at times very vain — to speak of spiritual things in others' presence, and sometimes even to instruct rather than be instructed; in their hearts they condemn others who do not seem to have the kind of devotion they would like them to have, and sometimes they give expression to this criticism like the pharisee who despised the publican while he

110

boasted and praised God for the good deeds he himself accomplished. . . . (*Collected Works*, "The Dark Night," Book I, chpt. 2.)

He also speaks of the pride that is caused by the devil's suggestions, and the unwillingness to have a spiritual director in times of need. The soul in this situation feels capable of directing himself, and therefore starts down the road to spiritual ruin.

> • **Spiritual avarice**. Sometimes many beginners also possess great spiritual avarice. They will hardly ever seem content with the spirit God gives them. They become unhappy and peevish owing to a lack of the consolation they desire to have in spiritual things. Many never have enough of hearing counsels, or of learning spiritual maxims, or of keeping them and reading books about them. They spend more time doing this than striving after mortification and the perfection of the interior poverty to which they are obliged. Furthermore, they weigh themselves down with overly decorated images and rosaries; they will now put these down, now take up others; now they want this kind, now they want another; they will prefer one cross to another because of its elaborateness. . . . (*Collected Works*, "The Dark Night," Book I, chpt. 3.)

St. John is warning us here about the dangers of the lack of appreciation for the grace that has been given us, of restlessness of spirit, and the exterior display some souls might have in "showing off" their devotion in order to impress others that they are truly holy. This, of course, runs contrary to the holy humility our Lord has taught us, and the display of that humility found in the lives of the stigmatists.

> • **Lust**. It happens frequently that in one's very spiritual exercises, without being able to avoid it, impure movements will be experienced in the sensory part of the soul, and even sometimes when the spirit is deep in prayer or when receiving the sacrament of penance or the Eucharist. They can proceed from the pleasure human nature finds in spiritual exercises. Some people are so delicate that when gratification is received from the spirit or from prayer, they immediately experience a lust which so inebriates them and caresses their senses that they become as it were engulfed in the delight and satisfaction of that vice. . . . (*Collected Works*, "The Dark Night," Book I, chpt. 4.)

Here we are reminded to take caution with emotional displays of frenzy when we are in the solemn mood of prayer, adoration or the like. Modern-day charismatics are particularly prone to these external displays of sensual gratification, and the effect of mass frenzy is sometimes evident. This is not meant to degrade authentic charismatic experience. Where true charismatic experience is evident, then moderation and control of one's emotions is needed in order to give God the due respect He alone deserves, and to allow some period of silence so that God may speak to us in the depths of our hearts. We also need to respect those in our midst who may be silently responding to God as well.

When the authentic gift of speaking in tongues is given to some, instead of everyone joining in simultaneously, rather let someone discern these words for the benefit of those who don't understand what is being said: "If any speak in a tongue, let there be only two or at most three, *and each in turn*; and let one interpret. But if there is no one to interpret, *let each of them keep silence* in church and speak to himself and to God" (1 Cor 14:27-28). Why does St. Paul exhort the faithful to do this? Because "God is not a God of confusion, but of peace" (1 Cor 14:33). I do not mean to offend sincerely gifted charismatics; I only serve to warn those who, though present at the gatherings, are not authentically gifted and abuse the moment of prayer about which St. Paul so strongly teaches.

> • **Anger**. Because of the strong desire of many beginners for spiritual gratification, they usually have many imperfections of anger. For when the delight and satisfaction procured in their spiritual exercises passes, these beginners are naturally left without any spiritual savor. And because of this distastefulness, they become peevish in the works they do and easily angered by the least thing, and occasionally they are so unbearable that nobody can put up with them. Some become angry over the sins of others; they reprove these others, and sometimes even feel the impulse to do so angrily, which in fact they do, setting themselves up as lords of virtue. . . . (*Collected Works*, "The Dark Night," Book I, chpt. 5.)

Some souls are also extremely impatient with themselves, wanting to become, as it were, saints in a day. They lack the virtue of patience, which can only grow through humility and a resignation to God's will.

> • **Spiritual gluttony**. There is hardly anyone among these beginners, no matter how excellent his conduct, who will not fall into some of the many imperfections of this vice. These imperfections arise because of the delight beginners find in their spiritual exercises.

> Many, lured by the delight and satisfaction procured in their religious practices, strive more for spiritual savor than for spiritual purity and discretion; some, attracted by the delight of their spiritual exercises, will kill themselves with penances, and others will weaken themselves by fasts and, without the counsel or command of another, overtax their weakness; some will even dare perform these penances contrary to obedience. . . . (*Collected Works*, "The Dark Night," Book I, chpt. 6.)

Here is stressed the need for a good spiritual director, lest the eager soul falls away from the path that leads to perfection. Practically all of the stigmatists have had this direction throughout their lives. The danger of not having guidance from one who is experienced in these matters is that the devil can deceive us into doing things we ought not do. We know very well

112

that this creature of darkness can easily transform himself into an angel of light (2 Cor 11:14), deceiving even the most chosen ones of God's special grace.

> • **Spiritual envy**. Many beginners will feel sad about the spiritual good of others and experience sensible grief in noting that their neighbor is ahead of them on the road to perfection, and they will not want to hear others praised. To learn of the virtues of others makes them sad. . . . (*Collected Works*, "The Dark Night," Book I, chpt. 7.)

Obviously, St. John is talking about jealousy, a temperament that runs contrary to holy charity (see 1 Cor 13:4). This jealousy is a holy envy, and hinders the soul's progression in the ways of the spirit. The soul who is guilty of spiritual jealousy is self-centered and possessive of all that he secretly wants for his own. It is a most pitiful condition, one that needs careful attention if one is to advance spiritually.

> • **Sloth**. Beginners usually become weary in the more spiritual exercises and flee from them, since these exercises are contrary to sensory satisfaction. Since they are so used to finding delight in spiritual practices, they become bored when they do not find it. If they do not receive in prayer the satisfaction they crave — for after all it is fit that God withdraw this so as to try them — they do not want to return to it or at times they either give up prayer or go to it begrudgingly. Many of these beginners want God to desire what they want, and become sad if they have to desire God's will. Beginners also become bored when told to do something unpleasant. Because they look for spiritual gratifications and delights, they are extremely lax in the fortitude and labor perfection demands. . . . (*Collected Works*, "The Dark Night," Book I, chpt. 7.)

To seek and follow God's will! This is a difficult challenge for all of us, yet it is one we are commanded to do: "Not my will but thine be done" (Lk 22:42). How many times do we seek God's will only when it will bring us pleasure or good fortune? How often do we proclaim to follow our Lord most intimately, yet fall away when challenge is there to confront us? The stigmatists, too, struggled with doing the Lord's will; they were often afraid that they might be seeking their own will at times, and lived in holy fear of offending God and disobeying His designs upon their souls. This holy fear is really quite beneficial, for it keeps one in a state of humility before God and frees us from selfish interests.

Let us look at how the stigmatists struggled with their own imperfections, and how they continually felt the need to purge themselves of all their earthly vices. This was always a source of extreme suffering for them, for they were never quite sure how they stood before God and His most holy judgment. Padre Pio of Pietrelcina once voiced this fear in a letter to his spiritual director:

> What am I to say about my present spiritual state? At present my soul is surrounded by a circle of iron. I fear, on the one hand to offend God in almost everything I do, and this fills my soul

with a terror that can only be compared to the sufferings of the damned. . . . (*Letter to Padre Benedetto*, March 11, 1915.)

The stigmatist St. Lydwine of Schiedam (1380-1433), one of the greatest suffering victims the Church has ever known, remarked when asked about her sense of personal sin:

> God alone knows, for I am but a poor being and it has cost me many chastisements to make me understand how much I am still subject to the infirmities of human nature. Praise God, and pray to Him for me! It is because of my sins that you see me so unhappy. . . . (*St. Lydwine of Schiedam*, J.K. Huysmans: TAN Books and Publishers, Inc., 1979.)

Even the great St. Francis was continually aware of his sin before God, and never took the graces God gave him for granted:

> O Brother Francis, thou hast done so much evil and committed so many sins here in the world that thou art worthy to go to hell. . . . (*St. Francis of Assisi*, p. 106, Johannes Jorgensen: Image Books, Garden City, N.Y., 1955 reprint.)

Imagine such a holy stigmatist fearing the fires of hell! We know that our dear saint was very pleasing to God, yet he did not allow himself to think too highly of his position before the Lord. This is humility in the highest degree, and serves as a reminder for us all.

The types of penances or mortifications that these holy stigmatists underwent are as varied as they are numerous. We will look briefly at some of the ways these souls have fought their sinful natures and strove to eliminate the imperfections that still remained to be purged. In some cases, it was a question of abstinence or self-denial; in others, a self-inflicting punishment served to purify their souls and chastise their bodies.

St. Teresa of Avila (1515-82), the Carmelite Doctor of the Catholic Church, gave words of sound advice to her convent sisters concerning the practices of mortification and penance. Teresa herself was most likely a stigmatist, for her heart and soul were permanently wounded by the hand of God (more on this later). Here are some of the counsels that Teresa gave to her followers concerning those who practice penance too severely, or not enough:

> It is amusing to see these persons and the torment they put themselves through. Sometimes they feel a desire to do penances without rhyme or reason, a desire that lasts a couple of days, so to speak; subsequently the devil makes them imagine that the penances did them harm. He makes them fear penance, and after some attempts they don't even dare carry out what the order commands. . . . (Kieran Cavanaugh, O.C.D. and Ottilio Rodriguez, O.C.D., *The Collected Works of St. Teresa of Avila*, "The Way of Perfection," chpt. 10; Institute of Carmelite Studies, Washington, D.C., 1976, 1980.)

Teresa reminds her sisters that the evil one interferes with good holy intentions to purge ourselves of sin. She admonishes them to not grow lax in their efforts to do penance for their bodies and souls. We see that the devil is sure to attempt to stop those who do penance. Yet the evil one is cunning and will work in the opposite way as well: he will try to encourage some to perform too many acts of penance, or penances too severe to discourage and weaken the soul on her way to perfection:

> He tempts us in regards to excessive penances so that we might think we are more penitential than others and are doing something. . . .

> We are so indiscreet that since the pain is sweet and delightful, we never think we can have enough of this pain. We eat without measure, we foster this desire as much as we can, and so sometimes it kills. How fortunate such a death! But perhaps by continuing to live we can help others die of desire for this death. And I believe the devil causes this desire for death, for he understands the harm that can be done by such a person while alive; and so at this stage he tempts one to perform indiscreet penances so that one's health will be lost, which would be no small gain for the devil. . . . (*Collected Works of St. Teresa*, "The Way of Perfection," chpt. 19.)

It is true that some stigmatists have undergone great penances in order to mortify their flesh; however, their mission was to suffer for others, so their reasons are entirely different than the average soul who seeks perfection. In any event, these victims always sought direction from their spiritual fathers in order to obey the laws of reason. If it was discerned that it was God's will to offer up more extreme penances, then this was usually done only through the advice and discretion of the director of the soul. This act of obedience is found in almost all of the authentic stigmatists; in turn, obedience to a good spiritual director is pertinent to all of the faithful, whomever they may be.

St. John of the Cross explains what should motivate the heart of the penitent, whether the penance be light or severe:

> The ignorance of some is extremely lamentable; they burden themselves with extraordinary penances and many other exercises, thinking these are sufficient for the attainment of union with the divine wisdom. But these practices are insufficient if a person diligently strives to deny his appetites. If these people would attempt to devote only a half of that energy to the renunciation of their desires, they would profit more in a month than in years with all these other exercises. The appetites are like a cataract on the eyes or specks of dust in it; until removed they obstruct vision. . . . (*The Ascent of Mount Carmel*, Book I, chpt. 8.)

It is very important to realize what St. John is saying here: that it's not enough to count the total number of penances done (or even their severity); rather, it is the intention to do away with the desires of the flesh that brings us merit and satisfaction. We can purge our souls continuously with the severest of acts, yet what good does it do if we haven't eliminated the desire from our hearts? It is there that we are tested (Ps 17:3), and we must create in ourselves a new heart (Ez 18:31). God is more concerned with what lies in our heart than with the many exterior acts we may show (2 Cor 5:12).

Yet this point is no way intended to undermine the necessity for penance or mortification! Just changing our attitudes cannot satisfy for the acts of sin already committed, for we must all satisfy for our past transgressions, either in this life or the next. A change of heart helps to satisfy for our ongoing imperfections and tendencies toward sin, but we also need to show our God that we are sincere by acts of loving sacrifice to Him. If done with a contrite heart, these acts may be applied to the satisfaction we all must make. The Venerable Louis of Granada, O.P. (d. 1588) was a favorite spiritual writer of St. John of the Cross, as well as two stigmatists of the same era: St. Teresa of Avila and St. Rose of Lima. He has this to say about the need for satisfying our sin:

> He who breaks the laws of God is obliged to the penalties which divine justice exacts. These penalties must be paid either in this life or in the next, that is, in hell, in purgatory, or in this world. In hell the penalty is eternal suffering; in purgatory the penalty is not eternal but is so intense that St. Augustine says that there is no suffering in this world which can compare with it. But we can avoid these penalties by fasting and ascetical practices in this life, although such sufferings are infinitely less than the former. God does not look so much to the greatness of the work as to *the will with which it is done*, for that which is suffered in this life is voluntary, while the suffering of the next life is obligatory. . . . (*Summa of the Christian Life*, Volume III, chpt. 45: TAN Books and Publishers, Inc., 1979 reprint.)

We will see later how deeply the stigmatists have applied their own wills with that of God's, only desiring to satisfy His demands with a pure heart and that which is born of true contrition and love.

What we have been talking about here is an *interior mortification* that seeks to eliminate the imperfections of the heart and soul. Those advanced in the spirit attempt to remove from their being those vices that, though sometimes hidden, are hindrances on the path to perfection: pride, impatience, envy, etc. The stigmatist mortifies himself through both exterior and interior practices, thus attempting to remove completely all vices of the body and soul. Through exterior practices (under the careful guidance of the spiritual director), he or she sometimes performs the severest of austerities, crucifying the body with fastings, vigils, hairshirts, disciplines, and other rigors. The body is restrained, denied all things that work against the path toward perfection.

Perhaps it is in the crucifixion of the will that the stigmatist performs his most austere mortification. To seek and to do God's will in perfect resignation — no matter the trial, no matter the cost — occupies his heart, mind and soul continuously.

The exterior mortifications are only means to arrive at the interior purgations. For it is in the very depths of the heart and soul that one learns to conquer self and to root out all evil habits, replacing them instead with holy virtues and the desire to only do God's will. Because the victim soul is so advanced in both exterior and interior mortification, he is usually capable of practicing those severe forms of penance that would only harm beginners. Their holy humility and pious fear of offending the Lord allows them protection against the complacency and secret pride that disillusions so many inexperienced souls.

Thus concludes the active night of the senses, a dark night that serves to rid the soul of those bodily and sensual imperfections which impede the progress towards perfection. The evil one, so alert to the good intentions and advancement of the soul, tempts these victims continuously in order to deter them from their goal. I have left an extensive treatment of his presence in the lives of the victim for a later chapter.

We now must look into the second stage of the dark night: that of the soul, whereby God in His infinite wisdom removes the deeper stains that must be purged, in order that the union with God Who is all Pure may be achieved. It is a state through which every victim must pass if he is to reach that loving bond with the divine that he desires; it is *the* great challenge of the stigmatist, who must be put through the crucible in order to be transformed into the Cross of Christ.

Dark Night of the Soul

After having gone through the active purgation of the senses, one must still await the more dreadful *dark night of the soul*, when God sees fit to purify the depths of the soul in order to prepare it for the divine union. As I indicated before, this night puts one in the state of *passive purgation* — a condition where one no longer actively pursues the elimination of his imperfections, but rather it is God himself who now does the purifying. This is the final act of purgation, and it is the most intense and painful.

Why does the soul in this state suffer so intensely if it helps bring him closer to God? It is because he or she longs for God in this darkness while feeling desolation and abandonment by Him. This night has also been described as the desert, the void and the abyss. This state is normally transitory because it can take place again after it has once subsided. Indeed, some mystics spend a greater part of their spiritual lives in this night, although it usually ends when the divine union is reached. Still, some have even experienced this sense of loss and abandonment by God amidst the union itself, where the soul simultaneously experiences joy and sadness, peace and desolation, or love and a sense of abandonment.

I once asked Father Joseph Martin, O.F.M. Cap. (Padre Pio's intimate friend and assistant) if the Padre still experienced the dark night later on in his years, even after reaching such extraordinary mystical heights. "Padre Pio lived in the dark night his entire life, even up to the moment of his death," Father Martin replied. It seems that this dark night, besides purging the soul of the stains of imperfection, also serves to keep these holy servants of God humble and fearful for any sin they still could commit, lest they should swell with pride or become too self-assured of their destiny. This would partly explain why some stigmatists oscillated between darkness and light, even while obtaining the divine union. This, in fact, is what Father Martin indicated about Padre Pio.

The dark night of the soul is really a blessing for the mystic, because by undergoing this painful state he is helping to pay for the just penalties that would one day become due in the purifying flames of purgatory, if he doesn't atone for them while still in this life (see last unit for more on satisfaction for sin). To further illustrate this point, Robert Broderick gives us this insight:

> The alternative is purgatory, which is purification without merit, and the way of sanctity is to be purified in this passive manner before death instead of after. . . . (*The Catholic Encyclopedia*, p. 152.)

The key point here is that while we are still alive, we can merit the cleansing action upon the soul through mortifications, sacrifices and penance. These meritorious actions through our own efforts serve to "cancel out" the debts due to sin that we must satisfy before being allowed to obtain heaven and the beatific vision. If we do not cancel these debts due to sin while still living our earthly lives, we must do so in the purifying state we call purgatory. Some holy souls still have some stain of imperfection when they die, and do not go directly to heaven until satisfaction is achieved. Others have canceled their debts while on this earth, and immediately ascend to heaven at the moment of death. They had not only reached the divine union while on earth, but the spiritual marriage and a level of the beatific vision as well. The Church honors these by declaring them *saints*.

The passive purgation (this dark night of the soul) in which God chooses to place the soul never precedes the night of the senses and rarely accompanies it; rather, it usually follows a period of spiritual delight and rest. This intermediate period of delight and consolation serves to build up one's confidence, increase faith, and allow the preparation needed for the trials yet to come.

When the darkness again unfolds, God removes the spiritual pleasures the soul had felt before and after the night of the senses. Before, the delights were in the meditations and sensible devotions. Now the sweetness of the contemplative experience is withdrawn, leaving him in total darkness and dryness. Although he still searches for God, he is unable to find Him in the ways he did formerly; hence, he feels abandoned by the Lord and searches even more desperately for His love which remains hidden, but nevertheless is ever-present. The soul cries out for God, unable to find Him anywhere but in a blind faith in which the God that they've known is now covered by a dense cloud that stills the night.

In order to know more about God as He is, one must strip away all preconceived notions he or she may have of the divine, for none of these thoughts or affections — however pious and sincere they might be — can fathom the essence of this pure and endless Love that is our Creator. It requires an "emptying" of self in order to allow God to manifest himself as He wants to be known. This concept has been known in mystical theology as "knowing by *unknowing*." The anonymous fourteenth-century mystic (author of the classic, *The Cloud of Unknowing*) described this experience as such:

> Be careful to empty your mind and heart of everything except God during the time of this work. Reject the knowledge and experience of everything less than God, treading it all down beneath the *cloud of forgetting*. And now also you must learn to

forget not only every creature and its deeds but yourself as well, along with whatever you may have accomplished in God's service. For a true lover not only cherishes his beloved more than himself, but in a certian sense he becomes oblivious of himself on account of the one he loves. This is what you must do. You must come to loathe and regret everything that occupies your mind except God, for everything is an obstacle between you and him. Long after you have forgotten every creature and its works, you will find that a naked knowing and feeling of your own being still remains between you and your God. And believe me, you will not be perfect in love until this, too, is destroyed. . . . (*The Cloud of Unknowing*, chpt. 43: transl. by William Johnston; Image Books, N.Y., 1973.)

The mystical author further stresses that we come to know and possess God and He us through love; knowledge in itself is not enough, because human knowledge operates through the natural intellect and physical senses — human channels that cannot come to know God's essence, purity or love. At best, we can only gain *concepts* of Him, not truths about Him as He really is. This author continues:

Why? Because nowhere, physically, is everywhere spiritually. Understand this clearly: your spiritual work is not located in any particular place. But when your mind consciously focuses on anything, you are there in that place spiritually, as certainly as your body is located in a definite place right now. Your senses and faculties will be frustrated for lack of something to dwell on and they will chide you for doing nothing. But never mind. Go on with this nothing, moved only by your love for God. Never give up but steadfastly persevere in this nothingness, consciously longing that you may always choose to possess God through love, whom no one can possess through knowledge. . . . (*The Cloud of Unknowing*, chpt. 68.)

One must desire to lose the knowledge and experience of self. This is essential in order to experience love as fully as possible in this life. One must realize that unless he loses himself he can never obtain that goal.

Thomas Merton (1915-68), respected author-theologian and mystic of our modern era, wrote a book in 1951 called *The Ascent to Truth*: a mystical exposition that relied heavily on the doctrine of St. John of the Cross, particularly the *Dark Night*. Merton talked about the void of obscurity one must enter in order to know something about God and His love — to know Him as He really is:

It is terrible to know God and not love Him. It is terrible to reach some speculative certainty concerning Him without any corresponding sense of the practical implications of that certitude.

If our conceptual knowledge of God is true and certain, then, by our very thoughts, we attain to Him, we touch Him. Yet He is untouchable and unattainable. But if that is true, how is it possible for us to think of Him without anguish?

Man was made to know truth, and his salvation consists in loving the highest Truth, which cannot be loved unless it is first known. But there is only one kind of knowledge that effectively confers upon man the light without which he cannot reach this supernatural end. This knowledge comes to him in the obscurity of faith. . . . (*The Ascent to Truth*, pp. 105,266: Harvest/HBJ, Orlando, Florida, 1981.)

This knowing of God through our unknowing was vividly described in the Sacred Scriptures through Moses' theophany experience on the mountain when he approached his God. Moses longed to speak to God — to know Him better — and this he did face-to-face, but in the darkness of the divine presence. This darkness, as we have seen, is like a cloud of unknowing: "Then Moses went up on the mountain, and the cloud covered the mountain. The glory of the Lord settled on Mount Sinai, and the cloud covered it six days; and on the seventh day he called to Moses out of the midst of the cloud. . . . And Moses entered the cloud, and went up on the mountain. And Moses was on the mountain forty days and forty nights" (Ex 24:15-16,18). Indeed, God told Moses that He would reveal himself only in the dark cloud of unknowing, as we see from the Book of Exodus: "I am coming to you in a thick cloud" (Ex 19:9). The word "thick" here could appropriately be called "dark," or "darkness." This is the same darkness that leads one to the divine presence in the contemplative experience. It is the same cloud that every mystic and stigmatist has entered in order to approach the divine; likewise he must pass through this mysterious cloud in order to become one with Him.

It is interesting to note the complete statement given by God to Moses in this Exodus experience: "I am coming to you in a thick cloud, that the people may hear when I speak with you, they may also believe you for ever" (Ex 19:9). This, of course, implies that the people will have faith in God himself ("also") through the cloud of unknowing, where paradoxically one comes to know and love his God. St. John of the Cross says almost exactly the same thing when he refers to this *pure faith* in the ascent to God:

Faith is dark night to the soul, and it is in this way that it gives it light; and the more (the soul) is darkened, the greater light comes to it. . . . (*The Collected Works*, "The Ascent of Mount Carmel," Book II, chpt. 3.)

Let us continue a bit further with this idea of a pure and dark faith leading one on to union with God. It is extremely important to understand this concept, for it becomes the basis for much of the experiences that the stigmatist must go through on his way up the mystical ladder. We will be encountering much of these dark experiences as we move further through this study.

Father George A. Maloney, S.J., describes the emptying of one's self as a type of spiritual poverty whereby a true inner silence becomes a loving surrender. In this state we have nothing to say to God:

Such inner silence is a relinquishing of all thoughts and images about God. It is an entering into a state of true knowledge of self and of God that is sheer gift of the Holy Spirit. This state is called "purity of heart" by Cassian and the other early Fathers and called "humility" in the total history of Christian spiritual writers. Evagrius writes of this inner stillness from all cares and all thoughts: 'You will not be able to pray purely if you are all involved with material affairs and agitated with unremitting concerns. For prayer is the rejection of concepts'. . . . (*Prayer of the Heart*, p. 55: Ave Maria Press, Notre Dame, IN, 1981.)

In short, this loving surrender and openness to God's presence is a *prayer of the heart*. The individual must retreat to a still silence and complete detachment from self and the world. This prayer of the heart requires a total emptying of one's self and a journey into darkness that removes the light of the intellect and makes room for the new Light, which is God. Such is a spirit of poverty, a nakedness of the soul, that allows God to reveal himself to the depths of our being. This self-emptying leaves the soul to suffer, for she weeps for God with tears of sorrow that are caused by this longing and sighing for her Creator: "We cry out for God to show himself in this night of the desert, and we gradually begin to understand our own absolute nothingness before God. Now we must dig roots and at long last opt for God alone! In deep, dark, stark faith we surrender to God as we cry out for his mercy, 'Lord, Jesus Christ, Son of God, have mercy on me, a sinner!' " (*Prayer of the Heart*, p. 75).

This is a true experience of the desert, the mystical *apophaticism* that the desert Fathers described some sixteen hundred years ago. This is the language of "knowing by unknowing," of finding life through dying to one's self (Mk 8:35). This apophatic knowledge of the desert Fathers was first described by Pseudo-Dionysius, the Athenian who was converted by St. Paul in his native Athens:

> God's presence in darkness breaks forth, even from the things that are beheld and from those that behold them, and plunges the true initiate into the darkness of unknowing wherein he renounces all the apprehensions of his understanding and is enwrapped in that which is wholly intangible and invisible, belonging wholly to him that is beyond all things and to none else (whether himself or another), and being through the passive stillness of all his reasoning powers united by his highest faculty to Him that is wholly unknowable, of whom thus by a rejection of all knowledge he possesses a knowledge that exceeds his understanding. . . . (Pseudo-Dionysius, *Mystical Theology*: from *The Soul Afire*, p. 49; ed. H.A. Reinhold, Image Books, N.Y., 1973.)

The transition from an active contemplation to a purely passive one is the beginning of an infused contemplative experience, whereby one is illuminated by God's direct activity upon the soul. It is then that we encounter divine knowledge through the love that is exchanged with Love. This is what Father Thomas Philippe, O.P., called *affective knowledge*, because its source is Love and its manifestation is charity acted out in the world. (For further information on this, see *The Fire of Contemplation*, Thomas Philippe, O.P.: Alba House, N.Y., 1981).

We end our discourse here on the cloud of unknowing in order to embark on the journey into the life of the stigmatist. Here we will see how this darkness plagues his soul with an intensity that makes him cry out for God's mercy. We will explore the various kinds of trials and sufferings that are an intimate part of most stigmatists' lives, including the moral sufferings that test each soul in order to purify him and prepare him for the living flame of Love which is God.

The moral sufferings that cause the spirit to struggle can be of every kind and of various intensity and duration. The evil one is also at the center of attack, ever-ready to tempt and to destroy. Let us look at some of the frightening ways in which the stigmatist Padre Pio had to encounter moral sufferings, as explained by Father Fernando of Riese Pio X, O.F.M. Cap. Father Fernando is a professor in the School of Theology of the Capuchin Friars in Padua, Italy; he was called to testify on Padre Pio's Cause for Beatification during its First Congress (San Giovanni Rotondo, May 1-6, 1972). Here is a list of the moral sufferings the good Padre endured during his perpetual dark night:

> frequent and violent temptations against faith, hope, and purity;
> fear of eternal damnation, of offending God, of his own poverty;
> anxiety and uncertainty if his desolation is God's work or a diabolical illusion, a grace or a punishment;
> fear of not being in God's grace, of abusing the sacraments, of being a burden on his brothers;
> desolation — the most desperate kind — when God hides himself from him;
> spiritual aridity, dark nights, profound blackness, darkness after darkness, the deepest obscurity;
> a continual state of war with the devil, who does not spare him attacks directed to the senses and to the external world from 1910 to 1916 and later directed to the superior part of his soul;
> the hell that hurled itself at him with fear, beatings, blows, and persecutions;
> sufferings during Mass, as he says, the "torment" of the Mass;
> thought and meditation on the Crucifix;
> the sufferings of a Confessor, in direct contact with evil;
> polemics, protests, and incredulity about the reality of his stigmata;
> disordered and noisy manifestations of the crowds and devotees who showed misplaced enthusiasm and fanaticism;
> the realization that he was a sign of contradiction and a cause of suffering to others;
> innacurate news and information which provoked incomprehension, double-meanings, and misunderstandings;
> medical examinations, visitors from the Holy Office, and from the Order;
> investigations and limitations, segregation, possibilities of transfer, and abuse of power;

being deprived of every priestly exercise;
prohibition of books and publications about him;
sufferings for the Casa Sollievo della Sofferenza;
sufferings proper to a celebrity. . . . (*The Mystery of the Cross in Padre Pio*, Fr. Fernando of Riese Pio X: *Acts of the First Congress of Studies on Padre Pio's Spirituality*, San Giovanni Rotondo, May 1-6, 1972. Used by permission from Fr. Joseph Martin, O.F.M. Cap., Our Lady of Grace Friary, San Giovanni Rotondo, Italy.)

There are several reasons why I have chosen to do such an extensive treatment of one stigmatist, Padre Pio, for material in this work: 1) he is a contemporary of our era (d. 1968); 2) he has become one of the most beloved souls of our century; 3) the vast amount of research and examinations that are available and well-documented; and 4) the amount of personal and intimate accounts of his spiritual life (particularly from the *Epistolario*, his spiritual letters to and from his directors, Padre Benedetto and Padre Agostino — well over one-thousand pages from this primary source alone!).

This list of sufferings is incredible, to say the least! Yet this inventory is certainly not complete, because Padre Pio zealously kept most of the trials of his soul a secret due to his profound sense of humility and simplicity of heart. Only out of obedience to his spiritual directors do we know what we do through these personal letters that have come down to us from Padre Benedetto and Padre Agostino.

We do know that this holy stigmatist friar also underwent great physical sufferings besides those caused by the stigmata. From his letters, one can readily observe some of the following: pains in the chest, in the back and in the left lung; gastric disturbances and coughs bad enough to break his chest; very bad headaches that became more and more unbearable; frequent high fevers; copious sweating; pulmonary infections and paralyzing rhuematism.

We also know that Padre Pio was a sickly young man, frequently suffering such high fevers that caused thermometers to break! His illness was so severe at one point that he was forced to leave the friary at San Giovanni Rotondo and return to his native Pietrelcina, near Benevento, Italy. Padre Pio's illness caused his early dismissal from the service, and many gave him up for dead. In his later years, his deteriorating eyesight gave way to a progressive blindness, and he was forced to use a wheelchair to move about.

These sufferings — both spiritual and physical — are common and familiar to those souls who journey through the dark and arid night. It's as though the Lord must prepare them for greater sufferings to come: for the mission of redemptive suffering that they are called to endure. This is an incomparable suffering whereby they become living crucifixes, voluntary martyrs who must sacrifice their blood from the wounds that pierce both their body and soul.

One thing remains certain for the stigmatist: in order for the wounds to manifest exteriorly on the body, they must first wound the soul, which is a deeper and more permanent wound: "Spiritual pains are reflected in the body because of that indivisible unity that the human being is. But more still because of the theological explanation that there is no visible stigmata that are not the result of a more painful interior stigmata of the soul — a stigmata which is more burning from love" (Malio Masci, *Padre Pio e gli altri stimmatizzati*, Rome, 1968: pp. 201-202).

Padre Pio himself tells us this:

> Don't believe that the body is not affected by such atrocious pains of the soul. No, the body takes part in them in a very surprising way that is not at all unknown to the sons of suffering. . . . (Padre Pio to Padre Agostino, May 9, 1915.)

Many other stigmatists have experienced a multitude of spiritual and physical sufferings throughout the course of their lives. One of the great trials they endure is persecution and suspicion from those that know them intimately. The Carmelite stigmatist, Mary of Jesus Crucified, was accused by her Superior of self-inflicted wounds that she said were caused with a knife, thus shaming and ridiculing her among her peers. She was exorcised, refused Holy Communion, and prevented from attending choir. Sister Mary had even been sent home to Pau, France, on a boat after a one-year stay in Mangalore, India.

Great aridity and dryness were trials that many stigmatists experienced as they hungered for a God who seemed to be so distant from them. Instead, they found themselves in a thick cloud of darkness. Sometimes these souls have great difficulty with prayer and meditation. Mother Louise Margaret Claret de la Touche (1868-1915), a victim soul who might have been a stigmatist, gives us these touching remarks:

> I have passed a Lent filled with so much exterior work and disturbance that I was thirsty for retreat and solitude; I shut myself up in my cell as much as possible during this Holy Week, seeking Jesus crucified and turning away from everything else. I suffered much, not so much corporally as interiorly. I had begun to suffer like that on Passion Sunday, and the suffering went on increasing up to Holy Saturday which I passed entirely on the Cross. A terrible weight seemed to crush my soul that day and I was in unspeakable anguish. It seemed to me that all the sins of the world came to me and enveloped me in a poisonous vapor which was suffocating me. However, I could not meditate either on the passion of Jesus, or on sin, or on anything. My adorable Master said to me in low tones: 'I will make you suffer, I will deprive you of support and help; you will feel yourself alone in difficulties and troubles; humiliation and suffering will press you on all sides, but I will be with you'. . . . (*The Love and Service of God*, Infinite Love, p. 127: TAN Books and Publishers, Inc. 1987.)

Like Jesus, all victims of divine love have been sujected to persecutions and isolation. They often are the source of contempt and ridicule to their neighbors, as well as to their families. Friends will frequently abandon them, and even their spiritual directors often misunderstand the mystery of their vocation.

St. Gemma Galgani (1878-1903), lay stigmatist from Lucca, Italy, was often misunderstood and ridiculed by others. She was a sensitive person who offered up her sufferings as reparation to God in union with Christ, who himself was the target of scorn and ridicule. Besides these sacrifices, Gemma was also rejected entrance into a religious order because of her failing health and weak disposition. She, too, offered this up for others to God in the spirit of reparation.

Henri Bremond, a famous mystical theologian, once made this claim: "The trial which is by far the greatest in the mystical life is that of being abandoned by a director."

The American stigmatist, Mary Rose Ferron (1902-36), suffered a variety of trials that caused her much pain and sorrow as a victim of God's love. As for her spiritual sufferings, we have this to observe:

> Doubts arose in her mind; she questioned her vocation; she wondered if she was not the victim of illusion; her sufferings were so intense, that she wondered for the remainder of her life, how she had been able to go through it all without losing her mind. . . .
> (*She Wears a Crown of Thorns*, Rev. O.A. Boyer, S.T.L, 1958.)

Of all the trials that these holy souls endure, one of the severest is being deprived of the Holy Eucharist. This can occur because of misunderstanding from one's pastor or director, or it may occur because of extreme illness that causes the victim to be bedridden and unable to attend Mass. Mary Rose Ferron was tried in this very way:

> The love of mystics for the Blessed Sacrament is general; but it varies in intensity, as in the case of 'Little Rose,' when in obedience to her confessor, they bear that privation of the Eucharist. But that does not mean that they do not hunger and thirst after it; they suffer all these things, but through their obedience, they obtain the grace to bear it.

> I have seen Rose forgetting her pain at the thought of receiving. When she expected to receive Holy Communion, and the priest did not come, her sufferings were beyond endurance, the very thought of it weakened her and made her gasp with pain. She was carried off by her unquenchable thirst for Jesus. No wonder she was perplexed when she knew she was too sick to receive. . . .
> (*She Wears a Crown of Thorns*, pp. 51-52.)

Another holy victim soul who was looked upon with suspicion by her pastor was the stigmatist St. Lydwine of Shiedam (1380-1433). She had been scorned and ridiculed, and later deprived of the Holy Eucharist, much to her sorrow and dismay. Like other victims, Lydwine literally craved the Body and Blood of the Savior Jesus and could not rest in peace unless she received Him on a daily basis. As we shall later see, this starving for the Body and Blood of our Lord is common among all the stigmatists.

Indeed, these trials of body and soul which the victim experiences during the dark night (and even after it) are so great that one can barely withstand them, were it not for a complete and loving resignation to the divine will. Marthe Robin (1902-1981), the lay stigmatist of Chateauneuf-de-Galaure, France, summed up her feelings in this way:

I feel that I am crushed, both physically and mentally. Everything causes me anguish and overwhelms me . . . I no longer know how to react. But so be it! But too much — too much about my poor self, and it seems it would be better for me to dwell more upon all that God is doing in my soul, and for my soul, every minute.

My soul is plunged into and, as it were, swept away toward that Jerusalem of Love, by the powerful allurements and inspirations of God himself, who now and then seems to desire to absorb me wholly into himself. I am afraid of this! . . . I am so alone, spiritually and mentally, and meanwhile I understand that I must abandon myself to Him without any reservations. . . . (*Marthe Robin: The Cross and the Joy*, Rev. Raymond Peyret: Alba House, N.Y., 1983.)

In spite of the tremendous trials and sufferings a victim soul must endure in the dark night, she willingly offers them up — even desires them — if she can help save sinners and live a life of sacrifice more intimately bound to our Lord. For this is her call: to share the Passion of Christ, to relive His sufferings, and to atone for others. It requires first and foremost a complete submission to the divine will, and this born out of compassion for others, as well as the deepest thirst for the divine love that is Christ's. Mother Louise Margaret Claret relied upon blind faith and love in the midst of these darkest of nights:

In the Christian soul which knows Christ and loves Him, suffering is a fuel for love; it serves marvelously to increase it. But at the moment when it makes itself felt in the soul, there is produced a sort of diminution of the loving forces. The light of love becomes veiled in a dark cloud, a cold feeling sets in; it seems to the soul, steeped in its suffering, that it no longer loves God as much as formerly. In prayer, at Holy Communion, every time that it approaches God, all that it is able to say to God is a resigned but sorrowful *fiat*. Love seems to be becoming extinct; it is not so, however; on the contrary, it is feeding itself on this suffering, and when the shadows which veil the light are dispelled, it will show itself to be stronger and more ardent. . . . (*The Love and Service of God, Infinite Love*, pp. 118-119.)

Note this loving attitude that is conveyed by Marthe Robin during her great trials:

Lord, take and sanctify all my words, all my actions, all my desires. Be for my soul its good and its all. To You I give and abandon it. I accept with love all that You send me: pain, sorrow, joy, consolation, dryness, shame, desertion, scorn, humiliation, work, suffering, trials, everything that comes to me from You, everything that You wish, O Jesus. . . . (*Marthe Robin: The Cross and the Joy*, p. 39.)

Perhaps the greatest of trials during the dark night are those brought

126

about by the evil spirit, who relentlessly pursues the victim through both physical and psychological attack. The stigmatist is a marked victim, and the devil does not fail to challenge his enemy with total hatred and pure vengeance, bent on destroying these pious souls through a never-ending battle of temptations and oppressions.

The spiritual warfare with this mystery of iniquity is profoundly real; it is a serious encounter with the enemy who spares no one who draws closer to God. He particularly loathes the stigmatist victim, whose very vocation serves to help destroy his kingdom through the victory of the Cross. Let us try to better understand this opposing spirit who never tires of attacking God's own. We now explore the spiritual warfare that every stigmatist is destined to encounter.

The Spiritual Warfare

For every reality in the universe, there has always been an opposing reality that seeks to disrupt the beauty and order of nature. In the beginning, we see how God created out of disorder and chaos a goodness and perfection in this universe He had made:

> In the beginning God created the heavens and the earth. The earth was without form and void, and darkness was upon the face of the deep; and the spirit of God was moving over the face of the waters. . . (Gn 1:1-2).

After all was completed, God found it to be "very good" (Gn 1:31).

In the spiritual world, God created pure angelic beings as part of the cosmic order. They were commissioned to praise and adore their Creator (Ps 89:6; 103:20; 148:2) and to assist the human creature through prayer (Tb 12:12), delivering messages (Mt 2:13-22; Lk 1:26-33; 2:8-14) and providing protection (Ps 91:11). In time, some of these beautiful creatures came to oppose God's natural and perfect order of creation. Satan and his cohorts were eventually banished from their exalted state, as the Scriptures have told us:

> Now war arose in heaven, Michael and his angels fighting against the dragon; and the dragon and his angels fought, but they were defeated and there was no longer any place for them in heaven. And the great dragon was thrown down, that ancient serpent, who is called the Devil or Satan, the deceiver of the whole world, he was thrown down to earth, and his angels were thrown down with him. . . (Rv 12:7-9).

We know from God's Word that the demons were destined for the fires of hell (Mt 25:41) and concurrently hold temporary dominion over the world in which we live (1 Jn 5:19). Why this remains so is a mystery of our Faith, but it nevertheless is with us until the consummation of the world through the coming of our Lord.

Though many question the reality of these spirits of darkness (especially liberal theologians who see all evil as strictly a product of human designs), the fact is that the Church has continuously taught that they do indeed exist, from the Apostolic era to our own time. As recently in Church history as 1972, Pope Paul VI spoke about this reality clearly and distinctly:

> Evil is not merely a lack of something, but an effective agent, a living spiritual being, perverted and perverting, a terrible reality, mysterious and frightening. . . . We know that this dark and disturbing spirit really exists and that he still acts with treacherous cunning; he is the secret enemy that sows errors and misfortunes in human history. . . . It is not a question of one devil but of many. . . This question of the devil and the influence he can exert on individual persons as well as on communities, whole societies, and events is a very important chapter of Catholic doctrine. . . . (*General Audience*, November 15, 1972.)

We will spend a great deal more time on this study of the world of darkness because of the grim reality it presents to the stigmatist, who must face the enemy throughout his earthly life. As we move through this discourse, it will become very apparent that the evil one attacks the stigmatist in a most profound and all-encompassing manner. The stigmatist is called to fight the forces of evil and to free souls from his domain; naturally, he is going to be a primary target that the devil seeks to destroy.

Before we turn to the devil and his role in the life of the stigmatist, let us take a look at what the Church has traditionally taught about the reality of these spirits of darkness, lest we reserve any doubt about their existence whatsoever. Scripture has given us ample evidence of the reality of these spirits of darkness, as we can readily see from the references given below. Here are some of the many descriptive names referring to the devil in both the Old and New Testaments:

Abaddon (Rv 9:11).
Accuser of our brothers (Rv 12:10).
Adversary (1 Tim 5:14; 1Pt 5:8).
Angel of light (2 Cor 11:14).
Angel of the bottomless pit (Rv 9:11).
Apollyon (Greek) (Rv 9:11).
Beelzebub (Mt 10:25; 12:27; Mk 3:22; Lk 11:15,18-19).
Belial (Jgs 19:22; 20:13; 25:17,25)
Dragon (Rv 12:4,7,13.16,17; 13:2,4; 16:13; 20:2).
Evil one (Mt 6:13; 13:19; Jn 17:15; 1 Jn 2:13; 5:18).
God of this world (2 Cor 4:4).
Huge dragon (Rv 12:3,9).
Liar (Jn 8:44).
Lying spirit (1 Kgs 22:22,23).
Master of the house (Mt 10:25).
Morning star (Is 14:12).
Murderer (Jn 8:44).
Old serpent (Rv 12:9; 20:2).
Prince of the demons (Mt 9:34; Mk 3:22).
Prince of the power of the air (Eph 2:2).
Prince of this world (Jn 12:31; 16:11).
Serpent (Gn 3:1,2,4,13,14; 2 Cor 11:3; Rv 12:14-15).
Son of the dawn (Is 14:12).

Tempter (Mt 4:3; 1 Thes 3:5).
Thief (Jn 10:10).
Unclean spirit (Mt 12:43; Mk 3:30; Lk 9:42).

All of the Biblical tradition overwhelmingly supports the existence of an evil force that is preternatural and an enemy to all of mankind. Imagine the special hatred these spirits of darkness unleash against God's chosen victims!

What characteristics do the demons have that make them so feared and detested by the saints and mystics of all ages? Here is a brief list that shows the evil tendencies that are a part of the very essence of the devil and his cohorts:

Accuser (Rv 12:10).
Anger (Mk 9:20,26; Acts 19:16).
Antagonistic (Mt 8:29; Mk 1:24; Acts 19:16; Rv 2:10).
Beguiler (Gn 3:13).
Betrayer (Jn 13:2).
Blasphemer (Rv 2:9).
Crazy (Mt 17:15).
Deceitful (Mt 13:19; Lk 8:12; Jn 10:10; 1 Tim 4:1; 2 Tim 3:13; 1 Jn 4:1; Rv 12:9; 13:14; 20:3,8).
Dishonest (Jn 10:10).
Hypocritical (1 Tim 4:2).
Jealous (Nm 5:14,30).
Liar (1 Kgs 22:22-23; Mt 13:22; Jn 8:44; Acts 5:3; 2 Thes 2:9; 1 Tim 4:2).
Loud (Mk 1:26).
Lustful (Jn 8:44).
Mean (Mt 8:29).
Murderer (Jn 8:44).
Revengeful (1Pt 5:8).
Seducer (1 Tim 4:1; 2 Tim 3:13).
Tempter (Mt 4:1,3; Lk 11:16; 4:2,13; 1 Cor 7:5; 1 Tim 4:1).
Troublesome (Mt 13:39).
Vain (Ez 28:17).
Vexed (Mt 15:22; 17:15; Lk 6:18; Acts 5:16).
Violent (Mt 17:15; Mk 1:26; 9:20,26; Acts 8:7; 19:16; 1 Pt 5:8).
Wicked (Mt 12:45; Lk 11:26).

Inspite of the total hatred and negative quality that is the evil spirit, he believes in God (Jas 2:19) and fears the fires of hell (Mt 8:29-31; Lk 8:31). We must not sell the powers of darkness short, however; they are much more knowledgeable than we are (Mt 8:29; Mk 1:24; Lk 4:41; Acts 19:15). Is it any wonder that we should shudder at the thought of their presence in our midst? And our fear is nothing compared to God's chosen victims, who invite the onslaughts of the spirits of darkness by virtue of their voluntary offering to atone for the sins of others.

Where else do we have support for the belief in these diabolical spirits? All of the great saints and theologians from the early days of the Church have recognized the work of the devil. We will explore several of the sources that acknowledged this reality through the words they have spoken:

Demons are everywhere, and the cursing of them is universal. . . . (Tertullian, *The Testimony of the Christian Soul* (third
century).)

The spirit of evil was from the beginning bent upon man's destruction. The demons, therefore, inflict upon men's bodies diseases and other bitter misfortunes, and upon the soul sudden and
extraordinary outbursts of violence. . . . (Tertullian, *Apology*,
The Fathers of the Church, Volume 10, p. 69.)

Regarding the devil and his angels, and the opposing influences,
the teaching of the Church has laid down that these things exist
indeed; but what they are, or how they exist, it has not explained
with sufficient clearness. . . . (Origen, *De Principiis*, Proem. 6
(third century).)

What else is waged daily in the world but a battle against the
devil, but a struggle with continual onsets against his darts and
weapons. . . . (Cyprian, *Mortality*, The Fathers of the Church,
Volume 36, p. 202.)

The devil is an apostate angel who seduces and withdraws man's
mind unto transgression of God's commandments, and gradually
blinds the hearts of such as make it their business to serve him,
to the forgetting of the true God, and the worshiping of Satan
himself as God. . . . (Irenaeus, *Against Heresies*, Library of Fathers, Oxford: James Parker, 1872, p. 506.)

Who is a worse enemy to the saints than the devil? Who is more
contentious toward them, more wrathful, jealous, and quar-
relsome?. . . . (St. Augustine, *City of God*, Book IV,chpt. 3.)

To the devil (who is the fallen Lucifer, now Satan) belong exclusively the plan and campaign of the demons' assaults upon
mankind. . . . (St. Thomas Aquinas, *Summa Theologica*, quest.
114, no. 2.)

In addition to these ancient sources, we know that the existence of
these spirits of darkness has been presupposed by the provincial Council of
Constantinople (A.D. 543) and by *The Decree on Original Sin* established by
the Council of Trent (A.D. 1546).

We will now turn briefly to statements from the modern era that
continue to support the ancient Church tradition that recognizes the
terrible forces of evil that are real and aggressive in the world in which we
live.

Father Delaporte of the Society of Mercy once claimed that our belief
in the evil one is rooted in the Scriptures themselves, and therefore, out of
obedience to divine faith, must be believed:

The belief of mankind is based on the Divine Word itself. For our
sacred books speak often of the devil, and St. John formally af-

firms not only that he exists, and that sinners are under his influence, but also that 'the Son of God appeared, that He might destroy the works of the devil' (1 Jn 3:8). . . . (*The Devil: Does He Exist and What Does He Do?*, p. 16: Original publication, 1871; reprint by TAN Books and Publishers, Inc., 1982.)

It is terribly important to establish without any doubt the position that the Church takes on the reality of this opposing force which seeks to destroy all mankind. For if we do not come to believe in the works of the spirits of darkness, then we will likewise have difficulty understanding much of the opposition the stigmatist undergoes throughout the course of his or her life. It is, therefore, imperative that we take seriously these warnings that the Church has given us. We will see in a while how real these spirits are as they wreak havoc in the lives of God's chosen victims, trying them both physically and spiritually in a never-ending onslaught that can make anyone shudder with fear.

We now turn to the Magisterium of the Church for further counsel on the existence of evil spirits:

It is the teaching of the Gospel and in the heart of the faith as lived that the existence of the world of demons is revealed as a dogma. . . . (S.C.D.W., *Les formes multiples de la superstition*, June 26, 1975.)

The Church teaches here that it is not merely a personal conviction to believe in the devil or his cohorts; in fact, it is an obligation on the part of the faithful, for it is a divinely revealed *dogma* of the Catholic Church.

We continue with more words from the Sacred Congregation for Divine Worship:

The Roman Missal of 1970 still bears witness to the Church's convictions regarding the activity of demons. . . . (S.C.D.W., *Les formes*, June 26, 1975.)

The Second Vatican Council did not fail to warn us against the activity of Satan and the demons. . . . (S.C.D.W., *Les formes*, June 26, 1975.)

The position of the Catholic Church on demons is clear and firm. The existence of Satan and the demons has indeed never been the object of an explicit affirmation by the magisterium, but this was because the question was never put in those terms. Heretics and faithful alike, on the basis of Scripture, were in agreement in the existence and chief misdeeds of Satan and his demons. . . . (S.C.D.W., *Les formes*, June 26, 1975.)

The belief that the devil is a creature and that he turned away from God by a free act had thus long been explicit elements in the faith of the Church. At the Fourth Lateran Council, therefore, these statements had simply to be introduced into the conciliar profession of faith; there was no need to document

them, because they represented beliefs which evidently were
held by the Church. . . . (S.C.D.W, *Les formes*, June 26, 1975.)

The Council of Trent, summing up the teaching of St. Paul,
asserted that sinful man is under the power of the devil and of
death. . . . (S.C.D.W., *Les formes*, June 26, 1975.)

When the Council of Florence spoke of the redemption, it
portrayed it in biblical terms as a liberation from the domination
of Satan. . . . (S.C.D.W., *Les formes*, June 26, 1975.)

We have here sufficient evidence that the Church believes firmly and
without reservation the reality and power of the spirits of darkness. Let it
serve as a chilling reminder to all the theologians who deny their existence,
lest they fall away from the official teachings of Holy Mother Church and
fall victim to the works of the evil spirit, who loves to teach distortions of
the truth (see Jn 8:44).

Perhaps it is fitting that we conclude this extensive treatment on the
reality of evil with a prayer that Pope Leo XIII (1878-1903) composed and
formerly said after low Mass in Catholic churches:

Saint Michael, the Archangel, defend us in battle; be our defense
against the wickedness and snares of the devil. May God rebuke
him, we humbly pray; and do thou, O Prince of the heavenly
host, by the power of God, thrust into Hell Satan and the other
evil spirits who prowl about the world for the ruin of souls. Amen.
(Pope Leo XIII, *Prayer to St. Michael the Archangel*.)

We have already discussed how the devil causes us to sin in an earlier
chapter. As a reminder of this, let us look at the words of St. Thomas
Aquinas:

In one sense the devil is the cause of every human sin, for he
induced the first man to commit the sin that has infected human
nature with the tendency to sin. . . . (*Summa Theologica*, Part
II, no. 80.)

Now we shall turn to the methods and ways that the evil spirit attacks
his victims. Then we will examine these types of assaults that are found in
the lives of the stigmatists.

Catherine Lassagne once described the method of attack as involving
the following:

There are two kinds of diabolical operations: those that are
ordinary and others of an extraordinary nature.
The devil acts on all men by tempting them; no one can escape
those attacks; these are his *ordinary operations*.
In other very much rarer cases, the devils reveal their presence
by troublesome vexations, which are more terrifying than
painful; they cause a great noise, they move, transport, knock
over and at times smash certain objects; this is what is called
infestation. Infestation is first among extraordinary diabolical

operations. Only in some very rare occasions does one become a victim of *external obsession*, during which the devil attacks, beats, and hurts the person obsessed. In ever rarer cases, *possession* can occur, whereby Satan seizes upon the human organism and makes use of its members, its tongue, in fact, of the whole body, which he moves according as he pleases. . . . (*Process de l' Ordinaire*, p. 481.)

Why are the stigmatists victims of Satan's attacks? Why aren't evildoers more prone to severe trials and sufferings that the evil spirit can give? St. John Vianney (the Curé of Ars) once described it as such:

The devil only tempts those souls that wish to abandon sin and those that are in the state of grace. The others belong to him: he has no need to tempt them. . . . (St. John Vianney, 1786-1859.)

For those living a life of sin, there is no threat to the devil because they will seldom win souls for God or challenge his earthly kingdom. Since they are already in his clutches, the evil spirit prefers to remain hidden, lest they find out and try to amend their ways. Indeed, we ought to worry if we are never tempted by the evil one, as the Curé of Ars continues his point:

The greatest of all evils is not to be tempted because there are then grounds for believing that the devil looks upon us as his property. . . .

Why are the holiest of souls tempted so severely? Is there any reason why they would not be relieved of their opposition at some point in their spiritual journey? One reason is that the devil is most furious toward those who work against his world of sin, oppression and deception; another reason is that the pious soul needs these trials in order to purify his soul, to humble himself, and to abandon himself unconditionally in the arms of the divine Savior. With the stigmatist in particular, nothing provokes the fury of Satan more than this victim soul who sacrifices his life in order to free others from the bondage of sin. And no one more than the stigmatist is expected to surrender unconditionally to the divine will, for much has been given him, and much will be expected of him.

Let us examine what some of the saints of the Church have said about temptation, as it is caused by the devil and allowed by God for the trial and purification of the pious soul:

God permits violent assaults and strong temptations only in souls whom He desires to raise up to His own pure and surpassing love. . . . (St. Francis de Sales, *The Devout Life*, Part IV.)

Fire tries iron, and temptation tries a just man. . . . (Thomas á Kempis, *The Imitation of Christ*, I, 13, 15th century.)

The devil is only permitted to tempt thee as much as is profitable for thy exercise and trial, and in order that thou, who didst not know thyself, mayest find out what thou art. . . . (St. Augustine, 354-430.)

The tempter, ever on the watch, wages war most violently against those whom he sees most careful to avoid sin. . . . (St. Leo the Great [d. 461].)

What can the devil succeed in doing to the soul who is on the road to perfection but still feels his temptations?

According to St. John Climatus (d. 649), "The devil flatters that he may deceive us; he charms that he may injure us; he allures that he may slay us." St. Ambrose tells us that we can be sure of our safety with the devil if we don't give in to his temptations: "The devil's snare does not catch you, unless you are first caught by the devil's bait" (*De Agone Christiano*, I,I, fourth century).

The saints of the Church have given us valuable insights in how to cope with the diabolical temptations in our lives. Let us turn to these pearls of wisdom for the help and guidance they give:

Turn your heart gently toward Jesus Christ crucified and lovingly kiss his sacred feet. This is so terrifying to the evil spirit that as soon as he sees that his temptations urge us on to God's love he ceases to tempt us. . . . (St. Francis de Sales, *The Devout Life*, Part IV.)

Again we hear words of wisdom from this most holy saint and Doctor of the Church:

This is the best way to overcome the enemy in small as well as in great temptations: the love of God contains within itself every perfection of every virtue and more excellently than the virtues themselves; it is also the sovereign antidote against vice of every kind. . . . (*The Devout Life*, Part IV.)

Prayer is particularly powerful against the snares and wiles of the enemy, as St. Bernard (1090-1153) so aptly states:

However great the temptation, if we knew how to use the weapon of prayer well, we shall come off conquerors at last; for prayer is more powerful than all the devils. . . .

Why, then, do some of our prayers go unanswered? What can we do when this is the case? Listen to the voice of the Doctor of the Church, St. Alphonsus Liguori (1696-1787):

It often happens that we pray God to deliver us from some dangerous temptation, and yet God does not hear us but permits the temptation to continue troubling us. In such a case, let us understand that God permits even this for our greater good. When a soul in temptation recommends itself to God, and by His aid resists, O how it then advances in perfection. . . .

We must remain firm in the faith despite our temptations, for "while the devil is able to tempt, he cannot extort our consent" (S.C.D.W., *Les formes*, June 26, 1975). We need not worry that we cannot bear these diabolical onslaughts, for St. Thomas Aquinas reminds us of the following: "God gives to men all requisite aid to repulse the assaults of demons, and to advance in grace and merit by resisting temptation" (*Summa Theologica*, Part I, no. 1).

We should not be surprised that our lives are filled with temptations from the devil, the world and the flesh. The Scriptures gave us plenty of examples to warn us about the realities of temptation, and how each soul who journeys toward perfection must encounter these trials on the way to the summit.

Temptation was the first means used by Satan to try to discourage Jesus from His obedience to the Father (Lk 4:1-13). He tempted Jesus to use His power to take care of himself (v. 3), to gain His end through false worship (v. 6-7), and to put God's care for Jesus to the test (v. 9-10). These we have discussed in greater detail in an earlier chapter.

Jesus warned His disciples that they would undergo a period of severe temptation at the hands of the devil (Lk 22:31). Ephesians 6:16 encourages Christians to defend themselves against "the flaming darts of the evil one"; in the Gospel of Luke, Christians are cautioned to keep alert and to pray in order to resist temptation (see Lk 22:46). Clearly, we are told to expect these things in the spiritual life, for they are the very things that our Lord himself had to endure for the sake of the kingdom. Because the stigmatist is expected to follow the life of Jesus most intimately, he in particular has had to fight the good fight and resist the continuous attacks from the darts of the evil enemy. It is here that we turn to examine the many temptations and oppressive attacks that these victims had to endure from the enemy throughout their earthly lives.

One of the ways the evil spirit infiltrates the life of the soul is through the psychological attacks he brings in the form of threats and harassments. This tactic is used to break down the will of the victim in order to oppress him and eventually to conquer him. Let's see how this verbal attack was used against many of the stigmatists. These verbal threats were very real to them, and often times extremely frightening:

> Excommunication, a thousand excommunications if you continue to write to your spiritual director! Already you are burning in Hell. Be converted, unhappy one! Be converted, miserable wretch! It is the affection I have for you that makes me speak in this way. I come now from your Christ who told me to take you, because he can no longer save you. He was distressed by your writings. . . . (*Alexandrina da Costa: The Agony and the Glory*; Francis Johnston, TAN Books and Publishers, Inc., 1979.)

Alexandrina was a lay person whose weekly Passion ecstasies have become well-known all over the world. Her Cause for Beatification is currently underway. She has never been labeled a stigmatist, but she certainly shared — at least interiorly — in the Passion and Cross of our Lord. It is in this respect that I include her in the list of stigmatists that the Church honors.

Here we can see that the evil one uses the state of her spiritual condition against her, especially in the eyes of her director; of course, her state is really quite pleasing to the Lord, but the devil makes her feel that

135

perhaps she is not living in a state of grace. This tactic has been used quite frequently by the devil against God's chosen ones in order to make them depressed and overscrupulous.

Alexandrina was tormented by these verbal assaults for many years. Here is another example of the diabolical attack at work:

> If it were not for that imposter which you hold in your hand, I would put a foot on your neck. I would reduce your body to a pulp. But you will see that He will do this to you himself. You will then wish to come to me, but I will not accept you. Thank that object of superstition. . . I don't fear it anymore, but I hate it!

The object that the enemy hates and refers to as an "imposter" is the holy crucifix she continually held in her hand for protection and strength. Many of the stigmatists held onto their crucifixes, especially during the course of their prayer. Some even kept them in their fingers throughout the night while sleeping.

The "He" that is referred to in the above verbal attack is none other than Jesus himself. The devil loves to make us think that Christ is not pleased with our spiritual state, or even worse, that He does not need or love us.

In one more excerpt from the enemy's verbal threats to Alexandrina, we hear the following:

> One moonlit night after prayers I felt a need to sleep, when suddenly into my room came a great darkness. . . I perceived a black shadow and saw it jump towards me, and it said to me, 'I come on behalf of your Christ to carry you to Hell, bed and all.' I kissed the crucifix and the voice continued, 'You kiss that wicked thing!' He then ordered me to do things that I cannot speak of. . . It was only when I took holy water that I was left in peace. . . .

Alexandrina continued:

> Every now and then I see a rapid light. Twice I have seen two very big eyes, wide open, staring at me, but they disappeared quickly. On Sunday, I heard a very sweet voice saying, 'My daughter, I come to tell you not to write anything of what you see: your sight is deceiving you. Don't you feel how weak you are? You displease me with this; it is your Jesus who speaks to you, not Satan.' I was suspicious and began to kiss the crucifix. The voice became enraged and thundered, 'If you continue to write I will destroy your body. Do you think I cannot do this?'. . . .
> (Exchange between Alexandrina and the devil, 1934.)

What is extremely frightening is the way the enemy can appear as an angel of light (2 Cor 11:14), deceiving even the holiest of souls. Here he appears with a reassuring voice, and even claims to come on behalf of the directions of the Lord himself! Equally terrifying is the way the evil spirit threatens to destroy the victim if she continues to follow the path of Christ. This is a test of one's faith that is perhaps unequaled in the normal state of life, and one many a stigmatist has had to undergo in order to remain firm in the faith. Some (including Alexandrina and Padre Pio) have been physically beaten by the evil spirit, with cuts, bruises, and even broken bones to show for their confrontation with the diabolical attacks. There's no doubt about it: the evil one and his threats are to be taken seriously; one can be certain that he is very capable of fulfilling these verbal threats. Satan is no one to take lightly, for in case our memory fails us, he is one of the most powerful angels that God created. He has been banished from his heavenly state, but he nevertheless retains his strength and power (being that the angelic essence does not change since their creation, but remains permanently fixed). This is an alarming but sobering truth for those who snear at his ways or attempt to challenge him!

Sister Josefa Menendez (1890-1923), stigmatist and Coadjutrix Sister of the Society of the Sacred Heart of Jesus, was the victim of the most severe diabolical attacks that a person can be subjected to. Listen to her description of the threatening and sarcastic voice of the evil one:

> You will be one of us . . . we shall tire you out . . . we shall overcome you. . .
>
> Don't let go of her; be on your guard . . . plague her in any way you can . . . so she must not escape . . . induce her to despair!. . .
>
> O! power and omnipotence of that God . . . He is stronger than I. There is only one left and she shall not escape . . . . (Josefa Menendez, *The Way of Divine Love*; Sunday, April 2, 1922: TAN Books and Publishers, Inc., 1981 reprint.)

These are the haunting words from the devil to Sister Josefa during her agonizing trial with the spirits of darkness. Notice how the evil one works with a multitude of helpers who are commissioned to carry out the destructive will of Satan. This is reminiscent of the Gospel story where the evil spirits admit to being many, while they work together in an attempt to destroy God's kingdom: "What have you to do with *us*, Son of God? Have you come here to torment *us* before the time?" (Mt 8:29). Or again: "What have you to do with *us*, Jesus of Nazareth? Have you come to destroy *us*?" (Lk 4:34). We also know from Sacred Scripture that many different demons can enter a man's body and possess his spirit: "And as he stepped out on land, there met him a man from the city who had demons" (Lk 8:27). The message is clear: Satan operates not alone, but with a body of demons who attack their targets ruthlessly and relentlessly. Josefa was often subject to such attacks in the course of her saintly life.

Many of the Church's stigmatists have been extraordinarily gifted with the discernment of spirits, and the ability to expel the demons from a particular person or place. Due to their personal holiness and profound piety, the stigmatist is often successful in commanding the evil spirit to leave with a simple word or two; sometimes his mere presence incites the fear of these enemies, who recognize in these saintly souls the image of Jesus Christ.

The devil is so hateful towards these victims that they are among the top enemies on his list to destroy. Many a stigmatist has been the target of not only verbal and psychological attacks, but physical ones as well. Padre

Pio had frequent bouts with the devil, sometimes lasting entire nights. The enemy would often pull him out of bed and beat him severely, leaving him with cuts and bruises over his entire body. Father Joseph Martin, O.F.M. Cap. (Padre's close companion the last three years of his life) explained to me that one night the devil beat him so severely that he fell on the floor of his cell and cut his head severely. The next morning, when Father Martin came to his aid and asked what had happened, Padre had told him the story. Furthermore, a blood-stained pillow (still seen to this day in his cell at Our Lady of Grace Friary) had been found underneath the Padre's head. When asked where it came from, he claimed that the Blessed Virgin Mary had placed it under his head during the night, while she consoled and comforted him.

Padre Pio was beaten many other times, as his personal testimony will reveal:

The ogre (devil) won't admit defeat. He has appeared in almost every form. For the past few days he has paid me visits along with some of his satellites armed with clubs and iron weapons and, what is worse, in their own form as devils. I cannot tell you how many times he has thrown me out of bed, and dragged me around the room. But never mind! Jesus, our dear Mother, my little Angel, St. Joseph and our father St. Francis are almost always with me. . . . (*Epistolario*: Letter to Padre Agostino, Jan. 18, 1912.)

Other letters from the Padre to his spiritual directors reveal diabolical assaults that are just as frightening:

The devil does not cease to appear to me in his horrible forms and to beat me in the most terrible manner. . . . (Letter to Padre Agostino, March 21, 1912.)

I had a very bad time the night before last; from about ten o'clock, when I was in bed, until five o'clock in the morning, that *wretch* did nothing but beat me continually. At five in the morning, when that *wretch* left me, my whole body became so cold that I trembled from head to foot like a reed exposed to a violent wind. This lasted for a couple of hours. I spat blood. . . . (Letter to Padre Agostino, June 28, 1912.)

Listen to what I had to endure a few evenings ago from those impure apostates. The night was already well advanced when they began their attack with a devilish din, and although I saw nothing in the beginning, I understood who was making the strange noise. Instead of being frightened, I got ready to fight them with a scornful smile on my lips. Then they appeared to me in the most abominable forms and to make me act dishonorably they began to present themselves to me all dressed up, but, thank heaven, I scolded them soundly and treated them as they deserve. Then, when they saw all their efforts going up in smoke, they hurled themselves on me, threw me to the ground and proceeded to beat me very severely, throwing pillows, books and chairs around the room, with desperate shrieks and most obscene language. . . . (Letter to Padre Agostino, Jan. 18, 1913.)

> Jesus never stops loving me in spite of all my shortcomings, for he allows those ugly-faced creatures to afflict me incessantly. For the past twenty-two days Jesus has allowed them to vent their anger on me continually. My body, dear Father, is bruised all over, from all the blows it has received at the hands of our enemies. More than once they even went so far as to pull off my nightshirt and beat me in that state. . . . (Letter to Padre Agostino, Feb. 13, 1913.)

> They flung themselves upon me like so many hungry tigers, cursing me and threatening to make me pay for it. My dear Father, they kept their word! From that day onward they have beaten me every day. . . . (Letter to Padre Agostino, Feb. 1, 1913.)

> Satan with his malignant wiles never tires of waging war on me and attacking my little citadel, besieging it on all sides. In a word, Satan is for me like a powerful foe who, when he resolves to capture a fortress is not content to attack one wall or one rampant, but surrounds it entirely, attacks and torments it on every side. . . . (Letter to Padre Benedetto, Aug. 4, 1917.)

As we have seen, Satan is a frightening adversary of all who advance in the spiritual life, but especially so to those victims who are called to atone for the sins of others . . . in particular, the stigmatist, whose very vocation threatens to destroy the chains that the evil one holds over his foes. No wonder he seeks all-out war with these holy saints!

The evil one is very powerful and should be taken seriously, as the good Padre had found through his many years of torment and struggle. Let us listen to the words of Padre Pio, who tells us just how powerful a foe we have in the devil:

> We must have no illusions about the enemy who is exceedingly strong, if we do not intend to surrender. In the light infused by God the soul understands the great danger to which it is exposed if it is not continually on its guard. . . Letter to Padre Agostino, May 9, 1915.

Other souls who bore the Sacred Wounds of our Lord have experienced similar assaults and beatings from the devil. Stigmatist Anne Catherine Emmerich (1774-1824) knew all too well the attacks that spring forth from the foe. She once received blows to the face from the devil who appeared to her in the form of a great, black dog. Another time, the evil one tried to hurl her down a ladder. She even experienced icy-cold hands grabbing at her feet, with the intention of throwing her to the ground.

Marthe Robin (1902-81), the lay stigmatist from the heartland of France, had the devil so enraged over her joining the Third Order of St. Francis that he had struck her a blow to the face, breaking two of her teeth.

The evil spirit tormented the stigmatist Josefa Menendez (1890-1923) with showers of blows that fell from invisible fists day and night, during her postulancy and especially during her time of prayer. She even experienced times when he snatched her away from the chapel! If that wasn't enough, the enemy tried to burn her to death by catching her clothes on fire. Josefa survived, but was severely burned in this attack.

Stigmatist Pudentienne Zagnoni, the seventeenth-century lay Franciscan, allegedly was dragged by the hair and tormented with blows from Satan.

It is obvious from these horrifying examples that the devil will not refrain from physical attacks upon his victims, especially if the psychological and spiritual attacks fail to stop the soul's advancement in the ways of perfection. More particularly, the evil spirit abhors those who are in any way associated with voluntary offerings to make amends for sinners. For this is his territory, and one who dares to trespass in it could encounter a full-scaled diabolical attack.

Yet this is not to suggest that one should not voluntarily offer his sufferings for the salvation of sinners! Each one of the stigmatists mentioned above had overcome the snares of the foe because of their unrelenting devotion to Christ and their deep commitment to the Faith that was the cornerstone of their lives. Although the enemy was constantly badgering them, Christ was equally present with the grace necessary to sustain these assaults for those who hold out to the end.

We are comforted with the words from the Psalmist, who reassures the faithful with these moving words:

> He who dwells in the shelter of the Most High,
> who abides in the shadow of the Almighty,
> Will say to the Lord, "My refuge and my fortress;
> my God, in whom I trust."
> For he will deliver you from the snare of the fowler, and from the deadly pestilence;
> He will cover you with his pinions, and under his wings you will find refuge;
> his faithfulness is a shield and buckler.
> You will not fear the terror of the night,
> nor the arrow that flies by day,
> nor the pestilence that stalks in darkness,
> nor the destruction that wastes at noon day.
> A thousand may fall at your side, ten thousand at your right hand; but it will not come near you.
> You will only look with your eyes and see the recompense of the wicked.
> Because you have made the Lord your refuge,
> the Most High your habitation,
> no evil shall befall you, no scourge come near your tent.
> For he will give his angels charge of you to guard you in all your ways.
> On their hands they will bear you up,
> lest you dash your foot against a stone.
> You will tread on the lion and the adder,
> the young lion and the serpent you will trample under foot. . .
> (Ps 91:1-13).

As we have seen, evil is a serious reality that all Christians must face, some more severely than others. Some who do not appear to be tormented by the devil are perhaps in his clutches already, and therefore do not need to be attacked by these spirits of darkness. Indeed, when one senses that the forces of evil are quiet and do not bother him, then he must be suspicious of his own level of spirituality and faith life. It is only those who strive for the greatest perfection (and who achieve a certain level of sanctity) that the enemy pursues with an onslaught of temptation and oppression. Yet we must not fear the dark of night, nor the arrows that fly by day, as the Psalmist tells us (Ps 91:5). Rather, we must seek refuge in the bosom of Christ, who promised to not let us be tempted beyond our strength. Faith in the victory of the Cross is the armor that will assure us protection against the forces of the world of darkness.

Illumination

Like all mystics on the road toward spiritual perfection, the stigmatist must pass through three stages that are usually progressive but sometimes overlapping: the first being the *purgative way*; the second, the *way of illumination*; and finally, the *unitive way*. Since we have covered the ways of purgation, let us now turn to the degree known as illumination (also called the *way of proficients*), whereby the soul begins to know Christ more intimately through the infused gifts of the Holy Spirit. This light is the very light of Christ, who told His closest followers: "I am the light of the world; he who follows me shall not walk in darkness, but will have the light of life" (Jn 8:12).

St. John of the Cross (1542-91) gave us these descriptions of the illuminative way that all souls who pursue the way of perfection must experience:

> Since faith is a dark night, it illumines the soul that is in darkness. The darkness is demanded on this road if the soul is to receive light. . . . (*Collected Works*, "The Ascent of Mount Carmel," Book II, chpt. 3.)

It's as though one cannot understand or appreciate the light unless he has first known the darkness; in order to know the good, one must have known the bad, or evil. For as St. John says, "The intellect is not illumined but in darkness" (*The Dark Night*, Book II, chpt. 13). It is through the darkness of the soul that God's transforming light is manifested. It is a question of spiritually "paying one's dues," of being tried and tested as gold in the furnace (Wis 3:5-6). Only then can the soul continue the ascent up the mystical ladder that leads to the divine union.

Our mystical Doctor of the Church continues in his description of this divine light that enters the soul:

> Although naturally speaking God is indeed as dark a night to the soul as is faith, it can be affirmed that He is less dark. God supernaturally illumines the soul with the ray of His divine light. . . . (*Collected Works*, "The Ascent of Mount Carmel," Book II, chpt. 2.)

These words tend to echo Isaiah's statements about the light that comes out of the dark: "then shall your light rise in the darkness and your gloom be as the noonday" (Is 58:10). This divine light is not obtained through one's personal efforts or reasoning; it is a gift from God, who delivers this grace to whomever He wills:

> The illuminative way, or the way of *infused contemplation* occurs when God himself pastures and refreshes the soul without any of its own discursive meditation or active help. Such is the sensory night and purgation of the soul. . . . (*Collected Works*, "The Dark Night," Book I, chpt. 14.)

In order for one to reach the illuminative experience, he must attain a high level of purity and holiness. This is why the purgative stages in the spiritual ascent usually precede the infusion of the heavenly Light, for one cannot come to appreciate the wisdom of divine knowledge unless his soul is empty of all self and receptive to the All Other, which is God. St. John of the Cross talks about this need for purity:

> Perfect transformation is impossible without perfect purity. The illumination of the soul and its union with God corresponds to the measure of its purity. The illumination will not be perfect until the soul is entirely cleansed, clear and perfect. . . . (*Collected Works*, "The Ascent of Mount Carmel," Book II, chpt. 5.)

> A man makes room for God by wiping away all the smudges and smears of creatures by uniting his will perfectly to God's. When this is done the soul will be illuminated by and transformed in God. . . . (*Collected Works*, "The Ascent," Book II, chpt. 5.)

This illumination creates a keen awareness of the divine will in one's life, known through the heavenly impulses, infused knowledge, and the gift of discernment which helps the soul to "know" God more intimately. This heavenly knowledge is based upon charity and the love of God for His own (St. Maximus the Confessor, *Centuries on Charity*, I,9: seventh century).

The grace of illumination usually gives the soul a deeper and more precise knowledge of the divine operations than he or she could ever possibly hope to attain through years of prayer and pious study. This is because it is a supernatural gift — a heavenly wisdom that can only claim God as its Source.

All the stigmatists agree that the knowledge God imparts to their mind and spirit is indescribable, simply because the intimate secrets they share with God are so sublime and personal; divine wisdom is so much more superior than human wisdom, and divine love is infinitely more perfect than human love.

Padre Pio, in his letters to his directors, Padres Agostino and Benedetto, revealed this inability to communicate what the divine has revealed :

Dear Father, what a terrible thing is spiritual suffering! I am
embarrassed by my failure to find suitable words in which to
explain myself. . .

Again, when I am busy about even indifferent things, a mere
word about God or the sudden thought of some such word effects
me so deeply that I am carried out of myself. Then the Lord
usually grants me the grace of revealing to me some secrets
which remain indelibly impressed on my soul. I am unable,
however, to describe all these secrets, for more often than not I
have not adequate words for the purpose. Even the secrets which
I succeed to some extent in putting into words lose so much of
their splendor that I regard myself with compassion and
disgust. . . . (*Letter to Padre Benedetto*, June, 1913.)

These intimate relations with God cause the soul to become completely
absorbed in His love and goodness, thereby rendering it difficult to
interrupt this divine state of intimacy for the sake of communicating it to
others; to do so would force one to leave this extraordinary state he or she is
so immersed in.

The stigmatist St. Gertrude (1256-1302) experienced similar anxiety
when the Lord requested that she write down for the benefit of the faithful
some of the illuminations she had received:

These words having depressed me, I began to consider within
myself how difficult and even impossible it would be to find
thoughts and words capable of explaining these things to the
human intellect without scandal. . . . (*The Life and Revelations
of St. Gertrude*, p. 93: Christian Classics, Inc., Westminster,
MD, 1983.)

Gertrude further adds:

It has not been possible for me, although I applied my whole
mind to it, to find a single word to express the things which on
the following day I could write freely. . . . (*Life and Revelations*,
p. 94.)

What type of knowledge or feelings does the stigmatist experience
during illumination? Although we've seen how difficult they find it to
describe such matters, some general thoughts have come down to us from
their pens. St. Gertrude once said that she learned of her nothingness
compared to God's greatness, because her sinful nature had been exposed
with the divine illumination: "After the infusion of Thy most sweet light, I
saw many things in my heart which offended Thy purity, and I even
perceived that all within me was in such disorder and confusion that Thou
couldst not abide therein" (*Life and Revelations*, p. 74).

Like other stigmatists before and after her, Gertrude saw a positive
growth amidst the toil; she reveals that illumination gives the soul a
profound knowledge of God and His love:

Thou didst give me a more clear knowledge of thyself, which was
such that the sweetness of Thy love led me to correct my faults

far more than the fear of the punishments with which Thy just anger threatened me. . . . (*Life and Revelations*, p. 75.)

St. John of the Cross described this immense gulf between the Creator and the creature that becomes known during the state of illumination:

God will give illumination by bestowing upon the soul not only knowledge of its own misery and lowliness but also knowledge of His grandeur and majesty. . . . (*Collected Works*, "The Dark Night," Book I, chpt. 12.)

Paradoxically the stigmatist feels an immense distance between herself and God, yet is motivated to love Him more because the illumination brings about an irresistible thirst for the divine love and purity which she hopes one day to call her own. Perhaps it is God's way of keeping the victim humble, while at the same time inflaming her heart, mind and soul with that fire for Love that consumes the victim with a passion to become more and more like the Beloved; it is a gradual preparation for the total immersion with the Lord that ultimately ends in divine union. Likewise, it is a preparation for the reception of the stigmata, for the victim must become one with Him in love and in suffering — to imitate His sacrificial life, even unto the Cross, for it is there that the supreme test of love resides.

For the stigmatist, the divine illumination is much more profound than it is for other souls, since he must be prepared for the greatest of humiliations, sufferings and sacrifices. To represent the Crucified Christ, the victim needs to be purged of even the slightest stains of imperfection, for Christ did not sin at all; therefore, the stigmatist must undergo the severest of trials in order to become a near copy of another Christ in our midst.

The illumination is frightening in the sense that the stigmatist's heart and soul are laid bare before the awesome reality that is God. Yet the illumination is equally consoling, for the divine comes to share His goodness and perfection with the chosen one who is destined for union and a mission of co-redemption.

The heavenly Light will thus help to make God's will clearer to the victim, in that he will be called to self-denial through a life of suffering that is not entirely his own, but rather that of Christ's; secondly, he will come to realize that his vocation is to suffer for the sins of others, and not for his own benefit or punishment. The stigmatist, more than anyone else, is not his own person, but is Christ's, Who chooses to use him as a vehicle for the salvation of others. The acceptance of this mission may take some time, for the strength and endurance that are needed are only developed through a long, intensive period that tries the soul and prepares it for this mystical crucifixion.

So far we have moved through the various stages that the victim normally encounters on his way to stigmatization. After he passes through the ways of purgation, the dark night of faith, and the diabolical assaults that attempt to set him back, God rewards him with the heavenly rays of light that begin to reveal the intimate ways of the divine to his soul. Many spiritual delights and consolations appear at this stage to comfort and strengthen his soul, yet the trials and tribulations continue to form him into the image of the Crucified Christ.

144

When the victim reaches this point in the spiritual ascent, the next way brings him into the states of spiritual ecstasy and rapture, whereby the soul becomes lost in the sea of God's infinite love. During these experiences the soul may start to receive heavenly visions, apparitions and divine messages for the world; he increasingly encounters the supernatural order of existence as he moves ever closer to the divine union. Normally, this union will occur during or after the heights of ecstatic experience, sometimes leading to the mystical marriage and the partial beatific vision, which would be the highest ascent that he could reach in this earthly life. The gift of the stigmata normally occurs during the intense contemplative ecstatic state, when the soul is already in union with the Beloved.

We will now turn to the next step in the mystical ladder that the stigmatist encounters: the states of ecstasy and rapture, where the soul really becomes immersed in the divine and in all of the supernatural order. These states are preludes to the divine union; however, as we've already seen, they continue to be experienced within the unitive way itself.

Ecstasy

Ecstasy is the state in the mystical life whereby the soul is enraptured in God through suspension of all exterior activities. Following the affective state of prayer, ecstasy is the first true stage of the divine union that involves the transmission of divine mysteries and impulses directly to the soul, as well as the infusion of divine love into the depths of one's very being. It is in the *ecstatic state* that one might receive visions and apparitions of Christ, His Mother Mary, the angels and the saints. As St. Teresa of Avila explains:

> Here in this ecstasy are received the true revelations and the great favors and visions — and all serves to humiliate and strengthen the soul, to lessen its esteem for the things of this life, and to make it know more clearly the grandeurs of the reward the Lord has prepared for those who serve Him. . . . (*Collected Works*, "Life" 21, no. 12.)

It is here, too, when wounds of love — including the Sacred Stigmata — impress themselves upon the body and/or the soul of the chosen one. Ecstatics often receive prophecies and revelations during this initiation into the divine union, both for private use and for public exhortation or instruction. And here the chosen soul begins to experience a host of supernatural phenomena, be they extraordinary charisms for the benefit of the faithful, or inspirations and delights that invite the soul to a more intimate relationship with God.

Let us listen to a description of the state of divine ecstasy, as given by the Doctor of the Church, St. Francis de Sales (1567-1622):

> An ecstasy is merely to go out of oneself. Men who have been touched by divine and intellectual pleasures and have let their hearts be ravished by such feelings are truly outside of themselves, that is, they are above their natural condition. This is a blessed and desirable departure and by it they enter into a nobler and loftier estate. . . . (*Treatise on the Love of God*, Book I, chpt. 10: TAN Books and Publishers, Inc., Rockford, IL, 1975.)

> As long as their ecstasy lasts those angelic men who are rapt up
> to God and heavenly things completely lose the use of sense,
> movement, and all exterior action. . . . (*Love of God*, Book I,
> chpt. 10.)

> The height of love's ecstasy is to have our will not in its own
> contentment but in God's. . . . (*Love of God*, Book VI, chpt. 11.)

Particularly evident is the knowledge or wisdom of things normally not known in the ordinary Christian state. Father Joseph Naber, director of stigmatist Therese Neumann (1898-1962) for over fifty years, said that Therese often told him things that she was completely ignorant of in her normal condition: knowledge of when and how a particular person had died; intimate details of the life of Christ that are hidden from the Gospel texts; the state of some of the poor souls in purgatory; etc. Therese experienced many insights into the mysteries of Christ's Passion and Crucifixion, as have all the stigmatists of every era.

Part of the ecstatic experience often involves the states of *elevated calm* and the *prayer of quiet*, when the soul loses all sense of time and place, being totally immersed in the divine presence. Father Naber observed this about Therese Neumann:

> In Easter week, when Therese was unable to go to church, she
> still saw our Savior every day at home, at the time of
> consecration, and quickly passed from a brief vision of the Savior
> into the prayer of quiet, which was the source of even greater
> happiness for her (she was in the state of elevated calm) than the
> vision of the Savior. May 24, 1931 (Pentecost Sunday): The
> previous night at about one o'clock, Therese had slipped into the
> church (they had allowed her to keep a sacristy key so that she
> could go in and out of the church for visits, even after the doors
> were locked, without being seen or disturbed — Author) and sat
> down on one of the choir stalls. There she had a vision of our
> Savior and passed into the prayer of quiet. It was not until they
> came to ring the Angelus that she slipped quietly away. Her
> longing for such quiet times alone with the Savior takes away all
> her fears, and makes her feel happy (The length of time involved
> on this occasion was at least four hours. — Author). . . . (*Therese
> Neumann: A Portrait*, Johannes Steiner; Alba House, N.Y.;
> copyright by the Society of St. Paul, N.Y., 1967.)

This sense of the suspension of time and space can take place suddenly and uncontrollably, as we hear from the words of stigmatist Anne Catherine Emmerich (1774-1824):

> I was frequently unable to resist the divine impulse, and I felt
> unconscious before my companions. I was in choir one day,
> though not singing with the rest, when I became rigid, and the
> nuns happening to push against me, I fell to the ground. Whilst
> they were carrying me out, I saw a nun walking upon the highest
> point of the roof where no one could go, and I was told that it was
> Magdalen dei Pazzi, who had borne the marks of our Lord's

wounds. Again I saw her running along the choir-grate, mounting upon the altar, or seizing the priest's hand. Her perilous flights made me reflect on myself, and I took every precaution not to yield to these states. My Sisters understood nothing of the kind and they, at first, reproached me severely for remaining in the chapel prostrate, my arms extended. But as I could not prevent those raptures, I tried to hide myself from them in a corner. Despite my efforts, however, I was ravished out of myself, sometimes in one place, sometime in another. I lay prostrate, stiff and immovable, or I knelt with outstretched arms. The chaplain often found me in this state. . . . (*The Life of Anne Catherine Emmerich: Volume I*; TAN Books and Publishers, Inc., Rockford, IL, 1976.)

The ecstasies of Anne, like so many other stigmatists, often came when she was alone, at work, in the Church before the Blessed Sacrament, and even in bed. She often thought that they were brief in duration, but she found out frequently that these ecstasies were much longer than what she once thought. So intense were her ecstatic moments that they often brought tears of joy to her eyes.

Although the ecstatic moments are generally short, nevertheless they affect the soul permanently with an infusion of the divine love that a lifetime of normal human effort could never achieve. St. Catherine of Siena (1347-80), Dominican nun who was both Doctor and stigmatist of the Church, revealed this:

Ecstasy cannot be continual. The soul, the spirit and the body which, by the abundance of these marvelous gifts, have received an increase of sanctity, must return to the customary works of this exile. . . But the Lord watches over them from on high . . . and He calls them anew and incessantly raises their spirit to himself until He adorns them with perfect purity and makes the soul and body both equally free from all the weaknesses of fallen nature. . . It is to this point that we are led by the love which the Lord deigns to bestow on us. . . . (Catherine of Siena, *Dialogue*, Book II, Chpt.I.)

Note that the saintly Doctor emphasizes the necessity of the soul to be purged of its imperfections in order to taste the sweetness of the divine milk. It is a continual journey for the soul who strives for perfection. This is one of the reasons why one cannot experience an ecstatic state for too long of duration: the soul is not purified enough to stand in the constant presence of God while in this earthly life; rather, some who have achieved extraordinary mystical heights through their saintly lives have been able to share but brief moments in the divine presence; even so, these short moments are indescribably sweet and delightful to the soul, and advance him toward the divine union much sooner than a lifetime of prayer, study or pious practices could ever achieve.

St. Catherine continues with this thought:

Who could worthily appreciate these marvelous communications between the soul and God? Who would not be inebriated with this happiness of holy love which is a prelude to glory?. . . . Ah, those joys and blessings are unknown to the world. They cannot be known by any save the privileged lovers of the Savior who here below lose themselves in the ocean of illuminations and delights which will never end. . . . (*Dialogue*, III,8.)

Some of the most profound ecstatic experiences that every stigmatist has known are those called the *Passion ecstasies*. In this state, the victim relives the Passion scenes of Gethsemani, the Way of the Cross, and even Calvary itself, where the "mystical death" occurs. Here the stigmatist participates in every suffering that Christ endured during those last moments of His life, almost as if he were taking the Lord's place, or was His constant companion, another Simon of Cyrene. Of course, no one could ever suffer the way that Christ did, but these victims relive His Passion most intensely, even to the point of receiving the same wounds, bruises and blood loss that our Savior experienced.

Saint Francis of Assisi (1182-1226), the holy Poverello who was the first officially recognized stigmatist in history, desired to suffer the pains of the Passion so strongly that he even asked our Lord to grant him this favor:

My Lord, Jesus Christ, I pray You to grant me two graces before I die: the first is that during my life I may feel in my soul and in my body, as much as possible, the pain which You, dear Jesus, sustained in the hour of Your most bitter Passion. The second is that I may feel in my heart, as much as possible, that excessive love with which You, O Son of God, were inflamed in willingly enduring such suffering for us sinners. . . . (*The Little Flowers of St. Francis*, Raphael Brown, p. 190: Image Books, Doubleday and Company, Inc., N.Y., 1958.)

We know that God granted Francis' request shortly thereafter by giving him His Five Sacred Wounds during the ecstatic state on Mt. Alverna, Italy, during the time of September 1224, or two years prior to his death.

The Poverello's devoted follower and fellow Franciscan, Padre Pio of Pietrelcina (1887-1968), also requested to share the Cross with our Lord, and he too was granted his request. The Padre had asked the Lord for years to allow him to participate in His sufferings of the Passion, in order to carry on the redemptive suffering of his Seraphic Father. We have seen this holy desire expressed in the *Epistolario* (letters to his spiritual directors) many times before he received the visible stigmata:

This desire has been growing continually in my heart so that it has now become what I would call a stong passion. I have in fact made this offering to the Lord several times, beseeching him to pour out upon me the punishments prepared for sinners and for the souls in a state of purgation, even increasing them a hundredfold for me, as long as he converts and saves sinners and quickly admits to paradise the souls in Purgatory, but I should now like to make this offering to the Lord in obedience to you. It seems to me that Jesus really wants this. . . . (*Letter to Padre Benedetto*, November 29, 1910.)

In fact, after this offering the Lord did grant his request. Sometime in that same year (1910), Padre Pio was given the first transitory signs of the visible stigmata, which later turned into the invisible wounds that caused him continual pain. (It wasn't until September 20, 1918, that he received the visible stigmata in a permanent form that lasted until the year of his death, 1968). From 1910 until 1918, Padre Pio had suffered the invisible stigmata continually during this pre-stage of the permanent crucifixion.

When ordered out of obedience to explain what had happened to him during this early stage, he told Padre Benedetto this:

> Yesterday evening something happened to me which I can neither explain nor understand. In the center of the palms of my hands a red patch appeared, about the size of a cent and accompanied by acute pain. The pain was much more acute in the left hand and it still persists. I also feel some pain in the soles of my feet. This phenomena has been repeated several times for almost a year now, but for some time past it had not occurred. . . . (*Letter to Padre Benedetto*, September 8, 1911.)

It was during his stay in Pietrelcina that Padre Pio first received the invisible stigmata. One day, having spent a long time in prayer underneath a tree in a place known as the Piana Romana (a field that was a short distance from the Forgione home), he experienced painful burning sensations in both of his hands. When coming home, his mother noticed him shaking his hands and questioned him on his peculiar behavior. It was then that Padre described the sharp pains that pierced his hands, not really aware of what was about to transpire in his life. This was in 1910, when the Padre (his last days to be known as Francesco Forgione) began to feel the first pains of the invisible stigmata. That same year, on August 10, 1910, Francesco became Padre Pio as he was ordained priest in the Benevento Cathedral.

Once again, these experiences occurred during the state of ecstasy, remarkable when one considers how young Padre Pio was when he attained such extraordinary spiritual heights!

Many such stigmatists have received the wounds of our Lord through the intense longings they have had for the Cross and the profound devotion they felt for the mystery of the Passion. Jesus himself told Padre that He longed for those victim souls who would voluntarily unite themselves to His Cross:

> My son, I need victims to calm my Father's just divine anger; renew the sacrifice of your whole self and do so without any reserve. . . . (*Our Lord to Padre Pio: Letter to Padre Agostino*, March 12, 1913.)

The reference to the renewal involves Padre Pio's statement written for the occasion of his first solemn Mass at Pietrelcina on August 14, 1910: "Jesus, my breath and my life. Today, with trembling hands, I elevate you in a mystery of Divine Love. May I, with you, be for the world, the way, the truth and the life, and for you a holy priest, *a perfect victim*" (*Padre Pio of Pietrelcina: Everybody's Cyrenean* p. 55; Allesandro of Ripabottoni: San Giovanni Rotondo, Italy, 1987).

Now we move into the nature of the ecstasies themselves. What occurs during these Passion ecstasies? How does the victim suffer, and what are the external signs of this suffering?

Again we need to be reminded of the total devotion these souls have for the Cross, involving a passionate and continual contemplation on the Crucified Lord and the mystery of His sufferings. The stigmatist becomes transformed in Christ, a living crucifix who has reached the highest ecstatic state possible in the divine union.

Returning to St. Francis, we see that his immersion in the state of ecstasy was total and complete, absorbed was he in the Crucified Lord:

> And the fervor of his devotion increased so much within him that he utterly transformed himself into Jesus through love and compassion. And while he was thus inflaming himself in this contemplation, on that same morning he saw coming down from Heaven a Seraph with six resplendent and flaming wings. As a Seraph, flying swiftly, came closer to St. Francis, so that he could perceive Him clearly, he noticed that He had a likeness of a Crucified Man, and His wings were so disposed that two wings extended above His head, two were spread out to fly, and the other two covered His entire body. During this apparition, all of Mount Alverna seemed to be on fire with very bright flames. . . . (*The Little Flowers of St. Francis*, p. 191; Raphael Brown: Image Books, Doubleday and Company, Inc., Garden City, N.Y., 1958.)

An angelic visitor is a very common experience to those souls who are deeply caught up in the ecstatic state. Let us continue to see how this experience led to the stigmatization of St. Francis of Assisi:

> Now when, after a long time and a secret conversation, this wonderful vision disappeared, it left a most intense ardor and flame of divine love in the heart of St. Francis, and it left a marvelous image and imprint of the Passion of Christ in his flesh. For soon there began to appear in the hands and feet of St. Francis the marks of nails such as he had just seen in the body of Jesus Crucified, who appeared to him in the form of a Seraph. For his hands and his feet seemed to be pierced through the center with nails, the heads of which were in the palms of the hands and in the upper part of his feet outside the flesh, and their points extended through the back of the hands and the soles of the feet so far that they seemed to be bent and beaten back in such a way that underneath their flesh — it would have been easy to put the finger of one's hand as through a ring. And the heads of the nails were round and black. Likewise in his right side appeared the wound of a blow and from which blood often issued from the holy breast of St. Francis and stained his habit and breeches. . . . (*The Little Flowers* p. 192-93.)

One of the greatest examples of the Passion ecstasies can be found in Therese Neumann, who experienced more than 700 separate visions of the sufferings of Christ from 1926 (the year she received the stigmata) up to her death in 1962. According to Johannes Steiner, these ecstasies were each divided into roughly 35-50 individual visions, lasting every week for half the year from Thursday evening through late Friday or early Saturday.

These Passion sufferings never occurred during the joyous liturgical seasons (Christmas to Septuagesima) and from Easter to the Friday after the Octave of Corpus Christi. Nor did they occur on the Fridays that fell on feast days. Therese's most intense sufferings occurred, as with all the stigmatists, during the season of Lent, especially during Holy Week. Father Naber once observed and recorded 46 separate visions of the Passion that occurred between 11:30 p.m., Holy Thursday, and 11:00 a.m. on Good Friday. According to Albert Vogl, lifetime friend of Therese, she suffered our Lord's Passion some 26-28 times every year, including all the sorrowful Fridays of the Catholic year (*Therese Neumann: Mystic and Stigmatist*, p. 27; Albert Vogl: TAN Books and Publishers, Inc., Rockford, IL, 1987).

The lay stigmatist Marthe Robin (1902-81) suffered the Passion ecstasies every week as well. Her agonies began each Thursday evening and ended on Friday night. On Saturdays, Marthe returned to her normal state, though at times this didn't occur until Sunday or even Monday. At the peak of these sufferings — the vision of the Cross — Marthe actually appeared to have died a mystical death, her head falling back as she sighed, "Father, into your hands I commend my spirit." Of course, she was not really dead, but mystically she had all the symptoms of expiring. Like other stigmatists upon the examination of competent doctors, Marthe Robin's pulse appeared to stop, as she remained for awhile in total stillness and silence. Miraculously, she is "revived" when the ecstatic state has ended, at least until the following Thursday, when it started all over again.

Alexandrina da Costa (1904-55) suffered our Lord's Passion for a number of years at her home in Balasar, Portugal, where she remained bedridden after a fall that left her body paralyzed for life. She apparently asked the Lord not to make the afflictions and wounds of her sufferings visible (the stigmata), and Jesus granted her request. Still, it is probable that Alexandrina bore the invisible stigmata, as continuous and intense as her Passion experiences were.

Here is what this pious victim said about her Passion ecstasies:

> On the morning of 2 October 1938, our Lord told me that I would have to pass through all of His Passion from Gethsemane to Calvary, but that I would not arrive at the *Consummatum Est.* He confirmed that I would begin on the following day and that I would repeat these sufferings every Friday immediately after mid-day, until three o'clock in the afternoon. I did not say no to the Lord. I warned my spiritual director of everything and waited anxiously for the morrow because neither of us could imagine what was going to happen. During the night of 2-3 October, my agony of soul was intense, but the suffering of my body was even greater. I began to lose blood and felt fearful pains. And it was in this suffering that I entered into my first crucifixion. That horror I felt deep inside. Oh, how unspeakable were my afflictions!. . . . (*Alexandrina: The Agony and the Glory*, p. 49; Francis Johnston: TAN Books and Publishers, Inc., Rockford, IL, 1982.)

All in all, Alexandrina suffered some 180 Passion ecstasies during her lifetime, which included the agony, the scourging, the crowning of thorns, and the vision of Mother Mary at the foot of the Cross.

It is the love of Christ that compels the greatest of saints to a passionate devotion to the Cross of our Savior and Redeemer; it is the surest way towards the divine union, a union that is based on the pureness of Love that is Christ. Let us hear some of the heartfelt words from the lips of the saints, as they reflect on the merits of true devotion to the Passion and Cross of our Lord Jesus Christ:

> Let the crucifix be not only in my eyes and on my breast, but in my heart. . . . (St. Bernadette, 1844-79.)

> It is loving the Cross that one finds one's heart, for Divine Love cannot live without suffering. . . . (St. Bernadette.)

> Life without a cross is the heaviest cross of all. . . . (St. Sebastian Valfre, 1629-1710.)

> Our joy depends upon the Cross, and our Lord would not enter His glory save by the way of bitterness. He leads you by the same path as the Saints. . . . (St. Vincent de Paul, 1580-1660.)

> Follow after Christ and carry your cross for your salvation, as Christ carried His Cross for your salvation. . . . (St. Anthony of Padua, 1195-1231.)

> The cross of Christ is both a mystery and an example: a mystery by which the power of God is shown forth; an example, by which man's devotion is aroused. . . . (Pope St. Leo I, *Sermons*, 72,I: fifth century.)

> It was such that brought the stigmata to the loving, seraphic St. Francis, and the Savior's burning wounds to the loving, angelic St. Catherine of Siena. In them loving complacence had sharpened the points of dolorous compassion, making the compassion felt for His afflictions infinitely stronger. . . . (St. Francis de Sales, *Love of God*, Book V, chpt. 5.)

> The death and passion of our Lord is the sweetest and the most compelling motive that can animate our hearts in this mortal life. . . . (St. Francis de Sales, *Love of God*, Book XII, chpt. 13.)

> Mount Calvary is the mount of lovers. All love that does not take its origin from the Savior's passion is foolish and perilous. Unhappy is death without the Savior's love; unhappy is love without the Savior's death. Love and death are so mingled in the Savior's passion that we cannot have the one in our hearts without the other. Upon Calvary we cannot have life without love, or love without the Redeemer's death. . . . (St. Francis de Sales, *Love of God*, Book XII, chpt. 13.)

Nothing is more to our advantage than to be like Him in His
Passion. . . . (St. Robert Bellarmine, 1542-1621.)

All of the great minds in the history of the Church are unanimous in
proclaiming that devotion to the Cross of our Lord is both meritorious and
necessary for the advancement in the spiritual life. This is one devotion that
every victim soul has made a vital part of their life, and one that every
Christian is called to follow, whether they follow the ordinary path that God
has willed for them, or for those called to the higher mystical states.

Rapture

The mystical phenomenon known as *rapture* (also referred to as *transport*,
flight, or *swoon*) is often difficult to separate from the state of ecstasy,
primarily because this spiritual flight takes place within the ecstatic state;
it is really a peak moment within the state of ecstasy, a kind of momentary
mystical height that draws the soul closer to God.

St. Francis de Sales (1567-1622) has said it well:

> An ecstasy is called rapture inasmuch as in it God draws and lifts
> us up to himself, and rapture is called ecstasy because in it we go
> out and above ourselves, and remain there so as to be united to
> God. . . . (*Love of God*, Book VII, chpt. 4.)

This holy Doctor of the Church further explains this sublime state:

> When union attains the perfection of keeping us held and
> fastened to our Lord, it is the same as spiritual rapture, transport
> or suspension of spirit; it is called union or transport only when it
> is brief, whereas when prolonged, it is called ecstasy or
> rapture. . . . (*Love of God*, Book VII, chpt. 3.)

Listen to the description given by the angelic Doctor, St. Thomas
Aquinas:

> Rapture is the state of being transported emotionally or
> spiritually; it is being carried out of oneself by a kind of ecstasy.
> It is the uplifting of a person by the Spirit of God to things
> supernatural. . . . (*Summa Theologica*, Part II, question 175.)

St. Paul once talked about this extraordinary state in his letter to the
Corinthians: "I must boast; there is nothing to be gained by it, but I will go
on to visions and revelations of the Lord. I know a man in Christ who
fourteen years ago was caught up to the third heaven — whether in the body
or out of the body I do not know, God knows. And I know that this man was
caught up into Paradise — whether in the body or out of the body I not
know, God knows — and he heard things that cannot be told, which man
may not utter" (2 Cor 12:1-4). This experience, as we have now seen, is
beyond the comprehension of those who practice the normal ways of
perfection, simply because it deals with the supernatural states reserved for
those called to a more intimate encounter with the Lord. This does not
mean that many are unable to attain this exalted state; no, it only means
that it is God and He alone who reserves these favors for the souls He has

specially chosen. Why He chooses whom He chooses must remain a mystery to us while we live out our earthly lives, for no one can know the ways of the Lord.

Frequently the soul who is caught up in the state of rapture loses all sense of time and reality, as if transported to another dimension. Furthermore, this condition is sudden and often uncontrollable, an irresistible urge from the divine impulse to lose one's self in the bosom of the Lord. St. Teresa of Avila (1515-82) tells us this:

> In these raptures most often there is no remedy; rather, without any forethought or any help there frequently comes a force so swift and powerful that one sees and feels this mighty eagle raise it up and carry it aloft on its wings. . . . (*Collected Works*, "Life," chpt. 20.)

> One sees oneself carried away and does not know where. . . . (*Life*, chpt. 20.)

Teresa explains that the rapture occurs unexpectedly, momentarily suspending all the human faculties:

> When the body is in rapture it is as though dead, frequently being unable to do anything of itself. It remains in the position it was when seized by the rapture, whether standing or sitting, or whether with the hands opened or closed. Ordinarily the soul is disoriented. . .

> This complete transformation of the soul in God lasts only a short time; but while it lasts no faculty is felt, nor does the soul know what is happening in this prayer. . . .

> After the soul returns to itself — the rapture has been intense — it goes about for a day or two, or even three, with the faculties absorbed or as though stupefied; it seems to be outside of itself. . . . (*Life*, chpt. 20.)

St. Margaret Mary Alacoque (1647-90), victim soul of the Visitation Order, was frequently found adoring the Blessed Eucharist in the enraptured state, often all night long. In one case, witnesses knew of this state lasting from 8 o'clock one evening until the next morning, where she remained kneeling motionless before the altar, lost in the sweetness of the divine presence. Many other souls have experienced these long periods of bliss as well.

Padre Pio of Pietrelcina (1887-1968) frequently fell into this sublime state while celebrating his holy Mass, especially during the consecration of the Eucharist. He became so caught up in the divine presence that others had to frequently encourage him to proceed with the rest of the celebration. Many of Padre Pio's Masses lasted for four hours because of his enraptured experience and pious devotion.

It was during one of these mystical experiences that St. Teresa of Avila was overcome by the divine love, resulting in a wound of her heart caused by the fiery arrow that pierced her soul and united her to the Sacred Heart of the Savior. In this respect, Teresa had borne the stigma of the heart, which remained with her for the rest of her life.

The stigmatist St. Gertrude (1256-1302) of Eisleben, Germany, experienced profound moments of rapture, especially when contemplating on our Lord's Passion. On one Good Friday, Gertrude's union with God became so engaging that she could not attend to anything exterior or sensible, remaining in rapture the whole day and through the next day (Holy Saturday): "She was perfectly united to and absorbed in God, by the tenderness of her compassion, that she was entirely dissolved therein" (*The Life and Revelations of St. Gertrude*, p. 390; Chrisitan Classics, Inc., Westminster, MD, 1983).

According to Venerable Marina de Escobar, the ability to see divine things more clearly is greatly illuminated in the light of ecstatic rapture:

> When in a profound ecstasy God suddenly unites the soul to His essence and fills it with His light, He manifests to it in an instant the loftiest mysteries, together with His secrets. The soul sees an immense unity and an infinite majesty. . . . (*The Mystical Evolution in the Vitality and Development of the Church: Volume II*, p. 354; Fr. John G. Arintero: TAN Books and Publishers, Inc., Rockford, IL, 1978.)

During the rapture one receives divine wisdom concerning the things of God. Suddenly everything is seen in a much clearer light, because now one is able to penetrate to the roots of these realities and understand them. This all takes place, not through ordinary means, but is infused knowledge given by God.

The holy Doctor of the Church, St. Bernard of Clairvaux (1090-1153) described this state as an intimate expression of love between God and the soul:

> During these assaults of love the soul cannot contain itself and, to alleviate the heart, it breaks forth into expressions of love which are without order, rule or human rhetoric. It often happens, also, that the soul is mute and can merely give expression to sighs. . . . (*On the Canticle of Canticles*, Sermon 67.)

Furthermore, as Father Arintero has described, the experience of rapture can totally overwhelm the soul, even making her "swoon and fall to the ground as if dead; rapture elevates one, transfigures and tends to lift him into the air." Others have experienced a feeling of the soul tearing away from the body, carried along in the flight phenomenon known as *elevation*, *levitation*, or even *bilocation* (more about this later).

During this time, all use of the senses may be momentarily suspended, and the face takes on a heavenly beauty that is filled with an unearthly radiance and serenity. Many of the stigmatists have been seen in this supernatural trance-like state. Padre Pio's face, particularly during the consecration of the Eucharist, has often been observed to take on a radiant glow, reflecting the joys of one as if in heaven; some witnesses claimed to have seen the likeness of Christ emanating from his holy face. This is like-wise true with the stigmatists St. Gertrude, Anne Catherine Emmerich, and St. Francis of Assisi.

Mystical Flights

Another unusual phenomenon that many of the stigmatists have experi-enced is the supernatural wonder known as the *mystical flight*. We will lim-it our concern in this unit with two of the most remarkable types of flight: that of *levitation* and *bilocation*.

Levitation involves the body being raised above the ground without any natural support. Sometimes the saint will soar high into the air. St. Francis of Assisi once levitated — quite literally — out of sight, according to his close companions; at other times one simply floats or glides above the ground (a condition often referred to as *mobile ecstasy*). Many have felt that these mystical transportations are examples of what we can expect one day in our glorified bodies, when no natural barrier will hinder the move-ments of the faithful who have risen in Christ. These flights are a kind of prelude to our future resurrection, a sign of God's promise so vividly ex-plained by St. Paul the Apostle (see 1 Cor 15).

All levitations are not signs from God, however. The devil is very capable of causing wonders of nature. That is why Pope Benedict XIV so prudently stated that proper Church authorities must investigate and even witness (if possible) any proclaimed levitations in order to be certain of their cause. Nevertheless, many well-known, authenticated cases in the lives of the saints have been claimed; e.g., Joseph of Copertino, Philip Neri, Paul of the Cross, Peter of Alcantara, and Stephen of Hungary. Many saints as well have been recognized for their gift of bilocation, such as: Nicholas of Myra, Anthony of Padua, Francis Xavier, Alphonsus Liguori, and others.

St. Teresa of Avila (1515-82) has perhaps the best-known explanations for these mystical flights, as St. John of the Cross once attested. Here is what she had to say about her own levitations:

Such great powers raised me up from the very soles of my feet. . . . (*Collected Works*, "Life," (Autobiography), chpt. 20.)

We are incapable, when His Majesty desires, of holding back the body any more than the soul, nor are we its master. . . . (chpt. 20.)

When one sees one's body so elevated from the ground that even though the spirit carries it along after itself, and does so very gen-tly if one does not resist, one's feelings are not lost. At least I was conscious in such a way that I could understand I was being elevated. . . . (chpt. 20.)

Yet, Teresa often felt uneasy about these transports, not wanting to disturb the recollection of her sisters who were often beside her, deeply engaged in prayer. She even pleaded with them at times to hold her down when the elevations were about to take place.

Teresa of Avila was only one among many of the victim souls who levitated at various times during their mystical lives. St. Catherine of Siena (1347-80), that holy stigmatist nun of the Order of St. Dominic, was known to have levitated many times throughout her life of mystical prayer. Now we will turn to the state of flight known as bilocation, where many examples are found in the Church's long history.

Bilocation is a type of mystical flight whereby the person is transported to another location, while he mysteriously continues to remain present at the site where he had first taken flight. In other words, he physically appears in two different places at the same time. Obviously, this is one of the most extraordinary charisms that a person could ever encounter; yet its occurrence has been so well-documented and thoroughly investigated that the reality of bilocations is an accepted fact in the history of the Church.

But why do some of God's saintly souls receive this mysterious gift? Normally, the person who bilocates is given this grace in order to help or to intercede for others; some do so for the edification and instruction of those to whom they bilocate. Never is the bilocation given as a gift for the benefit of the one in question alone, as the stigmata is never granted for one's own pleasure or self-advancement. As with all extraordinary charisms, the Lord grants them for the benefit of the whole universal Church.

The stigmatist St. Catherine dei Ricci (1552-90) often appeared to those who asked for her intercessions in order to console them or even to protect them on long journeys. Catherine had once bilocated to the victim St. Mary Magdalen dei Pazzi (1566-1607), who also suffered the Passion of our Lord.

Many of God's victims, such as Anne Catherine Emmerich (1774-1824), visited and participated in many of the Gospel scenes, especially those that involved the life of Christ or His Blessed Mother. It's as if they are transported back in time to witness these events while they actually occurred. These mystical "visions" are vividly real to these favored souls, as their testimonies clearly indicate. Many of the details they provide for us are not to be found in the Gospels themselves, yet nothing is found to conflict with the teachings of the Faith; furthermore, many of the particular facts revealed have been later verified, especially with events in the lives of the saints, who may have lived long before these visionaries. When the details are investigated, they have often turned out to be remarkably accurate — even down to the times, dates, names, and locations in question!

Therese Neumann's gift of bilocation was nothing less than extraordinary. Albert Vogl, her lifetime friend, once related this story:

> The day Cardinal Pacelli was to be crowned as Pope Pius XII, Father Naber told Therese to get some friends together in his rectory to listen to the coronation ceremonies from St. Peter's on the radio. They all listened intently for hours. When the time came and the new pope gave his blessing *'urbi et orbi'* — to the city (Rome) and to the world — Therese suddenly fell into ecstasy; her arms were outstretched, and her chair — with Therese in it — suddenly turned around, facing south. Even though all were accustomed to so many unusual happenings, this one came as a complete surprise. When Therese came back to normal after the exalted rest period, she told them that she had, indeed, been right there by the Holy Father and had seen all the people

around him. On one occasion Father Naber visited a friend in Berlin. There he said Mass each morning in a nearby church. When he got back to Konnersreuth, Therese described the church and its contents precisely, and also the conversations Father Naber had had with people while in Berlin. Therese had indeed been present in that city through bilocation. . . . (*Therese Neumann: Mystic and Stigmatist*, pp. 59-60, Albert Vogl: TAN Books and Publishers, Inc., Rockford, IL, 1987.)

Mr. Vogl told me personally that Therese continues to appear to some of her faithful followers to this very day.

As a final example of this mysterious charism, we cannot exclude Padre Pio, whose long personal history of bilocations are well-known. He, too, continues to pay visits to many of his spiritual children the world over, according to the numerous testimonies from those he has visited.

Many a time Padre Pio would come to the aid of those who were seriously ill or close to death. Mrs. Devoto of Genoa was one who was in danger of losing her leg, and she decided to call on Padre Pio for help, fearing that she may have to have her leg amputated. No sooner did she call on the holy friar than he appeared in her doorway. He told her to "wait for nine days," and then she would be cured. Exactly as predicted, Mrs. Devoto was miraculously cured without the aid of an operation! On the tenth day, her doctor verified that her leg had completely healed. All of this in Genoa, Italy, while others knew Padre Pio to be far away at that time in San Giovanni Rotondo, Italy!

Padre Pio has been reportedly seen in many different countries while others will testify that he was with them at the same time in the friary at San Giovanni Rotondo. Some of these reports include the countries of Austria, Uruguay and the United States. Countless testimonies come from all over Italy as well, where the holy friar has been seen to appear and heal the sick or dying.

There was once a case where Padre himself admitted to being in Milwaukee, Wisconsin, on June 25, 1950, to assist at the death of the father of a Capuchin. Once again, others knew him to be right where he always was at that time: in the small friary of Our Lady of Grace. In fact, Padre Pio never left this Franciscan friary (which is nestled high in the Gargano Mountains near the Adriatic Sea) for many years.

There are simply too many cases of the Padre's bilocations to repeat here. One can simply refer to the books on this saintly stigmatist that I have listed in the bibliography. There you will find thorough documentations for all of his extraordinary gifts, as well as the many stories of his exceptional life. (To order those official and reliable books that are printed straight from Our Lady of Grace Friary in San Giovanni Rotondo, I supply this address: Father Alessio Parente, O.F.M. Cap., general editor; Our Lady of Grace Capuchin Friary, 71013 San Giovanni Rotondo, Foggia, Italy.) Father Alessio speaks very good English, and would be more than happy to assist. In addition to these books listed in my bibliography, Father Alessio is the author of many fine books on Padre Pio; he's a definite authority on the Padre's life, for he was his personal aid and one of his closest friends the last six years prior to his death.

Visions and Apparitions

Perhaps the most commonly known phenomena associated with the mystical life are heavenly visions and apparitions. Practically every great mystic has experienced such things, and countless stories have been written from the pens of the saints themselves describing these wonders. Yet there are some popular misconceptions surrounding these mystical gifts. We will look at one of them in a moment, but for now let us attempt to provide a working definition for both of these graces as a starting point for this particular study.

There are basically three types of *visions* and *locutions* (a supernatural communication to the ear, imagination or the intellect): 1) *sensible* or external, whereby the communication is perceived by seeing or hearing; 2) *imaginative*, where all perceptions occur in the mind; and 3) *intellectual*, which does not involve any of the senses (internally or externally), but rather is a kind of intellectual vision that is purely spiritual in nature.

The first type is common to beginners, who still rely upon the senses for consolations, delights and inspirations. The second is common to more advanced souls, who are no longer as dependent upon sensual stimulation, but who nevertheless are still attached to some spiritual delight or consolation. The third type is experienced by those who have reached the heights of the mystical life, where the Spirit operates more purely in the soul and infuses the divine love and wisdom in such a way that no ordinary human effort could ever achieve.

Interior visions (illuminations) are usually given for the benefit of one's own sanctification; these differ from *prophecy*, which is normally meant for the universal Church's edification. Why does God choose to favor some souls with private visions that are meant for them alone? Because through them, some are inspired to climb even higher in their already-heightened mystical state; others need guidance or correction, and some need divine protection and discernment from the snares of the devil. At any rate, the Lord disposes His gifts to everyone according to His divine will (see 1 Cor 12:7-11).

The important thing to remember is that one should not desire these visions (especially bodily apparitions) because they are really not necessary for salvation. Furthermore, visions and apparitions can be misleading, misunderstood or misinterpreted. Worst of all, many of these celestial visions can be caused by diabolical intervention in one's life, so one must not believe in them too readily. Rather, the discernment of a good spiritual director who is wise in the ways of the spiritual life is crucial in order that one is not disillusioned with his own imaginations, nor deceived by the devil.

Listen to the wise counsel of that great master, St. John of the Cross:

> Besides the hardship of avoiding any error resulting from God's locutions and visions, there is also the difficulty of discerning those communications which the devil causes. For his usually have resemblance to God's. He imparts facsimiles of God's communications so that, disguised among the flock like the wolf in sheep's clothing, his meddling may be hardly discernible (Mt 7:15). Since the devil through conjecture makes many reasonable manifestations that turn out to be true, people may be misled, thinking that the revelations must then be from God. These peo-

ple do not realize the ease with which the devil with his clear natural light knows, through their causes, many past or future events. . . . (*Collected Works*, "The Ascent of Mount Carmel," Book II, chpt. 21.)

St. Teresa of Avila further warns us about the dangers of the evil one and the need for prudent counseling:

What is necessary, Sisters, is that you proceed very openly and truthfully with your confessor. I don't mean in regard to telling your sins, for that is obvious, but in giving an account of your prayer. If you do not give such an account, I am not sure you are proceeding well, nor that it is God who is teaching you. He is very fond of our speaking as truthfully and clearly to the one who stands in His place as we would to Him and of our desire that the confessor understand all our thoughts and even more our deeds however small they be. If you do this you don't have to go about disturbed or worried. Even if the vision is not from God, it will do you no harm if you have humility and a good conscience. His Majesty knows how to draw good from evil, and the road along which the devil wanted to make you go astray will be to your greater gain. . . . (*Collected Works*, "The Interior Castle," Part VI, chpt. 9.)

Let us remember, however, that authentic visions do exist, especially in the lives of God's favored souls. The extreme caution one must take concerning these holy images and the advice to not seek them does not always mean that one must never accept them, especially if they've been authenticated by the director of the soul. In this case, the visions or apparitions may be made known as an act of obedience to one's superiors if they felt it wise to disclose them.

Perhaps these visions were meant to be signs to the faithful of God's loving action; or maybe they contain useful counsels for the visionary himself. Again, the spiritual director must guide the soul and advise him accordingly.

Closely related to these celestial visions is the phenomena known as *apparitions*. We will avoid discussion of the diabolical apparitions, since this was treated in a previous unit (see "The Spiritual Warfare"). The apparitions we will examine are the *corporal visions* that deal with the physical representations of the material things of heaven and earth. Visions of *incorporeal substances* (angels and departed souls) cannot be seen in this earthly life because they are of the spiritual (and not natural) order. Yet on rare occasions, God sometimes allows these saintly souls to see heavenly or spiritual beings when He sends them as messengers, protectors, or to plead for the prayers and sacrifices of the chosen soul. When this happens the spiritual beings temporarily take on a material body in order for one to recognize and converse with them. Such is the case with guardian angels, the poor souls in Purgatory, the saints, Jesus, and the Blessed Virgin Mary. We will now investigate the many ways these heavenly beings (or those in Purgatory) have manifested themselves to the stigmatist, as well as the mystical visions associated with them.

One type of bodily apparition that frequently occurs to the stigmatist is that involving the poor souls in Purgatory, who often appear in recognizable form to the victim, asking for his or her prayers and sacrifices.

Stigmatist Anne Catherine Emmerich (1774-1824), one of the greatest visionaries the Church has ever produced, described these corporeal visions that the Lord had granted her. Some of these souls appeared to her buried in darkness, tortured with thirst, heat and sometimes extreme cold; other times these images appeared the color of grey. These darkened features are thought to reflect the state of their impure souls in Purgatory, burning from the flames of purification.

Often these poor souls are those whom the stigmatist once knew in this life, be it relatives, friends, immediate family, or neighbors. At times a familiar priest or Religious appear to plead for the victim's sacrifice and intercession on their behalf. Other souls that Anne Catherine Emmerich saw were kings, soldiers, peasants, and doctors.

An interesting description was made by Anne regarding these souls and how they were manifested to her in a vision of Purgatory:

> The saints were grouped according to their spiritual relationship: the religious in their Orders higher or lower, according to their individual merits; the martyrs, according to their victories; and laics of all classes, according to their progress in the spiritual life, the efforts they had made to sanctify themselves. . . . (*The Life of Anne Catherine Emmerich: Volume II*, p. 201; Very Reverend Carl E. Schmöger, C.SS.R.: TAN Books and Publishers, Inc., Rockford, IL, 1976.)

Furthermore, all of these souls were continually tormented by evil spirits, according to where they happened to be in Pugatory. Those who had sinned the most frequently or seriously were placed in the lower depths of Purgatory, which is very close to the borders of Hell. Here, the flames of purgation burn far more violently and the poor soul suffers more intensely and for longer periods of time, since they have more to atone for before they are released into heaven. In these lower levels, the evil spirits are able to attack their victims more directly and with greater force. Yet a poor soul is often able to appear to some on earth seeking prayers and sacrificial offerings, for God has allowed those here on earth to make atonement as satisfaction for their sin. They cannot help themselves, for the time of merited grace is during our earthly lives, not later.

Let us examine other visions from the holy stigmatists concerning Purgatory:

St. Mary Magdalen dei Pazzi (1566-1607) was once transported to Purgatory in a moment of ecstasy. There she saw everyone from Religious to simple souls, imprisoned in different levels of dark dungeons. They were screaming in pain, tormented constantly by demons and the burning flames of purifying fire.

St. Lydwine of Schiedam (1380-1433) was also transported to Purgatory, where she saw suffering souls trapped in various pits or wells. Some souls appeared as though on fire, and even took on the characteristic of molten metal, so much were they being purged for their transgressions. Lydwine also saw the guardian angels of these victims, who faithfuly stayed with them in their darkened wells. Lydwine was repeatedly asked to pray and suffer for them, and she did so heroically throughout the remainder of her life.

The holy stigmatist, St. Gertrude the Great (1263-1302), was once visited during an ecstasy by a former Religious from her own convent. This pious soul was surely thought by the sisters to be in heaven, but this nun from Purgatory explained how even the slightest stain of sin must be purged before one can enter heaven:

> The deceased sister was shown to her standing before the throne of God, surrounded by a brilliant halo and in rich garments. Nevertheless, she appeared sad and troubled; her eyes were cast down, as though she were ashamed to appear before the face of God; it seemed as though she would hide herself and retire. Gertrude, much surprised, asked of the Divine Spouse of Virgins the cause of this sadness and embarrassment on the part of so holy a soul. At this sight the saint addressed herself directly to the soul. "Ah! my dear Mother," replied the soul, "I am not worthy to appear before the Immaculate Lamb. I have still some stains which I contacted upon earth. To approach the Son of Justice, one must be as pure as a ray of light. I have not yet that degree of purity which He requires of His saints. Know, that if the door of Heaven were to be opened to me, I should not dare to cross the threshhold before being entirely purified from all stain. It seems to me that the choir of virgins who follow the Lamb would repulse me with horror." "And yet," continued the Abbess, "I see you surrounded with light and glory!" "What you see," replied the soul, "is but the border of the garment of glory. To wear this celestial robe we must not retain even the shadow of sin. . . . (*Purgatory: Explained by the Lives and Legends of the Saints*, pp. 71-72; Father F.X. Schouppe, S.J.)

For those who escape the flames of Purgatory, what joy must he or she experience! When St. Francis of Assisi had been assured in a vision that he was among the elect, he exclaimed in an ecstasy of heavenly delight: "Paradise, O Paradise! We shall enter Paradise!" (*Charity for the Suffering Souls*, p. 53; Fr. John A. Nagaleisen: TAN Books and Publishers, Inc., Rockford, IL, 1982). So great was his rapture at this assurance, that he henceforth despised all transitory things.

Many a stigmatist has experienced a bodily vision of St. Michael the Archangel, especially when warnings from God are involved or protection is needed against the spirits of darkness.

Father Pascal P. Parente, noted authority on the spiritual world, described Michael's role as such:

> Saint Michael has always been the warrior Angel, fighting first Satan and his demons from the beginning, then, in the course of time, all the enemies of God's own people. He is "the great prince, who standeth for the children of thy people." As of old, so today, Saint Michael is the great defender of the Church of Christ on earth. . . . (*Beyond Space: A Book About the Angels*, p. 85-86: TAN Books and Publishers, Inc., Rockford, IL, 1973.)

One stigmatist who had many apparitions of St. Michael was Anne Catherine Emmerich:

> The Venerable Anne Catherine Emmerich was frequently granted visions of the past and future combats of the Church. Repeatedly she saw St. Michael, in the form of a warrior, standing with blood-stained sword above the Church, replacing the sword in his scabbard as a sign of victory. She was also shown how, in the present-day struggles of the Church, St. Michael would bring about a most glorious victory. This thought should be consoling to all the faithful Christians who knew with alarm the many shafts of persecution now being directed against the Church. His assistance is needed by us, especially in these troublesome times when the legions of evil are almost visibly abroad over all the earth exciting the minds of men. . . . (*St. Michael and the Angels*, p. 84; Compiled from Approved Sources: TAN Books and Publishers, Inc., Rockford, IL, 1983.)

Angelic apparitions are frequent experiences in the life of the stigmatist, especially that of the guardian angel. Father Alessio Parente, O.F.M. Cap., speaks of Padre Pio's guardian companion whom he saw and conversed with daily. Padre's guardian angel delivered messages for him, protected him from the assaults of the enemy and often counseled him in his spiritual ascent.

Listen to these words involving the intimate relationship the Padre had with his guardian angel; in fact, the two were so close that he often questioned and corrected him, as if the angel were more like a close brother or friend than the majestic celestial being that he is:

> Angel of God, my Angel . . . are you not taking care of me? Are you a creature of God? Either you're a creature of God or a creator . . . You're a creator? No. Therefore you are God's creature and you have laws which you must obey . . . You must stay beside me whether you want to or not . . . He laughs . . . what is there to laugh about? Tell me one thing . . . you must tell me . . . who was it? Either Father Agostino or the Superior . . . tell me then . . . was it perhaps their secretaries? Answer me now . . . If you don't answer me I will say it was one of those four . . . He laughs . . . an Angel laughs! . . . Tell me then . . . I won't leave you until you tell me . . .

> If not, I will ask Jesus . . . and then you'll catch it! . . . Anyway, I won't ask that little Mother, that Lady . . . who looks at me so grimly . . . She's there in a bad humor . . . Jesus, isn't it true that your Mother is in a bad humor? . . . She laughs! . . . Now then, little man (his Guardian Angel), tell me who it was . . . No answer . . . he's there . . . like a fixture . . . I want to know . . . one thing I asked you and I'm here a long time . . . Jesus, you tell me . . . (It is assumed that there his Angel answers). It took a lot for you to say it, little man! . . . you made me chatter on a lot! . . . yes, yes, Father Agostino . . . very well, my Angel, will you

save him from the war prepared by the evil one? You must save
him. . . . (*Send Me Your Guardian Angel: Padre Pio*, Father
Alessio Parente, O.F.M. Cap., Our Lady of Grace Friary, San
Giovanni Rotondo, Italy, 1984.)

Note how the angel laughs, and how Padre corrects him like a father
would do to his small child. These words were taken down by his spiritual
director, Padre Agostino, during an eavesdropping of one of his ecstatic
visions.

At other times, the guardian angel would serve as Padre Pio's protector
against the spirits of darkness, as these words from the stigmatized friar
plainly reveal:

Jesus, will the evil one come tonight? . . . Well, help those two
who assist me, protect and defend them . . . I know, you are there
. . . but . . . Angel of mine, stay with me! Jesus, one last thing
. . . let me kiss you . . . Fine! . . . how sweet are those wounds!
. . . they bleed . . . but this blood is sweet . . . is sweet . . . Jesus,
sweetness . . . Holy Host . . . Love, Love that sustains me, Love
. . . until we meet again! (a rivederci) . . . November 29, 1911.

Remarkable as it may seem, the Padre was even known to have scolded
his guardian angel and reprimanded him in no uncertain terms:

My Jesus, why do you seem so very young this morning? You
have become so small. My Guardian Angel, do you see Jesus?
Well then, bow to him! That is not enough . . . Kiss his wounds
. . . Fine . . . Good! Angel of mine . . . Well done little child . . .
Now, now he becomes serious . . . he pouts . . . what am I to call
you? . . . What is your name? . . . But you understand, Angel of
mine, forgive me, you understand . . . Bless Jesus for me. . . .
(December 1911, as recorded by Padre Agostino.)

And once again:

I call you Angel and you don't come immediately to help me, I
have to beg you . . . I call you little boy . . . and you become
serious . . . what a way to behave! You understand, Angel of
mine, forgive me, you understand . . . Bless Jesus also for
me. . . . (December 1911.)

I rebuke him bitterly for having kept me waiting for so long when
I had not failed to call him to my assistance. To punish him, I did
not want to look him in the face; I wanted to get away; to escape
from him. But he, poor creature, caught up with me almost in
tears and held me until I raised my eyes to his face and found
him all upset. . . . (Letters I, no. 102.)

Many times, Padre Pio's protector also helped him to understand the
many letters written to him in foreign languages that he was not normally
familiar with.

Father Agostino of San Marco in Lamis (Padre Pio's confessor) once tested this gift by writing letters to Padre in Greek and in French, two languages that he did not know. Here is what was revealed about this:

> I, the undersigned, testify under oath, that when Padre Pio received this letter, he explained its contents to me literally. When I asked him how he could read and explain it, as he did not know even the Greek alphabet, he replied: 'You know, my Guardian Angel explained it all to me'. . .
>
> Signed
The parish priest Salvatore Pannullo. . .
Pietrelcina, August 25, 1919.

Padre Pio himself also made it very clear how he learned to decipher these foreign languages:

> The heavenly beings continue to visit me and to give me a foretaste of the rapture of the blessed. And while the mission of our Guardian Angels is a great one, my own Angel's mission is certainly greater, since he has the additional task of teaching me other languages. . . . (*Letter to Padre Agostino*, September 20, 1912.)

Padre's angel had often heard from the guardian angels of other needy souls, who implored their aid to act as messengers to the holy friar of San Giovanni Rotondo:

> On 25 October 1914, Padre Pio wrote once again to Raffaelina (one of his spiritual children): 'You tell me that in the midst of the sufferings that oppress you, you often turn to me in your thoughts and you call me. Well, your good Guardian Angel sometimes transmits these necessities of yours and then I, in my unworthiness, always do my duty with Jesus, recommending you to his Fatherly goodness'. . . . (Fr. Alessio Parente, O.F.M. Cap. on Padre Pio.)

Once again I must thank Fathers Alsessio Parente, O.F.M. Cap. and Joseph Martin, O.F.M. Cap. for their permission to quote all that I needed in order to help promote the good Padre's cause. They supplied me with many fine tapes and books on this saintly stigmatist, including the one from which this information came (Fr. Alessio's *Send Me Your Guardian Angel*). In fact, I was privileged to receive a blessing from his pen on the first page of a copy of this book, where he asked Padre Pio to guide me in my work. I hope that I have served him well.

Many of the stigmatists have had a close relationship with their guardian angel, similar to some of the experiences just described on Padre Pio.

St. Gemma Galgani (1878-1903), lay stigmatist from Italy, often conversed with her guardian angel, who protected, counseled and even scolded her at times. Gemma speaks constantly about her relationship with her angel in her diary. Her spiritual director, Father Germano, had once heard her arguing with this heavenly angel, and had to remind her to always show the deepest respect for all of God's celestial beings. Gemma's guardian was also present to help her into bed the same day she had received the stigmata.

St. Rose of Lima (1586-1617) once saw her guardian angel before the throne of God, pleading with him for help during her torments and trials: "My angel! Plead for me! you have helped me in the past!"

Therese Neumann often saw her guardian angel, but as Albert Vogl has said, she could recognize him in bright light, as he was of an indistinct nature.

Anne Catherine Emmerich was favored since youth with the guidance and protection of her guardian angel. God allowed her to entrust her will to this angelic creature, who in turn enlightened her to God's designs upon her soul. Anne even revealed that her angel often took her to various places during her ecstastic moments, throughout all of Europe and even to the Holy Land.

Often this favored soul would communicate with the poor souls in Purgatory via the guidance of her angel, who led her safely through this place of purification in order that she might visit those who implored her aid. In turn, Anne would pray and suffer in order to help free them from their pain and to help gain their entrance into the heavenly kingdom.

It is important to acknowledge the great good that our guardian angels do for us. We have seen how they protect God's favored souls in order that they may more successfully carry out their missions, especially where the counter-attacks of the evil one are concerned. Yet each one of us is aided by an invisible guardian, as the teaching of both Scripture and the Church has affirmed. In fact, it is a Church dogma that every one of us, at the time of baptism, receives an angel, who accompanies, inspires and guides throughout our entire life. These celestial beings are forever at our side, faithful to our welfare, and always ready to intercede for us if we implore their help. Because of this reality, the Church honors her guardian angels on the feast day of October 2.

The visions that the stigmatists have experienced do not stop with the angels. Many have seen apparitions of the saints, as we shall now encounter.

St. Catherine of Siena once saw St. Peter, St. Paul and St. John the Evangelist surrounding the heavenly throne upon which the Lord sat in all His majesty. What's more, this extraordinary vision occurred when Catherine was only six years old!

Anne Catherine Emmerich saw a tremendous number of saints during the almost continuous ecstatic visions she encountered throughout her holy life. Many of these she conversed with, and she often witnessed events in their lives as if she were right there beside them. The list is truly impressive, so only some of their names will be mentioned here: Jesus, the Blessed Virgin Mary, her guardian angel, St. Agnes, St. Agatha, St. Emerentiana, St. Paula, St. Dorothea, St. Apollonia, St. Benedict, St. Scholastica, St. Paschal, St. Cyprian, St. Isidore, St. Stephen, St. Lawrence, St. Nicodemus, St. Clare, St. Thomas Aquinas, St. Perpetua, St. Felicity, St. Justina, St. Denis, St. Ursula, St. Hubert, St. Gertrude, St. Cecilia, St. Catherine of Siena, St. Augustine, St. Francis de Sales, and St. Jane Frances de Chantal. And this is far from being a complete list! Anne Catherine Emmerich is considered to be one of the greatest visionary souls the Church has ever known; her visions of complete and detailed events in the lives of the saints are second to none.

St. Gertrude the Great was blessed with many visions and conversations with the saints, including St. Agnes, St. Benedict and St. John the Evangelist.

Therese Neumann was visited by her beloved saint, Thérèse of Lisieux (the Little Flower), on May 17, 1925, the day of her canonization. After having spoken to her, Therese Neumann was completely cured of a paralysis that had haunted her since her fall of March 10, 1918. The Little Flower had earlier cured Therese of blindness as well, on the day of her beatification ceremony in Rome, April 29, 1923.

The list does not stop with Thérèse of Lisieux, however. Therese Neumann was extraordinarily graced with many visions of the Passion scenes, as well as with apparitions from a host of saints. Here is a list of only a few of them: St. Francis of Assisi, St. Teresa of Avila, St. Helena, St. Aloysius, St. Peter, St. Paul, St. Wolfgang, St. Cecilia, St. Catherine of Siena, St. Francis de Sales, St. Barbara, St. Anthony of Padua, and St. Lawrence. And this list does not include the many visions she experienced of all Twelve Apostles, Jesus and the Blessed Virgin Mary!

Therese's visions included the following scenes: the stigmatization of St. Francis of Assisi; the martyrdom of many saints (including Sts. Lawrence, Cecilia and Barbara); deaths of various saints, such as Teresa of Avila, Francis de Sales, Aloysius, and Wolfgang; and entire narratives from the Gospels, including most of our Lord's earthly life.

If nothing else, these visions and apparitions in such great numbers help to verify the extraordinary favor that God has given these stigmatists. The remarkable supernatural phenomena surrounding these souls serve as signs to us all of their credibility, lest we doubt for a moment that the finger of God was upon them.

For our final glimpse at the visions and apparitions in the lives of the stigmatists, we will now turn to those visions of Jesus Christ and His Blessed Mother that these saintly souls have been blessed with.

Of particular interest and importance are the apparitions of the Lord immediately before or at the time of the impression of the Sacred Stigmata. The stigmatist normally always receives these heavenly visits in order to be warned of the mysterious grace that is about to take place; for others, the stigmata comes completely unexpected, but the Lord is there to console and comfort the victim soul. In some cases (such as with St. Francis of Assisi), a heavenly seraph appears to inflict the wounds upon the stigmatist. Even then, the seraph usually takes on the image of the Crucified Christ.

Padre Pio had been warned about the coming of the stigmata — at least indirectly — through several previous apparitions of the crucified Christ, as well as the appearance of an angel who had earlier pierced his heart with the wound of divine love. Here is how the Padre described these visions prior to and upon the reception of the Sacred Stigmata:

> While I was hearing the boy's confessions on the evening of the 5th, I was suddenly terrorized by the sight of a celestial person who presented himself to my mind's eye. He had in his hand a sort of weapon like a very long sharp-pointed steel blade which seemed to emit fire. At the very instant that I saw all this, I saw that person hurl the weapon into my soul with all his might. I

cried out with difficulty and felt I was dying. I asked the boy to leave because I felt ill and no longer had the strength to continue. . . . (Letter to Padre Benedetto, August 21, 1918.)

This letter was written by Padre Pio to his director two weeks after he received this permanent wound (presumably of the heart). Note that it does not disclose who the celestial person was: could it have been a seraphim, or was it an image of Christ himself? The Padre doesn't say. What is clear is that he was being prepared for the permanent stigmata that would occur on September 20, 1918, a little over one month later. This transverberation of the heart remained with him until his total transformation in Christ was complete:

This agony lasted uninterruptedly until the morning of the 7th. From that day on I have been mortally wounded. I feel in the depths of my soul a wound that is always open and which causes me continual agony. . . . (Letter to Padre Benedetto, August 21, 1918.)

After Padre Pio received the permanent visible stigmata, he again wrote to Padre Benedetto (out of obedience) and described what transpired on that fateful day of September 20:

While this was taking place, I saw before me a mysterious person similar to the one I had seen on the evening of 5 August. The only difference was that his hands and feet and side were dripping blood. . . The person of whom I spoke in a previous letter is none other than the one I mentioned having seen on 5 August. He continues his work incessantly, causing me extreme spiritual agony. . . . (Letter to Padre Benedetto, October 22, 1918.)

It is obvious that Padre is describing a vision of the Crucified Christ that appeared to him on these two occasions, whether it be from a seraphic figure or a representation of the Lord himself. The main point here is that Jesus often appears to these victim souls in His Crucified image, revealing to these souls that it is this likeness of the Savior they are to imitate. For them, it is not the glorified Christ that invites them to union, but rather the suffering, human Christ who will serve as a model for their lives as victims of love. This does not mean that the glorified Christ (Jesus as divinity) is less meaningful to the stigmatist than the human Jesus. No! It is the divine Christ who appeals to the human creature to take up His Cross, to share in His human suffering, and to do so with the love and the grace of the risen Lord, who calls them to a sacrificial life which is truly both human and divine. For the stigmatist, the divinized Christ — the Son of God, and God himself — is made known in His human nature, precisely because the victim soul is called to a human life of redemptive suffering in union with our Lord. That is his earthly mission: to represent the suffering Christ. Yet it is the divine Son of God who sustains and graces him. One day, when the stigmatist is called to his eternal reward, the mystery of the human-divine God will be revealed in all its fullness, as it will be to each of us who are destined to enter the heavenly kingdom.

Another victim soul who experienced frequent apparitions of the

Crucified Christ was stigmatist Josefa Menendez (1890-1923), the Coadjutrix Sister of the Society of the Sacred Heart of Jesus. We have these words from Josefa herself, who described the appearance of our Lord prior to and upon the impression of the Sacred Wounds:

> I offered myself to His sweet will, but as I was afraid of falling asleep, I asked Him to be kind enough to wake me. . .
> Hardly had I gone to bed than I fell asleep. . .
> I do not remember what the time was when I awoke at the sound of His voice calling me. 'Josefa!' Stupefied with sleep, I said: 'O, my Jesus, forgive me. What time is it?'
> 'What does that matter, Josefa? . . . It is Love's hour.'
> How beautiful Jesus looked. He was bearing His Cross . . . He gave me His Cross, which weighed me down, and I also felt the pain in my side, and my soul was overwhelmed with anguish. . .
> February 18, 1923. . . . (*The Way of Divine Love*, p. 240; Sister Josefa Menendez: TAN Books and Publishers, Inc., Rockford, IL, 1981.)

As in many apparitions to those receiving the Sacred Stigmata, Jesus often appears with His Sacred Heart all afire, a vision of the pierced heart that was wounded for the love of humanity:

> Suddenly He appeared . . . such loveliness! His garments seemed of gold and His heart one blaze of fire. . . . (March 17, 1923.)

Again, this vision of the Sacred Heart continued:

> His heart dialated in the midst of the flames. How lovely it was! No words can express it. . . . (March 28, 1923.)

Josefa revealed the vision of her Crucified Savior at the moment she was to receive the stigmata. She felt that these visions were given as testimony to other souls of His torments:

> He was nailed to the Cross. The Crown of Thorns encircled His brow and great spiky thorns furrowed deep into the flesh. One longer than the rest had pierced its way through His forehead and emerged near the left eye which was much swollen. His face covered with blood and filth leaned forward a little to the left. Though His eyes were very swollen and bloodshot, they were open and gazed earthwards. All over His wounded body were to be seen the weals and welts caused by the scourges which in some parts had torn away fragments of flesh and skin. Blood flowed from His head and from His other wounds. His lips were purple and His mouth slightly twisted. . . His once beautiful hair which used to add such grace to His person was all matted, tangled, and clotted with blood, and falling across His face. . . . (March 30, 1923.)

The lay stigmatist Marthe Robin (1902-81) received a vision of the Crucified Christ at the exact moment of her own crucifixion, as the Father Raymond Peyret points out:

> Sometime during the early part of October (possibly on the 4th, the feast of St. Francis, the stigmatized saint), Jesus Crucified appeared before the eyes of Marthe. At once he took her paralyzed arms, rigid since February 2, 1929, and opened them wide. At that moment a tongue of flame leapt from his side, separated in two, and struck both her feet and both of her hands; a third tongue of flame struck Marthe on the heart. She bled from her hands, her feet and her heart. . . . (*Marthe Robin: The Cross and the Joy*, p. 52: Alba House, N.Y.; copyright by the Society of St. Paul, 1983.)

Alexandrina da Costa (1904-55) suffered the Passion ecstasies of our Lord weekly for many years in her room. After a Mass had been said there in the autumn of 1933, Alexandrina had this vision of Christ:

> One night Jesus appeared to me in natural dimensions, as if he had just been taken down from the cross. I could see deep, open wounds in his hands, his feet and his side. The blood streamed from these wounds, and from the breast it came with such force that, after having drenched the garment around his waist, it flooded onto the floor. . . . (*Alexandrina: The Agony and the Glory*, p.28; Francis Johnston: TAN Books and Publidhers, Inc., Rockford, IL, 1982.)

In fact, entire Passion ecstasies that Alexandrina experienced have been filmed and photographed for observation by authorities in Rome. Father Pinho, Father Terca and Dr. Azevedo were present during an entire Passion ecstasy that took place on August 29, 1941. Father Terca (a Missionary of the Holy Spirit) kept a detailed diary of each ecstatic vision (forty separate scenes), which occurred every few minutes. Alexandrina had seen the entire Passion narrative from the Agony through the death on the Cross.

Listen to the description that Therese Neumann gave to the bishop's commission on January 15, 1953, concerning the first appearance of her stigmata:

> I saw Christ's sufferings in the Garden of Olives, and for the rest of that night (Lent of 1926), as far as the scourging inclusive; on the third Friday, I saw the sufferings as far as the crowning of thorns; on the fourth, which was Friday in Passion Week, I saw the entire Way of the Cross, up to the point where the Savior was thrown into an empty tomb to await the time of his own crucifixion; on the fourth Friday, which was Good Friday, I saw the entire Passion of Christ, down to the sealing of the tomb. During the nailing of the cross, the Savior looked at me with great love again (exactly as when I had received the wound of the heart) and at this moment I experienced a dull pressure of pain in my hands, at the very spot where ever since I have had the

mark of wounds. . . . (*The Visions of Therese Neumann*, p.39; Johannes Steiner: Alba House, N.Y.; copyright by the Society of St. Paul, 1976.)

Judgment of the Church

Therese goes on further to describe that her foot wounds occurred in the same way, after a vision of Christ's feet being nailed to the Cross. Therese received other wounds as a direct result of her ecstatic visions of the Passion; for instance, the crown of thorns and the scourge marks. She even cried tears of blood during these visions, just as Christ had shed at Gethsemani (Lk 22:44). Many remarkable photographs exist to verify these wounds, as Therese Neumann was one of the most thoroughly investigated stigmatists in the history of the Church. Thousands of pilgrims witnessed her Passion sufferings in her upstairs bedroom in Konnersreuth, as well as a host of medical doctors, theologians, psychiatrists, and authorities from Rome.

We now bring to a close the discourse on our Lord's appearances to these stigmatists, simply because there are so many of such cases that they would fill up many volumes by themselves. Let us conclude this section with a brief look at the appearances of the Blessed Virgin Mary to these victims of God's love.

Once St. Rose of Lima saw the Blessed Virgin appear to her as the Queen of the Most Holy Rosary, dressed in the Dominican habit; it was a reaffirmation that Rose was called to live the life of a Dominican Tertiary. Furthermore, our Lady appeared with the Infant Jesus on her knee. After giving Him to Rose, she embraced Him sweetly in her arms.

St. Gemma Galgani once saw the Blessed Virgin Mary drawing her close, then wrapping her inside her mantle. It was at this time that the Crucified Savior appeared to her and gave her the Sacred Stigmata. Mary had further comforted her after the reception of these wounds, reassuring Gemma of her love and support.

Our Lady had frequently appeared to Padre Pio, even as a young child. Along with our Lord, Mary consoled him and helped to reaffirm the Padre's choice to enter the Franciscan Order. Later, she comforted him when he recieved the visible stigmata, and remained close to him for the rest of his life. Padre Pio once claimed to a fellow friar that Mary was always present to him in his cell room at our Lady of Grace Friary, especially the last few years of his life. It is well-known that the Padre had constantly recited his beloved Rosary, and encouraged everyone to have a deep devotion to the Blessed Virgin. Rarely was he seen without the Rosary beads wrapped around his fingers.

It was Mary who placed a pillow under Padre Pio's head after he was attacked by the devil, thrown to the floor of his cell, and left alone, cut and battered about his head. The blood-stained pillow can still be seen to this day on the chair in his cell at the friary. This story was told by Padre himself to Fathers Alessio Parente, O.F.M. Cap. and Joseph Martin, O.F.M. Cap.

Our Lady often came to Josefa Menendez while she suffered the Passion of our Lord. Mary was there to console Josefa before the impression of the visible stigmata, and she was there after the grace was given. As Josefa herself has said:

> I saw near the Cross the Blessed Virgin, standing erect. She was gazing at her Son. She wore a purple garment and veil and spoke in a voice which was firm though full of deep sadness: 'See, my child, the state to which His love for souls has reduced Him! He whom you see in so sad and pitiable a state is my Son. Love is driving Him to His death, and it is love that constrains Him to make all men brethren by giving them all His own Mother'. . . .
> (*The Way of Divine Love*, Josefa Menendez, p.309.)

Our Lady is often present to these victim souls before our Lord visits them with the Cross. She comes to console and comfort them, and offers protection against the onslaughts of the devil. Mary is our Mother; she is Mother of the universal Church. As Mediatrix of all Grace, the Blessed Virgin is the aqueduct from which flows forth God's many blessings to His people. It is very evident that she plays a major role in the life of the stigmatist, primarily because it was she who shared so intimately the Passion of Her Son. It was Mary who stood at the foot of the Cross, and it was she who carried these sufferings in her heart, which was pierced with the sword of crucifixion (Lk 2:35). Our Lord's sufferings were her sufferings, the Savior's Cross became her Cross. One cannot separate the Passion of Christ from His Most Blessed Mother, for the blood He spilled was hers to begin with. Likewise, the Blessed Virgin is intimately present in the lives of the stigmatists, for they have come to unite themselves to the Cross of our Lord, where Mary has stood all along. To love the Savior is to also love His Mother; without love for Mary, there is no love for her Son.

Supernatural Communions

Many of the saints throughout Church history enjoyed the blessing of *spiritual Communions* — that is to say, the experience of the Holy Mass and the reception of the Sacred Species from afar, usually accomplished through a profound meditation and reinactment of the Mass, in the form of a vision that sweeps across the mind. It comes from the sweet desire to receive Jesus as the Bread of Life in order to nourish the body and soul, especially when one is deprived of attending Mass for one reason or another. Yet many souls have made spiritual Communions numerous times each day, so profound are their longings for the spiritual union with the Lord.

The real desire for reception of the Eucharist in the lives of these gifted souls should not surprise us, for the Lord himself has told us that His Body and Blood would contain the real food that gives eternal life: "For my flesh is food indeed and my blood is drink indeed. He who eats on my flesh and drinks my blood abides in me, and I in him" (Jn 6:55-56). Again we hear the words of the Lord: "He who eats me will live because of me" (Jn 6:57). This reception of the Eucharist from afar or as a result of a spiritual, mystical experience is a grace given to those chosen souls who are literally transformed in Christ; they live through Him, with Him and in Him, sharing in the most intimate union that is as mysterious as it is divine: "I have food to eat of which you do not know" (Jn 4:32).

An extraordinary phenomenon that occurs frequently in the lives of the stigmatists has come to be known as the reception of Communion "from a distance." In fact, more than 40 souls given the titles of Venerable, Blessed or Saint have experienced such a mystical grace. According to Dr. Imbert-Gourbeyre, 55 of the stigmatists he studied received Communion in this way, or one out of every six: five in the thirteenth century, seven in the fourteenth, six in the fifteenth, 22 in the seventeenth, seven in the eighteenth and eight in the nineteenth. Only three of those 55 examined had been men.

Out of the list of 321 stigmatists that Dr. Imbert-Gourbeyre identified, 27 had miraculous Communions only once, but 14 had this experience many times, and 27 frequently so.

How can the reception of Communion be of a miraculous nature? There are two ways that have been acknowledged: 1) sometimes the stigmatist receives the Sacred Host directly from the Lord, a saint or an angel, always during the state of ecstasy; or 2) the Host has been seen to suddenly disappear from the priest's hand, where it is instantly transported to the tongue of the stigmatist without the aid of the priest placing It there.

Although normally never as meritorious as the physical attendance of sacramental Communion which is celebrated by the priest, nevertheless great graces are given for these spiritual Communions. The Church has traditionally granted an indulgence of 300 days for every spiritual Communion that is made, as well as a plenary indulgence once a month.

We have these words from Jesus to the Venerable Jane of the Cross:

> As often as you communicate spiritually, you receive a grace similar to that which you derive from the sacramental Communion. . . . (*The True Spouse of Jesus Christ*, p. 587; St. Alphonsus Liguori: Redemptorist Fathers, Brooklyn, N.Y.,1929.)

Extraordinary cases of these spiritual Communions have been observed in the lives of many pious souls, such as Blessed Angela of the Cross, who reportedly made a hundred of these Communions every day, and then a hundred more each night!

St. Alphonsus Liguori (1696-1787), Doctor of the Church, tells of this inspiring case:

> How pleasing these spiritual Communions are to God, and the many graces which He bestows through their means, was manifested by our Lord himself to Sister Paula Maresca, the foundress of the convent of St. Catherine of Siena in Naples, when (as it is related in her life) he showed her two precious vessels, the one of gold, the other of silver. He then told her that in the gold vessel he preserved her sacramental Communions, and in the silver one her spiritual Communions. . . . (*The Holy Eucharist*, p. 121; St. Alphonsus Liguori: Redemptorist Fathers, Brooklyn, N.Y., 1934.)

Many unusual phenomena have surrounded the lives of various stigmatists who received Communion miraculously. One example is Louise Lateau (1850-83), the Belgian mystic of the nineteenth century. In January, 1876, Louise suffered so much from the stigmata in her feet that she was unable to attend Mass. Communion was then brought to her daily. One day, when the parish priest was about to say the prayers of the Ritual in her room, an unusual thing occurred: the Host that lay on the table miraculously leaped onto her tongue, though it had been some distance away!

Let us hear what a competent witness had to say:

> Immediately after Communion, Louise's mouth shut, all movement ceased absolutely, there was not even any movement of deglutition to swallow the Host. Doctor de Backer of Paris, who was present at the ceremony on Holy Saturday, 1883, testifies: 'I saw the Host in some way moistened, with no movement of the glottis in swallowing; there was a sort of spontaneous introduction of the Host into the stomachal cavity. . . . (*The Enigma of the Stigmata*, p.68; René Biot: Hawthorn Books, Inc., N.Y., 1962.)

Therese Neumann is another well-documented case of miraculous Communions. After her absence from all food since the mid-1920s, Therese lived only on the daily Communion she received from the hand of her priest and director, Father Joseph Naber. Usually, at the sight of the Sacred Host, Therese went into an ecstatic repose. When the Host was placed on her tongue, it immediately disappeared without any effort of swallowing; the Species spontaneously entered her body as fast as it was placed in her mouth.

Many other stigmatists had frequently experienced miraculous Communions, as in the following examples:

St. Mary Francis of the Five Wounds (1734-91) had experiences of the Host miraculously transported to her from various distant places. Even before the age of two, Mary Francis had an intense yearning for the Holy Eucharist. She bore the invisible stigmata, and lived for many years on nothing but the Holy Eucharist.

St. Catherine of Siena (1347-80) frequently received the Sacred Host from Christ himself, as well as from the angels, during her states of ecstasy. So did the stigmatist St. Gertrude the Great of Eisleben, Germany (1263-1302). Catherine was unable to take any food daily save that of the Most Holy Eucharist. Whenever the attempt was made to do so, she expelled the food from her stomach and received terrible pains. Blessed Raymond of Capua tells us this:

> Catherine was willing to appease their murmurs, and determined that every day she would go once and take a seat at the common table and endeavor to eat. Although she used neither meat, nor wine, nor drink, nor eggs, and did not even touch bread, what she took — or rather, what she tried to take — caused her such sufferings that those that saw her, however hard-hearted they were, were moved to compassion: her stomach could digest nothing, and rejected whatever was taken into it; she afterwards suffered the most terrible pains and her whole body appeared to be swollen; she did not swallow the herbs which she chewed, she only drew from them their juice and rejected their substance. She then took pure water to cool her mouth; but every day she was forced to throw up what she had taken, and that with so much difficulty that it was necessary to assist her by every possible means. . . . (*Life of St. Catherine of Siena*; Blessed Raymond of Capua: P.J. Kenedy & Sons, N.Y.)

Stigmatist St. Lydwine of Shiedam (1380-1433) existed entirely on the Holy Eucharist the last nineteen years of her life. Whenever she was deprived of the Sacred Species, her strength quickly deteriorated.

St. Rose of Lima (1586-1617) was frequently weakened from her severe fasts and self-imposed penances; however, upon receiving the Holy Eucharist, Rose regained her strength and restored her health.

Anne Catherine Emmerich (1774-1824), German stigmatist and extraordinary visionary, existed on only water and the Eucharist for the last twelve years of her life. Alexandrina da Costa (1904-55) subsisted solely on the Eucharist for three years, and Therese Neumann (1898-1962) for thirty-six years, from 1926 to 1962.

As we have learned from these many examples, the Lord invites us to partake in His Body and Blood in order to have eternal life, both with and through Him. As the Lord commanded (Mt 26:26-30; Mk 14:22-26; Lk 22:14-20), we are to share in His Body as one community in faith, as one Mystical Body, as long as we live out our earthly lives as a People of God. We have also heard how our Lord offers eternal life to those who partake in the Holy Eucharist (Jn 6:55-57), and even suggests that to not partake in this ongoing Supper could cost one his very soul: "Truly, truly, I say to you, unless you eat the flesh of the Son of Man and drink his blood, you have no life in you; he who eats my flesh and drinks my blood has eternal life" (Jn 6:53-54).

Although the great mystics and stigmatists are unusually gifted ones who have been known to receive the Eucharist in miraculous ways, nevertheless we are all called to the Lord's Supper to nourish and rejuvenate our souls. We may never experience these supernatural ways of receiving Communion, but we are all called to follow the example of these saintly souls, who placed the Eucharist at the center of their spiritual lives. As we have learned, the mere desire of the Eucharist brings great graces to all; the actual reception of the Host during the celebration of the Sacred Mass is even greater, for it is there that we share as a witnessing community the signs of our faith. For those unable to attend the Holy Mass, the spiritual Communion is important in order to keep the Lord in our hearts and in our souls, each and every day that we live to serve and to love Him. For it is there in our hearts that we find the Lord, and it is there that He unites himself with those who seek Him earnestly.

Kardiognosis

One of the unusual charisms that many of the stigmatists possess is known as *kardiognosis*, or the "reading of hearts." This gift gives one the ability to discern the condition of another's soul; for example, whether they are living in God's grace or in the state of mortal sin. Amazingly, some are aware of one's deepest secrets — in effect, they can read minds. Some of these gifted people have been able to see the intimate details of one's past, present or future. Many such souls have been equally as blessed in spiritual direction, especially as needed to help one understand God's will for him or to counsel him against the snares of the enemy.

Therese Neumann displayed a remarkable ability to read hearts and counsel souls accordingly:

In describing the state of elevated calm we understand that Therese, after her stigmata, was able to look into the inner heart of the person who was speaking with her. The person's thoughts and intentions were all known before being spoken, and even when they are not actually spoken at all. She also had a privileged knowledge of the individual's former life. But references to such knowledge, excepting for very exceptional cases, were made only when the individual was alone with Therese. Thus the only proof for the exercise of this faculty could come from personal experience, or from the strong emotion reactions of people who had experienced this knowledge, or from sharing experiences in conversation afterwards. Even in the childlike state of prepossession Therese possessed this faculty, whenever a person touched her finger. . . . (*Therese Neumann: A Portrait*, pp. 58-59; Johannes Steiner: Alba House, N.Y.; copyright by the Society of St. Paul, Staten Island, N.Y., 1967.)

In effect, the stigmatist who possesses this discerning gift is always concerned about the spiritual welfare of the soul. The reading of hearts is a charism that has charity as a cornerstone and God as its goal.

Archbishop Teodorowicz described Therese's charism as such:

Therese definitely has a very special and particularly acute sense of perception. The penetrating rays of her knowledge of human hearts illuminate the most mysterious and secret ways of the human soul, the ways of grace or the ways of sin, and these ways cannot be spied (upon) or discovered by any earthly organ. Everything — the story of their past life, the unveiling of the oppression within each individual soul — serves only as an external but very precious evidence of what constitutes the very heart of the gift of holy wisdom. . . . (*Therese Neumann: A Portrait*, p. 191: Johannes Steiner.)

What purpose does this gift serve outside of one's own interest? In Therese's case, she was able to help uncover those impediments which hindered the spiritual progress of the soul; furthermore, she helped to expose the types and degrees of personal sin in people with the intention of leading them closer to God. In addition to this, the positive workings of God's grace are also revealed, thereby inspiring the soul on the right road towards his or her sanctity.

The stigmatist is particularly sensitive to an awareness of a sinful nature in a person who asks for prayers, blessings or counsel. This stands to reason, for the primary mission of the holy victim soul is to counteract the effects of sin by making atonement for others before God.

Padre Pio was very much aware of those who came before him, secretly living in a state of sin. Oftentimes, he could be extremely harsh with these people, even refusing them absolution or spiritual direction until they mended their ways. Listen to a straight-forward approach he had to one of his beloved spiritual children, Raffaelina Cerase (1868-1916), the pious Third Order Franciscan whom he led to the heights of spiritual perfection:

I want to you to know that as long as you refuse to answer fully the questions I put to you in my second to the last letter, I'll be obliged, to my immense sorrow, to make you feel the effects of my silence. . . . (*Letter to Raffaelina Cerase*, June 25, 1915.)

Every good spiritual director must demand total obedience from his children, for God has placed them under his care at a particular point in their spiritual journey. It is the director who is representing God before them, and who helps them discern His most holy will for them according to their state in life and their calling.

Let us turn to another example of Padre Pio's blunt but honest assessment of Raffaelina's spiritual condition, as he replies to her challenges that hint of a stubborn disposition or secret pride:

You tell me that certain expressions I used were suggested to me by the devil. May the Lord look upon you with merciful eyes. He knows who placed those questions on my lips. It is evident, however, that you are always wide of the mark and continue to behave as a quite capricious and unmanageable child. Instead of deserving reproof, for me you are an object of compassion. I asked you such a question, not because you could, through your own fault, have considered interrupting our correspondence, for I hadn't the remotest notion of such a thing, but because I feared the devil might have suggested something of the kind to you. Judge for yourself, now, who was the true author of that question. May Jesus forgive you! You are accustomed to look at things from one side only, and hence you are very often mistaken in your judgment. . . . (May 23, 1915.)

Raffaelina was experiencing that dark night of the soul that all great mystics and favored ones go through at some point in their ascent to God. Padre — like all good directors blessed with the gift of kardiognosis — was able to point out one's strengths and weaknesses, thereby offering precious advice to help the soul advance in perfection. The key line in the above quotation from the Padre is this: "for me you are an *object of compassion.*" No matter how much he needed to correct or reprimand someone, it was always done out of a motive for charity. This is the mark of a special director who spares no feelings when it comes to helping others attain their union with God. It is a true sign of Christ's loving presence among us.

Padre Pio always made it very clear when he was directly commissioned by God to lead a soul through the ways of perfection. This he carried out only as a result of God's supernatural grace operating in his mission of service to others. Again we hear him speak to his beloved Raffaelina:

In order to avoid being deceived in actions which appear holy, you ought, on the contrary, to seek the opinion of the one who has charge of you. Do you understand?. . . (November 4, 1915.)

You have already consulted too many doctors without waiting for the consent and opinion of the one to whom God has entrusted you. . . . (September 7, 1915.)

Yet the demanding nature of the good spiritual director is always tempered with charity. As often as Padre Pio reproved his disciple, he showed his true motivation of love:

> Don't tell me this time also that I am too demanding in a matter which to an ignorant person would appear negligible. Jesus who reads the depths of the heart knows whether or not I am too pretentious in this. . . . (November 4, 1915.)

> I perceive in you a lack of docility since you fail to be convinced by my assurances. Do you not see that it is the devil who wants to make you lose at all costs that trust and abandonment towards the one who is your spiritual guide? Moreover, when all is said and done, this is a real waste of time and prevents you from advancing rapidly. I cannot spare you this time from a gentle brotherly reproof. . . . (June 21, 1914.)

This holy stigmatized friar of San Giovanni Rotondo knew the most intimate details in the lives of many of his spiritual children that he directed. Once again, note what he said to Raffaelina Cerase:

> Everything is known to me . . . your life and your interior feelings, everything because of divine mercy. . . . (January 23, 1915.)

The above correspondence was taken from the following source: *Letters: Volume II (Correspondence with Raffaelina Cerase, Noblewoman)*; Our Lady of Grace Friary, San Giovanni Rotondo, Italy, 1987 edition.

Kardiognosis, as we have seen, is an extraordinary gift given to some of God's favored ones for the sanctification of those whom He puts in their care. Never is such a gift (of any special charism, for that matter) given for one's benefit alone. This is the gauge by which we must judge the authenticity of God's actions among us.

Hierognosis

Hierognosis is a gift which many of God's victims have had; it involves the ability to discern holy things from those which are not holy, including the following: whether or not a Host has been consecrated; if an object has or has not been blessed: the presence of a good or evil spirit; and the ability to find lost or hidden objects and holy relics. This charism is closely related to the gift of kardiognosis, and is very common among God's stigmatists; therefore, it is only fitting to believe that souls who are unusually holy themselves would be able to sense when a holy presence is in their midst.

Johannes Steiner revealed this about Therese Neumann's gift of hierognosis:

> Therese Neumann, especially when she was in the state of "prepossession," enjoyed the faculty of recognizing relics, consecrations and blessings. When she was in this state, if someone touched a relic against her finger (generally her eyes would be closed), she would react negatively, or not at all, if the

relic was not genuine or only a facsimile. But if it was genuine, she would react positively and enthusiastically and frequently also tell where it came from; sometimes adding that "it was only touched to the relic." The same was true of blessed objects. With persons too, who would touch her finger, she could immediately tell if they were priests or laymen. . . . (*Therese Neumann: A Portrait*, p. 58.)

Anne Catherine Emmerich was unusually gifted in the discernment of holy things. Her remarkable ability to sense when an ordained priest was near (even when she did not see him), or the identification of relics or their whereabouts is well-documented.

Father Carl E. Schmöger, C.SS.R., described some of these discernments in his study of this most unusual stigmatist:

With the gift of prophecy, Sister Emmerich had also received the power of discerning holy objects, even by the senses. Blessed bells had for her a melody all their own, a sound essentially different from every other that struck her ear; her taste detected the blessing imparted to holy water as readily as others can distinguish water from wine; her sense of smell aided her sight and touch in recognizing the relics of saints; and she had as lively a perception of the sacerdotal benediction sent her from afar as when given in her actual vicinity. . . . (*The Life of Anne Catherine Emmerich: Volume II*, p. 394.)

Anne herself explained these holy things which she was able to distinguish, such as blessed objects or relics:

I see the blessing and the blessed object endowed with a healing and helping power. I see them as luminous and radiating light; evil, crime and malediction appear before me as darkness radiating darkness and working destruction. I see light and darkness as living things enlightening or obscuring. . . . (p. 395.)

I feel irresistibly drawn to look for these relics. They are attracted to me, and I sighed for them! It is easy to recognize them at such times, for they shine with a different light. I see little pictures like the faces of the saints to whom they belong, toward which rays of light dart from the particles. I cannot express it! It was a wonderful state!. . . (p. 417.)

Besides the ability to discern between holy and unholy objects, Anne could also sense the presence of a holy being, whether angelic or human:

I see the angels without aureolas. They appear to me, indeed, under a human form with faces and hair, but they are more delicate, more noble, more beautiful than men. They are immaterial, perfectly luminous and transparent, but in different degrees. I also see blessed souls surrounded by a material light, rather white than resplendent, and around them a many-colored glory, an aureola whose tints correspond to their kind of purification. I see neither angels nor saints moving their feet, excepting in the historic senses of their life upon earth, as men among men. I never see these apparitions in their real state speaking to one another with the mouth; they turn to one another, interpenetrate one another. . . . (p. 419-420.)

Many other stigmatists have been able to discern various relics that are venerated by the faithful: authentic pieces of the True Cross; other cherished relics of the Passion; bones and articles of clothing from various saints; relics of the Apostles; relics of the Blessed Virgin Mary; etc.

Miraculous Healings

Many a stigmatist has been known to possess an unusual gift of healing, especially of the miraculous order. Countless testimonies exist on these phenomenal cures which seem to defy all known laws of nature.

One of the more incredible gifts is that of raising people from the dead. As unbelievable as this might seem, many such cases are on record. Among such cases is the one in the Acts of the Apostles, where St. Peter had brought back to life a dead woman from Joppa:

Now there was at Joppa a disciple named Tabitha which means Dorcas or Gazelle. She was full of good works and acts of charity. In those days she fell sick and died. . . (Acts 9:36-37).

Later on in the same story, Peter is called by his disciples to come to her aid:

But Peter put them all outside and knelt down and prayed; then turning to the body he said, 'Tabitha, rise.' And she opened her eyes, and when she saw Peter she sat up. And he gave her his hand and lifted her up. Then calling the saints and widows he presented her alive. And it became known throughout Joppa, and many believed in the Lord. . . (Acts 9:40-42).

There are many such examples of God's holy souls who have raised the dead back to life. Jesus himself gave this power to His disciples as He prepared them for their mission:

And preach as you go, saying: 'The kingdom of heaven is at hand!' Heal the sick, raise the dead, cleanse lepers, cast out demons. . . (Mt 10:7-8).

Even before the coming of Christ, God had blessed some of His servants with the power to raise the dead, as in the case of Elisha who raised a boy back to life:

When Elisha came into the house, he saw the child lying dead on his bed. So he went in and shut the door upon the two of them, and prayed to the Lord. Then he went up and lay upon the child, putting his mouth upon his mouth, his eyes upon his eyes, and his hands upon his hands; and as he stretched himself upon him, the flesh became warm. Then he got up again, and walked once to and fro in the house, and went up, and stretched himself upon him; the child sneezed seven times, and the child opened his eyes. Then he summoned Gehazi and said, 'Call the Shunammite.' So he called her. And when she came to him, he said, 'Take up your son.' She came and fell at his feet, bowing to the ground; then she took up her son and went out. . . (2 Kgs 4:32-37).

Why does God give some chosen souls the ability to raise the dead? There are really several reasons: 1) in order to prove His power and glory to His people; 2) to substantiate St. Paul's claim that all the faithful will one day rise to a new life (see 1 Cor. 15); and perhaps most importantly, 3) to remind the people of Christ's glorious Resurrection and His eternal role as Lord of heaven and earth. Indeed, we all look forward to our own resurrection as the cornerstone of our faith, for as St. Paul has reminded us, our faith is in vain if Christ has not risen (1 Cor 15:14). Both Church Tradition and the Sacred Scriptures claim to await with confidence this marvelous promise from God to those who love Him:

> . . . And I look for the resurrection of the dead, and the life of the world to come. Amen. . . . (*The Nicene-Constantinopolitan Creed*, A.D. 381.)

> . . . everyone who sees the Son and believes in him should have eternal life; And I will raise him up at the last day. . . (Jn 6:40).

St. Catherine of Siena (1347-80), holy stigmatist Doctor of the Church, raised her dead mother Lapa Benincasa from the dead through her prayers and pious tears. Lapa lived on to the ripe old age of 89.

Stigmatist St. Teresa of Avila (1515-82), also a Doctor of the Church, reportedly raised her sister's son Gonzalo from his premature death. This occurred after Teresa covered the child with her veil, held him tightly and prayed that God would spare her sister and brother-in-law the agony of the loss of their beloved child. The Lord granted her request, for Teresa handed her revived nephew over to her sister after he had been taken for dead.

St. Rose of Lima (1586-1617) was also gifted with this extraordinary charism, but only after her own death and intercession from heaven. It is reported that Rose raised a dead daughter back to life after the mother placed a relic of Rose's on the girl's mouth. Her father and several others witnessed her resurrection and complete return to normal health.

St. Margaret of Cortona (1247-97), holy saint who bore the wounds of our Lord, was claimed to have cured the sick, secured the release of souls from Purgatory, and raised a dead boy back to life.

There have been stories that Padre Pio of Pietrelcina, one of the great miracle workers of our time, raised a dead man through his intercession (this report has not been adequately substantiated as of this time).

Many more examples of these miraculous resurrections exist in the lives of the stigmatists. What has been presented should be sufficient grounds to at least take these claims seriously.

Another area of miraculous healings can be found in cases of physical abnormalities, such as in paralysis, disease, physical injury or deformity, blindness, deafness, as well as in mental disorders. Let us take a brief glance at some of these wonders in the lives of the stigmatists.

St. Francis of Assisi (1182-1226), the first recognized stigmatist in Church history, had cured many people of various illnesses, diseases and deformities. One time Francis healed a man of his leprosy after washing him and rubbing sweet herbs on him with his holy hands.

Francis' devoted follower of the twentieth century, Padre Pio of Pietrelcina (1887-1968), has a long history of miraculous cures. Some of those people whose stories are well-documented and thoroughly examined are named as follows: the son of Count Marzotta (cured of blindness); Gemma Di Giorgi (born with no pupils but able to see after Padre's intercessions); Maria Giuliano of Ghizzano, Italy (cured of epithelioma, a severe tongue disease, in 1919); Preziosi Paolina of San Giovanni Rotondo, Italy (cured in 1925 of extreme pneumonia); Maria Pennisi of Pietrelcina (cured in 1922 of tuberculosis; Enrico del Fante (who was healed in 1930 of kidney failure); Countess Baiochhi of Gavinana (who had an incurable illness, but with Padre's intercession was completely healed); Annunciata Ventrella of San Giovanni Rotondo (cured of heart disease by Padre Pio); Elena Galeati of Imola (completely healed of a thyroid malady); Franco Angelini of Bologna, Italy (a baby who was cured of pneumonia after Padre Pio's picture was put under the child's pillow). Of course, this is only a small sampling of the incredible gift of healing that Padre Pio possessed. And to think that only two authenticated miracles through a soul's intercession are needed for Beatification and two more for Canonization makes this list (and others) impressive, indeed!

Stigmatist Marthe Robin (1902-81), the Third Order Franciscan from Chateauneuf-de-Galaure, France, once interceded for the cure of a Mrs. Octave of Vaulx-en-Velin, also of France. She had come down with puerperal fever after giving birth to a new son. There was no hope for her. Eventually, in June of 1941, Mrs. Octave was completely cured after some linens that had touched Marthe had been placed under her sick bed.

Many claims of total healing have come from the intercessions of stigmatist Mary Rose Ferron (1902-36), the "Little Rose" from Woonsocket, Rhode Island. A woman suffering from terminal cancer was reportedly healed, as well as a young lady who had been paralyzed since her birth.

Another area of miraculous healing that is often overlooked is that which concerns the conditions of spiritual bondage and diabolical oppression or possession; in effect, the gift of deliverance and/or exorcism. Let us conclude our study on this topic with a look at a few examples from the lives of the stigmatists.

Brother Rufino (a close companion of St. Francis of Assisi) was once being tempted and threatened by the devil. After imploring Francis' help, the devil left him alone because of his fear of confronting the holy stigmatist of Assisi. Francis frequently claimed victory over the evil one, and helped others to do so as well.

Stigmatist Josefa Menendez (1890-1923) was severely tried and beaten by the devil because of her heroic efforts to be God's victim for others. With the aid of our Lord and His Mother, Josefa courageously withstood the diabolical onslaughts and defeated the enemy's attempts to end her mission. As a result, Josefa had atoned for many a sinner and was responsible for numerous souls who escaped the clutches of Satan.

Many other victim souls have been assaulted by the evil spirit, yet through the grace of God they had withstood the warfare and helped many a soul on their way towards sanctification: St. Margaret of Cortona (1247-97), St. Veronica Giuliani (1660-1727), Anne Catherine Emmerich (1774-1824), Padre Pio (1887-1968), St. Teresa of Avila (1515-82), and St. Rose of Lima (1586-1617) are just a few of the stigmatists who have suffered the spiritual combat. In fact, all of them have done so in various degrees, only because their vocation as victim souls defeats the plan of the enemy, whose primary mission is to gain the very souls that these holy victims suffer to save.

Supernatural Sufferings

Because the stigmatist is a chosen victim and lives a life of reparative suffering, we should expect him to suffer every kind of trial, illness or physical pain. This is especially so for victims who suffer vicariously, voluntarily submitting themselves to God for satisfaction due to the sins of others. Once this offering is made, God is free to inflict upon the body and soul the same sufferings due to the one he is atoning for, and then again some for his own purification and sanctification. In effect, the victim becomes a living sacrifice, a victim of every trial and tribulation imaginable in this life.

There is another reason for the stigmatists' extraordinary sufferings: God must prepare a soul to be worthy to be His victim through these tests which are designed to strengthen him to a heroic degree. The victim must attain patience and endurance in order to withstand the severest of illnesses and physical pain, as well as the emotional and spiritual conflicts that are sure to come his way.

It is the normal lot for all stigmatists to have endured the most extraordinary sufferings possible in this earthly world — sufferings that can only be described as supernatural; God himself is the Author, inflicting many of the pains upon both body and soul to those who are called to a life of reparation.

Padre Pio's intense and prolonged illnesses are well-documented, coming from his own words to his spiritual directors, Padres Agostino and Benedetto, between the years 1910-22. High fevers plagued him almost daily since 1910, and these were usually accompanied by profuse sweating (*Epist.* 3/14/1910). Furthermore, the Padre suffered from continual pain in his chest and back; even his walking was undertaken with the greatest of difficulty. When he coughed (which was quite frequent), he said that it felt like it "almost splits my chest" (11/29/1910), so painful were these physical calamities.

The list of physical sufferings that this holy stigmatist endured just between 1910-17 (let alone his entire life) makes one shudder. This list includes all sufferings prior to receiving the external stigmata: stomach troubles (7/29/1910); difficulty with breathing (3/29/1911); intense head pains (3/29/1911); weakness (7/19/1911); burning sensations (9/8/1911); failing eyesight (12/16/1911); frequently confined to bed (5/2/1911); spitting blood (6/28/1912); bodily inflictions caused by the devil (8/26/1912); beatings from the evil one (11/5/1912); wound of the heart (12/3/1912); a continual feeling of dying (10/24/1913); difficulty with eating, drinking and sleeping (11/1/1913); prolonged influenza (10/17/1915); tuberculosis (11/18/1915); a severe case of pneumonia (2/23/1917); bronchial catarrh (9/4/1917); undernourishment (9/4/1917); and thorough exhaustion

(9/27/1917). All of these sufferings, not to mention the invisible Sacred Wounds that he carried with him since 1910, nor the visible stigmata after 1918! It seems safe to conclude that no one could ever sustain such sufferings in a lifetime were it not for the divine grace which provides supernatural strength and endurance beyond the natural order.

For the stigmatist, physical suffering is only one type of affliction he must endure. In order to take up the Cross of Christ more fully, he must bear contradictions, persecutions, scourgings, moral sufferings, and great spiritual trials. What man fails to inflict, God himself supplies by mysterious pains, agonies and the wounds of the stigmata, which will make him a living crucifix in the image of Christ.

Another intriguing case is that of the stigmatist St. Lydwine of Schiedam (1380-1433). One of the most extraordinary victim souls of all time, Lydwine's sufferings are described by J.K. Huysmans in his book, *Saint Lydwine of Schiedam*:

> She now seemed to have run the gamut of possible diseases. Far from it! To read the descriptions of her biographers (which I tone down), one would think one was in a clinic, in which the most terrifying diseases, the acutest kinds of pain, the rarest crises, pass before one in succession. Her chest developed blood-blisters, then coppery pustules and boils. Gallstones, which had tortured her in early childhood but disappeared, returned, and she evacuated stones the size of a small egg. Then it was her lungs and liver which decayed; then a cancer dug an ulcer. . . When the plague broke out in Holland, she was the first infected; two bubos appeared, one on the anus, the other in the region of the heart. . . . (*The Enigma of the Stigmata*, p. 57; Rene Biot: Hawthorn Books, Inc., N.Y., 1962.)

Incredible as this may seem, it is far from a complete list of the sufferings Lydwine had to endure. Besides the above mentioned, she also experienced the following: bodily parasites; a tumor on the shoulder; ergotism; neuralgia; loss of sight in the right eye; severe toothaches; bleeding from the eyes, ears, mouth, and nose; displaced chin and swollen mouth; twisted and broken nerves; worms that ate at her spine, forming holes in her body; loss of sleep; and of course, the pains of the stigmata. Indeed, these supernatural sufferings could only be tolerated with the aid of divine grace. These unusual phenomena — especially when taken together in one soul — seem to be signs to the faithful of God's special action in these favored souls.

It should be noted that for over thirty-three years Lydwine suffered these things which have no known natural origin (when taken together as a whole); it can only be assumed that divine providence was at work in her fragile body and soul, just as it is in every stigmatist who tolerates unheard of agonies for the sake of following the Cross.

Perhaps one other example would help us to understand the terrible sufferings that these victims are subjected to. Another great victim soul was Mary Rose Ferron (1902-36), the "Little Rose" of Woonsocket, Rhode Island. During her Passion ecstasies, witnesses have seen Mary Rose bleed from the Five Sacred Wounds of her stigmata, as well as from the eyes, cheeks, nose, and the mouth. Her bleeding crown of thorn wounds was very evident to many as well. She often suffered severe gastric pains that caused her stomach to tighten up like a knot. Mary Rose was also victim to a distortion of the feet and arms, and eventually she had great difficulty in moving them at all. Added to this was a terrible hemorrhage that she experienced the last year of her life. Bedridden and in extreme pain her last two years, Mary Rose Ferron was finally relieved as she passed to her heavenly home on May 11, 1936.

Many other stigmatists have suffered similar kinds of mystical illnesses and pains; St. Lywdine and Mary Rose are not the only ones. But they are certainly among the greatest cases of suffering on record. Therese Neumann of Konnersreuth was plagued by pains and illnesses that equal either those of Lydwine or Mary Rose Ferron; similar claims might be made as well for St. Margaret Mary Alacoque (1647-90), Anne Catherine Emmerich (1774-1824), Alexandrina da Costa (1904-55), and Padre Pio (1887-1968).

Inedia

One gift that has mystified the best minds from the world of science and medicine is that which is known as *inedia*, or the phenomenom of eating very little or nothing at all. Along with this rare and puzzling gift is the inability to retain any fluids in the body, save that of small amounts of water from time-to-time. As incredible as this may seem, many stigmatists have been known to survive on nothing but the Holy Eucharist for the remainder of their entire lives. Likewise, many have not swallowed any fluids except for a few drops of water for a number of years. These and other bodily phenomena have been observed in the homes of the victims, as well as in the best of hospitals for extended periods of time. Competent doctors, theologians sent from Rome, family and friends have observed the miracle of inedia in the life of the stigmatist, as well as agnostics and even atheists who have come away baffled and sometimes converted!

The stigmatist has lived, literally, on that Bread of Life which Christ promised in the Gospel of John: "I am the bread of life; he who comes to me shall not hunger, and he who believes in me shall never thirst" (Jn 6:35). Jesus echoes the words of the ancient prophet Isaiah:

> Ho, everyone who thirsts, come to the waters. . . . Hearken diligently to me, and eat what is good, and delight yourselves in fatness. Incline your ear, and come to me; hear, that your soul may live. . . (Is 55:1-3).

It must be understood that this suspension of eating is not what we normally associate with "fasting" or "abstinence." With some of the stigmatists, the total absence of eating has also included the absence of the elimination of any bodily waste, which has also been observed over long periods of time by highly competent medical authorities. These extraordinary findings are well-documented. We will now look at some examples of inedia in the lives of these holy victims:

Blessed Angela of Foligno (1250-1309), reported stigmatist, was the first person known in history to have lived with total abstinence. She survived this miraculous condition for twelve years, living on the Communion brought to her by the angels from heaven.

St. Catherine of Siena (1347-80) was reported to have gone without food for some eight years; Blessed Elizabeth of Reute (d. 1420) had lived for fifteen years without earthly food. Stigmatist St. Lydwine of Shiedam (1380-1433) went even longer without any normal bodily nourishment; incredibly, Maria Rose Andriani (1790-1862), the Third Order Franciscan stigmatist, survived twenty-eight years without eating save that of the Eucharist!

In more modern times, we have many cases of stigmatists whose inedia have been extensively investigated under rigorous conditions. Marie-Julie Jahenny, stigmatized victim of the twentieth century, allegedly ended her intake of food by 1874. This abstinence lasted for ninety-four days. Later on, Marie resumed her inedia for over five complete years. All during this time, her examiner, Dr. Imbert-Gourbeyre, reported no excretion of bodily wastes whatsoever.

Louise Lateau (1850-83), the Belgian stigmatist, ended her food dependency when she received the Sacred Wounds in 1868. By 1871, Louise could take no food except small pieces of bread or fruit; any attempt to eat more only resulted in sickness and vomiting.

Usually, this is how the stigmatist discovers his or her inability to eat or drink in the normal manner. If they attempt to do so, either by desire or through the efforts of others, then a series of symptoms takes place: high fevers, sickness, sweating, and profuse vomiting have often been observed. It is the Lord's way of weaning them from earthly nutrients in order to prepare them for the Sacred Bread of Life, the heavenly food that our Savior promised to give for eternal life: "This is the bread which came down from heaven, not such as the fathers ate and died; he who eats this bread will live forever" (Jn 6:58).

In order to be receptive to such a heavenly gift, the victim must be invited to live the Eucharistic Life, which includes a profound desire for the Sacred Species and an awareness of Its continual and saving presence within the body and soul. This occurs upon the reception of the Holy Eucharist, and results in a transformation of one's being. These blessed souls become so dependent upon this Sacred Bread that they become one with Christ. Eventually, to deny them this heavenly nourishment becomes painful and even life-threatening. At this stage of their spiritual transformation, they come to experience what St. Paul had proclaimed: "It is no longer I who live, but Christ who lives in me" (Gal 2:20).

Perhaps the greatest case of inedia on record — and one that has been the most thoroughly investigated — is that of the lay stigmatist, Therese Neumann of Konnersreuth, West Germany (1898-1962). Like many others, Therese (Resl) was weaned from food through a series of physical disorders that progressively worsened and weakened her so much that she could not swallow or even digest her food, if forced into her system. In 1922, four years before she received the Sacred Wounds of our Lord, Therese was stricken with a throat infection that made it impossible for her to swallow food or even a drop of water. From Christmas of the same year, a digestive ailment affected her ability to retain anything she ate, which caused her to vomit all that she injested, except for small amounts of mashed, husked barley. Stomach aches were soon followed by vomiting, which at times included blood. All medical treatment proved to be ineffective, a sign to her spiritual director that this was no ordinary illness, but one destined by God.

After Therese received the stigmata in March of 1926, she could only drink small doses of particular liquids: coffee, tea and juices. After Christmas of that year, no nourishment — food or water — was taken by Therese

Neumann, except for the Blessed Eucharist, right up to her death in 1962. What is even more remarkable is that Therese actually gained weight throughout these years, until her dying day; pictures of her in each successive decade between the 1920s and 1962 reveal a hefty woman "overweight" by today's standards! How did she gain this weight without the intake of calories? Why did this happen? Perhaps it was a sign of Providence that Therese's state was not of human or natural designs; rather, she had been touched and gifted by God, a sign for the world of Christ's living presence among us.

Many others on record had been given the gift of inedia, both stigmatists or other victims of love who did not receive Christ's visible wounds. Here is a list of only a few of the better known: Venerable Maria d' Oignies, St. Angela Foligno, St. Catherine of Siena, Blessed Elizabeth the Good of Waldsee, St. Colombe dei Rietie, Dominic dei Paradise, Blessed Marie Bagnesi, Francis of Jerrone, Louise of the Resurrection, Mother Agnes, Blessed Nicolas of Flue, and St. Peter of Alcantara.

Bodily Phenomena

Many unusual physical phenomena occur in the lives of the stigmatists, as if these were marks or signs of God's special grace — the "visible credentials" of predilection. In these holy victims, the laws of nature appear to be suspended; the scientific and medical worlds have been unable to explain the operations that lay behind these mysterious occurrances. Yet they have been authenticated through intensive observations under close scrutiny, whether it be in their homes or in the hospital.

One of the bodily phenomena that has occurred in these saintly souls is that which is called the *gift of perfume*, also known as the *odor of sanctity*. It involves the heavenly scent that issues forth from the body, a sweet and desirable scent often compared to the smell of fresh roses. Listen to the words of St. John of the Cross:

> He (Jesus) makes her so beautiful and rich and so imbues her with delights that it seems to her she rests upon a bed, made of a variety of sweet divine flowers, that delights with its touch and refreshes with its fragrance. . . . (*The Spiritual Canticle*, Stanza 24.)

Or again we hear him say:

> Sometimes the fragrance is so abundant that it seems to the soul she is clothed with delight and bathed in inestimable glory, to such an extent that the experience is not only within her but overflows and becomes manifest outside of her, and those capable of recognizing it are aware of her experience. It seems to them that she is in a pleasant garden filled with the delights and riches of God. . . . (*The Spiritual Canticle*, Stanza 17.)

Of course, these descriptions by the mystical Doctor are taken from the mystical Song of Songs: "Awake, O north wind, and come, O south wind! Blow upon my garden, let its fragrance be wafted abroad. Let my beloved come to his garden, and eat its choicest fruits" (Sg 4:16); "the scent of your

187

garments is the scent of Lebanon" (Sg 4:11); "I will lie me to the mountain of myrrh and the hill of frankincense. You are all-fair, my love; there is no flaw in you" (Sg 4:6-7); etc.

This aroma has been observed in some of the stigmatists while they were living (especially noticeable from the wounds themselves), and in others it is emitted after death directly from the body or from the site of the grave. In some cases (such as with Padre Pio and Therese Neumann), the scent is smelled as a sign of their presence, usually from bilocation, but sometimes after death when they come to the aid of a soul in need. At other times, the aroma stays for a length of time in a particular place that the stigmatist has visited or lived — a corridor, a room or even a church. Some who have touched the perfumed stigmatist have been known to carry the same scent on them, as if the stigmatist's "traces" were momentarily left in their midst.

Some of these victims were known for the sweet scented wounds which they possessed: St. Humiliane, St. Ida of Louvain, Dominic dei Paradise, Jeannie Marie de la Croix, as well as Padre Pio of Pietrelcina. Others emitted the powerful but pleasant aroma after their deaths: St. Teresa of Avila, St. Rose of Lima, and Blessed Catherine dei Racconigi, to name a few. These scents are reaffirmations that the wounds are of a supernatural origin, for normal wounds tend to fester and leave foul odors.

St. Teresa of Avila (1515-82) carried a sweet fragrance throughout her life and even after her death. Teresa's cell room was saturated with this heavenly aroma, and reports of her grave giving off the same scent are well-known. In fact, when this stigmatist's body was exhumed on July 4, 1583, Father Jerome Gracian, provincial of her Carmelite Order, noticed a strong but beautiful fragrance which lasted several days. As late as 1914, when Teresa's heart wound was examined by the sisters at Alba de Tormes, they noticed the same delicate scent coming from Teresa's incorruptible body.

St. Catherine dei Ricci (1522-90), the holy stimatized Dominican, was reported to have given off a flowery scent at the time of her death.

Many other saintly persons — stigmatist and non-stigmatist — have been known for their sweet bodily aroma: Pope Marcel, St. Aldegonde, St. Menard, St. Dominic, St. Catherine of Bologna, Blessed Lucy of Narni, Blessed Catherine dei Racconigi, St. Claire dei Rimini, St. Fine of Tuscany, St. Elizabeth of Portugal, St. Rose of Lima, St. Louis Bertrand, St. Joseph dei Copertino, St. Thomas of Villanova, St. Raymond dei Pennafort, St. Willibrod, St. Agnes of Montepulciano, and St. Mary Magdalen dei Pazzi are among the many of such privileged souls.

The gift of perfume is not the only bodily phenomena known in the lives of the stigmatists. Another mysterious one is the lack of sleep that some of these souls have experienced. Padre Pio was reported to have slept only a few hours each night. He would often study and pray until one o'clock in the morning, then arise at three o'clock to prepare for his 5:00 a.m. Mass! St. Catherine dei Ricci slept for one one hour every week. Others, such as St. Catherine of Siena and Therese Neumann, required little sleep as well.

Many of these victims' bodies were re-established in youth and beauty after their death, such as St. Francis of Assisi, St. Catherine of Siena, St. Catherine dei Ricci, St. Mary Magdalen dei Pazzi, and St. Rose of Lima — remarkable when one considers how much abuse and torment their bodies and souls went through as expiatory victims!

Another unusual phenomenon of the body was seen in Padre Pio of

Pietrelcina. The stigmatized friar had often been sick with extremely high fevers. When others tried to take his body temperature, the thermometer would break on occasion because of the unusually high readings: a temperature of 120-125 degrees was often reported through reliable sources! Of course, this cannot be explained by any natural means. The temptation would be to discredit such stories because we often tend to think in terms of human reason or the natural order. But these mystical charisms are above the natural order, given by the hand of God to His chosen instruments. Again, we must conclude that the extraordinary gifts that each stigmatist seems to possess in abundance are signs of God's special privileges in His favored souls, especially those who follow the Cross of His Son in order to cooperate in the redemptive plan of the world.

Incorruptibility

One of the most unusual phenomena associated with some of God's chosen souls — including a few of the stigmatists — is the condition known as *incorruptibility*, where the body of the person remains preserved and intact, in some cases even hundreds of years after his or her death.

How was this extraordinary miracle first discovered? In one sense, it was really accidental. For hundreds of years, it has been the practice of the Church to *exhume* the body of a potential candidate for sainthood, thus enabling him to be examined years after his death and original burial. (Many holy souls have been known to emit a heavenly perfume from their bodies long after they've gone; and many before have been found to be incorruptible. So, the practice continues.)

One practical reason for exhuming the body is that it had long been a practice to divide and distribute parts of the saint's body to many different churches throughout the Christian world; in this way, the faithful would be allowed to venerate them by paying visits and praying before their remains in the altars or in the crypts. An example of this is with Therese Neumann. Plans are currently underway to remove her remains from the cemetery in Konnersreuth in order to have her placed under the side altar of St. Therese of Lisieux inside the St. Lawrence Church. This is being done in order to accomodate the large groups of pilgrims who visit the town annually. It had also been Therese's wish long before she died, since she so loved the Little Flower.

Another reason for the examination of saint's bodies is that, unfortunately, relics were frequently stolen by grave-robbers and over-zealous souls who sometimes sold the precious remains for huge profits. In order to be certain that the remains were intact (or that they were even at a particular site at all), the Church found it necessary to verify if the saint was indeed still where he or she was originally buried.

So many factors had contributed to the exposure and/or removal of the bodies of the saints who had died long ago. Today, the Process for Beatification and Canonization can take decades to finish before a candidate is declared a saint. Therefore, plenty of time will have elapsed for evidence of incorruptibility to be affirmed.

Let us now examine a few of the more than 100 authenticated cases that claim incorruptibility in the bodies of God's holy souls.

The body of the Dominican stigmatist, St. Catherine of Siena (1347-80) was found to be incorruptible, and her head can still be seen today in the

Basilica of Sts. Catherine and Dominic in Siena, Italy. While in Siena, this author has also seen Catherine's finger preserved behind a glass encasing (although the skin is wrinkled and discolored, nevertheless this relic is fully formed; even her nail is still present!). The rest of her body is in safe keeping in Rome, where she had died.

St. Clare of Montefalco (1268-1308), Augustinian nun of heroic virtue, continues to mystify the faithful. Besides her body being incorrupt, this stigmatized saint has an image of the Crucifix imprinted in her heart. This relic has been examined and verified by authorities in the Church. She can be seen in the Church of the Holy Cross on Montefalco.

A thorn wound has been observed in the preserved body of St. Rita of Cascia (1381-1457). The Lord granted her a share in His Passion after she offered herself up to share in His sufferings. Her intact body — only slightly discolored after more than five centuries — can be seen in a glass case at the Basilica of St. Rita in Cascia, Italy. There are reports that her eyes have opened and closed several times over the years, and her body (according to eyewitnesses) has moved more than once.

The heart of the great St. Teresa of Avila (1515-82) was found to be preserved upon examination in 1872. This relic appears to be pierced with the wound of divine love, described once by Teresa herself in her autobiography (*Life*). Part of her remains were found to be still incorrupt after the last exhumation in 1914.

The Basilica of Prato, Italy, holds the incorruptible body of St. Catherine dei Ricci (1522-90), stigmatist who was inflicted with the Five Wounds of Christ, as well as the crown of thorn wounds. Though darkened with time, her body is available for the veneration of the faithful below the main altar of the basilica.

The partially preserved remains of stigmatist St. Rose of Lima (1586-1617), Patroness of the Americas, are occasionally exposed to the faithful in the Church of Santo Domingo in Lima, Peru. Part of her body rests here, while the remainder of her relics is located in a small church close to where Rose had once lived.

St. Veronica Giuliani (1660-1727), stigmatist who carried the Five Wounds of Christ as well as the crown of thorn wounds, was incorrupt for many years. Later, when the Tiber River overflowed and saturated her body, it was destroyed. Yet her heart was preserved, and remains intact to this day in the Capuchin Monastery at Citta di Castello, where her skull is also preserved.

Blessed Osanna of Mantua (1449-1505), like St. Catherine of Siena, received the Sacred Stigmata but requested that the Lord make them invisible, a request that was later granted. Osanna's body, displayed three times a year in the Cathedral of Mantua, is still well-preserved. Like St. Catherine, Osanna's stigmata later reappeared on her body, visible for all to see.

The question must be asked: why does incorruptibility occur? How can it possibly benefit those who have died, let alone those who are still living? One explanation is that God has left a sign for the faithful, indicating how He is Master of both body and soul, before and after death. Another reason is to reaffirm the teachings of St. Paul on the reality of the bodily resurrection the faithful will one day encounter:

There are celestial bodies and there are terrestrial bodies; but the glory of the celestial is one thing, and the glory of the terrestrial is another. There is one glory of the sun, and another glory of the moon, and another glory of the stars; for star differs from star in glory. So it is with the resurrection of the dead. What is sown is perishable, what is raised is imperishable. . . (1 Cor 15:40-42).

Our bodies will be changed into spiritual bodies not subject to corruption: ". . . this perishable nature must put on the imperishable" (1 Cor 15:53). But these risen bodies will nevertheless remain true bodies: "It is sown a physical body, it is raised a spiritual body" (1 Cor 15:44). One is reminded of this fact through the incident of our Lord's risen appearance to St. Thomas: "See my hands and my feet, that it is I myself; handle me, and see; for a spirit has not flesh and bones" (Lk 24:39); or the Transfiguration narrative: "And he was transfigured before them and his face shone like the sun, and his garments became white as light. And behold, there appeared to them Moses and Elijah talking with him" (Mt 17:2-3).

As incredible as incorruptibility may appear, it really ought not to cause us to doubt, for with God all things are possible. In fact, this phenomenon is nothing compared to the hope for what is yet to come: "What no eye has seen, nor ear heard, nor the heart of man conceived, what God has prepared for those who love him" (1 Cor 2:9).

The Divine Touch

The divine touch is a supernatural feeling imprinted upon the soul by God, distinguished by a greater or lesser degree of intensity. Sometimes these touches are delightful, at other times they cause the soul extreme pain or anguish. In order for the soul to receive this sublime touch from the heavenly Master, he or she must reach a high level of spirituality and an intensely intimate relationship with God.

The deeper mystical touches are called *substantial* because they seem to take place between two substances, God and the soul. What really happens is that God is acting upon the senses and has not yet fully penetrated the depths of one's spiritual being. Nevertheless, the soul does not acquire these touches on his or her own effort; rather, they are received passively, with God as the sole Initiator of this impression. This is an ongoing experience that is really an extension of the dark night of the soul, whereby the Lord does all the work to purify and ready the soul for the divine union. In this later stage of the spiritual life, God begins to let one experience heavenly joys and delights by caressing him with the pureness of His love. It is one of many loving encounters that God gives to the soul who will one day bear the wounds of the Sacred Stigmata.

Sometimes these persons experience what might be called the *kiss of love* from the heavenly Father. This sensation is a pure and penetrating touch so overwhelming that the victim is overcome and eventually consumed in the presence of God. St. Matilda once explained the intimate encounter in this way (described in the third person):

The Savior called her to himself and, putting His divine hands in hers, He gave her all the works which He had performed in His holy humanity. He fixed His eyes on hers in such a way that she could see through those same divine eyes. He pressed His mouth on hers and gave her, in compensation for her negligences, all the praise, thanksgiving, prayers, and exhortations which had come forth from His divine lips. Finally, He united His divine heart with hers and communicated to her His devotion and love and the plenitude of His graces. At the contact of the fire of His love, her heart melted like wax in fire. . . . (*The Mystical Evolution*: Volume II, p. 285; Fr. John G. Arintero, O.P.: TAN Books and Publishers, Inc., Rockford, IL, 1978.)

These divine kisses of love are totally spiritual, yet the closest image the mystic has to convey this supernatural (but altogether real) love is by way of comparison with the loving and intimate exchange between two lovers who lose themselves in a warm and sweet embrace. The divine union is infinitely greater, and the caresses from the heavenly Spouse are more profound and penetrate deeper into the soul of the dearly beloved. One can see the same mystical language of love that captivated the author of the Song of Songs: "O that you would kiss me with the kisses of your mouth! For your love is better than wine!" (Sg 1:1). The image of the mystical bride whom the heavenly Groom unites to His Sacred Heart is again depicted by the same author, who in turn describes the beauty of the divine kiss: "How sweet is your love, my sister, my bride! how much better is your love than wine, and the fragrance of your oils than any spice! Your lips distill nectar, my bride; honey and milk are under your tongue; the scent of your garments is like the scent of Lebanon" (Sg 4:10-11).

The divine love is so intense that it softens the victim's heart, molding it like a potter molds the clay. He touches the soul in order to purify it, preparing it to see and experience Him as He really is: pure and infinite Love. Before the soul is able to enjoy the sweetness of these heavenly delights, she must pass through the Lord's crucible in order to be worthy to share such a sublime love. This experience, as we have seen in the dark night of the soul, can be both sweet and painful, terrifying yet assuring.

The mystical Doctor, St. John of the Cross, tells us this:

> The touch of divine love and fire so dries up the spirit and so enkindles the soul's longings to slake its thirst for this love that a person will go over these longings in his mind a thousand times and pine for God in a thousand ways. . . . (*Collected Works*, "Dark Night," Bk. II, chpt. 11.)

The author of the Psalms expressed this feeling well: "my soul thirsts for thee; my flesh faints for thee" (Ps 63:1).

Yet this divine touch is subtle. According to the stigmatist St. Teresa of Avila (1515-82), it is "delicate," and one must be extremely sensitive to God's presence deep within the recesses of the heart. This can only come about when one has reached a high level of contemplation and an advanced degree of purity. Furthermore, the subject must be extremely loyal to following God's will, to look for it with every breath, to see it in every action. Then and only then can he experience Him as He is, a total Love that transcends anything the mortal mind can fathom. Because the divine touch is a grace freely given by God (and not earned by anyone), it is absolutely essential that the soul receives Him passively and allows God to work on the spirit as He wills. It is then that love can be exchanged unconditionally between the Lord and the soul whom He chooses for His own.

Once the soul tastes these pleasures in the depths of the heart, he or she is then able to transform their very being into the likeness of the Divine himself. The Holy Spirit will come and dwell in these privileged souls (Jn 14:23), allowing them to experience ever greater graces that He longs to bestow upon them. Such is the case with the stigmatist, who has been changed into the likeness of the suffering Christ.

Stigmatist St. Mary Magdalen dei Pazzi (1566-1607) once explained this transformation in this way:

> The Word loves the soul with such a love that He gives himself to it as its food. He unites it to His humanity in a most intimate manner; He communicates to it the ardent desires, pure affections, and holy words and works of His own humanity. In a word, He transforms it into himself. This transformation raises the soul to such a high degree of perfection that each one of its aspirations for God draws, in a certain manner, the Word from the bosom of the Father into its own. . . . (*The Mystical Evolution*, p. 285-86.)

St. Gertrude the Great (1256-1302), mystical Doctor who bore the Five Sacred Wounds of our Lord, gave us these insights into the way the stigmatist is transformed into Christ:

> The Holy Ghost inflames hearts with the fire of His love and leaves them like melted wax. Then upon them the Savior stamps His image like a divine seal. . . . (*The Mystical Evolution*, p. 285.)

Transverberation

The mystical *wounds of love* (of the soul or heart) are wounds that transform the victim soul into a receptacle of divine love. With these living flames of love, the soul is transported to an intensely intimate relationship with God. Normally, these wounds precede the impression of the stigmata upon the body or soul; they are a kind of preparation for the eventual and complete transformation of the victim into another Christ crucified . . . a living crucifix of redemptive love.

Technically, this phenomenom has been called *transverberation* of the heart. Some mystics have even experienced what is known as the *exchange of hearts*, whereby the Lord consumes the heart of the victim with the fire of His Sacred Heart, and the Lord likewise makes the heart of the victim His own.

Because the wound of love is a forerunner to the impression of the Five Wounds of the Sacred Stigmata, we need to take a closer look at what this wound does to the soul, and how it is initially received.

Before the wound appears, the victim has normally achieved a high degree of perfection, including advanced states of mystical experience. Indeed, few are the number who have reached this level and have been found worthy to receive such extraordinary graces.

Normally, the wound is given during the state of ecstasy, where the mystic is completely absorbed in the divine love, oblivious to all surroundings. He or she appears to be caught up in a different dimension of time and space, a state that betrays all normal human experience.

Blessed Angela of Foligno (1248-1309), holy victim of our Lord's love, expressed this state in the following manner:

> When the soul is elevated above itself, and, illuminated by the presence of God, enters into intimate communication with Him, it knows, enjoys and rests in a divine happiness which it cannot express, for it surpasses every word and every concept. Each ecstasy is a new ecstasy and all the ecstasies together are one inexpressible thing. . . .

After the victim experiences this level of mystical ecstasy, a heavenly being sent by God, or even the Lord himself, may pay a visit to this victim and impart a permanent wound in the heart or the soul by means of a spear, dart or arrow. St. Teresa of Avila was wounded in just this way, as she describes:

> I see beside me, on my left, an angel in bodily form. He was not tall, but short, and very beautiful. It must be those who are called cherubim. In his hand I saw a long golden spear and at the end of the iron tip I seemed to see a point of fire. With this he seemed to pierce my heart several times so that it penetrated into my entrails. When he drew it out, I thought he was drawing them out with it and he left me completely afire with a great love for God. . . . (*Life*, chpt. 29.)

This same celestial visit was experienced by Padre Pio of Pietrelcina (1887-1968), as he described in his letter to his spiritual director, Padre Agostino:

> I am led to manifest to you what happened to me on the evening of the 5th of this month and all day on the 6th.
>
> I am quite unable to convey to you what occurred during this period of utter torment. While I was hearing the boy's confessions on the evening of the 5th I was suddenly terrorized by the sight of a celestial person who presented himself to my mind's eye. He had in his hand a sort of weapon like a very long sharp-pointed steel blade which seemed to emit fire. At the very instant that I saw all this, I saw that person hurl the weapon into my soul with all his might. I cried out with difficulty and felt I was dying. I asked the boy to leave because I felt ill and no longer had the strength to continue.
>
> This agony lasted uninterruptedly until the morning of the 7th. I cannot tell you how much I suffered during this period of anguish. Even my entrails were torn and ruptured by the weapon, and nothing was spared. From that day on I have been

mortally wounded. I feel in the depths of my soul a wound that is always open and which causes me continual agony. . . . (August 21, 1918.)

This wounding of the heart in Padre Pio is remarkably similar to that which was described by St. Teresa of Avila. As we have seen before, St. Francis of Assisi also received his wounds from the appearance of a majestic, celestial being.

In many cases, the transverberation of the heart directly precedes the impression of the Five Wounds. (Note: sometimes this trasverberation is only felt internally and is not manifested on the outside of the body. In this case, the complete Five Wounds would appear at a later time. If the original transverberation did appear externally, then only the hand and foot wounds would manifest when the Sacred Stigmata appears, thus completing the major wounds of our Lord's Crucifixion.) We must also realize that many stigmatized souls — such as St. Teresa of Avila — never receive all of the Five Wounds, but only receive a portion of them: the heart wound, the hand wounds, the crown of thorns, etc.

Although many a stigmatist receives the transverberation or the complete stigmata from the hands of a heavenly figure, nevertheless sometimes it is the Lord himself who visits the soul to wound the heart with His divine love. St. Gertrude the Great heard these words from our Lord before she was permanently inflicted: "I desire to pierce thy heart through and through so that the wound can never be healed."

Paradoxically, these wounds are pleasant and desirable to the victim, even though they are intensely painful:

How sweet is that loving dart which, in wounding one with the incurable wound of divine love, leaves him forever sick and with such a violent beating of the heart that it leads to death. . . . (*Treatise on the Love of God*, Book VII, chpt. 10.)

Or again, the stigmatist St. Catherine of Siena (1347-80) had this to say:

Oh, abyss of charity! Thou art a fire that ever burns but does not consume; a fire filled with joy, happiness and sweetness. To the heart which is wounded with this arrow all bitterness seems sweet and all heaviness is turned into lightness. . . . (Letter no. 123.)

The pain these mystics describe is not merely a pain of the body or senses; it is a pain that penetrates the interior of the soul, causing it to moan, but with heavenly splendor. According to St. Teresa, they are like intense longings for God, similar to the beloved spouse who awaits the bridegroom. In mystical language, this spouse is the chosen soul, and the Bridegroom is Jesus himself.

If these mystical wounds are intense enough, they will appear in the depths of the soul, or they could manifest themselves outside the body. Sometimes this transverberation or wound of the heart is called the "Seraph's assault," because, as St. John of the Cross reminds us, the soul is interiorly attacked by a Seraph who pierces the heart or soul with a fiery dart, wounding it permanently but with a sweet delight.

If this wound becomes even more intense and penetrates the body so thoroughly that external manifestations of the wounds become apparent, the victim is sealed with the visible stigmata. Padre Pio once experienced such a similar prelude to his visible marks, as we have seen:

> From Thursday evening until Saturday and also Tuesday, there is a painful tragedy for me. My heart, hands and feet seem to be pierced through by a sword. I feel great pain on this account. . . . (Letter to Padre Agostino, March 21, 1912.)

This description was certainly a prelude to the permanent visible stigmata that Padre was to receive on September 20, 1918, a mere six years later.

It must be repeated that these heavenly wounds usually occur because of intense impulses of love on the part of those who are wounded. Again, Padre Pio expresses this keen desire: "My heart wants more and more to experience any affliction whatever if this pleases Jesus" (*Epistolario*, August 19, 1910); "I am suffering and would like to suffer even more. I feel myself consumed and would like to be consumed even more" (May 6, 1913); "I want to suffer: This is what I long for" (July 27, 1918).

These desires are not aimed at suffering for its own sake — this would be pathetic and perhaps even pathological. No, they are impulses for a share in Christ's Passion: their redemptive and purifying values are what is at stake. Only then does suffering take on a truly meaningful experience that transcends all earthly values. It becomes a supernatural value that stores up treasure in heaven for those who seek God with all their hearts, souls and minds.

All of us can benefit from these merits that the suffering victim souls earn for our salvation on behalf of Jesus; thus, we must hold in awe their very mission of self-sacrifice through suffering out of love for God and His people. The stigmatist's love is a sacrificial love spilled out for every soul in need of God's mercy, for a brokenness that cries out for healing and reconciliation.

Invisible Stigmata

Much has been said about extraordinary visible phenomena that, from time to time, holds the attention of the universal Church. The visible has always been observable, so naturally the faithful are captivated by the supernatural events that can be seen, heard or felt; extraordinary wonders of nature, miraculous healings and the visible stigmata are but a few of these observable phenomena that speak of the reality of God's presence among us.

Even so, there remains another level of reality present in creation — a reality unseen, but known through the experiences of those souls who are sensitive and open to God's work within them. It is the realm of the spiritual and the mystical: the way of the stigmatist, who experiences the divine presence most intimately and most intensely, not in external realities, but in the deepest recesses of the heart and soul: "The Spirit of truth, whom the world cannot receive, because it neither sees him nor knows him; you know him, for he dwells with you, and will be in you" (Jn 14:17). Again, St. John communicates to us these words from our Lord: "If a man loves me, he will keep my word, and my Father will love him, and we will come to him and make our home with him" (Jn 14:23).

With these thoughts in mind, let us move on to an internal but very real manifestation of Christ's Passion in His victim souls — that of the *invisible stigmata*. This is a condition whereby a stigmatist bears all or part of our Lord's sufferings and wounds intensely though invisibly in his or her body or soul. In fact, the sufferings can be as great or greater in these souls than in those who have visible, exterior stigmata.

Why is this so? Because the invisible stigmata reaches the deepest level of one's being. Christ truly dwells within them, and many of these souls suffer in obscurity for the remainder of their lives. Perhaps some stigmata remain permanently invisible as God's way of keeping the victim humble, lest he should fall prey to exhibitionism or harbor a secret, spiritual pride. Others have desired to keep their stigmata hidden as a voluntary act of humility. Some, such as St. Gemma Galgani (1878-1903), were granted such a request after asking our Lord to hide them from view; with others, such as Padre Pio of Pietrelcina (1887-1968), the Lord chooses to keep the wounds visible as a sign to the world (in Padre Pio's case, for fifty years, from 1918 until his death in 1968). Although we can guess as to why some stigmata remain invisible and some do not, many things remain mysteries reserved for the designs of Providence.

It is a general fact that most authentic stigmatists with visible stigmata have experienced the invisible wounds first before they are manifested exteriorly, as St. John of the Cross explains:

> As a rule, God bestows no favors upon the body without bestowing them first and principally upon the soul; the greater the delight and strength of love which causes the wound within the soul, the more it is manifested outwardly in the bodily wound, and if one grows, the other grows likewise. . . . (*Collected Works*, "The Living Flame of Love," Stanza II, no. 13.)

The mystical Doctor of the Church continues his explanation:

> If God sometimes permits an effect to extend to the bodily senses in the fashion in which it existed interiorly, the wound and sore appears outwardly, as happened when the seraphim wounded St. Francis. . . . (*The Living Flame of Love*, Stanza II, no.13.)

How does one know when the invisible stigmata is present? What are some of the prevailing signs that accompany this mystical state of suffering?

Padre Pio, the first stigmatized priest in history (who also had these wounds longer than anyone on record), described this state in his letters to his spiritual director, Padre Agostino. In a letter dated September 8, 1911, Padre revealed that his "whole body was burning in an indescribable manner." His face felt as if "on fire," and "acute pain" was felt in his hands and on the soles of his feet. At other times, Padre Pio called it a "consuming fire" that invaded his whole being, keeping him in "painful languor." We know from his letters that he received the invisible stigmata as early as August of 1910, although they appeared visibly a few times for a brief period, then remained unseen until his permanent crucifixion on September 20, 1918.

Many other cases of invisible stigmata have been observed since the time of St. Francis of Assisi (the time when the Church first started to keep records of this unusual phenomena). Such was the case with St. Catherine of Siena (1347-80). In 1375, when she was just twenty-eight, Catherine received the Five Wounds of our Lord during one of her ecstatic visions, but asked the Savior to make them disappear as an act of humility. This request was granted, but she continued to have the same intense pains of these invisible wounds as she had when they were visible. After Catherine died, her stigmata appeared outwardly again, and they were authenticated by Popes Urban VII and Benedict XIV.

It has been long known that the unseen wounds that afflict these victims are very real and ever as painful as those that are seen on the outside of the body. It is often the case (as we have just seen with St. Catherine) that these wounds manifest openly after the death of the stigmatist, most likely as a sign from God of their authenticity.

Many other saintly victims have had signs of possessing some or all of the invisible stigmata, as well as additional sufferings of the Passion deep in their souls: St. Catherine of Genoa (1447-1510) and Blessed Osanna of Mantua (1449-1505) are two of the better known.

Visible Stigmata

The *visible stigmata* are the various external wounds that appear on a vicitm's body as a sign of their union with the mystery of Christ's Passion. These wounds are the outward reflections of the Lord's Passion imprinted upon the soul, and can appear in a variety of ways. When only one wound is present, it is known as a *stigma* (literally, a "mark" or "impression"). The victim need not have all of the marks of the Crucifixion in order to be considered a stigmatist; thus, there have been over three hundred recognized stimatists (also known as *stigmatics*) since the time of St. Francis of Assisi, who received his Sacred Wounds on September 14, 1224. As was previously mentioned, Dr. Imbert-Gourbeyre listed over 321 such cases in his two-volume work, *La Stigmatization* (1894). Since then, many others have joined the list of authentic stigmatics.

If a soul has received one or several of the wounds of the Passion, he or she is considered to have a *partial* or *incomplete stigmata*; nevertheless, they are still true stigmatists, and should be treated as such.

The five classic points where the wounds have most commonly appeared are the side, the two hands, as well as both feet. These have been traditionally known as the Five Wounds, or the Sacred Wounds of our Lord, because they are the marks that occurred exactly at the time of the Crucifixion. Because our Lord suffered more than the Cross at the end of His earthly life, we consider the entire Passion when referring to His redemptive suffering that includes the following physical afflictions: the agony at Gethsemani (including the tears or sweating of blood); scourging; the crowning of thorns; beatings; the shoulder wound from carrying the Cross; and the Five Wounds inflicted during the Crucifixion itself.

No one has ever carried the entire sufferings of the Passion in his or her body, for Christ alone suffered incomparable atrocities for the love of humankind; indeed, that is why He is Lord and Savior, and we are mere human creations. A few of the stigmatists have come close to suffering all of the physical torments of the Passion, however, such as Therese Neumann of Konnersreuth, West Germany (1898-1962) and Mary Rose Ferron of Woonsocket, Rhode Island (1902-36). These two are among the most completely stigmatized souls in Church history, for their inflictions included all of the above wounds of the Passion. Yet even they could not come close to the moral and spiritual sufferings our Lord had to endure, let alone the psychological and emotional pains.

One of the most common wounds experienced in the stigmatist is that of the side. Close to 100 have been known to have it, alone or with several other wounds. Of these, 22 have had the wound on the left side of the body, while only 6 have had it on the right: St. Francis of Assisi (1182-1226), Blessed Dodo of Hascha, Blessed Ugolino of Mantua (d. 1471), Onofrio of Fiamenga (1566-1639), Angella della Pace (1610-62), and Marie Ock (1622-84).

The wounds on the head (the so-called *crown of thorn wounds*) are much less common, although they are still quite numerous. Usually, these wounds have the appearance of a cap placed over the head instead of an actual crown.

Many variations exist with the locality of these Sacred Wounds. Here are a few examples from Rene Biot:

> There is considerable variety in the combination of these different positions. For example, we find marks on one foot alone in the case of Catherine Perez of Carvalho, the Cistercian, while Mary of the Crown, a Dominican of the Seveda monastery, who died in 1554, had the marks on both feet, but no other wound. So had Jean Gray and Marie Marguerite of the Angels, a Carmelite, born at Antwerp in 1605, of the Valckenissen family, who had gifts of bilocation and prophecy: after her death her body gave out a fragrant oil which cured the sick. . . . (*The Enigma of the Stigmata*, p. 28: Hawthorn Books, Inc., N.Y., 1962.)

When do these stigmata appear in the bodies of these saintly souls? Is there any particular age or time period when they normally manifest? Doctor Imbert-Gourbeyre did an extensive study of this, and I will briefly summarize a few of his findings.

Basically, the stigmata comes to all ages and all types of people. Madeleine Morice, born in July of 1736, was a dressmaker who lived in poverty. She first received the stigmata when she was only 8 years old. These wounds disappeared after a period of time, but they reappeared again when she was 32. Another very young stigmatist was Angela della Pace, who was only 9 when she had the Sacred Wounds imprinted in her body. Angela's side wound issued forth both blood and hot water.

Many souls have received the stigmata while in the tender years of puberty: Mother Agnes of Jesus (1602-1634), the Dominican from Le Puy, received the wounds at age 12. In addition, Mother Agnes was known for her ecstasies and visions, as well as the gift of perfume; Marguerite of the Blessed Sacrament (1619-48), the Carmelite from Beaune, experienced the wounds for the first time at age 12. At the age of 14, Francesca de Serrone was given the Sacred Wounds; at 15, there was Blessed Stephana Quinzani; Louise Lateau was next at 18, followed by St. Mary Magdalen dei Pazzi,

Jeanne de Jesus-Marie, Crescentia Nierklutsch and Dominic Lazzari at 19; then at age 20, we have Blessed Lucy of Narni, St. Catherine dei Ricci, Etienne Guyot, Josepha Kumi, Sister Bernard de la Croix, and Mary of Jesus Crucified.

After the age of 20, many have received the stigmata, but rarely after the age of 40. Unusual cases of older stigmatists can be seen in the following: Christina Mary of the Cross (1242-1312) of Strumbele received the wounds when she was 65; so did the Franciscan Poor Clare, Pudenziana Zagnoni (1583-1650); Ursula Benincasa (d. 1662) received the Sacred Wounds at the age of 69; Delicia di Giovanni (1550-1622), the Domincan from Palermo, Italy, had the stigmata between the ages of 65-72. There is no record of anyone first receiving the stigmata after age 69. Padre Pio of Pietrelcina (1887-1968) is probably the oldest stigmatist on record: although his stigmata came in 1918, he was 81 when they finally disappeared just prior to his death in 1968.

Each wound of the stigmata does not always appear at the same time, nor do they bleed in exactly the same manner among the stigmatists. In the many cases where all of the Five Wounds appeared in these victim souls, most of them occurred simultaneously. Such is the case, for example, with St. Francis of Assisi (1182-1226), whose wounds appeared all at once. Yet with others it is quite different. Delicia di Giovanni received each of the Five Wounds, one in each succeeding year: the first year, the right hand, and in the second, the left; the third year saw the right foot wound, and with the fourth came the left; in the fifth year, Delicia received the wound of the heart; in her sixth year, she experienced the scourge marks; finally, in the seventh year, she received the crown of thorn wounds, thus completing her crucifixion.

How long does the bleeding and suffering last in these victim souls? Once again, there is a wide variety of experiences. When St. Francis of Assisi received his Five Wounds all at once, they were permanently fixed in his body. Padre Pio's wounds continually bled without any interruption the entire time he had the stigmata (1918-68). Francis had his wounds for only 2 years (1224-26), whereas Padre Pio's lasted for 50. The Belgian mystic Louise Lateau (1850-83) had the stigmata for 16 years, but her wounds only bled on several days each week (nevertheless, it is believed that she hemorrhaged more than 800 times in her life!). This was also the case with the following: Blessed Stephana Quinzani (1457-1530), St. Catherine dei Ricci (1522-90), and Therese Neumann (1898-1962). Some of these souls only bled from their wounds once each year during Holy Week of Lent, such as Domitilla Calucci (d. 1671), a Capuchin nun of unusual sanctity.

Where do these stigmatists come from? Once again, we must turn to the figures given by Dr. Imbert-Gourbeyre, whose statistics are the most complete available: 229 stigmatists from Italy, including 10 from Sicily; 70 from France, 47 from Spain, 33 from Germany, 15 from Belgium, 13 from Portugal, 5 each from Switzerland and Holland, 3 from Hungary, and 1 from Peru.

In terms of the Religious Orders that they come from, Dr. Imbert-Gourbeyre notes the following: 109 from the Dominicans, 102 from the Franciscans (a quarter of whom are Poor Clares), 14 Carmelites, 14 Ursulines, 12 Visitation nuns, 8 Augustinians, 3 Jesuits, and several from smaller religious affiliations.

Lay stigmatists are much less common than Religious ones, as the following observations make very clear: only 2 out of 18 were recognized in the eighteenth century, and 10 out of a total of 29 cases in the nineteenth century.

(Note that Dr. Imbert-Gorbeyre's studies do not include the twentieth century. Many other cases have been reported since his book was published in 1894, so all of the above figures are minimum statistics — there are now considerably more cases to add to his original lists of the total number of stigmatists and their respective Orders, as well as the total number of lay stigmatists.)

The Divine Union

The *divine union* is the highest mystical state that the soul can ascend to in his journey toward spiritual perfection. It is a state whereby God chooses to unite himself to the soul in a most intimate manner. When this occurs, the soul is transformed into the divine likeness and lives the life of a new, heavenly love that is incomparably greater than the human love once experienced. Included in this state of divine union is the mystical marriage of the bride to the heavenly Spouse, where the total spiritual transformation in God takes place (see next unit for a more detailed account of the mystical marriage). Indeed, this lofty state is so sublime and supernatural that the greatest of mystics have difficulty explaining it.

St. Teresa of Avila (1515-82) made this worthy effort of describing the state of the divine union:

> This state is a sleep of the faculties, which are neither wholly lost nor yet understood how they work. This seems to me to be nothing less than an all but complete death to everything in the world and a fruition of God. I know no other terms in which to describe or explain it, nor does the soul, at such a time, know what to do: it knows not whether to speak or to be silent, whether to laugh or to weep. . . . (*Collected Works*, "The Interior Castle," fifth mansion, chpt. 1.)

When does one begin to experience the divine union? It begins with the indwelling of the Trinity in the depths of the soul, where God promised to reside in those who love Him with all their hearts, souls and minds (Jn 14:21-23). Yet it is God who initiates this holy action, and it is He who calls His most favored ones to a deeper, more intimate relationship with the divine life. In fact, all are called to perfection: "For this is the will of God, your sanctification" (1 Thes 4:3); God has "saved us and called us with a holy calling" (2 Tim 1:9). It is acceptance of this indwelling presence that makes it possible to share in the divine life, action and power.

In a very real sense, all of the faithful are called to union with God, for we are all the living Mystical Body of Christ: "you are the body of Christ and *individually* members of it" (1 Cor 12:27); or again St. Paul tells us: "The body is one and has many members, and all the members of the body though many, are one body, so it is with Christ" (1 Cor 12:12).

First, we must distinguish between what is known as *ecstatic union* and *transforming union*: the ecstatic union is a prelude to the more complete and permanent transforming union. St. Teresa of Avila placed this mystical state in her sixth mansion in *The Interior Castle*, whereby one's senses are temporarily suspended as the soul is caught up in the divine presence and completely oblivious to her surroundings. Teresa said that these ecstatic unions are transitory, usually lasting for no longer than one hour, at the most. Listen to the description given by Reverend Dom Vitalis Lehodey:

> All the powers are absorbed in God. Here, the vividness of the light, the fire of love, the inebriating joy and the certitude of God's presence attain to a wonderful degree of intensity during prayer, and prepare the soul for an astonishing transformation in her conduct; this is what gives so high a value to the ecstatic union. . . . (*The Ways of Mental Prayer*, pp. 352-53; TAN Books and Publishers, Inc., Rockford, IL, 1982 reprint.)

The ecstatic union, as was previously mentioned, is really only a preparation for the complete absorption into the divine life. These early states are, for the most part, phenomena associated with the prayerful state. The transforming union, on the other hand, is a total way of being, found in the loving and constant presence of the indwelling Trinity, the source of the mystic's gradual deification. Yet it must be agreed that in proportion to the soul's advancememt, her union with God becomes always more spiritual and more perfect.

The soul's ultimate goal — and one which the stigmatist has reached — is that of the *transforming union, consummated union* or *deification*. This union is no longer transitory; it is stable. God has now captivated the will, and takes hold of the very substance of the soul and of its life (Father Dom Vitalis Lehodey). St. Teresa of Avila tells us this:

> The soul arrived at this state hardly ever again experiences those impetuous raptures of which she had spoken; ecstasies and even flights of the spirit become very rare, and hardly ever happen to her in public . . . God alone and the soul enjoy one another in a very great silence. . . . (*The Interior Castle*, seventh mansion, chpt. 3.)

Before, God favored the soul with spiritual delights, joys and heavenly raptures in order to inspire her and to strengthen her faith. Now, the mere resting in the presence of God is joy enough, for she has come to seek God for himself.

Although the soul in this state seldom encounters the usual aridities of the lower spiritual states, nevertheless he or she will experience occasional darkness because the Lord wants the soul to always remain completely dependent upon Him as the Source of all the grace he's been given; furthermore, God humbles the soul at different times to keep him always in a state of holy fear and respect for His eternal omnipotence, lest he fall from grace through self-presumption or secret pride. As was stated before, this is exactly what happened to Padre Pio of Pietrelcina, whose dark night of the soul and frequent depressions remained with him throughout the course of his extraordinarily holy life, even in the midst of the highest state of divine union.

Now we will turn to the apex of this mystical state known as the transforming union, whereby the soul receives the blessing of the spiritual marriage with the heavenly Spouse as a sign of her total union with God. As a groom becomes one with his earthly bride, so the mystical Groom seals the union with his favored spouse by rewarding her with the promise of peace, love and joy in the eternal kingdom where the Lord and Savior resides.

The Mystical Marriage

We have now come to the last treatment of the many mystical charisms that are typically found in the lives of the stigmatists. As we have seen, some of these souls have experienced all of these graces, while others have been favored with several of them during the course of their extraordinary lives. Let us now take a brief look at the highest mystical state that is possible in this earthly life, one that is a seal of the divine love upon the soul: that of the *mystical* or *spiritual marriage*, whereby one is united to the Lord in mind, body and spirit and receives a taste of the heavenly embrace.

Many such souls have experienced the *mystical espousal*, a state where the Lord gives the victim His symbolic ring that solidifies a type of "love pact" with the one He chooses to unite himself to most intimately. This occurs only after the soul has been purified and beatified, as much as the heavenly union is possible while she is still on this earth. This mystical ring is really the stamp of approval that the Lord gives to those precious few who live totally with Him, in Him and through Him, and who have abandoned themselves completely into the arms of the divine will. These souls who are truly God's chosen ones, blessed with the rewards of a lifetime of complete fidelity and submission to God; the Holy Spirit has come to dwell in their hearts because of their pure and unconditional love (Jn 14:21-23), much as a groom comes to unite himself to his bride.

In order to better understand the sublime nature of the spiritual marriage, let us hear the words of the great Doctor and stigmatist of the Church, St. Teresa of Avila (1515-82), who herself enjoyed this heavenly state:

> The spiritual espousal is different in kind from marriage; the spiritual joys the Lord gives when compared to the delights married people must experience are a thousand leagues distant. For it is all a matter of love united with love. . . . (*The Interior Castle*, V, chpt. 4.)

Teresa described how the Trinity comes to dwell in the deepest recesses of the soul, as the folllowing words explain:

> In the spiritual marriage, the secret union takes place in the very interior center of the soul, which must be where God himself is. . . . (*The Interior Castle*, VII, chpt. 2.)

Teresa is literally describing a union so great that it reaches such a high point as to make the spirit one with our Lord; hence, the term, "mystical marriage."

What exactly occurs in the mystical marriage? What is required of a soul to reach this heavenly state? St. John of the Cross (1542-91), perhaps the greatest mystical Doctor and theologian ever produced by the Church, gives us these revealing insights:

In order that the soul reach Him, it is necessary for her to attain an adequate degree of purity, fortitude and love. The Holy Spirit, He who intervenes to effect this spiritual union, desires that the soul attain the possession of these qualities in order to merit this union. . . . (*Collected Works*, "The Spiritual Canticle," Stanza 20, no. 2.)

The mystical union with the divine is a reinactment of the Blessed Virgin Mary's *fiat* to the Lord, of whom she gave herself freely, totally and unconditionally. Mary was found worthy to share in the divine union, and God placed His heavenly seal upon her soul by uniting her to himself. In this way, she was found worthy to be the Mother of God: in a sense, Mary was espoused to God her entire life by sharing with His Spirit in the creation of the only begotten Son. Our Mother Mary is the prototype of all heavenly spouses who are joined to the Love that is God, so intimately absorbed in the divine was she. Yet Mary remains singularly the most perfect of all heavenly spouses because of her unique role as the sole Mother of God and all His children. Many holy souls — and a good number of stigmatists — have been invited to share in the Virgin's divine espousal, thus becoming a part of the heavenly family of God.

St. John of the Cross reiterates this point about the necessary *fiat* that all the heavenly spouses must submit to before the Lord can solidify His union with them:

She (the soul) must hold the door of her will open to the Bridegroom that He may enter through the complete and true "yes" of love. This is the yes of espousal which is given before the spiritual marriage. . . . (*The Spiritual Canticle*, Stanza 20, no. 2.)

What occurs in the souls of those precious few who taste the heavenly union while still on this earth? Let us hear once more from the lips of the mystical Doctor:

Few in this life reach spiritual marriage. What God communicates to the soul in this intimate union is totally beyond words. For in the transformation of the soul in God, it is God who communicates himself with admirable glory. In this transformation the two become one, but this union is not as essential and perfect as in the next life. . . . (*The Spiritual Canticle*, Stanza 26, no. 4.)

In this state of spiritual marriage the sensory and lower part of the soul is so purified and spiritualized that it recollects the sensory faculties and natural strength so that they may thereby share in and enjoy in their own fashion the spiritual grandeurs which God is communicating in the inwardness of the spirit. . . . (*The Spiritual Canticle*, Stanza 40, no. 5.)

Indeed, the mystical union so intimately joins the bride with the Bridegroom that the two really become as one: "All mine are thine, and thine are mine" (Jn 17:10). The reciprocal love that is shared between the soul and the divine Spouse involves the free and unconditional surrender of both to each other, as St. John of the Cross indicates in his *Living Flame of Love* (stanza 3, no. 79).

Returning to that seal of divine love — the mystical ring — we find that there have been many such stigmatists who were so favored by God, according to Dr. Imbert-Gourbeyre. He had once compiled a list of close to 100 persons who were admitted to the mystical nuptials, some who have experienced the heavenly espousal and some the heavenly marriage itself. In his study, Dr. Imberty-Gourbeyre found 55 examples of those who have received the mystical ring, and 43 of those were stigmatists.

How does this mystical ring appear to the stigmatists and to others? With some, such as St. Catherine of Siena (1347-80) and Blessed Osanna of Mantua (1449-1505), it was only visible to them alone; for others, such as St. Catherine dei Ricci (1552-90), it was often visible to others. Let us look at a few of these examples a bit more closely.

St. Catherine of Siena claimed to have received a gold ring from our Lord as a sign of her mystical union. According to Catherine, there were brilliant stones set within the ring, including a large diamond in the center. Although she alone could see this ring, it nevertheless remained with her throughout the rest of her life.

During Holy Week of 1542, on Easter Sunday, St. Catherine dei Ricci entered into complete union with the divine when Christ appeared to her with the sign of the mystical espousal: He took a ring from His finger and placed it on the forefinger of Catherine's left hand. She once described this ring as made of gold with a large diamond in the middle. It appeared to others (some who could see it) as a swelling and reddening of the same finger, and some had even seen a bright light emitting from the left hand. This mystical ring was even seen after Catherine's death at the age of 79; incredibly, she was only 19 when she first received this grace!

St. Gertrude the Great (1256-1302), mystical Doctor and stigmatist, had an extraordinary experience concerning the reception of the mystical ring:

> I perceived thereon seven golden circlets, in the form of rings, one on each finger, and three on the signet finger; which indicated that the seven privileges were confirmed to me, as I had asked. . . . (*The Life and Revelations of St. Gertrude*, p. 115; Christian Classics, Inc., Westminster, MD, 1983.)

When a stigmatist has been favored with the mystical marriage, the Lord has often appeared with the Blessed Virgin Mary in a heavenly celebration that witnesses the divine espousal between Christ the Groom and His beloved, spotless bride. Many heavenly saints were present during such visions at the time of the spiritual marriage: St. Catherine dei Ricci (1552-90) once saw the presence of St. Thomas Aquinas (1225-74) and St. Mary Magdalen; St. Catherine of Siena (1347-80) had Sts. John, Paul and even Dominic (1170-1221) in her midst; St. Mary Magdalen dei Pazzi (1566-1607) described the appearances of St. Augustine (354-430) and St. Catherine of Siena; Marina of Escobar enjoyed the company of St. Joseph on her heavenly day of union. In fact, Marina celebrated the mystical marriage not once but twice — at the ages of 48 and 57.

To understand a bit more about how the soul is transformed in God with the arrival of the mystical marriage, let us hear from the words of stigmatist St. Mary Magdalen dei Pazzi:

> By means of the union and transformation of thyself into the soul and of the soul into Thee, here on earth through grace and in heaven through glory, Thou dost deify the soul. O deification! The soul which has the happiness of arriving at the state of being made God, like a sphere irradiating the rays of the sun, is made luminous and resplendent as the sun itself. We are transformed into Thy very image, from clarity to clarity. . . . (*Euvres*, IV, chpt. 16.)

According to Blessed Angela of Foligno, the divine transformation can occur in three different ways:

> The first unites the soul to the will of God (the *conforming union*); the second unites the soul with God himself (the *mystical union* and *espousal*); the third unites the soul in God and God in the soul (the *spiritual marriage*). The first transformation is the imitation of Jesus crucified, for the Cross is a manifestation of the divine will. The second transformation unites the soul with God and its love is then not only an act of the Will, but the fountain of deep feeling and immense delight is opened, although there yet remains room for word and thought. The third transformation so fuses the soul in God and God in the soul that at the great height at which the mystery is effected all words and thoughts vanish. Only he who experiences these things understands them. . . . (*Visions*, chpt. 64.)

The great spiritual master, Father John G. Arintero (1860-1928), had this to share concerning the transformation of the soul which leads to the heavenly marriage:

> Signs accompanying the celebration of the marriage are: First, the entire Blessed Trinity dwells in the soul as on its throne; secondly, the soul experiences a divine transformation which leaves it entirely deified and it feels . . . that the purification and transformation which are experienced leave the soul impeccable, as it were. By means of the secret knowledge which is imparted to the soul at that time, it clearly understands that what it is experiencing, tasting and feeling is an anticipated joy of the happiness of heaven. This is the most certain sign of the actuality of the marriage. Thirdly, the soul feels that it is continually nourished and enraptured by wisdom and love, and there are infused into the depth of the soul certain secrets of knowledge of our holy religion and the divinity and nature of God. Now the soul is no longer burned or wounded as it was in the espousal . . . but there are divine touches which neither burn nor wound, but deify. . . . (*The Mystical Evolution: Volume II*, p. 247; Fr. John G. Arintero, O.P.: TAN Books and Publishers, Inc., Rockford, IL, 1978 reprint.)

Some souls who have been graced with the mystical marriage are quite certain of their state and special blessing from God. Stigmatist St. Rose of Lima (1586-1617) once told ecclesiastical judges who were examining her life that she was sure she was confirmed in grace and knew from God that she would never lose Him, but would always be intimately united to Him. In fact, God even let it be known to her that she would never have to suffer the pains of Purgatory, so favored was she with this mystical state.

Venerable Mary of the Incarnation had this to say about the mystical marriage:

> Divine matrimony is the most sublime of all states. God takes possession of the soul in such a way that He becomes the very basis of its substance, and what transpires there is so subtle and divine that it is impossible to describe it. It is a permanent state in which the soul lives peacefully and tranquilly in perfect union with God. . . . (*The Mystical Evolution: Volume II*, p. 223.)

Yet as wonderful as the mystical espousal and marriage are, nevertheless it is not always absolutely stable or indissoluable, according to Father Arintero. Even in these highest of states the soul can experience darkness and aridity; furthermore, one is always in danger of sinning against God while here in this earthly life. Great prudence and careful discernment from a wise spiritual director are vitally important to anyone who reaches the heights of the mystical ladder, lest they fall to a depth lower than that of the ordinary person, for much more will be expected of those whom God so highly favors.

We know that many favored souls (such as the stigmatist Padre Pio) were never totally sure of their condition before God, and they frequently lived in fear of offending the good grace that was given to them. Some of these souls periodically fell into the dark night of the soul, even when they were transformed in the divine union or the mystical marriage. Perhaps this occurs to keep them humble before others, and to make them continually aware that they are nothing and God is everything in Whom they must depend for their redemption and salvation.

Even in the heights of the mystical life, there are both mountains and valleys, deserts and oases. Not until the arrival in heaven can anyone live in a perfect state of rest and calm, nor bask in the endless joy of perfect love as is seen in God. The complete and total transformation — the fulfillment of the glorified beatific vision — is reserved according to God's mysterious designs for the life hereafter. This observation in itself ought to keep the greatest of souls humble, and the most hardened sinners aware of the need for continual conversion and reconciliation with their Lord and Savior until He comes again in the fullness of His glory.

CHAPTER 4

Explaining the Stigmata

Science and Medicine

Throughout the course of this study, we have attempted to explain the meaning of suffering in the lives of God's victim souls, the nature and characteristics of the stigmata from the vantage point of the stigmatist and theologian, and the charisms associated with the stigmatists in general. Now we turn to the world of science and medicine for an evaluation of this phenomenon from the eyes of objective observers who have examined some of the stigmatists we've encountered in this work — those who have established themselves in the specialized fields in which they work.

One legitimate question concerns the theological implications behind the mystery of the stigmata itself: is the Sacred Stigmata a scientifically unprovable phenomenon? Does this mystery belong exclusively to the realm of Christian faith? The answer is really yes and no. On the one hand, regardless of what the world of science has to say, it cannot prove or disprove in the end anything connected with the experience of the supernatural; this is God's domain, and certainly no one can second-guess the workings of Divine Providence. On the other hand, the scientific and medical world have the obligation to investigate and report on the nature of things that people want to and have the right to know about. The world of science really poses no problem to the faithful, for the evaluations and conclusions that it has drawn are very supportive of the authenticity of the stigmata, if for no other reason than to admit that nothing known in the natural order can explain the mystery of this extraordinary grace.

In terms of the theological arguments that favor the reality of the stigmata, we only have to look to the Gospel accounts of the Passion narrative to see that the need for co-redemptive suffering and atonement for sin are important aspects of our Christian faith.

Those theologians who would argue against the authenticity of the Sacred Stigmata usually emphasize the one-time role of Christ as the sole Mediator between God and humankind for the satisfaction of sin and the salvation of the world. This theological position is weak for several reasons: 1) nothing in Scripture states that the Crucifixion of Christ would end all need for conversion, forgiveness and reconciliation for every person for all time; 2) sin has not been eliminated from the world, in spite of the offering that Christ had given to free man from the very things he continues to commit; and 3) we cannot presume that God would not allow human beings to help in Christ's redemptive mission in the world. If we are truly the Mystical Body of Christ, then the Lord can use whatever means He chooses to include His Body in the plans He has predetermined for all who desire to follow Him.

Let us look to the evidence that has been brought forth concerning several stigmatists who have been extensively investigated over the years. In particular, we will focus on the natue of the wounds themselves.

One of the most thoroughly investigated cases in history is that of Padre Pio of Pietrelcina (1887-1968). After having examined Padre's wounds in June 1919, Dr. Romanelli of Barletta concluded the following: "From all I knew or could tell, these lesions could not be classified among the ordinary injuries" (*Acts of the First Congress of Studies on Padre Pio's Spirituality*, p. 129: San Giovanni Rotondo, Italy, May 1-6, 1972). He described the side wound as a "clean cut parallel to the ribs, seven or eight inches long," which bled profusely and appeared to be sore even to the lightest touch.

The hand wounds were described as such: "They were covered by an inflated membrane that was a reddish brown color; there was no bleeding, no edema and no inflammation in the surrounding tissues. I had the conviction, indeed the certainty, that these injuries were not superficial because if I exerted a certain pressure with my fingers and squeezed the thickness of his hand between them (always in correspondence to the two lesions), I had an exact idea of the empty space that there was between my fingers" (*Acts*, p. 129). After fifteen months of examinations, Dr. Romanelli never found any clinical explanations that could classify these wounds.

Padre Pio's side wound had been observed by countless doctors, among them being Dr. Festa. Here he describes the wound he personally examined:

> The wound on the left side still has as in my first examination the form of an upside down cross whose longitudinal bar has the same characteristics as before. But the transverse bar is perhaps somewhat wider and longer. It has a pale pink color like that of a scar of recent formation. . .
> We had to remove from his side a little cloth much larger than the ordinary handkerchief in order to examine the wound. The cloth was entirely soaked with blood, and he had put it on only the day before. . . . (July 15, 1920. *Acts of the First Congress of Studies on Padre Pio's Spirituality*, p. 132: San Giovanni Rotondo, Italy, May 1-6, 1972.)

Another distinguished physician who examined the wounds of Padre Pio was Dr. Sala, Padre's personal doctor in the last years of his life. Here is what Dr. Sala observed concerning these wounds:

> Padre Pio had wounds of circular shape . . . of two centimeters on the back of his hands and his feet on the palms and the soles. . . A look at his hands, which was possible on certain occasions, showed clean injuries, with tissues of a vivid dermal color. Shining blood flowed from them, and they were surrounded by clotting which was layered irregularly. There was no sign of circumscribed inflammation or secretion of pus. The margins of the injuries were clear. . . .
> The injury on his side was seven centimeters long and had the shape of a slightly oblique rhombus. It was located horizontal to the fifth space between the ribs. It began at the left sternal margin. It was obviously deep with clear borders and without

formations of crust. . . . His hands and feet, especially the left foot, were edematous, and did not have a cyanotic color. . . . July 7, 1969. *Acts*, p 138: San Giovanni Rotondo, Italy, May 1-6, 1972.

Perhaps one of the most extraordinary observations of Padre Pio's wounds occurred shortly before and immediately after his death in 1968. Unlike Therese Neumann of Konnersreuth (1898-1962), whose stigmata were plainly visible even after she had been placed in the casket, Padre's wounds completely disappeared. In fact, there were no signs at all of scar tissue or bleeding — not even a scratch! This was remarkable, to say the least, for the Padre had carried the deep wounds with him for fifty years of his life. This is what Dr. Sala testified about his examinations of Padre Pio in 1968:

Some months before his death, his feet became dry, and there were no more of the above-mentioned symptoms, which had been evident up to that time. But his hands still showed the same symptoms up to the day before his death. On this day there was an accentuation of the pallor of the skin, a diminishing of the formations of crust, and the disappearance of the wounds on the backs of his hands. During his short agony the palm on the left hand still had a crust (which remained and was collected after his death). Ten minutes after his death Padre Pio's hands, thorax and feet were held up by me . . . and were photographed by a friar in the presence of four other friars. His hands, his feet, his thorax, and every other part of his body did not show any trace of injury, nor were scars present on his hands and his feet, neither on the back, nor on the palms, nor on the soles, nor on the side. The skin on the above-mentioned parts was the same as on every other part. It was soft, elastic, and mobile. . . .
Such syptoms and behavior . . . must be considered as outside of every type of a clinical nature. They have an 'extra-natural' character. . . . (July 7, 1969. *Acts*, pp. 138-39: San Giovanni Rotondo, Italy, May 1-6, 1972.)

Photos by Father Giacomo Piccirillo in the *Acts* clearly reveal these miraculous healings that Dr. Sala had spoken of. Others have witnessed the same mysterious disappearance of the wounds and all traces of bleeding, including Padre Pio's closest aids and daily companions, Fathers Alessio Parente, O.F.M. Cap. and Joseph Martin, O.F.M. Cap., who spoke to me about this in the summer of 1988 in San Giovanni Rotondo. It's as though our Lord left us a "double sign" of the authenticity of these Sacred Wounds, just as an extra reassurance to the faithful that they were indeed of a supernatural origin. In reality, there were three miraculous signs associated with the Padre's stigmata: 1) the very reception of them on September 20, 1918 (after many had known him before they appeared); 2) the unbelievable length of time that Padre was wounded (fifty years); and 3) their miraculous disappearance on the eve of his death.

Along with Padre Pio, Therese Neumann was perhaps the most extensively examined stigmatist in Church history. In addition to the dozens of highly qualified doctors, scientists and theologians who observed her wounds and her actions, hundreds of thousands of people had visited her home in Konnersreuth, West Germany to serve as witnesses to her miraculous condition.

The distinguished Dr. Seidel made the following observations in the examination of Therese Neumann's wounds:

> As for the stigmata, we must point out that the wounds which remained the same for almost eleven years, never becoming inflamed or infected, and on the other hand resisting the application of any medication or treatment, are not the wounds known to the world of medicine. Anyone who really thinks that Therese Neumann's stigmata might have arisen through a process of autosuggestion needs only to look at the compresses which lay directly over the heart wound on Good Friday, 1936; they have been preserved by her sister Marie. The blood clotting that built up in the wound remained sticking on the compress and it gives a clear picture of the size of the wound. In comparison to such a wound, all the wounds and bleedings that are produced by a process of suggestion (psychogenic) can only be called ridiculous. This argument has even greater weight when we consider the sum total of the wounds from which Therese Neumann bled on last Good Friday: their size can still be clearly judged from the blood stains on her bed jacket and head cloth. . . . (*Therese Neumann: A Portrait*, p. 233, Johannes Steiner; Alba House: copyright by the Society of St. Paul, Staten Island, N.Y., 1967.)

Doctor Leo Ritter of Regensburg, West Germany, once wrote to Father Naber (Therese's spiritual director): "For me, Resl's stigmata has no 'natural' explanation, and Professor Tschermak von Seyssenegg is in perfect accord with this position, to say nothing of the lack of nourishment intake which a few other stigmatics besides Resl have also experienced" (April 15, 1949).

Other credible witnesses to the case of Therese Neumann are given below. Here I quote excerpts that focus on the Sacred Wounds themselves.

Dr. Louis of Versailles had visited Therese Neumann in 1930 to examine the wounds in her hands, which were rare in the sense that they had the same characteristics as those of St. Francis of Assisi: actual nails had penetrated her hands, instead of the more common bleeding holes that accompany most stigmatists throughout history:

> On the back of the left hand I see a head of a nail, rectangular in form, slightly longer than wide in the direction of the hand. The rectangle which it forms is admirably regular and has its edges delicately adorned with zig-zag borders. It is about 15 mm. by 10 mm. These borders are slender and sharp like the edges of a nail forged with a hammer. The head of the nail itself is slightly arched and is round like a dome. The top of the dome itself is about two or three millimeters in thickness. It shows flat marks in several places resembling those produced by a blacksmith's hammer on a piece of iron. The color is reddish brown like a seal of ancient wax. . . . (*Who Is Teresa Neumann?*, p. 39: Radio

Replies Press, Inc., St. Paul, MN; reprint by TAN Books and Publishers, 1974.)

Doctor Louis also described his vision of the nail wounds that penetrated the palms of the hands:

> I now examine the point of the nail on the palm of the left hand. It is lying on the skin in the hallow of the hand, turning obliquely down as if by a hammer, with the point turned towards the outside of the hand. It emerges, thus bent, for a length of about 15 mm. It adheres completely to the skin. It is about 4 mm. in thickness and is rough and round in form. It is of the same brownish color as the head of the nail. . . . (1930.)

We know from many accounts that these hand wounds of Therese's were formed over a period of time: they first appeared on the backs of her hands, and only later did they penetrate through to her palms. In fact, the wounds in the back of Therese's hands are very close to the wrist area, whereas the penetration in the palms occurs much closer to the center of the hands, as if the nail had been driven in at an angle.

Albert Vogl, lifelong friend of Therese Neumann's while he was still living in Bavaria, West Germany, made these exact observations about each of the wounds that appeared in Therese's body: right hand wound, one centimeter long; left hand wound, one and one-half centimeters long; the heart wound, three and one-half centimeters long by one-half centimeter wide (taken from *Therese Neumann: Mystic and Stigmatist*, p. 88-143).

Can we be certain that the investigations of these stigmatists were properly conducted? How extensive were they? In the case of Therese Neumann, an investigation under the authority of Archbishop Michael Buchberger of Regensburg, West Germany, indicates the most thorough study possible. Between July 14 and July 28, 1927, the following rules were to be followed. These examinations were to be conducted and recorded by the following experts: a professor of the Federal Psychiatric Research Clinic at the University of Erlangen; Dr. Seidl from Waldsassen, West Germany; Dr. Ewald, M.D., who headed the investigation; four sisters; and other doctors, all who were sworn to testify under oath as to their findings:

1. The sisters were to work in two shifts, two sisters in each. All occurances were to be recorded on paper.
2. Therese was not to be left alone, day or night.
3. She was to be bathed with a damp cloth; a sponge, which might have held some water, was prohibited.
4. Water used in cleaning her teeth had to be measured before and after.
5. The amount of water used to enable her to swallow the Host was to be measured.
6. Any bodily discharges were to be carefully reserved for measurement and chemical analysis. After 1930 Therese had *no* natural eliminations from her body — including urination, stool and menstruation.
7. Temperature and pulse were to be checked periodically each day.

8. The blood shed during her sufferings was to be carefully caught, measured and analyzed.

9. Very accurate and detailed descriptions were to be recorded in writing of the bleeding periods during the Friday ecstasies.

10. The cloths used to cover the head and heart wounds were to be saved.

11. Photographs were to be taken of the stigmata and, circumstances permitting, also of various phases of the ecstasies.

12. Observations and recordings were to extend to Therese's religious life, as well as to her behavior toward her family and visitors.

13. Dr. Seidl was to remain immediately available, to enable the sisters to relate their observations with technical accuracy and to clear up any questions of the relevancy and significance of what was observed. . . . (*Therese Neumann: Mystic and Stigmatist*, p. 81; Albert Vogl: TAN Books and Publishers, Inc., Rockford, IL, 1987.)

(The following information was taken from Albert Vogl's biography on Therese Neumann, and I am deeply grateful. Mr. Vogl is a dear friend of mine, and I know that he would expect only the most accurate information to be printed in this work on his lifelong friend from Konnersreuth. There is no doubt whatsoever, according to Mr. Vogl's direct and intimate observations, that Therese Neumann's stigmata and other mystical graces were both authentic and of a supernatural order.)

One of the most surprising results of these tests were in Therese's body weight. In spite of not eating anything save the Holy Eucharist, Therese's weight remained constant (121 lbs.) between July 13-28, 1927: a fact that doctors have acknowledged as miraculous in itself. No further investigations were opened by the Archbishop of Regensburg, so satisfied was he that the testing was extremely accurate and well attested for. Many other such rigorous tests were conducted on both Padre Pio and Therese Neumann throughout their saintly lives. Not one test produced any evidence to suggest that the wounds of the stigmata (and all the extraordinary gifts associated with them) were explainable through any natural or medical means.

Do we have expert testimonies concerning stigmatists other than Padre Pio or Therese Neumann? Yes, there are many such cases, especially in the twentieth century, when science has become such an exacting discipline; also, the Church has increasingly demanded more thorough investigations in the lives of these souls, simply to establish with reasonable certainty the nature of these gifts.

A case in point is that concerning the stigmatist Mary Rose Ferron (1902-36), the "Little Rose," of Woonsocket, Rhode Island. Many qualified doctors had witnessed the sufferings of Mary Rose, including the wounds of her stigmata. Some of these doctors, in fact, were her personal physicians: Dr. Constantineau, Dr. McLaughlin, Dr. McCarthy, and Dr. George H. Gendron, D.M.D., all who believed that Mary Rose's stigmata were authentic. It is reported that even Therese Neumann knew of her through a mystical discernment from Konnersreuth, West Germany.

Doctor Gendron once made these testimonies concerning Mary Rose Ferron:

> I have seen Rose many times, in fact, I was a frequent visitor. Besides seeing her in a coma, with her eyes upwards, I also observed the stigmata of her forehead and those of her hands. . . . (*She Wears a Crown of Thorns*, p. 115; Rev. O.A. Boyer, S.T.L.: Villa Pauline, Mendham, N.J., 1958.)

A dear friend who knew her intimately between the years of 1927 and 1936 made these comments concerning Little Rose:

> Sister Mary Angela of the Sacred Heart visited Rose on many occasions. She lived in Quebec, Canada, at the Poor Clares Convent, but had known Rose because of her one-time residence in Woonsocket, Rhode Island. Here is what she said about her experiences with Rose:

> I did not revisit my sweet invalid until 1927, certainly before June 21, because I did not know that it would be our last meeting. Rose showed me the red spots which appeared on her hands, and told me of inflamations which began to encircle her head painfully. 'I believe that our Lord wishes me to share His Crown of Thorns,' she told me simply. . . . (*She Wears a Crown of Thorns*, p.147.)

Detailed descriptions of the stigmata have actually been kept since the time of the first stigmatist, St. Francis of Assisi (1182-1226), although not as thoroughly as in recent times. Thomas of Celano, author of the first biography on St. Francis, described his wounds in such manner:

> His hands and his feet seemed to be pierced through the midst with nails, the heads of the nails showing in the palms of the hands and the upper side of the feet, and their points showing on the other side; the heads of the nails were round and black in the hands and feet, while the points were long, bent, and as it were turned back, being formed of the flesh itself, and protruding therefrom. . .

This description is remarkably similar to the one on Therese Neumann mentioned earlier in this chapter.

Thomas of Celano further emphasized that Francis' closest companions were very much aware of his stigmata:

> Those who lived with him knew that his mind dwelt constantly on Christ. Jesus filled his heart, was on his lips, and before his eyes; his bodily members, like the powers of his soul, were as though marked with the seal of Christ. . . . (*St. Francis of Assisi: A Biography*, pp. 235-36; Omer Englebert: Servant Books, Ann Arbor, MI, 1979 reprint; original copyright: Franciscan Herald Press, 1965.)

Another intensely investigated stigmatist was Anne Catherine Emmerich (1774-1824) of Flamske, Westphalia, West Germany. In 1813, Anne was an object of ecclesiastical and medical inquiry lasting for five months. According to Dr. Imbert-Gourbeyre's study, this inquiry reported the the stigmata on her hands and feet were formed of scabs and dried blood, very thin, resting on a superficial wound, itself covered with a little blood and an aqueous liquid. In addition, the stigma on her side was three inches long, crescent-shaped, covered with scabs of dried blood. The skin was reddish in color, with no cuts except some roughness of the epidermis, which was observed with a magnifying glass.

In more recent times, stigmatist Louise Lateau (1850-83) of Bois d'Haine, Belgium was intensely examined over many years; in fact, along with Padre Pio and Therese Neumann she may be the most thoroughly investigated stigmatist of all time. The distinguished commission that was ordered to investigate her case including the following: Cardinal Deschamps, Archbishop of Malines; Monsignor Labis, Bishop of Tournai; and Dr. Lefebvre, professor at Louvain University and a member of the Belgian Academy of Science. In addition to this original inquiry, Dr. Lefebvre set up another inquiry on Louise Lateau for further examination, 1874-76. His reports, taken from Dr. Bourneville's pamphlet, "Louise Lateau ou la stigmatisee belge" (Progress Medical, Paris, 1875), are thoroughly documented. I have included a few of the major conclusions of these highly qualified investigative teams:

1. After Louise showed the first signs of bleeding on April 24, 1868, she continued to bleed every week until her death on August 25, 1883. All-in-all, the total number of bleedings was approximately 800.
2. Louise first felt the burning pains of the stigmata on Tuesdays, and this continued through Thursdays. Come Thursday, these pains turned into blisters which would form over the stigmata, especially evident on the back of her hands.
3. The wounds that formed on her hands and feet were of a dark red color that was circular in fashion.
4. Intense bleeding usually occurred from Thursday or Friday nights through Saturday. The beginning of the bleeding normally started between midnight and one in the morning.
5. About 250 grams of blood was lost during each Passion ecstasy.
6. The wound on Louise's side was located between the fifth and sixth ribs, a little below the left breast.
7. The foot wounds were located between the third and fourth metatarsals. Both feet (as well as the hands) were marked with the same identical wounds.
8. The crown of thorn wounds was seen as a circular pattern of some twelve to fifteen points that formed around the forehead. This area was painful and swollen.
9. The scalp showed evidence of hemmorhaging as well.
10. A fresh lesion was observed on the right shoulder, a reminder of the Cross that Christ carried on His way to Calvary.

These are only a few of the many stigmatists who have been subjected to the greatest of inquiries under the watchful care of respected authorities in various fields. Many such investigations occurred in their lives, sometimes for months at a time. There is simply no known scientific or medical answer to these phenomena, and only the most hardened skeptics would doubt their supernatural origins (especially in the well-documented cases that we've seen above). The job of the skeptic is really much more difficult than that of the believer: it appears much easier to prove that the stigmata is not the result of natural causes; therefore, how does the critic begin to justify what others cannot?

We will now turn to a brief discourse on the psychological evaluations done on various stigmatists to see if this provides any support or condemnation of the subjects involved.

Psychological Evaluations

As with the medical and scientific examinations done on the stigmatists, many detailed psychological evaluations have given support to the authentic nature of the mystical wounds that these holy victims possessed. They have also exposed the cases of *false stigmatism*, which can be caused by neurosis, psychosis, and even the devil himself, who frequently attempts to deceive the faithful by appearing as an angel of light (2 Cor 11:14).

First, let us begin this study on false or *diabolical stigmata* before we treat the legitimate stigmatists in this same unit. We know that the devil is capable of producing the marks of the stigmata, for he has done so many times in the course of Christian history. As Cardinal Bona (1609-74) once stated: "The marks of the wounds of Christ can be imitated and impressed by the fiend, as so many examples too painfully have proven" (*De discretione spirituum*, Chapter VII, Rome, 1672). Although the Cardinal admits to the imitation and impression of the wounds caused by the evil spirit, he does not say that the devil can cause permanent, deep wounds that bleed continuously for many years; on the contrary, these false wounds are always transitory, although they have been known to last for a few years in some special cases. Even then, it is an off-and-on again occurance.

One well-known example is that of Magdalena de la Cruz, born near Cordoba, Spain, in 1487. For more than fifty years Magdalena was under the oppression of the evil one. She even showed signs of bleeding wounds for thirty-nine years, but these occurred intermittently. It's interesting to note that when she finally confessed to the cause of her wounds and repented shortly thereafter, the wounds disappeared (1643), never to be seen again! Magdalena died in 1560. This case is admittedly rare, for most diabolical wounds do not last for very long. Even in this case, the wounds were superficial and subject to irregularities that an authentic stigmatist would not encounter.

Other causes of false stigmata are neurosis and psychosis. We know that certain blisters or reddening of the skin can be caused by a biological or mental imbalance. Indeed, there have been cases where some overly fanatic souls have so desired the Sacred Stigmata that they have intentionally wounded themselves with knives, picks, etc. in order to produce false impressions to others that they were extraordinary saints! These souls, however, are soon recognized for their inconsistent behavior and self-centered ways. In addition to this, none of these false, hysterical "stigmatists" are blessed with any of the other extraordinary supernatural gifts that usually accompany the authentic stigmatists: bilocation, the reading of hearts, discernment of spirits, healing, inedia, and so on; in other words, a tree is known by its fruit.

What are some of the signs of stigmata that are not authentic? How can we determine if these wounds are above the natural order, or whether they are products of neurosis, psychosis or even the devil? Here are some of the characteristics that help distinguish false stigmata from authentic stigmata:

False stigmata

1. These wounds are transient, usually lasting for brief intervals (though in rare cases, for months or for years).
2. The wounds are superficial and the color of the blood flow is not as clear or bright as that with authentic stigmata.
3. Lack of other extraordinary supernatural gifts in the alleged stigmatist.
4. A propensity towards "showing off" the wounds to others, or the desire to draw attention to them. This usually occurs when the wounds are self-inflicted.
5. The wounds do not appear to cause very much pain to the alleged stigmatist.
6. Wounds may appear or vanish through hypnosis or auto-suggestion.
7. Wounds are often more like small punctures, abrasions or scratches; never are they deep (much less do they penetrate all the way through the hands or feet).
8. Hysterical symptoms are usually evident.
9. These superficial wounds can be altered with the applications of various medicines or chemical treatments.
10. Odors might accompany the wounds; pus tends to form and infection often sets in; some scar tissue may be evident.
11. The wounds do not match those described in the Gospel narrative, nor do they share many exact characteristics with the wounds of other legitimate stigmatists.
12. These wounds tend to appear outside of an ecstatic state. Often the victim will fail to have a deep spirituality in his or her life.

Authentic stigmata

1. These wounds are deep; in the case of the hands or feet, they usually penetrate all the way through the limbs.
2. Authentic stigmata are usually always accompanied by states of ecstasy or rapture, especially when they are intially received.
3. The wounds are subject to severe bleeding, often daily, in most cases weekly for years or decades.
4. The wounds appear fresh and the blood is of a very bright color.
5. The wounds do not appear to be affected by any chemical or medical treatment.
6. There is often a sweet odor much like perfume that comes

from the wounds; never do the wounds have a foul odor, nor do they tend to fester or scar.

7. The wounds occur spontaneously, though not always simultaneously.

8. Blood flow from the wounds often goes against the laws of gravity.

9. The wounds tend to appear in places where the skin is thickest and most resistant.

10. Intense pain is caused by these wounds, which remains constant throughout the entire course of the stigmatism.

The question of hysteria as an identifiable cause in the appearance of some stigmata has been verified through many isolated cases which prove to be inauthentic. Conversely, psychiatric evaluations have also proven that authentic stigmatists remain sound in character and well-balanced mentally and emotionally.

Many of the stigmatists in the past have been accused of neurotical or hysterical behavior, such as St. Teresa of Avila or St. Lydwine of Shiedam. For some peculiar reason, St. Francis of Assisi was exempt from these kinds of accusations. A likely reason for this is that Francis is portrayed as a happy saint, whereas others have been misunderstood because of their prolonged and intense experiences of the dark night of the soul which St. John of the Cross speaks about. Because of this, many misconceptions have occurred concerning the mental and emotional stability of some stigmatists, such as in the case of Padre Pio of Pietrelcina. Since Padre's supernatural state often coincided with moments of anxiety and depression during the continual dark night that plagued his soul, he would often appear imbalanced if his life or his writings were taken out of context; yet many of the highly qualified psychiatrists who have examined him described a stable, serene and well-balanced character.

The same can be said for the psychological evaluations done on Therese Neumann over the years. Here are a few statements from distinguished doctors who personally examined Therese:

My investigations into Therese Neumann's credibilty have arrived at the following result: There are no serious grounds for considering her as an hysteric and thus a conscious or unconscious liar. Quite the contrary, we must, from the very outset, credit her with the reliability of any person who is sound in mind and soul. . . . (Dr. Fritz Michael Gerlich, 1929.)

I must honestly confess that I have observed not the least sign of hysteria in Therese Neumann, no suggestion or auto-suggestion, hypnosis or deceit, or for that matter, possession by the devil. The young lady gives the impression of being a perfectly sound and normal person, in the opinion of everyone who has ever had an opportunity to see her and speak with her in her normal state. . . . (Dr. Karl Cardinal Kaspar, 1930.)

In my judgment, Therese Neumann has an uncommonly clear mind and judges her own person and her own personal graces with amazing objectivity and sobriety. Her will is powerful, masculine even, and oriented solely towards fulfilling the will of our Savior in all things, out of love for him, and bringing all men everywhere closer to him. . . . (Dr. Franz X. Mayr, Professor of Chemistry, Biology and Geology, 1937.)

Even Archbishop Teodorowicz had these nice things to say about Therese Neumann's mental, emotional and spiritual state:

Naturalness, love of truth, but especially simplicity — these are the three principal qualities I have noted in Therese. But simplicity of soul does not consist, as do some other virtues, in special activities which are verified only on the proper occasion. Simplicity is the whole cast of her soul, her spiritual health; it streams out of her very person and is shared by everyone who speaks of her or observes her. Her simplicity is in her eyes, in her every motion, and it rules over the exterior as well as the interior part of her soul: it resides in her deepest thoughts and feelings. Other virtues, such as humility and patience, could all be artificial, but every artificial attempt to feign simplicity quickly betrays itself. . . (1936).

Again we hear the words of Archbishop Teodorowicz:

The spiritual life of Therese Neumann appears harmonious and balanced, despite the variety of her moral and spiritual characteristics. Thanks to this simplilcity and straight-forwardness of her whole being, the supernatural world, as she describes it in answer to our questions seems to be reduced to a natural world, or to put it much better, it seems as though the partition between these two worlds has disappeared under the breath of this simple and childlike soul. . . (1936).

Stigmatist Marthe Robin (1902-81) had been examined by many people, and she was found to have a very stable character. Note what author Father Raymond Peyret had to say about Marthe:

She was simple as a dove, much too simple to play a role for fifty years! The truth always leaks out through the holes, in the end. It seems unthinkable that Marthe could have deceived her parents, her family, her neighbors, her friends, numerous doctors, the members of the "Foyer," a realistic man like Father Finet, theologians, philosophers, and thousands of visitors, while simultaneously exercising so much patience, rising above suffering, and paying such attention to others. . .
It seems psychologically untenable that a faker could have sowed all around her hope in God, the desire to pray, the joy of loving and peaceful hearts. The fruits of the Spirit, enumerated by St. Paul, are too abundant to allow of any suspicion of deceit. . . .
(*Marthe Robin: The Cross and the Joy*, p. 133; Rev. Raymond Peyret: Alba House; copyright by the Society of St. Paul, Staten Island, N.Y., 1983.)

Favorable words have also been spoken about the personality of stigmatist Mary Rose Ferron (1902-36) of Woonsocket, Rhode Island:

> Humility and generosity mingled with a sense of humor made Rose one of the most charming and beautiful characters you could meet. Her modesty and her deep humility, together with a fear of vanity, kept her from making a show of herself. . . . (*She Wears a Crown of Thorns*, pp. 125-26; Rev. O.A. Boyer, S.T.L.: Villa Pauline, Mendham, N.J., 1958.)

Anne Catherine Emmerich (1774-1824), extraordinary visionary and stigmatist, was once the subject of intense ecclesiastical and medical evaluations. This is only natural, for anyone so highly favored with constant states of ecstasy and hundreds of supernatural visions needs to be evaluated by the proper Church authorities; yet a Dr. William Wesener, upon examining her, said the following: "In our communications, I always found Sister Emmerich simple and natural, kind and gracious toward everyone" (March, 1813). Listen to the remarks made by Father Carl E. Schmöger, C.SS.R.:

> Not only in the spiritual life was Sister Emmerich passively obedient to her confessor. In everything without exception, she sought to regulate her conduct by his directions. Her longing for religious obedience had increased with her inability to practice it . . . her humble forgetfulness of self led her friends to look upon her not as sick and requiring special care . . . simple, obliging and industrious, never did she aspire to notice. . . . (*The Life of Anne Catherine Emmerich: Volume I*, p. 334.)

We have looked at many examples of stigmatists who have been authenticated through the scientific and medical fields, as well as through intensive psychological evaluations conducted at the request of the Church. Although these facts in themselves can never totally prove each supernatural action in the lives of the stigmatist (some things are unproveable and rest with Divine Providence), nevertheless they help to substantiate the reality of God's action and grace working through these humble and pious souls. When we have the assurance of the Church that these souls are worthy of our admiration, imitation or devotion, then all of the faithful can greatly benefit from the inspiration these chosen ones have given for all who seek the way of perfection and the unity with God's love. Here lies one of the most important values of the stigmatist for the world today: these are extraordinary souls who live in an ordinary world, seeking nothing but God's will and love; in turn, they express this love through charity towards their neighbor, in whom they see the living Christ. They are sources for our own inspiration and motivation to seek the narrow road that leads to eternal life — to be more Christ-like in our everyday faith experience. Because they were human, the stigmatists offer each of us hope in moving closer to God and to each other as we make our way through life's journey.

Portrait of the Stigmata: The Holy Shroud of Turin

Ever since the recent controversial findings surrounding the Holy Shroud of Turin in Italy, I had seriously debated whether or not I should include this section in my work on the Sacred Stigmata. In the end, a "sixth sense" convinced me to proceed with my original intentions, whatever the final judgment may prove to be concerning this holy relic. I decided that even if the Church concludes one day that the Shroud is definitely the image of a crucified man from the thirteenth or fourteenth century (and not that of Jesus of Nazareth), it would still not devalue the comparative studies of the image on the ancient cloth with the marks of the Passion in the various stigmatists throughout the history of the Church.

What important role does the Shroud (or *sindon*) play with respect to the Sacred Stigmata? Is there any meaningful correlation between the two? If we can at least presume that the image on the Shroud is that of a real crucified man (and that has not been denied, even if some do not believe it could be Jesus Christ), then the evidence on this cloth helps to reaffirm what really occurs in the bodies of those who bear some or all of our Lord's wounds as a result of their own living crucifixions. The detailed images on the Shroud can also help us to understand more clearly what the wounds of a real crucifixion look like, how the blood flows or clots, and how a contorted figure appears as a result of a painful and total consummation upon a cross. Finally, let us not forget that the Shroud (if not the real image of the Crucified Christ) certainly helps us to understand His Passion more intimately. However, I am still not convinced that the image is not that of Jesus Christ, as we shall see later on in this discourse.

Medical authorities, anatomical experts, and top theologians have all agreed that the hundreds of details revealed on the Shroud through the aid of the most advanced technological resources leave no doubt that the Shroud image portrays an extremely accurate picture of the effects of a crucifixion upon a person. If this is true, then we can be assured that the same characteristics on the Shroud image should be present in the bodies of the stigmatists as well. Since no one has yet been able to disprove the fact that a real man was crucified as a result of the evidence on the Shroud, or furthermore, how it got there (even if some have disputed its age), we should feel confident in making this comparative study. To put it bluntly, it's the best representation we have ever had of the Passion of Christ, so why discard it?

I must confess that my first reaction to reading about the negative findings from the recent research teams concerning the Shroud of Turin (summer of 1988) was disappointing. I suspect that countless others have felt the same way. This is especially so for my wife Kathy and me, since we were just in Turin (Torino), Italy, in July of 1988 to examine the place where the Shroud has been kept since 1578. Many devout pilgrims were there to pay their respects, as millions have before them.

After attending Mass at the Cathedral of St. John the Baptist, we gravitated toward the high altar at the back of the church where the Shroud has been kept since 1578 (it may not have been there at the time we were because of the summer investigations that were taking place; however, it might well have been, because only a sampling of the cloth was taken for examinations, and then for only a brief period). The Shroud is housed in a silver casket behind a large grille which is secured with three locks. In turn, three separate Church officials possess each of these keys. Inside the casket, the Shroud is covered with red silk and rolled on a wooden spool. Because of obvious security reasons, public displays only occur on rare occasions, in some cases not for several decades. The 1978 public display was only the third showing this century (the other two being in 1931 and 1933).

Many traditional stories have linked this burial cloth to the times of Jesus Christ. We are on firm historical ground at least since 1357, when the Shroud was obtained by Geoffrey de Charny in Lirey, France. At this time, King Philip VI supported the construction of a church in Lirey to house this holy relic. By 1453, the Shroud was purchased by the Duke of Savoy and the House of Savoy has owned it ever since.

The Shroud of Turin is an ancient linen cloth believed by many to have been the burial shroud of our Lord, Jesus Christ. It measures fourteen feet three inches long by three feet seven inches wide. The Shroud is hand-woven, made in the form of an ancient three-to-one herringbone twill weave-pattern. It appears that this cloth had come from a flax that was common in the first-century Middle East or Mediterranean basin.

The image that is formed on the Shroud is of a naked man who appears to have been scourged, wounded around the head in a circular pattern and crucified. Two images actually appear head-to-head on the long cloth, one half which is placed under the body, the other half which covers the front of the man.

What really astounded the scientific world was when an accidental discovery was made that continues to baffle the best of minds: in 1898, a photographer named Secondo Pia had taken a picture of the Shroud. When he examined the negative, the entire image became much clearer than it looked when seen with the naked eye. In effect, the clear image of the Shroud is really a photographic negative — the exact opposite of what one would expect from a photographed image; in other words, the positive image is in fact a true negative! Even today, no one has been able to duplicate this unusual effect as clearly as it appears on the Shroud. In fact, when the cloth is seen with the naked eye, the image is very faint (like a negative would be). It is only clearly visible at distances of three to six feet, and fades from view after more than thirty feet away.

Equally as startling is the fact that through modern technology, a complete enhancement has made the Shroud appear as a three-dimensional image! This was discovered by the Shroud of Turin Research Team during their experiments in 1978. The question remains: how does a positive image form within a negative print which also contains three-dimensional characteristics? Who could have known of this (let alone duplicate what we cannot) in the 1200s or 1300s?

Doctor John H. Heller, former Professor of Internal Medicine and Medical Physics at Yale University and member of the 1978 Shroud of Turin Research Team, once revealed the startling fact that the apparent blood stains on the Shroud are real, discrediting the theory that the Shroud of Turin was a painting. Here is what he reported:

Test confirming the presence of whole blood on the Shroud:
1. High iron in blood areas by X-ray florescence;
2. Indicative reflection spectra;
3. Indicative microspectrophotometric transmission spectra;
4. Chemical generation of characteristic porphyrin florescence;

222

5. Positive hemochromogen tests;

6. Positive cyanomethemoglobin tests;

7. Positive detection of bile pigments;

8. Positive demonstration of protein;

9. Positive indication of albumin;

10. Protease tests, leaving no residue;

11. Positive immunological test for human albumin;

12. Microscopic appearance as compared with appropriate controls;

13. Forensic judgment of the appearance of the various wound and blood marks. . . . (*Report on the Shroud of Turin*, pp. 215-16; Dr. John H. Heller: Houghton Mifflin Company, Boston, 1983.)

Obviously this positive identification rules out the fact that the Shroud was a deliberate forgery, for back in the 12-1300s the only way one could forge an image on a cloth was by painting, drawing, etching, etc. Besides, other reports from the same 1978 team reveal that the image on the Shroud is only on the top surface — it does not penetrate throughout the cloth, which advanced microscopes and computers would be able to detect if there was paint or pigment of any kind; furthermore, other tests show that there is no smear or smudge marks whatsoever on the cloth, which would be impossible if the cloth was laid over a dead man and then taken off later to produce an illusion of Christ's image. It is facts like these that don't seem to square with the findings of the 1988 teams.

Several other interesting facts are known that rule against deliberate forgery:

Detailed. The Shroud image is extraordinarily detailed. For example, scientists could count the number of scourge marks on the man's back, and even distinguish tiny scratches within the marks.

Directionless. The process that formed the image operated in a non-directional fashion. It was not generated according to any particular directional pattern as it would have been if applied by hand. . . . (*Verdict on the Shroud*, pp. 66-67; Kenneth E. Stevenson and Gary R. Habermas: Servant Books, Ann Arbor, MI, 1981.)

Perhaps most amazing of all is the mathematical computations done on the probability factor of someone else's image other than Christ's being on the Shroud:

Several Shroud researchers and scientists have already tried to compute such a probability. One is Francis Filas, professor of theology at Loyola University and a long-time investigator of the Shroud. Father Filas believes that there is very little chance that the man buried in the Shroud could be someone other than Jesus. Citing the correspondence between the Shroud and the irregularities of Jesus' crucifixion, Father Filas computes the total possibility that the man on the Shroud was not Jesus as one in ten to the twenty-sixth power, thereby virtually identifying the Shroud as Jesus' burial garment.

A more conservative figure was devised by Vincent J. Donovan. Donovan was also impressed by the ways irregularities in Jesus' crucifixion correspond to the Shroud, especially the crown of thorns, the fact that Jesus' ankles were not broken, the spear wound, and the incomplete burial. Donovan concludes that there is a probability of 1 chance in 282 *billion* that the person buried in the Shroud was someone other than Jesus. . . . (*Verdict on the Shroud*, pp. 124-25.)

If these figures seem too unrealistic or incredible to believe, rest assured that many others have also come up with unbelievable odds. Professors Tino Zeuli and Bruno Barbaris, who are two members of the science faculty at the University of Turin, came up with a 1 in 225 *billion* chance that someone other than Jesus was buried in the Shroud! Obviously, not much better odds. The most *conservative* estimate by the many different teams who used statistical probability on the Shroud, according to the *Verdict on the Shroud*, was 82,944,000 to 1! If statistics can lie (as we've often heard they do), then what about the probability factor of human error in the 1988 research findings that discredit the Shroud? Certainly this would be much more likely to believe than the other odds, which are billions-to-one!

Now we will proceed to the nature of those images on the Shroud that correspond to the same wounds found in the different stigmatists throughout the centuries.

One interesting correlation is that of the hand wounds with those of stigmatist Therese Neumann (1898-1962) of Konnersreuth, West Germany. The Shroud shows the wounds to be in the wrists and not in the palms of the hands, as traditional paintings and statues have portrayed. Although Therese's hand wounds are located in a different spot, she reaffirms the position on the Shroud, as we will soon see. Dr. Pierre Barbet, famed for his study of the Shroud and experiments on cadavers to better understand the effects of crucifixion, once nailed a cadaver through the palms to see if they would sustain the body weight and pressure while suspended upon a cross. It was found that the nails ripped through the palms and therefore the victim could not have been supported in this manner. Yet when nailed through the area of the wrist known as the *point of Destot*, the body held up fine under the pressure. This little-known fact until recent years is identical with that on the Shroud's image! Dr. Barbet said this about Therese Neumann's wounds:

It is the opinion of the stigmatists themselves that their wounds have only a mystical value for them. I will only quote one, Therese Neumann, whose supernatural manifestations seem to be nowadays well confirmed by the proper authorities. Therese said to one of her friends: 'Do not think that our Savior was nailed in the hands, where I have my stigmata. These marks only have a mystical meaning. Jesus must have been fixed more firmly on the cross'. . . . (*A Doctor at Calvary*, p. 105; Dr. Pierre Barbet: Image Books, Doubleday and Company, Inc., Garden City, N.Y., 1963 reprint.)

Here Therese confirms that the Shroud's depiction of the wounded wrists is probably correct. What she means here is that the stigmata will normally appear in the places where one has traditionally felt them to be, or where one envisions them to be in his or her contemplative experiences and profound devotions to the Passion of our Lord. We must remember that grace works upon nature as it is and does not always change it. God often adjusts His gifts to the constitutions of the one who is favored. This is because He is a respecter of persons and loves them for the way they are — the very way He created them, strengths and weaknesses included. Because the wounds have a very personal meaning for the stigmatist who receives them (even though they are meant for the universal Church), many of these souls experience the Passion in slightly different ways, and some exhibit differences in the type or amount of wounds. Perhaps this is an indication that Christ's Passion and Crucifixion are truly unique, and can never be exactly duplicated; He is God, and there is no other. The stigmatist is a follower of Christ like anyone else, yet more intimately so than most of the faithful.

To continue with our point, St. Bridget (1303-73) was once told the following by our Lady:

'My Son's hands were pierced at the spot where the bone was most solid'. . . .

Let us conclude this point about the hand wounds by quoting from Dr. Barbet:

It is permissible to believe that the impression was usually made at the spot where the stigmatists believed that our Savior received His wounds. This would appear to be necessary and providential, so that the stigmatist should not be bewildered at these manifestations and so that they should retain their mystical meaning for his soul. And let us also own that we understand nothing about this mystery. If, for example, such an ordeal was imposed on me, I think that the stigma would be perhaps . . . not in the wrists, but in the palms of the hands, just in order to teach me humility! In any case, the sacred texts, to which we must give our complete submission, are not so explicit. They do not speak of the palms, but of the *hands*. It is for anatomists to say what is meant by the word hand. Those of every age and every country are agreed on this point: the hand consists of the wrist, the metacarpus and the fingers. . . . (*A Doctor at Calvary*, pp. 105-06.)

This last statement by Dr. Barbet is very important. It goes to show that not only are Therese's "hand" wounds perfectly justified where they are, but it also reaffirms the validity of the exact location of those wounds on the Shroud.

Other wounds depicted on the Shroud are remarkably similar to those stigmatists who bore the same wounds or who have felt the same pains during their Passion ecstasies. Therese Neumann described these visions of the scourging which produced in her body the same effects that are seen on the Shroud:

Beneath the repeated blows, the skin first swells up and is then torn; the blood flows so that His whole body looks terrible and red with wounds and blood. When the soldiers have fully satisfied their cruelty, they untie our Savior and He falls down; it is a heartrending sight. . . . (*The Holy Shroud and Four Visions*, p.26; Radio Replies Press, Inc.; reprinted by TAN Books and Publishers, Inc., Rockford, IL, 1974.)

Therese's visions were reproduced in her body during the ecstasy of the Passion; they also confirm what the Shroud reveals about the scourge marks.

Stigmatist Anne Catherine Emmerich (1774-1824) described her Passion visions in a similar manner, also consistent with the evidence on the Shroud:

Two fresh executioners used scourges composed of small chains, or straps covered with iron hooks, which penetrated to the bone and tore off pieces of flesh at every blow. . . . (*The Holy Shroud of Turin and Four Visions*, p.27.)

Indeed, under laboratory studies by enhancement of the scourge images, the marks on the Shroud do appear to be made from small metal objects that tore off pieces of flesh.

The crown of thorn wounds as depicted on the Shroud was also explained by these two stigmatists, who in addition to receiving the Five Sacred Wounds of our Lord, also suffered the head wounds themselves. Therese tells us this:

The crown of thorns which is now ready is placed on our Lord's head like a helmet; it is not just a crown as we see it depicted in our pictures. One of the soldiers presses the crown of thorns firmly on His head. The blood flows down His whole face which shows signs of intense pain during this terrible treatment. . . . (pp. 31-32.)

If one looks at the head image on the Shroud (both front and back), it is very clear what Therese is talking about. There does appear to be more than just a thin, circular crown, judging by the wounds and blood stains. Rather, a good portion of the head appears to be wounded and bloodied. Again, we have a confirmation of a fact probably unthought of in the thirteenth century: a different but more realistic image of the crown on our Lord's head. How would a forger know about this (let alone the anatomically correct placement of the wrist wounds)?

Anne Catherine Emmerich's visions (and subsequent sufferings) are very similar:

The crown of thorn wounds was made of three branches plaited together, the greatest part of the thorns being purposely turned inwards so as to pierce our Lord's head. . . They put a reed in His hand. They then seized the reed from His hand and struck His head so violently that His eyes were filled with blood. . . . (p. 31.)

226

Many stigmatists have been known to shed blood from their heads and faces, including the eyes. This phenomenon has been associated with the Agony of Christ in the Garden, or the beatings from the crowning that was just described. The Shroud shows evidence of deep head wounds that appear to have been forced, judging by the amount and direction of the blood flow. Who in the thirteenth century could have suffered such an unusally cruel crucifixion to be recorded on a burial cloth that exists today in Turin? This is really beside the point, because crucifixions went out with the Roman authorities centuries before. If nothing else, by the time of the Middle Ages criminals were usually sentenced to death by hanging, burning or some other cruel method of execution. As far as this author knows, people then were sentenced to die upon a stake (as in the case of the Inquisition), but not nailed to a cross, crowned with thorns, or speared in the side *after* death (which is clearly depicted by the analysis of the blood clots, blood flows, and water contents, according to anatomical experts).

The side wound on the Shroud reveals a piercing between the fifth and sixth ribs on the right side, with an opening that comes through on the back side, as though the wound went straight through the heart, which is confirmed in the Gospel (Jn 19:34). The side wound of both Therese Neumann and Anne Catherine Emmerich were reportedly in the same identical location and had the same characteristics of that which is shown on the Shroud. Anne tells us this:

> The officer seized his lance and rode up to the mound where the Cross was planted and taking his lance in both hands, thrust it so completely into the right side of Jesus that the point went through the heart, and appeared on the left side. . . . (p. 53.)

Again, Therese's description is similar to Anne's:

> When the sacred side of Jesus is transpierced with the lance, I see that the lance is vigorously thrust through the right side opposite the heart. The lance comes out on the other side, but only a little shows. . . . (p. 53.)

We must take the visions of these two stigmatists seriously, for they themselves had the same wounds that are described in their Passion stories. It is the same description of the wound characteristics on the sacred cloth at Turin.

To sum up our descriptions from Therese Neumann and Anne Catherine Emmerich, the visions they have had of our Lord's foot wound (wounds they themselves bore) perfectly match those on the holy Shroud of Turin: the left foot being nailed over the right with one nail, and the right leg in a straight position while the left is slightly bent to accomodate the position on the Cross. If the sacred image on the cloth is a forgery, then the forger must have designed his blueprint from the lives of the stigmatists, for they are replicas of that sacred image depicted on the Shroud. We have a paradoxical situation here: on one hand some are discrediting the Shroud as a Medieval forgery, while on the other hand the Church has authenticated many stigmatists who are near living copies of the very same images portrayed on the Shroud! Did a stigmatist pose for hours before a forger in order to allow him to copy the exact images on a thirteenth-century cloth?

Unlikely conclusion, to say the least, since the means to thoroughly examine stigmatists under prolonged observations by medical and scientific experts were not available in the thirteenth century. It is really only the past several centuries that we've come up with detailed descriptions.

Other wounds revealed on the Shroud (and many that different stigmatists have experienced) have been noted by Dr. David Willis. Here he gives a list of the facial wounds of the cruified man on the cloth:

1) Swelling of both eyebrows;
2) Torn right eyelid;
3) Large swelling below the right eye;
4) Swollen nose;
5) Triangular-shaped wound on right cheek with apex pointing to nose;
6) Swelling to left cheek;
7) Swelling to the left side of chin;

These injuries are readily in harmony with the Gospel accounts of Christ being struck repeatedly on the face, both at the hands of the High Priest's men and Pilate's soldiers, prior to the sentence of crucifixion. . . . (*The Shroud of Turin*, p. 36; Ian Wilson: Image Books, Doubleday and Company, Inc., Garden City, N.Y., 1979.)

Besides explaining the realistic sufferings that are known from the Shroud, this type of information reveals the extensive sufferings that the victim soul goes through as well, for the same wounds are often seen on the stigmatist during his or her Passion experiences.

Shroud scientist Giovanni Tamburelli of the University of Turin gave this list of twenty features of suffering on the facial image of the Shroud, through the aid of a three-dimensional enhancement:

1. A clot of blood on the left cheek near the side of the nose;
2. Blood clot on the right cheek;
3. Blood and swelling at the point of the left cheekbone;
4. Bloody cuts on the point of the left cheekbone;
5. Clot of blood at the edge of the left eyelid;
6. Streams of blood flowing from each nostril;
7. Blood under a split upper lip;
8. Blood at the right edge of the upper lip, strongly three-dimensional;
9. A pointed drop of blood emerging from the right nostril;
10. A clot of blood on the right side of the upper lip;
11. A clot of blood higher on the left side of the upper lip;
12. A clot of blood on a possibly burst lower lip;
13. Flowing blood from the left corner of the mouth;
14. Depressions on each side of the bridge of the nose, possibly indicating a crushed cartilage;
15. A deep cut across the bridge of the nose;
16. Abrasion of the skin of the nose;
17. The tip of the nose is out of alignment (a deviated septum?);
18. The beard is drenched with blood on the right side;

19. Blood and possible depression on the right cheek;
20. Circle on the middle of the right eyelid, which may be a coin. . . . (*Portrait of Jesus?* p. 121; Frank C. Tribbe: Stein and Day, Inc., N.Y., 1983.)

Hopefully we can begin to better appreciate the tremendous sufferings our Lord went through during His bitter Passion, all for the sake of the people He loved so dearly.

After all the extensive studies that have been done on the Shroud of Turin in the twentieth century, this author is not yet ready to claim that this revered relic is inauthentic, much less a hoax or fraud. There are simply too many opposing factors at this time to reach this final conclusion.

What exactly did the 1988 research teams conclude about the Shroud of Turin? The teams who undertook the extensive studies in the summer of 1988 were from the University of Arizona, Britain's Oxford University, and the Federal Institute of Technology in Zurich, Switzerland. According to *Time* magazine's October 24, 1988 issue (p. 81), Arizona Physicist Douglas Donahue claimed that all three teams reached a "remarkable agreement" in estimating the dates within 100 years of each other: a date somewhere between 1200-1300; furthermore, Mr. Donahue claimed that these estimates had a 95-100 percent probability of accuracy. Anastasio Cardinal Ballestrero of Turin, Italy, claimed that the scientific tests proved that the Shroud could not have been the burial cloth of Jesus Christ, and admitted that it indeed dates back no earlier than six or seven centuries.

The new carbon-14 dating technique that was used on the Shroud — the so-called AMS (accelerator mass spectrometer) — was developed only this past decade, and is supposed to be quicker and more reliable than the older system.

The problem with the *Time* article is that it is only seven paragraphs long, or a mere half-page of page eighty-one in the October issue. There is simply not enough information to rely on concerning proof for the verdict on the Shroud. The title of the article, in my personal opinion, is a cheap shot: "Debunking the Shroud of Turin." Debunking, according to one *Merriam-Webster Dictionary* definition, means "to expose the shame or falsehood of" (1974 edition, p. 189). Certainly no shame was brought about because of these recent reports, nor do the reports prove any falsehood whatsoever. All they can do is predict an age range for the Shroud of Turin, and no one can claim 100 percent certainty from a single series of tests. There is also the problem of the dating technique used, which we will discuss in the remainder of this discourse. Finally, we must consider carefully the theological and scientific credentials of the authors of these articles: Are they qualified to write about the subject matter involved, or are they just on a job assignment? Do they have extensive theological or scientific backgrounds of one sort or another? The reader needs to keep these things in mind in order to keep the circulated information in proper perspective.

One uncertainty rests with the recent conclusions from the 1988 research teams. In light of all previous tests and extensive evidence (particularly from the Turin Commission, 1963-73, and the Shroud of Turin Research Project, 1978), the conclusions of the latest teams seem to ignore and oppose all former testimony from the best scientific experts in the world today. These earlier team members collected an impressive amount of evidence — historical, chemical and anatomical — to indicate the image on the Shroud would have to pre-date the 1200-1300s, at least from the standpoint of common reason.

Because the 1988 teams have based their key dating technique on the Carbon-14 method (or so the newspapers report), it poses several problems that we should examine: 1) Carbon-14 dating has always been highly controversial, since major errors in its use have been admitted in the past. Even the 1978 team acknowledged its shortcomings; 2) Since the December 4, 1532, fire that deeply scourched the Shroud's longitudinal folds, how can we be absolutely certain that the heat and smoke did not alter the carbon content or decay ratio in the part of the cloth that was tested? Heat, of course, can affect the nature of carbon or a host of other elements, and smoke infiltration must affect the internal composition as well; 3) Can we be absolutely certain that the small strip taken from the Shroud for the 1988 testing was not from a repair patch used to replace the burnt areas in the 1532 fire? This added linen most likely dates to the same century. Former researchers have identified this patch work as a linen "square weave" (not the herringbone weave of the original Shroud); 4) Since the Shroud has many water stains on it as a result of the attempt to extinguish the 1532 fire (and there had been at least one other fire before 1532), could a part of this earlier saturation have found its way into the samples that were tested? Like heat, water can affect the contents of elements, too; 5) It is known that several nuns of the Poor Clares reinforced the *entire* backing with more linen after the damage from the 1532 fire. Was part of this backing tested instead of the true Shroud material underneath?; 6) Can extremes in climate conditions (caused by humidity, rainfall, pollution, or intense heat) affect the carbon content or its decay ratio over hundreds of years? It is well-known that at least since the 1300s the Shroud has been subjected to many moves in different areas, including frequent handling and exposure to different elements; and 7) Can we be certain that the prior testing done on the Shroud has not affected any of the carbon characteristics? Here we might consider the effects of photographic light, X-rays, physical handling, etc. And what about the effect of carbon on an object that is tightly enclosed for hundreds of years (in this case, a metal casket)? Does carbon remain built up in unusual quantities if it cannot escape in normal, open surroundings?

Not everyone is completely satisfied with the recent findings. Father Albert Dreisbach, a priest who is in charge of an organization in Atlanta that is devoted to studying the Shroud, had this to say: "It will be the carbon-14 dating and not the authenticity of the Shroud" that will be tested in coming months. Father Dreisbach claims that the strip of cloth which was tested came from the outer edge, a section that is one of the most contaminated in the entire Shroud; furthermore, he believes that we cannot be certain if the piece that was taken for testing is of the original cloth because of the patch work added due to the 1532 fire, as well as the reinforcement backing that was added to repair the Shroud.

Assuming that human or mechanical error are not factors in these findings, there are more serious problems with accepting the recent reports that the Shroud is inauthentic. I take these factors from conclusions drawn by the 1978 Shroud of Turin Research Project and put together by Frank C. Tribbe. Here is a summary of all the unusual characteristics of the Shroud that make a forgery or hoax very unlikely:

1) The body images are photographic negatives;
2) They are superficial, and run only one or two fibrils deep into the threads;
3) The images encode three-dimensional data that a computer can translate into a relief image;
4) The images are non-directional, showing a total absence of brushstrokes or other indication of physical application;
5) They are pressure independent, with front and back views compatible;
6) There is a lack of image saturation;
7) Variation is by shading and density without change in color;
8) There is exact anatomical and pathological data and lack of distortion;
9) They were not made by paint or other additive;
10) Actual primate blood, probably human, has made the photographically positive blood images;
11) The blood in many areas has penetrated to the reverse side of the cloth;
12) The bloodstains relate to four different periods covering about twelve hours;
13) Bloodstains and blood clots, whether fresh or dried, are un-broken and unsmeared (experimentation proves there is no way a cloth like the Shroud could be lifted from a body or a statue with-out smearing or breaking bloodstains or blood clots that are 36 hours old or less);
14) The Shroud images are consistent with Roman practices, with Jewish ritual, with history, and with the Bible. . . .
(*Portrait of Jesus?* pp. 252-53; Frank C. Tribbe: Stein and Day Publishers, N.Y., 1983.)

We can also summarize the Shroud's likely origins with these following points:

1) The weave (3-to-1 herringbone twill) had been used in the Middle East of the first century, but was at that time unknown in Europe;
2) Cotton traces in the linen cloth meant that it had been woven on a loom previously used to weave cotton — virtually precluding European production;
3) It almost certainly was made in the Near East (Syria to Mesopotamia to Egypt) and could have been made in the first century;
4) The Z-twist thread was distinctive of the Near East of the first century, but was then unknown in Europe. . . . (*Portrait of Jesus?* p. 253.)

If we assume that the Shroud is a fake, then someone had access to advanced knowledge in photography, anatomy, physiology, theology, chemistry, physics, and other scientific disciplines that were unheard of until the twentieth century. Furthermore, he would have had the information about scientific wonders that even today we cannot explain. The forger of the Shroud would have had to know several important things:

the exact methods of crucifixion in the first century; knowledge of a modern surgeon; how to fool computers in an age over six hundred years ahead of his time; and unparalleled wisdom concerning photography (which they hadn't even invented yet), painting or sculpturing. If we can believe this, then we've lost an advanced civilization somewhere in the past seven hundred years!

The question remains: Do the findings of the 1988 research teams prove beyond all doubt that the Holy Shroud of Turin is a hoax? No, certainly not a perpetuated hoax; for, along with Dr. John H. Heller (famed member of the 1978 Shroud Research Team), all that can still be concluded about this revered cloth, even after the 1988 investigations, is that it "remains a mystery."

Can we say with certainty that this thirteenth or fourteenth century piece of linen is inauthentic? It depends on what we mean by "inauthentic." If we are asking, "Does it prove or disprove Christ's Crucifixion or Resurrection?", then the answer would still have to be no.

Even if the Shroud does prove to be beyond all doubt a thirteenth or fourteenth century relic, one still cannot discount the possibility that our Lord miraculously placed His crucified image upon this cloth in the 1200-1300s as a sign to the skeptics of the world of the victory of His death and the glory of His Resurrection. Yes, even in that time — or any century, for that matter — God can and often does leave behind signs of His presence among us.

Let us not forget that a very similar phenomenon occurred in 1531 at Guadalupe, Mexico, when the Blessed Virgin Mary's image was miraculously imprinted on another ancient cloth — the cloak of the peasant Juan Diego — 1500 years *after* our Lady's departure from this earthly life! Why, then, is it so hard to believe that the same could have happened in an earlier century with an image of our Lord on a linen cloth?

With these possibilities in mind, let us not prematurely judge or discredit the Holy Shroud of Turin, for one never knows if we are in fact looking at a real image of Jesus Christ himself, regardless of how old the cloth proves to be. The action of Christ supercedes the laws of nature, as well as human reason and the instruments of modern technology. It is simply too soon to prejudge a relic that has been beloved by millions for centuries, and that has inspired countless souls onward in their faith.

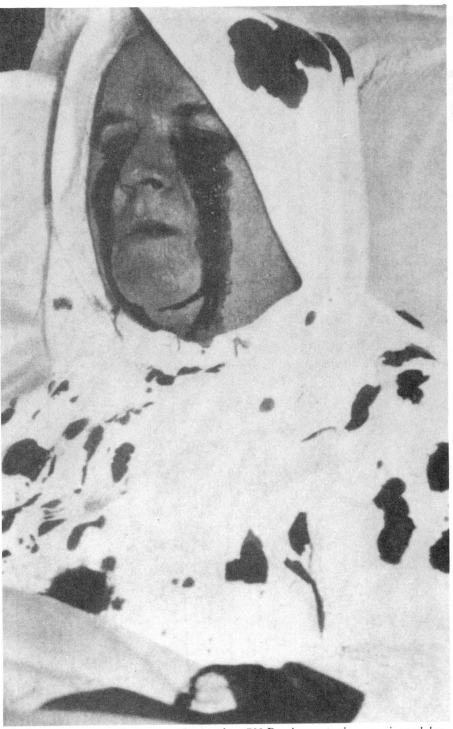

Therese Neumann suffering one of more than 700 Passion ecstacies experienced during her lifetime.   (reproduced with permission of Albert Vogl)

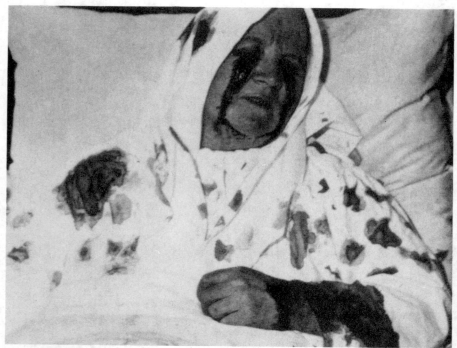

Therese Neumann's ecstacies continued until her death in 1962.

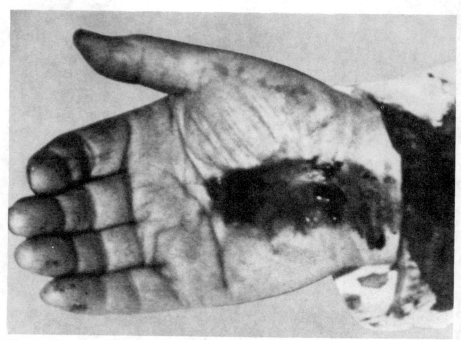

The hand wound of Therese Neumann; note the darkened, nail-like object that is bent back toward the skin.

Two early photographs of Therese in her younger years. She received the stigmata during Lent 1926. She was 28.

September 22, 1966; Therese died four days earlier.

St. Lawrence Church in Konnersreuth, Bavaria, West Germany. Therese attended Mass here throughout her life. (photo by author)

Therese Neumann's home in downtown Konnersreuth. The two upper windows were those of her bedroom. Note the crucified head of Christ between the windows.

St. Catherine of Siena (1347-80). She is one of only two women in the Catholic Faith proclaimed as Doctor of the Church. (OSV photo)

St. Catherine received the sacred stigmata from our Lord during a visit to Pisa in 1375.

(OSV photo)

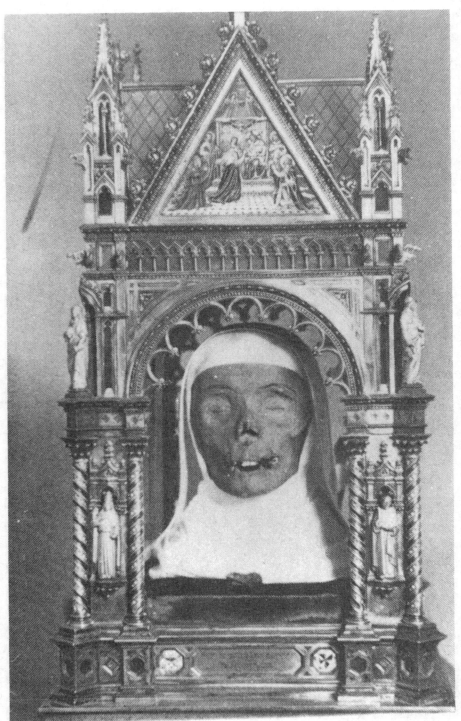

The incorruptible head of St. Catherine as seen in the Basilica of Ss. Catherine and Dominic, Siena, Italy. (OSV photo)

St. Paul the Apostle: perhaps the earliest stigmatist.

Sister Josefa Menendez (1890-1923) began her vocation as a Sister of the Society of the Sacred Heart of Jesus. She died December 29 at the age of 33.

Gemma Galgani (1878-1903) received the stigmata on June 8, 1899.

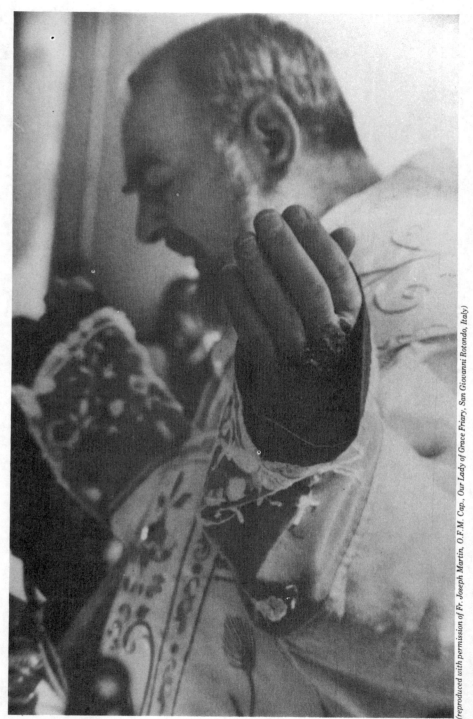

Padre Pio, perhaps the most celebrated stigmatic, celebrates one of his extraordinary Masses.

(photo by author)

Crucifix from which Padre Pio received his visible stigmata on September 20, 1918. It is located in the choir loft of the old church of Our Lady of Grace Friary, San Giovanni Rotondo.

Pietrelcina-Piana Romana. The chapel built on the spot where Padre Pio received the invisible stigmata in 1910.

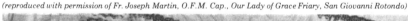

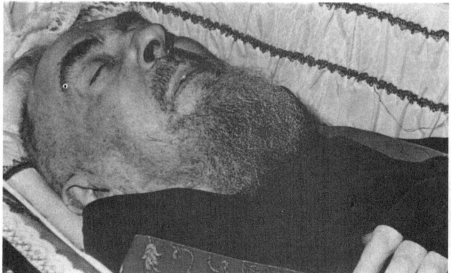

Padre Pio died on September 23, 1968.

The chair in which Padre Pio died. The blood-stained pillow (seen on chair) was placed under Padre's head one night by the Blessed Virgin Mary after he was beaten by the devil. (photo by author)

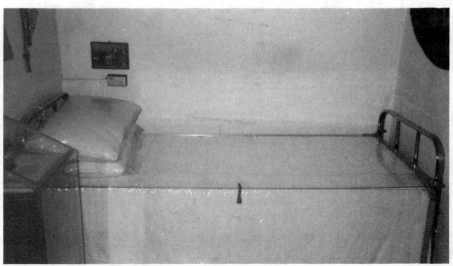

Padre Pio's bed in his cell, Our Lady of Grace Friary. Note the blood-stained pillow.

(photo by author)

Rare photo of Padre Pio taken by Padre Placido of San Marco in Lamis soon after Pio received the visible stigmata.

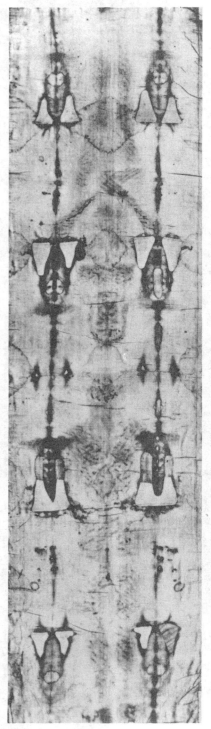

(OSV photo)

Positive (above) and negative (below)
images of the face on the shroud.

(OSV photo)

The Shroud of Turin.   (OSV photo)

Fresco of St. Francis of Assisi (1182-1226).   *(OSV photo)*

The crypt of St. Francis in the Lower Church of the Basilica of St. Francis, Assisi, Italy. Close-up of crucifix, below, left.

The Church of San Damiano, Italy

The Cross of San Damiano in the Basilica of St. Clare, Assisi, Italy. This is the original 13th century crucifix through which Jesus spoke to St. Francis: "Francis, rebuild my Church."

(photo by author)

Church of the Portiuncula where St. Francis established his order's headquarters. It is housed within the larger church of Our Lady of the Angels.

(OSV photo)

St. Francis received the stigmata on September 17, 1224. He is the first recognized stigmatic in history.

St. Teresa of Avila (1515-1582) was one of the greatest mystics of all time. (OSV photo)

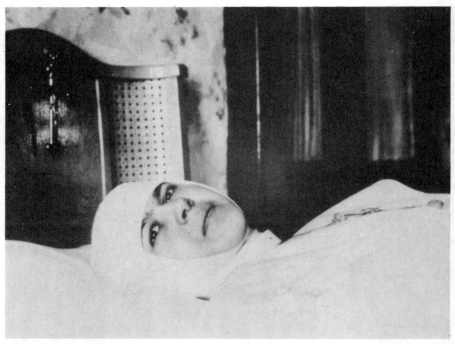

Mary Rose Ferron (1902-1936) received the stigmata in stages during 1927.

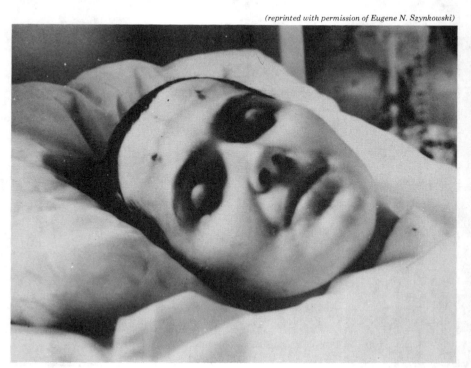

She died in May of 1936. Note the crown of thorn wounds.

Profiles of Victim Souls (Stigmatists)

Medieval Stigmatists (12th-17th Centuries)

St. Francis of Assisi
Italy
(1182-1226)

Francis Bernardone was born to a wealthy silk merchant family in Assisi, Italy. His mother desired that his name be John, but father Bernardone insisted on Francis, thus leaving him with a first name that would one day be recognized the world over.

As a frivolous youth, Francis spent his time seeking out the pleasures of life, with no concern for his father's business; nor was he particularly religious. For this ambitious man, chivalry was very much alive as he dreamed of immortality as a knight in shining armor. During his brief period as a soldier in the army, Francis was taken prisoner in 1202. In spite of confinement and a series of illnesses, the young trooper continued his services in war until 1205. Soon an event would radically change his life forever, turning him into one of the great Christian soldiers in Church history.

The first step in Francis' conversion occurred after a vision of Christ in Spoleto. However, it was not until the Lord spoke to him in the Church of San Damiano (St. Damian) that Francis turned his entire life around. One day, while praying in the ancient church that lay down the hill on the outskirts of Assisi, Jesus spoke through the Cross of San Damiano, telling him the following: "Francis, rebuild my Church." At first Francis thought our Lord wanted him to repair the worn out church buildings that surrounded the country in which he lived, especially that of St. Damian's Church. He eventually did repair that church with money he earned by selling his father's fabrics, which later caused friction between the two and resulted in Mr. Bernardone's disowning the young saint and demanding restitution for the "misappropriated" funds. It was too late. After 1206, Francis stripped himself of all money and possessions, taking up the evangelical life of chastity, poverty and obedience at the Benedictine abbey on Monte Subasio, called the Portiuncula ("little piece"), which was about two miles from Assisi. Later, the Benedictines gave the young Francis the chapel at the Portiuncula in order that he might have a home base for his newly-founded Franciscan Order.

In 1209, Francis received approval from Rome to start his own Religious order that demanded simplicity and, above all, spiritual poverty. By 1210, Francis gained the blessings of Pope Innocent III for the first General Chapter which would draw up the rules and principles of his Order at Portiuncula. Eventually, in 1221, a revision of the General Chapter was made for the ambitious young Franciscans, and finally again in 1223. The original name of the Order was the Brothers and Sisters of Penance.

In 1209, the first group of Franciscan brothers was formed (Friars Minor who were "poor servants" in the tradition of the begging mendicants). By 1212, Clare formed a second Order of St. Francis for Religious women. This Order eventually came to be known as the Poor Clares. About 1221, the Third Order of St. Francis was formed for the lay members who chose to follow St. Francis within the secular world.

Francis left behind many memorable things during these formative years. In 1223, he built a nativity scene at Grecchio which honored the baby Jesus, a practice that continues to this present day.

Francis also left us the beautiful "Canticle of Brother Sun," an inspiring piece of literature that praises the Lord's Creation: appropriately so, for he was so fond of animals and nature. Some of the verses are worth repeating here:

> 1. Praise be You, my Lord, with all your creatures, especially Sir Brother Sun;
> 5. Praise be You, my Lord, through Sister Moon and the stars, in heaven You formed them clear and precious and beautiful;
> 6. Praise be You, my Lord, through Brother Wind. . .;
> 7. Praise be You, my Lord, through Sister Water. . .
> 8. Praise be You, my Lord, through our Sister Mother Earth,
> who sustains and governs us. . . . (*Francis and Clare: The Complete Works*, pp. 38-39: Paulist Press, Ramsey, N.J., 1982.)

In 1224, the holy Poverello from Assisi retired from his intensely active missionary work that resulted in a thriving, new Order. He now decided to devote his time to prayer and practices of penance, leaving the supervision of the Order to Brother Elias. Francis retreated to Mount Alverna to live a life of strict self-discipline and to lose himself in the Crucified Christ.

On September 14, 1224, at Mount Alverna, Francis received the Sacred Stigmata from an angelic figure who appeared in the form of Christ himself. Deacon Francis (who felt unworthy to ascend to the priesthood) became the first recognized stigmatist in history. He suffered the wounds of our Lord for two years until Sister Death called him home on October 3, 1226, at the age of 44. Later, Pope Benedict XV was to call Francis "the most perfect image of Christ that ever was." His remains are now placed in an altar in the

Basilica of St. Francis, Assisi, Italy. Pope John Paul II has visited his tomb in 1978 and in 1982. Francis was canonized a saint only two years after his death.

St. Gertrude the Great
Germany
(1256-1302)

This Benedictine Abbess was born in the small town of Eisleben in the county of Mansfield, Germany (the same birthplace as the Protestant founder, Martin Luther). The exact birthdate of Gertrude is unknown. Most think it to be in the year 1256, while some others have favored the year 1263.

When Gertrude was only 5 years old, she was placed in the Benedictine Abbey of Rodersdorf in the Diocese of Helfta, later to be joined there by her sister Mechtilde. The abbess in charge of young Gertrude was Gertrude of Hackeborn (often confused with St. Gertrude herself).

From a very early age, Gertrude showed signs of being extraordinarily gifted and favored by God. Her intellectual abilities were far beyond her years, as she learned to speak and read Latin fluently as a young child. In addition to this, the saint was well-versed in Sacred Scripture, the Fathers of the Church, and other theological studies, all during the tender years of childhood.

Gertrude's visions of our Lord began in her 26th year, and continued on for the remainder of her life. According to our saint, the Lord appeared to her one evening after she had been ill for about a month. While Gertrude was paying respect by bowing to an elderly nun in the abbey, she looked up and saw our Lord, who appeared to her as "more beautiful than all the children of men." The Lord had great designs upon her soul, and from then on continued to favor her with illuminations that quickly brought her to the heights of the mystical world. Gertrude's ascent to the divine union was often hard and painful, but she eventually became transformed into the image of Christ.

Because of Gertrude's profound devotion to the Sacred Heart of Jesus, our Lord favored her by imprinting His Five Sacred Wounds in her heart, permanently wounding her with His divine seal of predilection.

St. Gertrude experienced the Infant Jesus lying close to her bosom during one of her many ecstatic states; another time, she claimed to have seen Christ face-to-face during the celebration of the Mass. So close was Gertrude to our Lord that she often felt the imprint of the Trinity within the depths of her soul.

By the age of 38, Gertrude was chosen to be Abbess of her monastery in 1294 because of her reputation for extraordinary virtues. As Superior of her fellow sisters, she led many a soul in their spiritual ascent to God.

Gertrude died near Eisleben on November 16, 1302, at the age of 46. In 1677, Gertrude was declared a saint by the authorities in Rome. By a request from the King of Spain, Gertrude was also declared Patroness of the West Indies. Her feast day is celebrated each November 16 in the liturgical calendar of the Church.

Gertrude was known for her brilliant spiritual writings that soon became classics in the annals of Christian literature. Among the better-known works are: 1) *Book of Extraordinary Grace* (*Revelation of St.*

Gertrude); 2) *Liber Specialis Gratiae*; and 3) the *Exercises* (or *Spiritual Exercises*).

St. Catherine of Siena
Italy
(1347-80)

Catherine was born to Jacomo and Lapa Benincasa as the youngest of 25 children on March 25 in Siena, Italy. Her extraordinary graces begin at the early age of six, when she had her first vision of the Lord. This occurred near a church in the Valle Piatta, and accompanying Christ in this vision were Sts. Peter, Paul and John the Evangelist. In some mysterious way, this experience gave Catherine a divine wisdom beyond her years; in fact, she soon made up her mind after this occurance to join the Order of St. Dominic, in spite of her mother's wishes that she marry and raise a family instead. She succeeded in becoming a Tertiary of the Third Order at the age of 17. There her activities centered around visiting the sick and the poor, distributing alms, and gaining personal disciples who would one day become devoted followers.

Throughout these formative years, Catherine was deeply committed to a life of prayer and fasting. She had frequent visions of Christ, the Blessed Virgin Mary and many of the saints, as well as diabolical illusions from the hand of the devil. Like all the great mystics, Catherine suffered the painful dark night of the soul during the course of her early life.

Catherine was an unusually gifted soul, one of the most favored mystics of all time. She frequently experienced levitations, performed exorcisms, possessed the gift of healing, existed on nothing but the Holy Eucharist for years, and had heavenly apparitions almost on a daily basis. One of the greatest graces bestowed upon Catherine by our Lord was the spiritual marriage, whereby Christ gave her the mystical ring of gold adorned with beautiful jewels as a sign of His union with her. Although no one ever saw the mystical ring except Catherine, she claimed that it was upon her finger for the rest of her life.

During a visit to Pisa in 1375, Catherine received the Sacred Stigmata from our Lord. After she prayed to the Lord that He remove the exterior signs of the Crucifixion because of her great humility, her request was granted. From then on until the end of her life, Catherine bore the invisible stigmata, but it appeared outwardly again at the time of her death.

Catherine was known for her heroic efforts to bring the papacy back to Rome during the Great Schism (1378-1417). Her attempts eventually proved successful when, on November 11, 1417, Pope Martin V was elected to the throne of Peter, thus ending a 39-year papal domination from Avignon, France, that had the Catholic Church in a state of upheaval. Catherine had visited Avignon, pleading with Pope Gregory XI to return ecclesiastical power back to Rome. By 1378, she had visited Rome, urging the support of Pope Urban VI and the return of the papacy to the holy city. Her death in 1380 prevented her from seeing the fruits of her efforts, which were rewarded with the coming of Pope Martin V.

Catherine's life was prematurely shortened when she suffered a paralytic stroke on April 21, 1380, while in Rome crusading for the return of the papacy and an end to the schism. There she died only eight days later on April 29.

During the course of her brief life, Catherine's spiritual writings quickly gained the admiration and praise of the entire Catholic world, including those in the city of Rome: There was something truly extraordinary about her profound wisdom and spiritual insights, a gifted writer who was obviously guided by the hand of God. Some 400 of Catherine's letters to various people are still extant. Perhaps the most famous of all her writings is the classical *Dialogue*, a treatise on her conversations with the Lord during her many ecstatic states. Because of this spiritual masterpiece and others, Catherine was proclaimed a Doctor of the Church in 1970, only one of two women ever given this honor (St. Teresa of Avila was proclaimed Doctor of the Church at the same time in 1970, also by Pope Paul VI).

Catherine of Siena was canonized in 1461 by Pope Pius II, and was declared Patroness of Italy by His Holiness Pope Pius XII in 1939. The Church celebrates her feast day on April 29 each year. The house where she died can still be visited by pilgrims on Via Santa Chiara in Rome.

The incorruptible head of St. Catherine can be seen at the Basilica of Sts. Catherine and Dominic in Siena, Italy. Also at the basilica is the remains of her incorruptible finger, enclosed in a glass container in a remarkable state of preservation. The remainder of Catherine's body is kept in Rome.

St. Lydwine of Shiedam
Holland
(1380-1433)

Lydwine was born at Shiedam, Holland, on Palm Sunday during the Great Schism and one day after the Feast of St. Gertrude, another medieval stigmatist. Lydwine was the fourth of nine children born to Pierre and Petronille, poor people whose families once enjoyed a modest prosperity. Records of the saint's ancestry are scanty, according to one of her biographers, Thomas á Kempis (probable author of *The Imitation of Christ*).

Lydwine's entrance into the world seemed to be prophetic. The name she received (Lydwine, Lydwyd, Lydwich, Liedwich, Lidie or Lidwine) comes from the Flemish word *lyden*, which means "to suffer." Also, at the moment of her birth, a song about the Passion of our Lord was being sung during the High Mass in town on the very day of the Feast of Psalms. Clearly, there was something special about this new child of God's.

As early as the age of seven, Lydwine had a profound devotion to the Blessed Virgin Mary, as well as a deep commitment to prayer and practices of mortification.

After she reached the tender years of puberty, many a young man proposed to this beautiful saint. Committing herself to God through a private vow of virginity, she declined all offers, despite her parent's encouragement to marry and raise a normal family. In fact, after too much pressure from her family to find a husband, Lydwine threatened to ask the Lord for a gross physical deformity, if necessary, to end the marital pursuits once and for all. Indeed, God did hear her prayer, which started her on a life of pain and suffering to a degree that is seldom known in the annals of Church history. Lydwine was to become God's victim soul: a living crucifix of sacrificial love.

When she reached the age of 15, Lydwine fell while ice skating and broke her rib, leaving her confined to her bed in excruciating pain. She would remain there for the rest of her life. This once beautiful young maiden was hardly recognizable anymore; part of her body had swelled, while other parts had contorted. Soon a mysterious illness dealt by the hand of Providence left her in a pitiful state. This was to be the start of a series of physical calamities that makes one shudder. Some of the sufferings that Lydwine experienced are as follows: tumors on her body; infestation of intestinal worms; open and bleeding sores; bones that protruded through the skin; gallstones; discolored skin; horrendous toothaches; paralysis of bodily limbs; abscesses; bone fractures; boils; gangrene; severe ulcers; putrefaction of the bone marrow; decay of both liver and lungs; bleeding eyes, nose and mouth; dislocations; partial blindness; neuralgic pains; twisted and broken nerves; and violent headaches. Lydwine also suffered many of the diseases that invaded her country, such as the great and dreadful plague that killed so many of her time.

Like all great mystics, Lydwine was plunged into the purifying dark night of the soul that included feelings of abandonment, aridity and desolation. This terrible night of dark purgation is necessary in God's plans for His most favored souls in order to try and cleanse them, and to prepare them for the reception of the Sacred Stigmata.

Lydwine was the object of violent diabolical attacks throughout her saintly life, as is so often the case with God's chosen victim souls. Frequently harassed and beaten by the evil spirits, she courageously looked to the Cross for her liberation.

From 1407 on, our saint began to experience ecstasies and visions of Christ, the Virgin Mary, the angels and saints. She was also privileged to see Purgatory and Heaven during her extraordinary life.

One day, some heavenly angels appeared to Lydwine and mystically imparted on her soul and body the wounds of our Lord's Passion. Her crucifixion had come to its completion. Lydwine would bear the pains of the divine imprint for the rest of her life.

Lydwine was favored with many other supernatural gifts. For the last 19 years of her life she existed on nothing except for the Blessed Eucharist, and she did not sleep for the last 7 years until her death. Lydwine was also favored with the gifts of prophecy, discernment and the sweet odor of sanctity. In reality, her entire life was a gift in itself, whereby God offered many souls the satisfaction for sin due to her heroic submission and abandonment to the works of Divine Providence.

An ecclesiastical commission was appointed to investigate the unusual life of this holy woman from Holland, and her cult was officially approved on April 14, 1890. Lydwine died in 1433 at the age of 53.

St. Rita of Cascia
Italy
(1381-1457)

St. Rita was born at Roccaporena near Spoleto, Italy, of elderly parents, who gave her the name Marguerita. Later, this name was shortened to Rita, and it is by this which she is known. Her parents had desired that she marry at a young age (perhaps worried that their deaths would leave her alone and lonely), and against her natural inclinations, Rita gave in. She married at the age of 12, had two sons, but was widowed 18 years later when her husband (Paola Ferdinando) was killed in a brawl. Their marriage was never a happy one, for Rita was frequently mistreated and abused. Even so, Rita continued to pray for him, and he did experience a conversion before his tragic death.

After the unexpected death of her two sons, Rita committed herself to the service of God, seeking entrance into the Augustinian convent called the Santa Maria Maddelina, located in Cascia. At first, Rita was denied admittance, but was later accepted after the nuns had learned that the bolted doors to the monastery were miraculously opened one night by Rita's patron saints, Augustine, Nicholas of Tolentio and John the Baptist. She finally became a nun there in 1413, after three refusals to enter the Order. The reason Rita was not accepted at first was because the rule of the Augustinian Order only permitted virgins to enter. Once again, God's miraculous intervention overcame a difficult if not impossible situation.

In time, Rita became known for her austerities, penances, prayers, and a deep concern and love for others. Her holy example led many a soul back to the faith. Because of her extraordinary reputation for piety and sanctity, the Augustinian monastery in Cascia would eventually be renamed in her honor.

In 1441, after hearing an inspiring sermon from St. James of the Marches on the crown of thorns, Rita implored our Lord to let her participate in some of the sufferings of His Passion. Her prayer was answered as God imprinted upon her forehead a thorn wound, which became infected and emitted such a foul odor that she was obliged to spend the next 15 years in total seclusion. Many claimed that they saw a powerful light coming from this myterious wound, a sign of God's intervention in the life of this holy victim soul.

Three days before her death, Rita experienced visions of Christ and His Blessed Mother. After she had died, witnesses experienced a heavenly perfume — the odor of sanctity — coming from her cell. Rita died on May 22, 1457, in Cascia at the age of 76. She was canonized in the year 1900 and is venerated as a saint of desperate causes. In 1946 a basilica was built in Cascia to honor this saint, and her incorruptible body rests there inside a golden shrine.

At the time when Rita's miraculously preserved body was exhumed prior to her beatification on July 16, 1627, many claimed to have seen her eyes open and roll around; in the years since her body has been placed in the glass case at the Basilica of St. Rita for public display, her body has reportedly shifted positions unaided many different times.

Many bees continue to reside at the basilica in Cascia, where they have been for several centuries. There is unusual story connected with the appearance of these bees. When Rita was just an infant, some bees had flown around her mouth, attracted to something she had been eating. About 200 years after she died, a swarm took up residence in the fifteenth-century wall at the Basilica of St. Rita, and have been there ever since. What's more amazing, they hibernate for most of the year, but emerge every Holy Week! The bees have never left the basilica since their arrival, yet the nuns currently at the convent do not consider this presence anything more than coincidental. After the Feast of St. Rita, May 22, the bees return to their hibernation for the remainder of the year.

Blessed Osanna of Mantua
Italy
(1449-1505)

Born in 1449, Osanna was an extremely pious child at an age when most children seldom think of the wonders of our Faith. In fact, she was so young that she was denied entrance into many different convents. Highly motivated and fiercely determined, Osanna finally was accepted into the Third Order of St. Dominic at the tender age of 14; however, she still wasn't allowed to make her solemn profession until years later. Through the many obstacles which Osanna had to face to become a Religious, God was gradually guiding this young soul and preparing her for the heights of the spiritual life. Although misunderstood, Osanna courageously practiced virtuous acts and held strong to the vocation she was certain God had given her.

Part of the misunderstandings surrounding Osanna centered around the many ecstasies and raptures that even as a youth she had been frequently favored with. Many accused her of possessing an overly zealous nature, as well as being one who was prone to bouts of exhibitionism. Many of her fellow nuns were jealous of Osanna's reputation for sanctity, since numerous people would often come to her for guidance and inspiration.

Although her many obstacles delayed her solemn profession until her 55th year (the very year that she died), an unusual mystical experience occurred that reassured her of her calling. The Blessed Virgin Mary herself and some of the angels had witnessed and approved of her intentions, and she was professed into her Order in a mysterious, heavenly way. It was God's way of confirming His intentions upon her soul, and from then on Osanna felt forever united to her Religious vocation as a Third Order Dominican.

Because of her deep desire to pray and suffer for sinners and the poor souls in Purgatory, Osanna begged our Lord to let her share His Passion in order to make atonement for their sins. After two years of such pleading, Jesus answered her by giving her His crown of thorn wounds, and later, the Five Sacred Wounds of the Crucifixion. Osanna's stigmata would remain with her for the rest of her life, although they were hardly noticeable to others. Immediately after her death, the wounds became very clear and left no doubt of their authenticity.

Osanna died on June 18, 1505. Originally buried in the Church of St. Domenico, her remains were later transferred to the Cathedral at Mantua. It was during this transfer that her body was found to be incorruptible. Pilgrims can still see her three times a year when she is displayed in a shrine beneath the altar of Our Lady of the Rosary. The incorruptibility of her body was reaffirmed when examined again in 1965. Pope Innocent XII confirmed her cult in 1694, and her feast day is celebrated on June 18.

St. Teresa of Avila
Spain
(1515-82)

Teresa was born at Avila, Castile, Spain, on March 28, the daughter of Alonso Sanchez de Cepeda and Beatrice Davila y Ahumada. An extremely pious child, at the age of seven, she was already devoted to reading the lives of the saints; at the same age, Teresa attempted to run away with her brother to convert the Moors.

Teresa received her early education from the local Augustinians, but was forced to leave their convent in 1532 because of a serious illness. Another blow struck at the age of 12 when her mother died, leaving Teresa to look toward the Blessed Virgin to be her mother from then on. For the remainder of her life, Teresa would have the deepest devotion towards our Lady, who often appeared to her and reassured Teresa of her love and maternal care.

God had great designs on this extraordinary soul, and her long desire to become a Religious was soon to be realized. In 1537, Teresa was professed into the Carmelite Order in Avila, an Order that would eventually proclaim her as one of its better-known and beloved saints.

Illness again visited Teresa soon after, and she was forced to leave the convent in 1538; however, by 1540, she returned. From 1555-56, Teresa experienced a series of heavenly visions which disturbed her and caused her great anguish; however, St. Peter of Alcantara, who became her spiritual director in 1557, convinced her that these visions were genuine.

After living in comfort in the midst of great laxity for some 27 years, Teresa felt the need for a change within her Order, especially in the area of rules and regulations. Inspired by a reading of Augustine's *Confessions*, Teresa sought to reform the Carmelites into a more strict Order. She founded St. Joseph Convent at Avila in 1562, where complete enclosure was to be the rule. In time, with the blessing of the prior general of the Carmelites, Father Rubeo, she founded 16 more reformed convents that were much more demanding than the one she had just left.

It was during the founding of her second convent at Medino del Campo when Teresa met a young friar by the name of Juan Yepes (St. John of the Cross). He would eventually start her first reformed Order for men by opening the Carmelite monastery at Duruelo in 1568. In time, Teresa turned the administration of these reformed male monasteries over to St. John, who successfully oversaw their growth and development.

Teresa was a tireless woman who traveled across Spain, forming new convents and attempting to reform the traditional Carmelites. It was no easy task, and members of the older Order fought her tooth-and-nail. Word eventually reached Father Rubeo, who was forced to put restrictions on her group from 1575-80. Finally, in 1580, Pope Gregory XIII recognized the fruits of Teresa's work, and he approved the new Order under the title of Discalced Reform.

It was during these bitter struggles and endless travels that Teresa wrote some of the works that would eventually go on to become classics, masterpieces on spirituality and the ways of perfection. Indeed, she would one day be honored as Doctor of the Church, one among only two women ever given this distinct title (St. Catherine of Siena was the other). Pope Paul VI proclaimed this title upon her in 1970.

Many of Teresa's writings are known the world over: her *Autobiography* (1565), *The Way of Perfection* (1573), and the *Interior Castle* (1577) are the works that have gained her a place among the greatest of saints and teachers that the Church has ever known.

Besides being a gifted writer and Church reformer, Teresa was one of the greatest mystics of all time, favored with many unusual gifts. Her incorruptible body was found to emit a sweet odor of perfume after her exhumation. Even her cell at the convent was filled with this heavenly aroma immediately after her death, according to many observers. With the last exhumation of her body in 1914, Teresa's remains were still found to be remarkably preserved, and the same sweet-smelling odor was evident from her coffin.

Perhaps the most remarkable grace bestowed upon Teresa was that of the transverberation, the mystical wounding of the heart. Upon examination of her body in 1872, three physicians from the University of Salmanca verified that she indeed had a perforation of the heart. Teresa talked about this stigma in her *Autobiography*. Her heart is now kept in a reliquary at Alba de Tormes, the location of one of her convents.

Pope John Paul II visited the tomb of the saint in 1982. His Holiness paid visits to both Alba de Tormes and the Convent of the Incarnation (where the saint had lived), celebrating the 400th anniversary of Teresa's death.

St. Catherine dei Ricci
Italy
(1522-90)

Alexandrina was born in Ricci, Italy, to a prominent family of wealth and honor. The life of social importance and prestige, however, was not to be for this pious young woman, who committed herself to a Religious life at a very tender age. When she turned 13, Alexandrina became a sister at the convent of San Vincenzio of the Dominican Order in Prato, Italy. After the initial year of Religious life, she took on the name of Catherine and quickly became known for her severe practices of penance and mortification. Catherine began to encounter many mystical experiences even at this stage of her spiritual ascent, and was deeply devoted to meditations on the Passion of our Lord.

Catherine's direct participation in the share of Christ's Passion began through her ecstatic raptures by the time she turned 20. It was in 1542, during the Holy Week, when Catherine first experienced the entire events of our Lord's suffering and Crucifixion in a series of scenes that started each Thursday and ended on Friday at 4:00 p.m. These mysterious sufferings went on every week for the next 12 years, according to the many souls who had witnessed this supernatural state. Catherine Dei Ricci was chosen by our Lord to be His victim for the salvation of sinners, sharing in His Crucifixion in order to make atonement and satisfaction for the transgressions of many.

The stigmata that Catherine received from our Lord were the Five Sacred Wounds of the hands, feet and side; she also was given the crown of thorn wounds, all which were seen by many different people during her exceptional life. Some had even claimed that a brilliant light shone from these wounds, bright enough to cause the eyes to wince.

It was during Easter of 1542 that Catherine experienced the divine union in a most intimate way: Jesus invited her to share in the spiritual marriage with Him. He took the mystical ring from His finger and placed it on Catherine's forefinger of the left hand, a sign which sealed their mystical espousal and brought them together as one. Many had noticed a reddening and swelling on her finger, but Catherine saw a golden ring which was set with a large, beautiful diamond, clearly visible to her throughout the remainder of her life.

Many other extraordinary phenomena were experienced by Catherine during her saintly life, such as the mystical visits she encountered with St. Philip Neri. These occurred while he was in Rome and she was in her convent in Prato, and several reliable witnesses have testified to being present during their conversations; St. Philip himself admitted to these visits, even though they had never physically met each other.

Catherine was extremely devoted to the poor and the sick, who often came to her for prayer and consolation. Many souls had visited this saint who was known for her great sanctity, including three different cardinals, each of whom would later become Pope.

Death came to this victim of God's love at the age of 68 after a long illness. She departed for her eternal home on the Feast of the Purification of the Blessed Virgin, February 2, 1590. Her incorruptible body is kept in a reliquary at the Basilica of Prato, which is exposed for the veneration of the many pilgrims who come to pay their respects. Catherine was declared a saint in heaven in 1747.

St. Mary Magdalen dei Pazzi
Italy
(1566-1607)

Baptized with the name Catherine, Mary Magdalen was born to a wealthy family of Florence, Italy. In 1582, she entered the Carmelite Order at St. Mary of the Angels Convent (also in Florence) after having refused several proposals for marriage. For this humble servant of the Lord, a life of prayer and penance would prove to be the way to a more perfect life in imitation of Christ.

St. Mary Magdalen encountered all the joys and trials of the spiritual life, as she quickly climbed the heights of the mystical ladder. She experienced many extraordinary graces from the Lord, such as locutions, visions of Purgatory and miracles. Prior to her reception of these unusual gifts, Mary Magdalen became seriously ill, fought bouts of depression and entered into a dark night which lasted from 1585-90. In time, the Lord granted her a share in His Passion as a victim of His divine love. During this time when she received the stigmata, Mary had numerous visions of Christ and the Blessed Mother, and she received many heavenly prophecies and revelations.

Death came on May 25, 1607, in her convent after suffering from a chronic illness which lasted over three years. It was reported that a sweet odor of sanctity was emitted from her grave. Her body was examined three different times — 1612, 1625 and 1663 — and it was discovered that it had been miraculously preserved, even though it was never embalmed.

Another phenomenon occurred after her death when her remains were examined. Several nuns observed that a sweet liquid seeped from parts of the body, especially from the knees. Subsequent tests have failed to identify the source or nature of this unusual aromatic fluid.

Mary Magdalen dei Pazzi was canonized in 1669, less than 70 years after her death. Her preserved body rests in the Carmelite Church of Florence, Italy.

St. Rose of Lima
Peru
(1586-1617)

Originally named Isabel de Santa Maria de Flores, St. Rose was born tenth
of 13 children of Spanish parents in Lima, Peru. She was known to be an extremely beautiful girl (hence, the name "Rose," which was really a
nickname), and had many a young man propose to her, but God had other
plans in store for this highly favored soul. Instead, Rose chose to live a quiet
life at home, helping to support her parents with needlework and the growing of flowers. Eventually, Rose lived a life of seclusion in a shack in the garden where she so often spent her time. A soul of unusual sanctity, Rose
eventually became a Third Order Dominican after having been so deeply
devoted to St. Catherine of Siena, both who were destined to become stigmatists of the Order of St. Dominic.

It was during her tender years that Rose began to practice severe acts of
penance, and she was profoundly devoted to prayer. Many mystical graces
visited this poor girl in the form of visions and ecstasies. Despite her absorb-
ing spiritual life, the saint found time to help destitute children and the
elderly of her community, and her social services became widely known in
her area. Her mystical gifts were so frequent and so extraordinary that the
Church sent the proper authorities to investigate this unusual prodigy of
God. Members of the Inquisition even kept a close eye on her, but after the
investigations the Church declared that her mystical experiences were
authentic.

After Rose's reputation for holiness spread throughout Lima, her
beloved "cloistered garden" became a kind of spiritual center for many
souls. Remarkable miracles of intercession were soon attributed to her. For
example, when many earthquakes had demolished surrounding areas but
left Lima relatively untouched, many credited the miraculous escape to the
prayers of their dear Rose. Through the blessings of the child Jesus, Rose is
reported to have been instrumental in the cures of many souls who were afflicted with chronic diseases.

Like all the great mystics and stigmatists, Rose was plunged into the
purifying dark night of the soul and suffered extreme anguish in this state
for many years. Her bouts with the devil are well-known, who frequently
threatened and assaulted this child-like saint of God.

Because of Rose's profound devotion to the Passion of our Lord and her
heroic efforts to associate herself with those who suffered, Jesus gave her a
share of His Cross by imprinting the Five Sacred Wounds in her heart. Rose
may have received the crown of thorn wounds from our Lord as well, which
completed her crucifixion in union with Christ.

This Patroness of the Americas experienced many more unusual gifts,
such as bilocation and the odor of sanctity. She knew the exact time when
she was going to die, even to the very day she had once predicted. Death
came in 1617 when Rose was only 31 years old, and she was recognized as a
saint just 54 years later on April 12, 1671, by Pope Clement X. She was
buried in the St. Dominic Church. In addition to being declared Patroness
of the Americas, Rose has also been proclaimed Patroness of Peru, the Indies and the Philippines.

After Rose's body was exhumed in 1630, she was found to be in a semi-
preserved state, and her relics are now located in two different places: her

skull is kept in the Dominican Church of Santo Domingo, while the rest of her remains are housed in a small church a few blocks away on the very spot where Rose once lived.

St. Margaret Mary Alacoque
France
(1647-90)

St. Margaret Mary was born on July 22, 1647, at L'Hautecour, Burgundy, France, to Claude Alacoque and Philiberte Lamyn, the fifth of seven children. Her baptismal name was Margaret, and the name Mary was not added until she was confirmed in 1669. As early as the age of four, Margaret made a private vow of chastity to our Lord, although she was not fully aware of the implications until later on. Even as a youthful child, Margaret was extremely devoted to the Blessed Virgin Mary and to the Blessed Sacrament. After her father died when she was eight years old, Margaret was sent away to the Urbanist Nuns school at Charolles, and it is there that she received the only two years of schooling she ever had in her life.

When she turned nine, the holy child had her first Communion, and soon thereafter was stricken by a mysterious illness that kept her bedridden for four years. Consequently, her stay at the convent came to an end, as did her brief education. Desperate because of her new condition, Margaret implored the aid of the Blessed Virgin, promising that if she would cure her, she would devote herself to one of the Marian Orders. The Mother of God soon answered her prayer, completely curing Margaret of all symptoms of the illness she had endured for several years.

In time, Margaret was drawn to profound meditations upon the sufferings of our Lord and derived great consolation from her mental prayers. Soon she would suffer from misunderstandings caused by some of her close relatives, and her soul was plunged into darkness. Satan was not long in seizing the chance to drive her to despair, and he attacked her spirit relentlessly, suggesting to her that her devotions were wrong and bringing to mind her past sins. Undaunted, the courageous saint applied anyway for admission to the Ursuline Order at Macon, but was called home before she had a chance to enter. Clearly, God had other plans in store for her.

Her home would be at the Visitation convent in Paray, where she eventually took the habit on August 25, 1671, and was professed on November 6, 1672. There she would live a life in close union with the suffering Christ, experiencing numerous ecstatic states and mystical graces. It would be Christ himself who would direct her soul throughout the rest of her life, teaching her the messages of the Sacred Heart for which she would later become so well known. Starting on December 27, 1673, Margaret began experiencing visions and messages from our Lord which lasted over a year and a half. Our Lord asked for a Nine Fridays devotion and the Holy Hour, as well as a feast day set aside in honor of His Sacred Heart (which was officially approved in 1765 by Pope Clement XIII). Since Margaret Mary's time, devotion to the Sacred Heart of Jesus has flourished throughout the entire Church, which owes its success to this humble maiden of the Lord.

There is evidence from many letters to her superiors and friends that Margaret Mary experienced the sufferings of our Lord's Passion continuously, bearing the invisible stigmata which included the crown of thorn wounds. In fact, her *Autobiography* mentions these words from our Lord:

"Receive this crown, my daughter, as a sign of that which will soon be given thee in order to make thee conformable to me." Her sufferings must have been immense, for she persistently refers to them in these letters of correspondence (see *Jesus Reveals His Heart: Letters of Saint Margaret Mary Alacoque*; transl. by Clarence A. Herbst, S.J.; St. Paul Editions, 1980: the Daughters of St. Paul, 50 St. Paul's Ave., Boston, MA, 02130).

Margaret Mary was the director of novices at the convent in Paray from 1685-86. It was also at Paray that the first public honor was given to the Sacred Heart in 1685. St. Margaret Mary died there on October 17, 1690, where her body still rests. She was declared Venerable in 1824, Blessed in 1864 and Saint on May 13, 1920.

St. Veronica Giuliani
Italy
(1660-1727)

Veronica was born in Mercatelli, Italy. When she was just four years old, her mother Benedetta was dying and entrusted each of her five daughters to one of the five wounds of Christ. Veronica was entrusted to the wound below Christ's heart. This act on Benedetta's part proved to be prophetic, for later on Veronica would become avidly devoted to the Passion of our Lord, even to the point of sharing His sufferings as she strove to imitate His life.

At the age of 17, Veronica was professed into the Order of Poor Clares, the second Order of St. Francis set up exclusively for women and directed by the Capuchins. As in so many cases with the stigmatists, Veronica's father wanted her to marry, but she was determined to follow the life of chastity, poverty and obedience. Her first duties in the convent were to work in the kitchen and to serve as a portress. When she turned 34, Veronica was made novice mistress, a position she was to hold for 22 more years. By the time Veronica turned 37, on Good Friday in 1697, she received the stigmata from our Lord.

The marks that Veronica received were an answer to her mother's prayer, for the Five Sacred Wounds were imprinted directly upon her heart. Earlier, Veronica was given the crown of thorn wounds, thus completing her own crucifixion.

After the news reached the Church authorities concerning the supernatural events surrounding this saintly soul from Mercatelli, the Holy See ordered the bishop of her diocese to examine her thoroughly and report on these unusual experiences. She was to give up her role as novice mistress, and was kept away from Mass except on Sundays and holy days. Her wounds were found to be open and bleeding, and all attempts to stop this phenomenon failed. Because of this and her submissive behavior towards authority, the Church authenticated her extraordinary experiences.

Many have considered Veronica to be another St. Teresa of Avila, in the sense that she was a great administrator and was blessed with so many supernatural gifts. In the last 11 years of her life (and against her wishes), Veronica was appointed abbess of the monastery at the age of 56. As busy as she was, Veronica still found time to write a ten-volume diary which was to serve her Cause for Beatification and Sainthood. She was eventually canonized in 1839.

Veronica died in 1727 from apoplexy. During an exhumation of her body, her heart was found to be incorrupt, and the examiners indeed found the Sacred Wounds imprinted there. What is remarkable is that the wounds match the drawing she had once made to describe them!

St. Mary Frances of the Five Wounds
Italy
(1734-91)

St. Mary Frances was given the name Anna Maria by her middle-class parents in her birthplace of Naples. Although her father agreed to a marriage proposal from a rich young man, the 16-year-old Anna refused his proposal, claiming that she intended to remain a virgin for life and dedicate herself to God. Her dream was realized when God called her to the Franciscan Order as a Tertiary. However, her father was angry that she had gone against his wishes. After he found out that his daughter insisted on becoming a Franciscan, he locked her in her room and beat her. Later, when the young Anna was unmoved by his threats and beatings, he finally gave in and allowed her to join the Order, provided that she would stay at home. Anna agreed, and spent her life devoted to prayer and penance, taking on the name Mary Frances as she entered her new life under the rules of the holy Poverello from Assisi.

Mary Frances suffered a great deal during those many years at home. Her brothers and sisters did not make life easy for her, nor did her obstinate father. Even her confessor misunderstood this child of God for a long time, as in the case with so many favored souls. Yet Mary Frances would continue to follow the Franciscan life, devoted to works of charity among those who were in need. She was very helpful towards the sick and homeless around Naples, and performed great acts of penance for their sake.

Devoted to the Passion of our Lord and continuously praying for the poor souls in Purgatory, God approved her sacrifices and sufferings for them and allowed her to feel the pains of His Passion by placing the stigmata on her hands, feet and side. Mary Frances was blessed with many other extraordinary graces. She experienced the Passion ecstasies every year during her lifetime, and was reported to have had the gift of prophecy. She was canonized in 1867.

Modern Stigmatists
(18th-20th Centuries)

Anne Catherine Emmerich
West Germany
(1774-1824)

Anne Catherine Emmerich was born on September 8 at Flamske, near Coesfeld in Westphalia, West Germany, to a small farming family. Her parents, Bernard Emmerich and Anne Hiller, were poor peasants, but very pious. They had Anne Catherine baptized at the St. James Church at Coesfeld.

Anne spent a good deal of time in her childhood as a maid and seamstress until her entrance into the Augustinian Order on November 13, 1803. She joined the Convent of Agnetenberg at Dulmen, which is also in Westphalia. Even during these youthful years, Anne was extraordinarily gifted with ecstasies and visions of Christ, the Blessed Virgin Mary, her guardian angel, and many of the saints. Although never given an adequate education, Anne had perfect recollection of her childhood days, and she could understand Latin from the very first time she attended Mass. Almost from infancy Anne reportedly had the gifts of discerning holy from unholy objects, consecrated objects or locations, and the identification of relics and from which saints they came. Also during these early years, Anne was often seen making the entire Way of the Cross in her bare feet, even when the snow had covered the ground.

In 1811, Anne was forced to leave her convent along with all the sisters when King Jerome Bonaparte closed all of the Religious houses during his reign. Four years before the suppression of her convent, Anne made a visit home with her family in Flamske. One day while she was kneeling and praying for hours before the Cross of the Church of St. Lambert at Coesfeld, Anne had asked our Lord for a share in His Passion as a sacrifice for the sake of her convent. From that time on, she began experiencing terrible pains in her hands, feet and side, an indication that God had given her the invisible stigmata. On August 28, 1812 (the Feast of St. Augustine), God imprinted a cross-shaped wound on her breast directly above the heart. Later that same year, Anne Catherine Emmerich received the visible stigmata in the hands, feet and side. In time, she would suffer the crown of thorn wounds as well, thus completing the marks of the crucifixion on her body.

In 1813, Anne was examined by competent Church and medical authorities, an inquiry which lasted for five months. The reports revealed that her hand and foot wounds were scabbed over with dried blood, and the stigma of her side was some three inches long. The blood that flowed from these wounds was of a bright, reddish color. The cross on her breast was shaped exactly like the one she saw in a vision.

From the moment she received the Sacred Wounds until her death, Anne Catherine Emmerich took no solid food, existing only on the Sacred Host. Miraculously, Anne could not even drink a few drops of water! During her last few years, she did not sleep at all, a miracle in itself according to the testimonies of many doctors. She was given shelter by various charitable people in the area, and was bedridden for the rest of her life. God had chosen this gifted soul to become His victim, and she voluntarily suffered and sacrificed as a means of atonement and expiation for the souls that were living in sin.

Because of the great trouble caused by her visible stigmata, Anne implored our Lord to remove them, a prayer which was granted — at least partially — starting in 1819. Over the next seven years, her wounds became less visible until finally they disappeared, except for on special occasions or particular feast days of the Church calendar. They would reappear and continue to bleed, however, during each Lenten season, particularly on Good Fridays. There were other occasions when Anne Catherine Emmerich's wounds would manifest and bleed severely, including some Holy Thursdays and a few Fridays outside of Lent. Yet she was never without the stigmata, for the rest of the time they were invisible but equally as painful.

Perhaps the most extraordinary gift that Anne possessed was that of her visions. Many have considered her to be the greatest visionary in Church history. During Anne's almost continuous state of ecstasy, she received private revelations from Christ that covered the most intimate details of His entire life, as well as a complete vision of the Gospel story. Other visions of Anne Catherine Emmerich include those of Heaven, Hell, Purgatory, the Passion, as well as intimate details in the lives of past saints. In addition to these, she received many prophecies about future events. Many of these revelations have come true, sometimes with remarkable accuracy.

Anne (who would one day be given the title of Venerable) died on February 9, 1824. It was during the last five years of her life that she began to write down the history of her visions for the benefit of the faithful.

Louise Lateau
Belgium
(1850-83)

Louise Lateau was born at Bois d'Haine, Belgium, in the year of 1850. She is one of the most thoroughly examined stigmatists of all time, having been subjected to countless tests and investigations by Church authorities, medical experts and psychologists. Most of the reports have authenticated the supernatural phenomena associated with her holy life. One of the most complete reports ever given on Louise was done by Dr. Lefebvre, a one-time professor at the Catholic University in Louvain. Even Dr. Imbert-Gourbeyre (famed researcher and author of the classic two-volume *La Stigmatization*, 1894) visited Louise when traveling to Belgium in 1818 (he was born not far from Louise, at Riom). Doctor Imbert-Gourbeyre was a professor at the Medical School in Clermont between 1882-88, so he is well-qualified to have done such an extensive examination of Ms. Lateau.

Already as a child, Louise showed signs of unusual mystical graces; one was that of *inedia*, or the lack of eating. According to Dr. Lefebvre, Louise's family was very poor, and as a result she lived on a little coffee with milk in the morning, soup in the afternoon, and some vegetables each evening. She never did eat meat. In April 1868, when Louise was 18 (and the same year that she received the stigmata), she limited her food intake even more, due to a series of bodily ailments. From the beginning of her stigmata, she ceased eating any foods on Fridays. By March 3, 1871, Louise could no longer eat any amount of food without it causing sickness or forcing her to expel it from her system. All that she survived on was the Blessed Host, yet she never appeared unhealthy nor did she lose much weight.

Louise first began to suffer the pains of the Passion on January 3, 1868, and on every following Friday until April 24, when blood began to flow from her side. On the following Friday, May 1, blood began to flow from the upper surface of the feet. On May 8, the hand wounds appeared, thus completing her stigmatization. The pain caused by these wounds became so intense that she was no longer able to attend Mass in the church; instead, Communion had to be brought to her every day in her own home. Louise often experienced the reception of Communion from a distance, whereby the Host miraculously traveled into her mouth from places far away or beyond her reach.

According to Dr. Lefebvre, Louise hemorrhaged some 800 times from the wounds of her stigmata, which bled weekly from April 24, 1868, until her death on August 25, 1883. He even reported that on one day the blood flowing from the wounds was about 250 grams.

In addition to receiving the Five Sacred Wounds, Louise Lateau experienced the crown of thorn wounds. There were 12 to 15 circular marks around the head that frequently issued forth blood.

St. Gemma Galgani
Italy
(1878-1903)

Born at Camigliano in Tuscany, Italy (near Lucca), on March 12, 1878, Gemma was a favored soul since her early childhood. With a deep love for prayer and an intense devotion to the Cross, this saint had an unusual reputation for piety even before her First Communion (which occurred on June 17, 1887, at the tender age of nine). During the early years of youth, Gemma had intimate communications with the Lord, who invited her to a life of sacrificial atonement for the sake of other sinners. She voluntarily accepted this offer, and from then on was a victim of most extraordinary sufferings. Throughout her life, Gemma had numerous illnesses that weakened her body, one that even forced her to quit her schooling before she completed her studies. Gemma was also refused entrance into the Religious life because of her frail condition.

After her father died in 1897, Gemma, at the age of 19, was left to care for her seven brothers and sisters (her mother had died when Gemma was very young). Left penniless due to her father's debts, she was faced with a poverty that made life trying and difficult. Finally, she and her brothers and sisters moved in with an aunt and uncle, who helped to take care of the newly orphaned family. However, Gemma was uncomfortable with their fast social life, so she returned to her parent's home to pursue a quiet life of prayer and devotion.

New illnesses began to plague this chosen soul, who accepted them heroically, remembering her voluntary vow to suffer for our Lord. She came down with meningitis, lost her hearing, and had to face total paralysis for over one year. She was being prepared for the Cross that our Lord was about to give her.

On June 8, 1899, the Blessed Virgin Mary appeared to Gemma along with Jesus her Son. She saw flames of fire issuing forth from His wounds, which suddenly wounded her in both hands, feet and the side. Blood flowed from Gemma's mysterious affliction, and she realized that Jesus had given her the visible stigmata.

In time, out of obedience to her director who wanted her to refuse them, Gemma asked our Lord to remove the visible wounds. Her request was granted, but not until the last three years of her life. Even then, she continued to have the invisible stigmata, which lasted until her death on April 11, 1903.

During those early years, Gemma's stigmata only appeared visibly each week between Thursday evening and Saturday morning, when blood flowed freely from the wounds during the heights of ecstasy. The rest of the week, the wounds were closed, with only white marks left as a sign of the deeper wounds which inflicted her continuously.

Gemma was favored with many other unusual phenomena during the course of her earthly life: daily conversations with her guardian angel; knowledge of future events; the ability to see the condition of some people's souls; and frequent visits from our Lord and the Blessed Virgin Mary.

In 1903, Gemma Galganni died from a chronic case of tuberculosis. She was canonized on May 2, 1940, less than 40 years after her earthly life had ended.

Sister Josefa Menendez
Spain
(1890-1923)

Josefa Menendez was born in Madrid, Spain, on February 4, 1890, the eldest of four surviving children. Her parents, Leonardo Menendez and Lucia del Moral, arranged for her baptism in the Church of San Lorenzo, on February 9, 1890, where she was given the named Josefa Maria. After her father died while she was still a youth, Josefa helped her mother take care of the family, eventually becoming its sole supporter through her work as a seamstress. Brought up in a devout Catholic family, Josefa made her first confession in 1897, and at the age of 11 she received her First Communion, a time when she privately vowed to dedicate her entire life to God. It was then that she heard the response, "Yes, little one, I want you to be all Mine;" Josefa's vocation had been confirmed.

Seeing something special in this child of God, Father Rubio agreed to be her confessor and director throughout these formative years, teaching her the methods of prayer and guiding her spirituality. Even at this time in her life, Father Rubio noticed that Josefa had a profound devotion to the Child Jesus and the Passion of our Lord, the latter which would prove one day to be the designs God had placed upon her soul.

By the age of 29, Josefa's vocation began as a Coadjutrix Sister of the Society of the Sacred Heart of Jesus. Josefa began her novitiate in the Religious life at the convent in Les Feuillants, which was located at Poitiers, France. All during this time she experienced great temptations against her vocation, particularly from the onslaughts of the devil, who would hound her soul throughout most of her remaining life. Her dark night was as intense as it was long. The devil physically assaulted her on numerous occasions, once even causing her clothes to catch on fire which resulted in severe burns to her body. There are few who have experienced as many diabolical attacks as this humble victim soul of God!

Josefa's mission as a member of the Society of the Sacred Heart would be twofold: to be a victim and messenger of God's love. Her private revelations from our Lord (given between 1920-23) would eventually find their way into the work that would make her known the world over, *The Way of Divine Love*. These messages of devotion to the Sacred Heart are an extension of St. Margaret Mary Alacoque's, which started in 1673. Many consider Margaret Mary the original messenger of the Sacred Heart (although it can be traced as far back as St. Gertude the Great in the thirteenth century). It is a message of God's love and mercy for the universal Church.

Paradoxically, although Josefa's message would eventually be heard by millions throughout the world, she herself lived a life of silence and obscurity within the confines of her convent. God weaned this saintly soul from the world and caused her to rely on his Providential guidance alone. In fact, very few of her own Religious sisters knew of her extraordinary graces or the mission with which she was entrusted. She was often ridiculed by others who misunderstood her vocation, a very heavy cross to bear, indeed! Yet this was not her only cross to carry; our Lord deemed to unite His favored spouse with a share of His Passion and Crucifixion, thus imprinting the Sacred Stigmata upon her body and soul.

Over a period of time, Josefa received the different marks of the stigmata. Particularly painful to this holy virgin was the crown of thorn wounds our Lord had asked her to bear. Part of her mission was that of expiation and reparation for the sinners of the world, as well as the poor souls of Purgatory. Josefa was one of those privileged few who was mystically taken down to Purgatory to see the suffering souls. Pitying their state, she constantly implored our Lord to release them through her expiatory sufferings. Jesus granted her request, for she was made to know that because of her heroic sacrifices and prayers many souls were released into their heavenly home. Josefa also experienced visions of Hell during her remarkable but brief life. These and other meritorious acts certainly contributed to the cause of the devil's vengeful hatred towards Josefa.

Josefa died at the age of 33 on December 29, 1923. As with her life, Josefa's death was marked by silence and obscurity to all except her director, confessor and superior. Yet after her message spread, her reputation became such that Cardinal Pacelli (later Pope Pius XII) wrote a letter of praise for the published account of her life. Josefa's Cause for Beatification is currently being promoted.

Mary Rose Ferron
United States
(1902-36)

Mary Rose Ferron was born on May 24, 1902, at St. Germain de Grantham, Quebec. Her father, Jean-Baptiste Ferron, was a blacksmith by trade, and her mother, Delima Matthieu, was a woman of good virtue and strong Christian values. The tenth child of the family, Rose (better known as "Little Rose") appeared to be a normal little girl, for she loved to play, dance and sing like all the other children. Yet Rose was very special, for God had His hand upon her from the moment she entered the world.

By the age of three, she was already devoted to St. Anthony of Padua, Italy. She would always call upon this saint whenever anyone lost something of value, and he would always help her find what had been lost. At the same age Rose had a vision of the Child Jesus, Who appeared to her with an image of the Cross. This would prove to be a sign to Rose of the suffering that lay in store for her in the years to come. God would eventually call her to a life of union with the Cross of Jesus in order to be His victim of love.

By the time Rose turned 10, she had made her First Communion. Because of her great respect for the Eucharistic presence of Christ, she insisted upon wearing only the finest of clothes for this glorious occasion. Her mother gave her a silk outfit, and this she kept only for First Communion and subsequent Masses.

Realizing that her family was struggling to make ends meet, Rose courageously applied for work at the age of 12. She was not only helping to provide for the family, but also saving up for a dowry one day. Rose had decided to enter the Religious life. After working some 12 months caring for a lawyer's children, Rose fell victim to a serious illness that was to change the course of her life. Suddenly she became prone to high fevers and had to be placed in bed. Then her hands and feet became paralyzed, which forced her to use crutches to get around. Upon attending a Mass one day, Rose put her numb hand in the holy water at Mass, believing this would help her. Immediately upon doing so, she regained the use of her hands. This all occurred while she was living at Fall River in St. Roch's parish.

Rose came to live in Woonsocket, Rhode Island, in the year 1925. She was still unable to walk unaided, and had to rely upon crutches to move about. Otherwise, Rose was permanently confined to bed, a condition that had haunted her now for almost three years. At this time, two local priests would be highly influencial in Rose's life: Father Pot and Father Gauthier. Through their careful discernment and spiritual direction, Rose came to accept the fact that God had chosen her to be His suffering victim. Soon she learned to embrace the crosses that Jesus sent her with great courage and patience.

It was not long before many in the area had heard about this saintly young woman who suffered so much. Many people came to ask of her prayers and guidance. One was Bishop Hickey. When the Sentinellist movement had gained a strong following, Bishop Hickey was a favorite target for public condemnation. He decided to ask Rose to help him through prayer and voluntary suffering to heal the wounds. She agreed, and presented her petitions to the Father. The Lord accepted them, and Rose became a victim for her diocese and for all its priests.

During this time, Rose would often meditate upon the Passion of our Lord and the wounds of His Sacred Body. In fact, her devotions proved fruitful, for with the permission of her Bishop, she would found a Religious organization called the Sisters of Reparation of the Sacred Wounds of Jesus. Rose took her solemn vows on December 8, 1928.

Rose was extraordinarily blessed with many mystical gifts: partial abstinence from food for many years; *hierognosis* (discernment of holy things); the reception of Holy Communion without deglutition; ecstasies; visions; prophecies; revelations; the odor of sanctity; and the Sacred Stigmata.

Rose's stigmata did not appear all together at once, but rather progressively: in 1927, she experienced the pains of the scourging; several days later, the marks appeared on her hands. It was not until October of 1927 when Rose received the wounds on her feet. Sometime in October or November of the same year, Rose received the wound of the heart, thus completing the Five Sacred Wounds of our Lord. In addition to these, Rose began to suffer the crown of thorn wounds by January of 1928. Between June and November of that year, many witnesses claimed to have seen two distinct, heavy chord-like marks across her forehead. Rose would have these marks for the rest of her life, as photographs have plainly revealed. Indeed, these chord-like markings look very similar to overlapping branches. Incredible as it may seem, Rose was also marked with a shoulder wound and a separate wound (a half-inch wide) that ran from the hairline down towards the top of the nose. This latter wound bled copiously.

By the time of her death, all of the visible signs had disappeared except the crown of thorn wounds, which she would carry to her grave. Yet Rose continued to bear the invisible stigmata even when the outer marks had disappeared. God had made her His victim, and victim she would always remain.

Rose suffered many other illnesses and physical deformities during her life of sacrificial suffering. Her feet had become grossly distorted, and at one point even a bone penetrated the outer skin. Near the time of her death, progressive paralysis had set in, her stomach was burning and her fevers ran incredibly high. Rose had also lost her hearing, her sight and her speech. Jesus called this saintly woman home in May, 1936: Her mission upon the Cross had come to an end.

Sister Faustina H. Kowalska
Poland
(1905-38)

Helen Kowalska was born in the village of Glogowiec, Turek County, Lodz Province, Poland, on August 25, 1905. The third of 10 children, Helen was baptized on August 27, 1905, in St. Casimir Church in Swinice Warcskie, which is located in the same county. It was not long before Helen heard the call of God: by the age of seven, the call to a more perfect life came from an interior voice, and by the time she was 15 she told her parents that she intended to enter a convent (against their wishes). Receiving little formal education as a child, Helen started to work at the age of 14, first in Aleksandrow, Lodz, and then in Lodz itself, still yearning for a Religious life.

After many struggles and long delays, Helen was finally accepted into the Congregation of the Sisters of Our Lady of Mercy on August 1, 1925 (10 years after her desire for the convent had started). Her postulancy period was served in Warsaw, and then she was transferred to the novitiate house in Cracow, where she took the name of Sister Mary Faustina, a name that would become so well-known only a few decades later. Finally, on May 1, 1933, Faustina took her perpetual vows.

Things did not go smoothly for Sister Faustina however. By 1927, she started to experience the dark night of the soul. This trial would last until the end of her novitiate. Other sufferings accompanied this beautiful young woman: In 1934, her first bout with asthma occurred, as it did again in 1937. Up until the day of her death, asthma would haunt Faustina and severely try her heroic patience.

On April 16, 1928 (Good Friday), Jesus' divine flame of love suddenly filled her entire soul, giving her some strength and inspiration during these years of trial and torment. By this time she was receiving many visions of Jesus that reassured her of her mission.

It was on February 22, 1931, when Faustina began to receive instructions from our Lord on the specific mission He had given her. She was to spread the message of His Divine Mercy throughout the universal Church. In 1934, this servant of God began her *Diary* of all that Jesus had taught and showed her (later, under obedience to her superiors, Faustina would expand the *Diary* to include her entire life's story, with all its supernatural graces). The year of her death (1938) fills up the last part of her *Diary*, which ended up being 697 pages when printed by the Marian Press in 1987 (see *Divine Mercy in My Soul: The Diary of Sister Faustina M. Kowalska*; Marian Press, Stockbridge, MA, 01263: 1987).

By March 29, 1934, Faustina had voluntarily offered herself up to become God's victim of love. He would accept her offering, and the servant of God made use of her sufferings to sacrifice for the sinners of the world. She would become Christ's co-redemptrix, an assistant to the Lord's redemptive mission of the Cross by experiencing His Passion and Crucifixion. Sister

Faustina would become a stigmatist in union with our Lord.

It was in April of 1936 when Faustina began to feel the pains of the Passion in her body. She claims that after her annual vows while she was deeply immersed in prayer, brilliant rays of light completely enveloped her; suddenly, she felt intense pains in her hands, feet and side, then the sting of thorns around her head. These pains were repeated during the Mass on Friday, then several more Fridays after that. In the future, she would continue to experience the Passion of our Lord every Friday, but the wounds would never appear outwardly. Faustina would bear the invisible stigmata until the end of her life.

Unusual heavenly graces would continue to be given to Faustina, including visions of Purgatory and Hell on November 27, 1936. Two days later, our Lady appeared to her with the Infant Jesus in her arms. These were only some of the many extraordinary visions granted to Faustina over the years, including frequent visits from our Lord and His Blessed Mother.

At 10:45 p.m., after many long years of suffering, Faustina died on October 5, 1938, in Cracow, Poland. Her funeral took place on the first Friday of the month and the Feast of Our Lady of the Rosary. Sister Faustina is buried in the convent cemetery in the garden of the Congregation of the Sisters of Our Lady of Mercy in Cracow. The Process for the Beatification of this servant of God was formally inaugurated on January 31, 1968.

Berthe Petit
Belgium
(1870-1943)

Berthe-Frances-Marie-Ghislaine Petit was born on January 23, 1870, at Enghien, Belgium. Her parents were Monsieur Petit, a lawyer, and Jeanne Meys. From her earliest years Berthe was an unusually gifted child. At the age of four, she experienced her first vision of the Blessed Virgin Mary while in a state of ecstasy. Soon afterwards, another vision in the Chapel of the Sisters of the Union of the Sacred Heart revealed the Infant Jesus coming towards her out of the tabernacle, saying: "You will always suffer, but I shall be with you."

By the age of 15, Berthe made her first Communion. From that moment on, she knew that she had a vocation towards a religious life. By 1884, her world suddenly shattered when a severe bout with typhoid fever nearly cost Berthe her life. After the doctors had given no hope for recovery, Berthe's mother went to Lourdes to implore our Lady's help. The request was granted and Berthe was healed, although she continued to have a delicate disposition from that moment on.

Berthe's vocation as victim was discerned by Father Godefroid, O.F.M Cap. After hearing her confession on September 8, 1888, Father Godefroid told Berthe that she would be a "crucified spouse" of Christ, a victim soul for many sinners. Berthe accepted this discernment, and heroically endured the life of suffering which was soon to follow. After becoming a Franciscan Tertiary, Berthe mysteriously suffered one illness after another: endocarditis, jaundice, abscess of the liver with vomiting, angina, hemorrhages and possible tuberculosis.

By 1908, when Berthe was 38, she could no longer retain any food in her system (*inedia*) save that of the Sacred Host. She lived from age 38 to 73 on nothing but one cup of coffee in the morning (rejected by her body later in the day), a small amount of white wine in the afternoon, and some water with a bit of lemon juice in the evening. Jesus himself became her sole nourishment.

It was during 1909-10 that Berthe received her mission in the world from a series of private revelations from our Lord. Jesus asked Berthe to start and spread the devotion to the Sorrowful and Immaculate Heart of Mary. To confirm the reality of these visions, the Blessed Virgin Mary appeared to her on the 24th and 25th of August, 1910, and showed Berthe her wounded heart (the same one that the prophet Simeon predicted in Lk 2:35). This devotion is being spread today through the efforts of *The World League of Reparation to the Sorrowful and Immaculate Heart of Mary* and other organizations in many countries such as: the United States, Canada, England, Italy, France, Spain, Portugal, India, Morocco, Burma, Haiti, Algeria, the Congo, and even Vietnam.

On December 29, 1930, our Lady told Berthe to prepare for "nothing but suffering," and on Good Friday of the following year she experienced the pains of the invisible stigmata in her hands, feet and side. She begged Jesus to keep her crucifixion hidden, and He did, except for occasional moments. On many Fridays of the year (especially Good Friday), friends have told how the wounds in Berthe's feet and hands bled and caused her tremendous pain. Many other Passion sufferings were experienced during her lifetime: the crown of thorns (which St. Catherine of Siena reportedly placed on her head during an ecstasy), bleeding from the lips and tongue, tremendous thirst, etc.; indeed, Berthe was Jesus' holy victim of love.

On March 26, 1943 (the anniversary of her mother's death), Berthe gave up her spirit to God. Her mission had been successfully completed. Like Jesus, immediately before her death she was heard to cry, "I thirst. Give me to drink!" Berthe's body was visited by hundreds of people before she was laid to rest. On April 8, a Requeim Mass was celebrated in her honor in the Church of the Annunciation in Brussels. Berthe is buried under a small chapel in a cemetery at Louvignies.

Alexandrina da Costa
Portugal
(1904-55)

Alexandrina Maria da Costa was born on Wednesday of Holy Week, March 29, 1904. She was the second child born to devout peasant parents of Balasar, Portugal. On April 2 of the same year, Alexandrina was baptized in St. Eulalia Church near the Este River (which is really a stream). Although a tomboy during her youth, Alexandrina was also a very spiritual and favored soul. She was devoted to the Blessed Sacrament, the Mass, Our Lady of the Rosary, and St. Joseph. This child was continually immersed in prayer, and she frequently prayed for the needs of others.

When Alexandrina was only nine years old, she was sent to work on a local farm. Her employer there tried to assault her. She fought him off with the rosary clutched tightly in her hands, and soon increased her adorations of the Blessed Sacrament. Then severe illnesses began to plague this victim of God's love. Later in the same year, she came down with typhoid and almost died. For her treatment, she desired nothing but Jesus in the Eucharist. Eventually she recovered from this illness, but remained virtually an invalid. Alexandrina took up sewing with her sister as a means of work in Balasar.

In March of 1918 an event would occur that would lead her on a mission that nobody anticipated. While she was alone and in prayer at her family home, her former boss came to the door and demanded entrance. He was accompanied by others with clubs, as they managed to break into the house. Frightened, Alexandrina jumped some 13 feet from her bedroom window down to the ground outside. Somehow this courageous young lady managed to return to the house with a club of her own. She must have been fiercely determined, for the men suddenly fled and never bothered her again! Yet the fall was not without its consequences: Alexandrina's spine had became permanently damaged. In 1923, she became totally paralyzed, and on April 14, 1924, Alexandrina became bedridden for life.

After a series of intense prayers imploring our Lord for a cure, Alexandrina realized that it was not God's will. She resigned herself to suffer as the Lord had arranged, and offered herself up to God to be His victim of love. In 1931, Jesus appeared to Alexandrina and asked her to use her sufferings with acts of reparation for others. Once she had submitted to Providence, Alexandrina continued to suffer more intensely through the coming years. By 1934, this victim of God would begin to experience the Passion of our Lord through her many ecstatic visions. Alexandrina literally felt each of the scenes she saw. On September 6, 1934, Jesus appeared to her and offered her a share of His Cross. She bravely accepted, and from then on this servant of God felt the pains of Christ's wounds in her hands, feet and side, as well as the crown of thorn wounds and the scourging. These Passion ecstasies would continue weekly for the rest of her life, although her stigmata never appeared outwardly. Alexandrina was called to bear the invisible stigmata, and to live a hidden and obscure life of expiatory suffering.

It would not be long before the devil came into the picture. Seeing how Alexandrina was beginning to save sinners from her sacrificial reparation, he began to torment her with suggestions and horrendous temptations. This started in 1935. Later on, the devil progressed to outright threats and then physical beatings. Alexandrina, forever with the crucifix in her hands, fought off the assaults of the evil one with great tenacity of spirit. He continued his attacks for the next 10 years, when finally the servant of God broke loose from his chains.

Alexandrina continued to have the Passion ecstasies, some 180 total throughout her life. They usually began on Thursday afternoon and ended on Fridays about 3:30 p.m. During her ecstasies, many have witnessed her various sufferings: vomiting, the twisting of bodily limbs, groans of excruciating pain, bleeding, and swelling of the facial area (including bruises that she sustained). The ecstasies were divided into approximately 40 separate segments of the Passion scenes, with only a slight break between each segment. Alexandrina could be heard repeating the words of our Lord from the Gospel narratives, even to its conclusion: "It is finished." There Alexandrina would appear as if dead, only to revive a bit later and resume her normal state of consciousness.

Many other extraordinary phenomena were experienced in Alexandrina's life. During her last 13 years on earth, she ate and drank nothing except the Holy Eucharist. Medical authorities could find no natural explanation after intense investigations over many years. She continued to have daily conversations with our Lord, and frequently received visits from the

Blessed Virgin Mary, the angels and some of the saints.

Alexandrina died on October 13, 1955, at the age of 51, the anniversary of the miracle of the sun at Fatima. Before her death, she had asked to be buried in the gown of a Daughter of Mary. Her request was granted. Her tomb is located in St. Eulalia's Church in Balasar, Portugal. As she had earlier predicted, her body would not remain incorruptible, but would turn to ashes without any signs of decomposition. Upon later investigation, her prophecy proved to be true, impossible from the view of medical experts! Alexandrina's ashes have been known to emit a heavenly perfume.

This servant of God's Process for Beatification is now underway. Her writings were approved by Rome in 1979.

Therese Neumann
Germany
(1898-1962)

Therese Neumann was born on Good Friday, April 8, 1898, in the small Bavarian town of Konnersreuth, West Germany. She was the eldest of Ferdinand and Anna Neumann's 10 surviving children (one son died in infancy). On Easter Sunday, April 10, young Resl (Therese's childhood nickname) was baptized at the Church in Holy Baptism. She grew to be a strong and robust child, for she had been used to working long hours helping her father on the Fockenfield farm. Therese had desired to become a missionary sister in Africa, but God would have other plans for this humble young servant.

On March 10, 1918 (the same year that Padre Pio received the Sacred Stigmata), Therese began her life of suffering that eventually included the reception of the Five Sacred Wounds. On this fateful day, a fire broke out on Mr. Neumann's farm, and Therese was called to lift heavy buckets of water up to the helper at the top of the stable; he in turn emptied them on the burning flames. After two hours of fighting the fire, Therese's back gave out and she was later confined to bed. A later fall from the cellar stairs at her home caused her further damage. This paralysis caused by her back injury lasted for seven years. Subsequent falls affected her eyesight, eventually resulting in total blindness for Therese on March 17, 1919.

The mysterious sufferings continued. After the accident on March 10, 1918, Therese's health quickly deteriorated: her digestive system malfunctioned; she came down with acute appendicitis; sores began to cover her now-frail body; and she had troubles with her hearing and breathing. She accepted all of this as God's will, heroically embracing her many crosses.

God's finger was clearly on this exceptional soul, for a series of miraculous cures were soon to follow, all due to the intercessions of her beloved saint, Thérèse of Lisieux (the "Little Flower"). On April 29, 1923, the day of the Little Flower's Beatification, Therese Neumann's blindness was cured. On May 17, 1925, the date of the Little Flower's Canonization, her paralysis and back ulcers were completely healed. Other cures were not long to follow: November 7, 1925, the cure of her appendicitis; on November 19, 1926, her lungs were restored to health.

Yet the greatest trials were still to come. During Lent of 1926, Therese received the Sacred Stigmata, permanently impressed upon her body until her death in 1962. In addition to these, Therese received eight or nine crown of thorn wounds on November 5, 1926, and by March of 1929 she experienced the shoulder wound. Finally, on Good Friday, 1929, Therese's stigmata included the scourge marks which completed her crucifixion. The number of wounds or marks that have been observed are as follows: two on the hands; two on the feet; one wound on the heart; 30 scourge marks, including the shoulder wound; and nine distinct head wounds from the crown of thorns. All-in-all, at least 45 distinguishable marks of the Passion. Therese also bled profusely from the eyes during her ecstastic vision of Christ's shedding tears of blood at Gethsemani (Lk 22:44). Dozens of excellent photographs exist as a result of the extensive examinations of Therese during her ecstatic sufferings, as well as film footage. Literally thousands have seen her experience the Passion sufferings, including doctors, theologians, priests, scientists, and faithful pilgrims.

Therese's hand and foot wounds were unusual in that, like St. Francis of Assisi (1182-1226), there were actual nail-like objects that completely penetrated her palms and soles. The nail heads can be clearly seen on the back of her hands, and on the palms the points of the nails are bent in toward the skin. Few stigmatists in history outside of St. Francis or Therese have been known to have wounds with nails protruding through them (exactly as Christ would appear on the Cross). Most of these victim souls have penetrating wounds that are more like openings or holes that never completely close.

Therese was one of the most extraordinarily gifted souls in Church history. Besides having the Five Sacred Wounds and others of the Passion, she was also blessed with the following: *inedia* (her lack of eating continued from 1926-62!); little or no sleep; survival on only the Eucharist; the gift of perfume; reading of souls; bilocation; visions; apparitions; and prophecy.

Therese Neumann died on September 18, 1962, at her home in Konnersreuth, West Germany. This was only two days before the anniversary in which Padre Pio received his stigmata on September 20, 1918. Over 10,000 people paid their respects at Therese's burial in the cemetery of Konnersreuth. (Plans are currently underway to remove her remains and place them beneath the altar of St. Thérèse of Lisieux in the St. Lawrence Church at Konnersreuth).

Therese's Cause for Beatification is currently being promoted. All pertinent records of her life and experiences are kept in Eichstätt, West Germany, with the "Konnersreuth Circle."

Adrienne Von Speyr
Switzerland
(1902-67)

Adrienne was born on September 20, 1902 (the anniversary of Padre Pio's reception of the visible stigmata in 1918), in the city of La Chaux-de-Fonds, Switzerland, the second daughter of a surgeon. Adrienne was very much influenced by her father Theodor's work, for she frequently spent time as a child visiting the sick. During these early years, Adrienne already experienced visits from Mary, the angels and many saints (particularly St. Ignatius of Loyola). This was all the more remarkable when one considers that Adrienne was raised a Protestant and didn't convert to Catholicism until 1940 — thirty-eight years after her birth!

For many years, Adrienne planned on becoming a doctor just as her father had. She studied hard, although her mother set her plans back by not supporting her ambitions. In addition to this obstacle, Adrienne was beset with many illnesses that often kept her down.

In 1927, Adrienne married Emil Dürr, a widower with two children and the dean of history at the University of Basel. He died unexpectedly in 1934, and Adrienne remarried Werner Kaegi, chairman of the same department, in 1936.

A fateful moment in Adrienne's vocation occurred upon the meeting of Father Hans Urs von Balthasar in 1940, the year of her conversion. This renowned Swiss theologian directed her spiritual life and became one of her closest friends. Even to this day, Father Balthasar (now deceased), through his work, remains one of the leading Catholic theologians in the world, and one of the best in the twentieth century. Pope John Paul II has called him his favorite theologian. Father Balthasar would later write a biography of this holy soul, called *First Glance of Adrienne Von Speyr*.

Over the course of a great number of years, Adrienne was privileged to have visions of Jesus and Mary quite frequently. The list of other heavenly visions is extraordinary in itself: Catherine of Siena, Elizabeth of Thuringia, Jeanne de Chantal, Hildegard, Bernadette, Anthony of Egypt, Peter Claver, Benedict Labre, John Vianney, and many of St. John the Apostle. Prior to these visions, Adrienne knew little about the lives of these saints. Yet later she would prove to know more than most who have studied their lives extensively.

Adrienne was baptized a Catholic on All Saints Day, 1940. By this time she had already been working as a doctor, fulfilling a life-long dream of helping the sick and suffering. Ironically, Adrienne herself fell victim to much suffering during these early years. It happened one day in the spring of 1941 when an angel suddenly appeared to her. The angel was sent by God, asking Adrienne's full consent to share in whatever sufferings the Lord had planned for her soul. She willingly agreed, and this point marked the start of the many Passion ecstasies she would be called to experience in the years to come.

In July of 1942, Adrienne received the visible stigmata from the Lord. Several people did see the wounds, but they were not very large. Because of her humility, Adrienne kept the wounds covered with bandages or gloves so as to not draw attention to herself. She prayed fervently for their disappearance, and later they did become less visible, appearing only on the days of her Passion ecstasies. When the wounds became hidden, Adrienne still felt as much pain as she had when they were visible. Her crown of thorn wounds remained invisible, but she could feel the sensation of blood oozing out of them.

In time, Adrienne was to suffer even more. In 1940 she had a severe heart attack that kept her bedridden for the entire summer. By 1964, her eyesight started to fail, and her arthritis became so advanced that she was barely able to move her bodily limbs.

In spite of all the pains that Adrienne was subjected to, she was an avid writer throughout her life. What is amazing is that she read few theological works, but relied upon her visions and heavenly insights to instruct her in the teachings of the Faith. She was a gifted theologian of enormous output, having written an incredible number of works during the course of some 20-25 years: 10 complete books in manuscript form (including her autobiography); close to 30 commentaries on Sacred Scripture; nine published articles; 12 volumes of "posthumous" works; and 24 other theological writings, making a grand total of 83 separate works! These have been carefully preserved and examined by Father Balthasar (prolific writer in his own right), who hoped to see them all published one day. Many are already available in English, though it will take years to translate the entire works.

Adrienne died at the age of 65 on September 17, 1967, the Feast of St. Hildegard, who, like herself, had been a doctor and great contemplative. A symbol of the Trinity was carved on her tombstone by Albert Schilling. Upon her death, Adrienne spoke these last words: "How beautiful it is to die."

Padre Pio of Pietrelcina
Italy
(1887-1968)

Padre Pio was born at Pietrelcina in the Province of Benevento, Italy. He came from a poor family, hard-working people devoted to God. Padre was baptized Francesco Forgione (after the beloved St. Francis of Assisi) and spent his formative years in Pietrelcina. His parents, Grazio Maria Forgione and his wife Maria Giuseppa, were deeply religious people who instilled a strong faith in young Francesco from his earliest days. They had two sons and three daughters, two others having died during infancy.

Padre Pio was markedly different than his childhood companions. He was extremely pious and prayerful and preferred to be alone with God to the company of others. Young Francesco was on fire with the love of God; particularly evident was his devotion to Mary, a life-long affection that would eventually make him known as the "living Rosary." His vocation to the Religious life was never in question.

His father entered him in the monastery of Marcone in 1902 to prepare him for his novitiate in the Order of St. Francis. From Marcone he went to Panisi, and then to Venafro. Eventually, after transfers to Serra Capriola and Montefusco, Padre ended up at Our Lady of Grace Friary in San Giovanni Rotondo, Italy, where he would remain for the rest of his life — more than 50 years behind the monastery walls in the rugged country of the Gargano Mountains in Southeastern Italy.

Francesco began his novitiate with the Franciscan Capuchins on January 6, 1903. By January 22, he took the habit and changed his name to Brother Pio da Pietrelcina. By 1907, he had made his solemn vows with the Franciscans, and left for Foggia to begin his theological studies. In 1909, he became a deacon at the celebration in Marcone. The moment of his ordination to priesthood came on August 10, 1910, in the Cathedral of Benevento. Padre's first solemn Mass was said at Pietrelcina on August 14 of the same year.

During these early years, Padre Pio began to suffer a number of mysterious illnesses that left him wracked with pain: High fevers, intestinal problems, excruciating headaches, and asthma attacks were some of the early sufferings that plagued him continuously. It was in 1910 that Padre first felt the burning pains of the invisible stigmata. At times red and swollen patches would appear, then they would disappear. His superiors had seen these patches themselves, which he tried to conceal from everyone else.

When he was sent to Venafro in 1911, Padre experienced such ill health that he was ordered back to Pietrelcina, where his superiors thought the air would be better for him. By 1916, Padre Pio was assigned to the monastery in San Giovanni Rotondo, Italy, where he lived the remainder of his 81 years. When he entered the military in 1915, Padre was in and out of the service because of his frail condition. Finally, on March 16, 1918, Padre Pio was permanently dismissed because of a double bronchial pneumonia.

During these long years of suffering, Padre was guided by Padres Agostino and Benedetto, both from San Marco in Lamis, Italy. From the years of 1910 to 1922, the letters between Padre and his two directors were preserved. These invaluable writings contain the history of Padre Pio's spirituality, covering 635 letters between Padre and both directors. The material has been published as the *Epistolario*, which is over 1500 pages long. A second volume, *Letters of Correspondence with Raffaelina Cerase: Noblewoman*, is now available in English; and, a third volume has been printed for the years beyond 1922, but at this time only in Italian.

Padre Pio was frequently attacked mentally and physically by the devil and he endured many temptations and injuries from the spirits of darkness for the remainder of his life. He was a marked target of the evil one, who certainly recognized this privileged soul as a special instrument chosen as a victim of God's love. Padre Pio remained loyal to his Maker, enduring these diabolical attacks with tremendous courage and strength. Because of his deep love for sinners and his intense devotion to the Passion of our Lord, Padre saved countless souls from ruin and damnation: the obvious reason for the devil's fierce attempts to destroy his will and eventually his life.

Perhaps the most remarkable event in Padre Pio's life occurred on September 20, 1918, when he received the visible stigmata. This happened while he was in prayer before our Lord's crucifix in the choir loft at the old monastery. A heavenly visitor came and pierced his body with the Five Sacred Wounds of Christ; he would carry them with him until shorty before his death: the first priest in history to receive the stigmata, who also had them the longest time — 50 years (1918-68).

Few of God's servants have been blessed with as many extraordinary gifts as Padre Pio. The list is staggering: the reading of souls; prophecy; visions of Jesus and Mary; daily communications with his guardian angel; bilocation; discernment of spirits; the odor of sanctity; spiritual direction; little sleep; partial-inedia; miraculous healings (hundreds reported); the hearing of confessions between 14-16 hours per day; and of course, the Sacred Stigmata.

Padre Pio died at 2:30 a.m. on September 23, 1968, with the rosary beads clutched firmly in his hands. He is buried in the lower level of Our Lady of Grace Friary in San Giovanni Rotondo. The last words heard from his lips were, "Jesus! Mary!" His Cause for Beatification is currently underway.

Marthe Robin
France
(1902-81)

Marthe Louise Robin was born at home at 5:00 p.m. on March 13, 1902 in Chateauneuf-de-Galaure, France, the last of six children. Her parents were simple, humble peasants who saw to it that their family received a solid Christian foundation. On Holy Saturday, April 5, 1902, Marthe was baptized in the church of St. Bonnet-de-Galaure.

One day the well which provided water to the local community became contaminated, causing an epidemic of typhoid fever that cost the life of Clemence (Marthe's brother) at the age of five. Marthe herself came down with the disease. Although she recovered, it left her frail thereafter.

Marthe started school when she was six years old, but missed many days because of her weak and sickly condition. Her own illnesses provided the background for a sympathetic attitude towards the sick, whom she later prayed and suffered for as a victim of God's love. Marthe did not receive her diploma because she was sick on the day of her final examination.

In 1911, Bishop Chesnelong of Valence confirmed Marthe in the Faith, and on August 15, 1912, she received her First Communion. Even this day was postponed for Marthe because again she was sick with the measles. From that moment on, Marthe felt a calling from God which was to begin the course of her life in union with Him. In 1916, when she was 14, Marthe finished her schooling and devoted her time to helping her parents around the house and the fields. It was during these many silent hours in the open air that Marthe developed a capacity for mental prayer and contemplation.

Marthe's sufferings would continue to plague her throughout her life. On November 25, 1918, she fell in the kitchen without any prior warning; her legs were paralyzed and she suddenly went unconscious. Nobody ever figured out what was ailing this poor girl. She continued to experience these same mysterious attacks until 1922. The pain she suffered during this time was immense. Confined to bed for most of the day, young Marthe took up reading and embroidery to pass the time, as well as prolonging her devotion and prayer time.

On March 25, 1922, the Feast of the Annunciation, the Blessed Virgin Mary appeared to Marthe and interceded for her. After she received the Sacrament of the Sick, Marthe was cured of her four-year malady.

Marthe made many pilgrimages to nearby shrines whenever her health would allow her to do so. She was particularly fond of the Marian shrines and visited as many as she could.

By October of 1925, Marthe had made a decision that would direct the course of her life as a victim soul: she voluntarily offered up her sufferings in union with Mary for the sake of helping Jesus to save souls who had sinned and needed satisfaction for their transgressions. After this complete abandonment to Divine Providence, Marthe had many apparitions of Thérèse of Lisieux, who was one of her favorite saints. Thérèse assured her that God would continue to allow her to suffer for others. Indeed, this prophecy came true, for by March 25, 1928, Marthe's legs became completely paralyzed. It was from this moment on that she would be bedridden for the rest of her life.

Many unusual phenomena surrounded Marthe during this period of her spiritual journey. By 1928, she had given up eating altogether except for the Holy Eucharist. This lack of food continued until her death in 1981! If this weren't miraculous enough, after 1928 Marthe ceased to sleep as well. According to doctors, the prolonged absence of sleep is even more incredible than the lack of food. God was looking out for this favored soul.

The devil was quick to prey upon this victim soul who was taking sinners away from him through her sacrificial sufferings. One night, Satan had struck her in the face, breaking two of her teeth. After she entered the Third Order of St. Francis (the Order for lay people) in November of 1928, he continued to manifest himself, threatening to destroy her if she continued to serve God. But Marthe was a strong-willed soul with a divinely-guided mission. In the end, the devil would lose out to this faithful young woman.

Total paralysis of Marthe's legs set in by February 1929, and she lost as well the use of her hands. Marthe offered them up in sacrifice to the Lord, and He took her at her word. Her state was pitiful: her legs were partly bent, her body was twisted and she could hardly move. Yet the consummation of her suffering was yet to come.

At the end of September 1930, Jesus appeared to Marthe and asked her: "Do you wish to become like Me?" Marthe readily consented, preparing herself for the union with the Cross. Then on October 4, 1930, Jesus appeared again, and a flame lept from His side, hands and feet, piercing Marthe in the same locations. She had received the wounds of the stigmata. Later on, our Lord also gave Marthe the crown of thorn wounds. After her stigmatization, she suffered the pains of the Passion every Friday during her ecstatic states.

Marthe died on February 6, 1981, at 7:00 p.m. in her bedroom after weeks of agonizing suffering. She was buried next to her family in Saint-Bonnet-de-Galaure, finally at rest in the bosom of the Lord.

Living Stigmatists: a Special Report

While I was in San Giovanni Rotondo in July of 1988, I asked Father Joseph Martin, O.F.M. Cap. what he thought about my including a good deal of information on reported living stigmatists in my book; after all, there seemed to be a number of them who were getting favorable responses from their communities and even from some Church authorities. Should I discuss them in my book, or would it be best to leave them out altogether?

Back in the United States, I had been given several names of alleged living stigmatists in Europe. From some reliable sources, I was even provided with names, address, and in one case, the home phone number of one of these people. It had crossed my mind to visit several of them for interviews and pictures. Most importantly, I wanted to see for myself if these claims appeared to be authentic and if they showed signs of bearing good fruit. Interestingly enough, all three of the alleged stigmatists that I was given the names and addresses to were from the country of Italy.

I decided to try to visit at least one of them while I was in Italy, if time permitted. My schedule was heavy, and my meetings with Father Ulrich Vey, O.F.M. Cap. (Altötting, West Germany), as well as with Father Alessio Parente, O.F.M. Cap. and Father Joseph Martin, O.F.M. Cap. (San Giovanni Rotondo, Italy) would take priority. These men were highly qualified spokespersons for two of the most well-known stigmatists of this century: Therese Neumann and Padre Pio. In fact, each of these priests had known these stigmatists personally, and were primary sources that I could trust completely.

When I was in Altötting on July 15-16, 1988, I had been talking with Father Veh; somehow, the same conversation came up concerning stigmatists who were thought to be in our midst. Father Veh had told me that he knew of a lay stigmatist — a married man — who now lives in a suburb of Munich, Germany (which was only some 40 miles west of Altötting). I asked him if he had met him, and he said yes. My impression was that this person may have the invisible stigmata, which can be difficult to authenticate. Because Father Veh is a most humble and sincere Capuchin, I believed him when he revealed this to me. Yet even he was a bit cautious in explaining the story, realizing that no final statements could be made about one who is still living and who hasn't been authenticated by the Church.

On the other hand, Father was more than willing to discuss everything he knew about Therese Neumann, and at one point he even showed me his prized possession of two of her relics: one, a blood-stained and swollen shoe that she had worn (caused by her foot wounds), and a head scarf that had circular blood stains in the form of a crown of thorns.

What is the main point here? It is this: Therese Neumann died in 1962, and her entire life has been investigated thoroughly. Her Cause for Beatification is currently underway, so he feels safe to talk about her and to promote her Cause. The hesitation was not there like it was for the man near Munich. I was beginning to understand. This was not the first time that caution was shown by some who are careful about making any premature judgments concerning reported living stigmatists.

As circumstances would have it, I was unable to visit several stigmatists I was hoping to interview. Too many important places to go and people to see prevented me from contacting them. One was living in San Stefano, another in Rimini, and the third was located at San Vittorino (Father Gino Burresi, probably the most well-known reported stigmatist of our era). As of this writing, Father Gino (formerly Brother Gino) has been transferred to Austria. However, these are by no means the only claims of living stigmatists. Many other cases have been brought to my attention from various countries, including the United States (a living stigmatist has been reported from California). Yet most of the claims still come primarily from Italy. Germany or France would have to be second on the list, as they have been in centuries past.

Father Martin, O.F.M. Cap. (who was Padre Pio's daily companion and assistant the last three years of his life) shed some important light on the entire situation. One of the things that concerned him was the fact that reported living stigmatists were just that: *still living*. Because the Church has not had the necessary time to investigate their lives thoroughly, their authenticity can not be confirmed. The Church has never authenticated a stigmatist while he or she is alive, partly because one always runs the risk of falling from God's grace at any time before his or her death. It would be premature, therefore, to risk honoring a chosen soul (mystic, saint or stigmatist) as an exemplary model for others to imitate or follow without being absolutely certain beyond all reasonable doubt that their entire lives were examples of heroic virtue, faith and love. To do so without the entire life having been thoroughly examined would not only risk the credibility of the Church's judgment, but it could also mislead the faithful. In other words, we must proceed with optimistic caution when dealing with reported cases of living stigmatists.

A paradoxical situation seems to be at work here: on the one hand, we must not be too ready to admit the authenticity of any reported living stigmatist, no matter how sincere they or others who know them appear to be. It is for the Church to decide in the end. So we must remain cautiously optimistic, yet careful and patient.

It seems like a double-edged sword, for on the other hand, the faithful have a right to know about people who are reported to have been specially graced by God and are in their midst. Why? Because if these souls are authentic, then their gifts are not for them alone; rather, they are for the universal Church. Nor is their vocation theirs and theirs alone: it is also for the benefit of the faithful. God does not give His graces for people to use exclusively for themselves. No, we are always called to share our gifts and our love with one another, for we are a Body of Christ, a community of faith, a people of God. We have a right to know about any extraordinary claims that occur within the Church, lest the faithful are misled or disillusioned. In the end, that has to be the primary concern.

Holy Mother Church, through the wisdom and guidance of the Pope together with the Magisterium, seeks all truth concerning Christ and His people. It is with them that final decisions concerning these mystical graces must rest, for they are Christ's representatives on earth. We have to keep an open mind until the Church decides on the matter (which could take years, for ecclesiastical investigations are most thorough and time-consuming). Let us remember that a tree is known by its fruit. If good fruit is born, then the tree will eventually be recognized for what it is.

Does this mean that we disregard them altogether until they have died? Not at all. Again, a tree is known by its fruit, and patience in discernment has always been a virtue. Therefore, it is my conclusion that it would not be appropriate to include anything but the most general information concerning these living victims, lest some of them turn out to be inauthentic and the credibility of those who *are* recognized is damaged. That is the key point.

It is my sincere hope that all of the reported stigmatists living in our era are very real and specially graced by God. There is always the possibility that every one of them proves to be authentic one day; a greater possibility exists that at least some of them are. Yet it is not beyond the realm of reason that every one of them could be false stigmatists. Although I lean towards the positive approach, the negative cannot be discounted (call it a healthy negative criticism, if you will). This author will be the first to promote any person whom the Church one day declares a saint or authenticates a stigmatist.

I apologize to those friends or relatives of reported living victims who are loyal to these people in question. But I would regret more fully a premature stand on a living stigmatist if one day the Church declares them to be something other than what was believed. Again, I call it cautious optimism (for lack of a better word). Am I riding the fence? Certainly. I am just as concerned about misjudging an authentic stigmatist as I am a false one; in fact, perhaps more so. Nothing could be worse than to discredit God's action among His people. That is why I lean towards a positive approach while keeping one foot back, like the devil's advocate during the Process for Canonization.

I must confess that I believe entirely in the cases I've presented in this book. All of the stigmatists mentioned have been well-known, thoroughly investigated, and most of them have been authenticated. The ones that have not are those who haven't been declared saints yet, or whose Process for Beatification or Canonization is not yet completed. However, this does not necessarily imply that they do not meet with favorable reception from the Church. There have been many stigmatists who have never been canonized (at least yet) — Padre Pio or Therese Neumann, for example.

Yet the Church has spoken out strongly in support of their saintly lives and Christ-like examples. I have attempted to be very particular in whom I include in a work such as this, for one can never be too cautious when dealing with the supernatural mysteries of our faith.

I firmly believe that the Sacred Stigmata is a real grace bestowed upon a few chosen souls by the hand of God himself; I have come to believe that these victims really do participate in God's plan of redemption for the world through sacrificial suffering in union with the Cross. I am convinced that this occurs through voluntary sufferings in the form of atonement, reparation and expiation. Only those whom God selects are given the Sacred Stigmata — nobody earns it or deserves it. It is a free gift and extraordinary grace reserved for those whom He wills.

Why does God choose some and not others? All that I can conclude after my intensive studies on this topic is: I don't know. Nobody does. It is a mystery of Divine Providence, one that cannot be known unless He chooses to reveal it to us. Yet God does not always reveal His mysteries, because they fall within the realm of pure faith. Furthermore, there are always some things that no mere human can comprehend because, after all, we are not God: a moving thought to humble the wise! In the end, the Sacred Stigmata — though authentic beyond all reasonable doubt — remains a mystery of our Faith.

Appendix

Up Close: Padre Pio of Pietrelcina

High in the Gargano Mountains in Eastern Italy, where the blue-green
Adriatic Sea calmly meets the shore, lies the town of San Giovanni Rotondo
in the Province of Foggia. It is one of the most beautiful spots in all of Italy,
surrounded by pine-covered mountains and air that is both fresh and clear.
This town of over 20,000 people was also the home of stigmatist Padre Pio of
Pietrelcina (1887-1968), who spent 50 years here in the Capuchin Friary of
Our Lady of Grace. It was here that I met Fathers Alessio Parente, O.F.M.
Cap. and Joseph Martin, O.F.M. Cap., intimate friends and daily compan-
ions of Padre during the last few years of his life.

I found both Fathers Alessio and Joseph to be the kindest of people, extremely generous with their time and helpful beyond all my expectations.
Father Alessio was very shy upon our first encounter, but I believe this was
due to his sincere humility and simplicity of heart. After the ice had been
broken and he understood my intentions in the promotion of Padre Pio, he
relaxed, opened up, and over several cups of coffee told me many precious
stories concerning his recollections of Padre Pio. Father Alessio was Padre's
personal daily assistant for the last six years of his life, and he was probably
closer to him than anyone who ever knew him in those later years. Father
Alessio has written many good books on Padre Pio, and is currently the editor of *The Voice of Padre Pio*, a publishing house located right next to Our
Lady of Grace Friary and devoted to the promotion of Padre Pio (much of
the material gathered and printed there is being used in the current Cause
for Padre's Beatification).

I have nothing but the kindest respect for Father Joseph Martin.
Besides giving me many tapes and books concerning Padre Pio, he spent
half of two days with me, giving me several tapes worth of interviews that
are honest, first-hand accounts of one who knew Padre Pio on an intimate
basis; besides, they are priceless possessions. Father Joseph was Padre's aid
and companion the last three years of his life, and was with him in his cell
on the day that he died. Jovial and very down-to-earth, he makes one feel
right at home with his warm personality. I cherish the new friendship I have
made with Father Joseph. I sincerely hope that I have done him justice on
my treatment of my spiritual Franciscan Father, Padre Pio of Pietrelcina.

Interview with Father Alessio Parente, O.F.M. Cap.
(July 22, 1988)

AUTHOR: We all know of Padre Pio's extraordinary gifts, his gift of humility, most importantly. But I haven't heard too many people talk about the
human side of Padre Pio. Do you know of any weaknesses that Padre had?
FATHER ALESSIO: The last three years of his life, Padre became very
sick. Since then, he clothed himself in a kind of silence. . .
AUTHOR: Depression?
FATHER ALESSIO: Depression for some problems . . . problems of old
age, you know. With so much suffering, really. . .
(Father Martin interjects: He was very withdrawn because he knew the day

he would die. And as that was approaching, he was preparing for death. At that point, he was very quiet. All the supernatural things in his life he would no longer talk about. In the last years of his life, Padre Pio starved for affection . . . that personal, human thing. This revealed his human side. . . .)

AUTHOR: What do you think Padre Pio's main mission was for people in our particular era?

FATHER ALESSIO: First of all, I think God sent him because of the world. It was in a state of chaos. The first thing that Padre did was to bring people back to God and to prayer. This was especially true during the war (WW II). I think his mission was also to bring back to God many people through the Sacrament of Penance. People were impressed by his humility and simplicity.

AUTHOR: Would you say that one of his main missions was to hear confessions?

FATHER ALESSIO: We know that he heard confessions up to 12, 14 hours a day. How did he do it? It is a gift. . . .

AUTHOR: Did Padre Pio sleep very much?

FATHER ALESSIO: According to my time, he would only sleep in bits and pieces . . . perhaps two hours a night, that's all.

AUTHOR: What did most of the letters to Padre Pio say from his followers? What did they thank him for?

FATHER ALESSIO: About 70 percent of them had thanked him for graces received through his intercession.

AUTHOR: Everybody says how Padre Pio was so humble, which is extraordinary considering the attention that constantly surrounded him. In what way have you seen his humility come through? Do you have a specific memory that comes to mind?

FATHER ALESSIO: I was assisting him, helping him into bed. He would hug me, almost crying because of his appreciation for others who would do things for him. I would say, "Father, this morning I said Mass for you," and he would cry out of joy to think that others would treat him this way. He had great simplicity and humility. . . .

AUTHOR: Did you ever see Padre Pio's expression change during Mass?

FATHER ALESSIO: Yes, I would see him change all the time when he approached the altar, he would seem like Jesus on the Cross. Then, during the consecration, his face would become beautiful and ecstatic.

AUTHOR: Are you planning on keeping Padre Pio's body where it presently exists here in the friary?

FATHER ALESSIO: Yes, I think so. We will open the tomb next year to see if his body is incorrupt.

AUTHOR: Is that a normal procedure during the Process for Beatification?

FATHER ALESSIO: Yes, when the Process is finished. We think the Process should be finished by the end of this year. Once they finish the Process they have to do that . . . to open the tomb and check his body so that Rome knows . . . it's standard procedure.

AUTHOR: If Padre's body is found not to be incorrupt, will that have any bearing on the outcome of the Process?

FATHER ALESSIO: No, that would not affect anything. That is a small concern in the Process.

AUTHOR: Was Padre more comfortable around older people or children?

FATHER ALESSIO: Oh, children especially. He would not pass by a child without giving him a kiss. Parents used to push their child in front of him, and he would always give them a kiss or caress or do something nice. He had a special love for the children.

AUTHOR: I sense a very strong resemblance of Padre Pio to St. Francis of Assisi: his attitude about people, nature, his humility. He is almost like a St. Francis for the modern world. I believe that's why a lot of people are attracted to him.

FATHER ALESSIO: Yes, he imitated Francis in everything: his joy, suffering, his love for animals, etc.

(Father Joseph interjects: There were some birds in the nest near here in the spring who were making disturbing noises in the evening. Once we had visitors here and they were making the same noises when Padre suddenly told them, "Will you be quiet," and there was silence until they left. This happened at least twice that I'm aware of.

AUTHOR: Do you have any examples you would like to share about Padre Pio's charity towards others?

FATHER ALESSIO: One day, a boy like you came by and was pulling and tugging on Padre Pio, trying to touch him. Later on when he left, Padre told me, "What are you doing? Don't you see that I'm being pulled apart?" I later said to that boy, "Don't do that again, or I'll have to teach you a lesson." By this time Padre Pio got real mad. The next day, this boy started to kiss him again. At that time, I just didn't care about anybody, not even Padre Pio. I jumped in front of Padre Pio, I took this boy from that door and threw him across the room to the other door. Later, Padre Pio said to me, "Boy, you are strong." (We all laugh). But then we went in, I shut the door, and Padre Pio said to me, "I don't care for the way they treat me; but don't do that again! That's not charity."

AUTHOR: I'm sure we can all learn a lesson of charity from this example! Thank you, Father Alessio, for sharing your memories.

Interview with Father Joseph Martin, O.F.M. Cap. (July 22, 1988)

AUTHOR: Father, did Padre Pio ever have a sense about a vocation of suffering? Did he ever mention this to you?

FATHER JOSEPH: Yes. Someone once asked him why he wanted to suffer so much. He said ,"I like to help my brothers in exile, and the holy souls in Purgatory. If we knew the value of suffering, we would ask for nothing else."

AUTHOR: Where does Padre's Cause for Beatification stand at this time?

FATHER JOSEPH: They are currently finishing up this Process in Rome. I have no idea when he will be Beatified; it could take years.

AUTHOR: In my current work on the stigmata, I am trying to stay away from a sensational approach. I would like this work to be a serious effort at understanding this extraordinary grace from God. One of the interesting things I've observed in my studies is the number of Franciscan stigmatists and victim souls who have appeared throughout Church history: St. Francis of Assisi, Padre Pio, Therese Neumann, etc. Is there any significant relationship between suffering and the Franciscan vocation?

FATHER JOSEPH: Yes, Franciscan spirituality is very much based on the Crucifixion.

AUTHOR: Why do you think there are so many stigmatists from Italy?

Why are there more from this country than anyplace else?

FATHER JOSEPH: Well, I think it has to do with the character of the people here. They're more emotional, and therefore they love easier. Actually, there are more women stigmatists than men, probably because they are more sensitive and emotional.

AUTHOR: Father, why do you think there are differences in the appearances or locations of the wounds on many of the stigmatists? We often hear of some stigmatists who receive the hand wounds in the wrist area, for example, while others receive them on the palms.

FATHER JOSEPH: It is because the stigmatist receives the wounds according to his or her understanding of the Passion; the information on ancient crucifixions is very recent. Each individual has a different state of mind according their participations in the Passion visions.

AUTHOR: I am including a unit in my book on the Holy Shroud of Turin as a comparative study with the Passion sufferings of the stigmatists. Do you believe that the Shroud was the true burial cloth of Christ?

FATHER JOSEPH: I believe that it is definitely authentic, since the Gospel tells us that His followers found the linen sheets in the tomb after the Resurrection. The Shroud is a testimony of the whole life of Christ, not just the Crucifixion. One thing they have proved about this Shroud is that it is not a painting, despite what the recent investigations may find . . . the blood on the Shroud was definitely found to be human blood.

AUTHOR: Getting back to Padre Pio, how long did you know him?

FATHER JOSEPH: I lived with him for the last three years of his life.

AUTHOR: Is it true that Padre Pio's wounds virtually disappeared moments after or even a little before his death?

FAHTER JOSEPH: Exactly when Padre Pio's wounds disappeared, no one knows, and I was with him every day, including the night he died. When they undressed the body — he died in the habit — they discovered that his wounds had completely healed, all five of them, and there were no scars or any signs that he had ever had them.

AUTHOR: Why do you think some stigmatists such as Therese Neumann still had their visible wounds when they died and even thereafter, whereas the wounds of some such as Padre Pio disappeared? Do you have any explanation why some have had their wounds appear and disappear intermittently, while with others they are permanently visible?

FATHER JOSEPH: No, I really can't explain it. But it is true that the stigmata in different stigmatists have appeared for different lengths of time.

AUTHOR: What about the invisible stigmata? Are these wounds hidden because the victims have implored our Lord to remove them out of humility?

FATHER JOSEPH: That is probably one of the reasons. But the visible stigmata is given as a sign to people of God's presence among them. It was not a sign just for Padre Pio; he tried many times to have his wounds concealed through his prayers to God, but it did not happen. Sometimes God will conceal the wounds but the pains remain continuously there.

AUTHOR: Why is it that most stigmatists are women or simple lay people? Why not the Pope? Why not cardinals, bishops or more priests?

FATHER JOSEPH: Because their mission is different. The stigmatist must be one who prays and suffers; he cannot be tied down to administrative work or other things that would keep him from his main mission.

AUTHOR: Father, I know that I owe my Franciscan vocation to Padre Pio. He has been a real inspiration to me, and I have often felt his presence, even though I live in the United States. And I don't know why. It's uncanny to me how someone can affect me as much as he has. There is something about him that is special above most of the saints I've admired. You know, I take my vocation seriously and would one day like to become a deacon. Yet the opportunity has not been available for me to do so. Perhaps God has given me this vocation to write as a means of serving Him at this moment in time.

FATHER JOSEPH: Yes, I believe you're right. Perhaps if you had become a deacon at this point of your life, you would not have been able to spend the necessary time on your writing. To write a serious work on the stigmata is really an extraordinary thing. When one comes to understand the mission of the stigmatist, he will see that it is to help mankind. You are really doing the same thing by becoming a kind of instrument for them by explaining the stigmata to others.

AUTHOR: Would Padre have approved of my writing a work that might help to promote his Cause?

FATHER JOSEPH: Well, he, out of humility, would not be involved. He would not even talk to the friars about his extraordinary life. But you are trying to do something to help the Church, so I would think he would have been delighted.

AUTHOR: What about his struggles with the dark night of the soul?

FATHER JOSEPH: His whole life long he experienced the dark night of the soul.

AUTHOR: It seems that Padre Pio was very much influenced by the writings of St. John of the Cross.

FATHER JOSEPH: And Teresa of Avila. . . .

AUTHOR: Do you find it strange to think that some of these gifted souls so advanced in the spiritual life could still experience darkness and frustration?

FATHER JOSEPH: To keep them humble, I think, is one of the reasons. I believe that this is why God chose to take the stigmata away from Padre Pio just before his death — to keep him humble, although he really didn't need it, as far as I'm concerned. The foot wounds actually started to close about three years before he died, although the feet were still swollen and the suffering was still there. You see, all the stigmatics always have a slight doubt, because Satan can give the wounds. . . .

AUTHOR: It has often been said that Padre Pio was very devoted to Mary. Can you describe something about his relationship with the Blessed Virgin?

FATHER JOSEPH: The reception of Padre Pio's stigmata is also tied up with Mary. She's in and out of his life constantly; she came with Christ to the stigmatization. As far as I know, this has not occurred with other stigmatics. Have you ever heard of such a thing in the story of stigmatics?

AUTHOR: No. I've heard of Mary coming before as a warning, or St. Michael the Archangel, but no . . . not that I'm aware of.

AUTHOR: How many Rosaries did Padre Pio say each day?

FATHER JOSEPH: Oh, he said an immense number of Rosaries a day. I have heard that Padre Pio was dispensed by the Blessed Mother from saying the whole Hail Mary — that he could just say the names of Jesus and Mary — and she would count that as the full Hail Mary. He was so devoted to the Rosary and said it so often. If this is true, his Rosary was the our Father, and 10 times saying Jesus and Mary, and the Glory. He said a fantastic number of Rosaries a day. He told the friars a number of times that sometimes he said 90 Rosaries a day. How could he do it if he heard confessions all day? Although he did have the gift of doing two things at once; because you could see him praying constantly, even when he was talking to you. He would be fingering his beads all the time.

AUTHOR: I wanted to ask you about the gift of bilocation. Was that still going on in his later years?

FATHER JOSEPH: Yes. Once Padre was asked by the friars about the nature of these bilocations — whether it was the body that actually moved. Padre said, "No, it is not the body that moves, it is the spirit that moves. How could so many miracles take place if only the body moved?" When the spirit moves, God incorporates it into a body for those who he appears to.

AUTHOR: We know that Padre Pio was often attacked by the evil spirit. Can you speak a bit about the reality of the devil in the world today?

FATHER JOSEPH: You must remember that Satan and his cohorts are just creatures subject to God, the Blessed Mother and so forth; if one starts to intrude in our lives because of study, and so forth, then they're annoyed by that; because you see, a human being is a creature of love. They are creatures of hate; they cannot love. They are incapable of love — just solid hate, you see? We are living at the end of the Apocalyptic age, and the diabolical forces are very strong now. But don't worry about it. They can't do anything against you.

AUTHOR: Why would the evil spirits attack the holiest of people — for example, the stigmatists or saints?

FATHER JOSEPH: Because they are more capable of love.

AUTHOR: Aren't they more afraid of God's holy ones because they are less able to stop them?

FATHER JOSEPH: Well, yes they are, but at the same time their rage becomes so much that it boils over.

AUTHOR: Father, what are your feelings about apparitions? We know that Padre Pio had many such experiences in his life, almost on a daily basis.

FATHER JOSEPH: I believe in some of them, but you can't believe in everything. Not even the saints can. Even Father Pio's confessors said, "You are always to be guided by your right reason and not by apparitions or voices because it is too risky." For instance, Bernadette at Lourdes. At times she would see the real Virgin Mary, and at other times she would see the figure of a woman, who was the devil. After she sprinkled holy water when she saw these apparitions, the diabolic woman fled. The evil spirits are always trying to get into the act.

AUTHOR: Would you please share some insights on how Padre Pio received the visible stigmata? Did it really occur while he was praying before a crucifix in Our Lady of Grace church?

FATHER JOSEPH: Yes, that is where it happened. Padre Pio would come to what we call the choir loft here in the same church where he said daily Mass. The friars would often go there to have privacy while saying the Divine Office. Padre used to pray before this crucifix here after each Mass in thanksgiving. You must remember that the Crucifixion has always played a major role in Capuchin spirituality; therefore, the crucifix was a center for everything. When Padre Pio received the stigmata from the crucifix here in the choir loft, it literally came alive to him at the moment he was given the wounds.

AUTHOR: Father, are there any other stigmata besides the Five Sacred

Wounds that Padre Pio suffered? Were there any that we may not be familiar with?

FATHER JOSEPH: Well, he did suffer the shoulder wound which bled on occasions. Many times his night shirt would be filled with blood from this area which was caused by the flagellation.

AUTHOR: Which of the wounds caused him the most pain?

FATHER JOSEPH: He never did make any comment about that. . . .

AUTHOR: What about Padre's heart wound? Did it bleed severely?

FATHER JOSEPH: Sometimes Father Pio would have to change his bandages four times a day because they became so saturated with blood. It is a clear indication of how much he suffered. He lost a tremendous amount of blood, especially from the heart wound. About a cup of blood would come from this wound every day.

AUTHOR: Did the foot wounds make it very difficult for him to walk?

FATHER JOSEPH: Yes, very much so. His sandles were very swollen and blood-stained . . . unbelievably swollen.

AUTHOR: Are there any particular illnesses that Padre suffered in his later years?

FATHER JOSEPH: He had a continual cough caused by his asthma. He was advised to spit up all that he could due to the amount of flem that would build up in his throat.

AUTHOR: Would you talk a little bit about the chair in Padre's cell?

FATHER JOSEPH: Yes, the chair that is now located in Padre's cell is the one that he died in. You see, he died at the age of 81 from asthma. About an hour before his death, he was in that chair. He said to me, "I see two mothers." One of them was his earthly mother, and the other was the Blessed Mother. There is an interesting story behind the cushion (pillow) on the chair. At ten o'clock one night in July of 1964, the friars heard this great noise and came running in. Father Pio had been in bed, was thrown out of bed, and wound up on the floor. This cushion was under his head. And over his head was a cut that the doctor had to come and put two stitches in. His eyes went black, and he was unable to celebrate Mass for three days. What had happened was that evil spirits entered the room and physically fought with him. They say that the Blessed Mother came and they fled. She acted like a mother would do when her child would fall. She took the cushion from the chair and put it under his bleeding head, and that's how the friars found him when they arrived. The blood stains can be seen to this day on the cushion in his cell.

AUTHOR: Did Padre Pio remain social and active towards the end of his life? I know that his health was rapidly deteriorating and he suffered immensely.

FATHER JOSEPH: During the last three years of his life, he no longer went to the refectory. He was really withdrawing from everything he had enjoyed in life. He did love the people and the friars, going into the garden, and so forth. But these last years he would eat alone here in his cell.

AUTHOR: Besides his old age what do you think finally caused Padre's health to deteriorate so rapidly?

FATHER JOSEPH: For many years, Padre Pio would eat very little — he nibbled at his food, actually. That coupled with sleeping no more than two hours a night, not taking a day's vacation in half a century because he didn't want to do it, plus the continual bleeding from his body for so many years finally caught up with him.

AUTHOR: Thank you, Fr. Joseph, for your insights on Padre Pio.

Interview with Mr. William Carrigan
(June, 1988)

I initially came into contact with Mr. Carrigan through a phone interview. He was stationed in Italy during World War II, and had the privilege of meeting Padre Pio there. He eventually introduced the U.S. troops to Padre Pio while they were stationed in Italy. Mr. Carrigan became a friend of Padre Pio, a personal relationship that he cherished for two years.

Mr. Carrigan sent me a series of photos of Padre Pio that he had taken while stationed in Italy, pictures that reveal an intimate side of the Capuchin friar from San Giovanni Rotondo. Two of the most beautiful pictures I have ever seen of Padre Pio were copies of mosaics that he had sent. I am deeply grateful for his generosity.

Mr. Carrigan was a member of the 99th Bomb Group during the Second World War. Below I combine his recollections of Padre Pio from our phone interview and from the material that I was given.

AUTHOR: What do you think Padre Pio's main mission was in the world?
MR. CARRIGAN: God had given us Padre Pio to teach us through suffering; he is a sign of conversion and faith.
AUTHOR: Did Padre ever say anything to you about his visible wounds?
MR. CARRIGAN: Yes. Padre Pio was always the most humble of men. He once told me: "I find them embarrassing."
AUTHOR: Why do you think Padre Pio was given the stigmata?
MR. CARRIGAN: I think the wounds were only given for others — not for Padre Pio — as signs of God working among us.
AUTHOR: Do you think that Padre Pio will be remembered as an exceptionally favored soul?
MR. CARRIGAN: I'm confident that one day Padre Pio will be canonized a saint, and will go down as one of the greatest saints for all people.
AUTHOR: Do you feel that Padre is still spiritually among us?
MR. CARRIGAN: Padre Pio is definitely still with us, leading us closer to God.
AUTHOR: How would you describe Padre's role as a priest?
MR. CARRIGAN: He was the ultimate priest.
AUTHOR: How would you describe Padre Pio's Mass?
MR. CARRIGAN: His Mass was an unforgettable experience. The sermons stirred the depths of one's soul and awakened a dormant faith in the heart. Yet he preached not a word! There was always a crowd at Padre Pio's Mass. It was often two hours long, but no one minded the time. During the consecration he was literally on the Cross with Christ. The sufferings in his hands, feet and whole body were obvious to all. His pain was so great at the words of the consecration that it was difficult for him to say them. He would repeat a word many times, rest and go on to the next one and repeat it again. After the elevation he seemed to be lost to the world and pleaded with Christ for the needs of his vast spiritual family.
AUTHOR: Did Padre Pio wear gloves during Mass to cover his wounds?
MR. CARRIGAN: He wore fingerless gloves at all times except at Mass. Many sought the opportunity to kiss his hands while he was unvesting be-

cause he put on the gloves as soon as he removed his alb.

AUTHOR: Was Padre Pio friendly towards those who came to see him? How did he treat those who were foreigners?

MR. CARRIGAN: His engaging smile and simple humility drew everyone to him. There were always interpreters around, should anyone wish to ask questions, but for the boys who spoke Italian he was a special interrogator. It was he who did the questioning.

AUTHOR: How would you best describe Padre Pio's role as a spiritual director?

MR. CARRIGAN: Padre Pio was a great designer of souls. Great artists are rare in this field. Would you not like to have your soul designed by so great a spiritual artist? Think about it.

AUTHOR: Indeed, Mr. Carrigan, I shall. Thank you for your time and concern.

All materials related to Padre Pio may be obtained from the following centers:

USA and CANADA:
National Center for Padre Pio, Inc.
Vera M. Calandra, Directress
11 N. Whitehall Rd.
Norristown, PA 19403

AUSTRALIA:
Padre Pio Center of Australia
Brother Allen Kennedy, O.F.M. Cap.
Capuchin Friary, 96
Catherine St., Leichhardt
2040 N.S.W.

Padre Pio Center
Mr. Paul MacLeod, Director
P.O. Box 1041
2 Hawthorn Ave., Belmont
3216, Geelong, Victoria 3216

ENGLAND:
Padre Pio Information Center
Stella and Anthony Lilley, Directors
Kingsdown Park House
Whitstable, Kent
CT5 2DF

Padre Pio Bookshop Center
10 Upper Tachbrook St.
London, SW1V ISH

IRELAND:
Irish Office for Padre Pio
Eileen Maguire, Directress
58 Dufferin Ave., S.C. Rd.
Dublin 8

NORTHERN IRELAND:
Northern Ireland Office for Padre Pio
101 Andersonstown Rd.
Belfast BT. 11 8GW, N.
Ireland

SOUTH AFRICA:
South Africa Center for Padre Pio
Barbara Potgieter, Directress
P.O. Box 1380
S-West 7130, Cape

Up Close: Therese Neumann of Konnersreuth

Father Ulrich Veh, O.F.M. Cap. is a Franciscan monk who lives in St.
Konrad Monastery in Altötting, Bavaria, West Germany. Altötting is about
40 miles east of Munich, and it is the home of Our Lady of Altötting, West
Germany's national shrine which is visited by hundreds of thousands of pilgrims each year. His Holiness, Pope John Paul II, came here in 1980 to pay
his respects.

Father Veh is the current Vice-Postulator of the Cause for Beatification
of Therese Neumann, the lay Franciscan stigmatist from Konnersreuth,
West Germany. I had the pleasure of getting to know Father Veh through
my good friend Albert Vogl of San Jose, California, who was a lifelong friend
of Therese's.

When my wife Kathy and I arrived at St. Konrad Monastery on July
15, 1988, I expected to record an hour's worth of interview material and to
take a few pictures for my work on the stigmata. Little did I know that Father Veh would spend the greater part of the day with us; in fact, he gave me
four solid hours of interviews (he speaks English well) between 11:30 a.m.
that morning through the following morning before we left. In addition to
this, I also received several dozen critical reports on Therese Neumann that
date back to the late 1950s. Needless to say, I was very blessed by Father
Veh's kindness and generosity. He is truly a humble and loving man, and I
cherish my new friendship with him.

Father Veh is part of the "Konnersreuth Circle" which gathers material on Therese Neumann to be evaluated during the Cause for Beatification.
This group is located in Eîchstatt, West Germany, half way between Konnersreuth and Altötting.

The one thing that remains in my memory about Father Veh is his
beautiful laugh and warm smile. He truly lives the Franciscan way of life, so
giving of himself without expecting anything in return. His brown habit,
long gray beard, and sandles make him look like something out of the medieval world, when monks would live a life of quiet solitude in prayer and contemplation. He is one of those rare people you run into a few times in your

whole life who really make a lasting impression upon your mind and spirit. I have nothing but the greatest respect for him; he is a saint in his own right.

This information on the stigmata and Therese Neumann came from the hours of conversations we shared at the monastery. Father has provided some interesting insights on the meaning of the Sacred Stigmata and its value for the world today.

Interview with Father Ulrich Veh, O.F.M. Cap.
(July 15-16, 1988)

AUTHOR: Father, you have been assigned to be Vice Postulator for the Cause of Beatification for Therese Neumann. Father Anton Vogl (Pastor of St. Lawrence Church in Konnersreuth) is the current Postulator. How far along is this Process now?

FATHER VEH: The Cause for Therese's Beatification is still in the beginning stages. It is not yet officially underway, although we're working on gathering the information now for her Cause.

AUTHOR: Are most of the people associated with the promotion of Therese's Cause in Konnersreuth or Altötting?

FATHER VEH: Some are there, but most of the information on Therese is kept in Eichstätt. Many who knew her when she was living are there, as well as some scholarly people who had been involved with her life (Eichstätt is a religious center with a cathedral and a Catholic college).

AUTHOR: How well did you know Therese Neumann? Were you a good friend of hers?

FATHER VEH: No, not a good friend, but I did know her. I spoke to her at times and I saw her as well. Yes, I knew Therese, but I know others much better who were very close to her.

AUTHOR: How often did Therese suffer from the Passion scenes?

FATHER VEH: Every week from 1926 until her death in 1962. Therese would go into ecstasy by Thursday night and would continue through the entire crucifixion with Jesus until Friday afternoon. She would revive, return to a normal state, and begin again the next Thursday.

AUTHOR: Would you tell us something about Therese Neumann's wounds? What were they like?

FATHER VEH: (He brings in two of Therese's relics for me to observe and photograph: her shoes and her blood-stained head scarf.) These were given to me by a friend of Therese's. I was told to guard them with my life! (He laughs). Notice the blood on her shoes . . . she suffered a lot from her foot wounds. Also see the circles of blood on her head scarf. These are the crown of thorn wounds from one of her Passion sufferings. Notice how several circular rings of blood overlap at each point. This happened because she would often bleed, come out of her ecstatic sufferings, then the blood would stop. Later, with the same scarf on, it would happen again in almost the exact same spot, but the scarf may have been put on in a slightly different position than before. This explains the overlapping circles from several different times that she bled.

AUTHOR: What are these blood stains on the edges of her scarf?

FATHER VEH: Those are stains from where she had cried tears of blood, just like Jesus at Gethsemani. Part of the blood (he points to a corner spot) is probably from her shoulder wound that she frequently suffered during her Passion ecstasies.

AUTHOR: I notice that her shoe is rather stretched. Why is this so?

FATHER VEH: Because of Therese's suffering, her feet wounds often swell, making it very difficult at times to walk.

AUTHOR: Father, what do you think of the stigmatists who are reported to be living among us today? How much attention should we be giving to them at this time?

FATHER VEH: We must be very careful when we hear a claim of a living stigmatist. Sometimes the devil can cause the wounds, so the Church wisely proceeds with great caution.

AUTHOR: Father, what do you think about the Shroud of Turin? Do you believe that it is the burial cloth of our Lord?

FATHER VEH: I think that maybe it is not necessarily the cloth in which Jesus was buried in the tomb, but rather the linen sheet that he was wrapped in when they took Him down from the Cross. Perhaps they wrapped the entire linen around Him there at the Cross, because it was an ancient tradition that one does not touch a dead body. This, I believe, is what happened. When they laid Him in the tomb, they could have taken the linen off of the body and laid it to the side, as the Gospel of John tells us. The sheet had to come off because the women at the tomb anointed His body. This was a standard custom of the day.

AUTHOR: You know, St. Paul once said that even though Christ died once and for all for our sins, nevertheless some souls are called to make up for what is lacking in the sufferings of Christ for His Church. Do you think it's possible that St. Paul might have been a stigmatist himself?

FATHER VEH: Oh yes, I do believe that. At the end of the letter to the Galatians, Paul had said that he bore in his body the marks of Christ. You can think otherwise, but Therese Neumann through her ecstasies knew that he was.

AUTHOR: Why is it that most of the stigmatists seem to come from small, out-of-the-way places instead of large population centers?

FATHER VEH: Sometimes it is easier for the people to visit the stigmatist in a smaller location than it would be in a larger, more busy city. Also, a smaller place is more quiet and is the ideal environment for the stigmatist to pray and suffer in — to grow spiritually, to lead the contemplative life that they are called to.

AUTHOR: Why do you think there have been more women stigmatists than men?

FATHER VEH: Women have been called to love in a more sensitive way than most men. They seem to be able to suffer more at the same time they love. A woman is a great lover.

AUTHOR: Thank you, Father Veh, for your time and your kindness. I hope that all goes well with the Promotion for the Cause of Therese Neumann. I will be keeping in touch with you.

Glossary of Mystical Terms

ABANDONMENT.
The total renunciation of one's will to that of God's. It involves self control and discipline, and the willingness to accept all of our crosses as a sacrifice to God. In the way of spiritual perfection, abandonment (also known as **self-abandonment**) involves the voluntary acceptance of the various trials one encounters in both the active and passive states of purification or purgation, be they physical or spiritual.

ACTIVE PURGATION.
The process whereby one attempts through his own efforts to rid himself of those imperfections that hinder his spiritual progress. This is done through voluntary acts of penance, fasting, mortification, prayer, self-imposed disciplinary measures, and the like. This is the first stage in the contemplative life known as the **dark night of the senses**; here, one attempts to deny himself the sensual pleasures that he has come to rely on in order to be free of all impediments that keep him from coming closer to God and to doing the divine will.

ADORATION.
The act of honoring God alone because of His divinity and perfection. Adoration is the highest form of veneration (often called **latria**) because through this act one acknowledges both internally and externally the supremacy and omnipotency of one God the Father.

AFFECTIVE PRAYER.
Movements of the soul that are emotional and inspired by the love for God. Affective prayer can take the form of sudden impulses that produce a few words (or even one word) of praise and adoration in the realization of God's infinite love, goodness and mercy. Often the affective prayer is an act with no words at all. When this is the case, one has reached the preliminary stages of contemplative prayer.

AFFLICTION.
Usually refers to the trials and sufferings imposed upon the body or soul during the active and passive states of purification. When the senses are deprived of their normal appetites or pleasures, the body rebels until he has conquered himself through control and self-denial. The soul feels afflicted when God himself chooses to purge it of all imperfections in order that the divine union may be achieved. The latter type of affliction usually occurs only with those who have reached a higher state of spirituality.

APPARITION.
A mystical vision of a supernatural character, usually representing an angel, a saint, the Virgin Mary, one of the Apostles, a soul in purgatory, or Jesus Christ himself. There are two types of apparitions: 1) **corporeal**, where one experiences a real person who can be talked to and even touched; and 2) **sensible**, where the vision is more of a luminous nature shown in the form of a mental picture. This often occurs in a dream to the visionary; nev-

ertheless, it is very real to the one perceiving it. Appparitions — even ones that the Church has authenticated — are not accepted as articles of faith, and the faithful are free to not believe in them if they choose. This is because all apparitions are of a private, mystical nature, and are usually not given to the public at large or in a public setting (although many have claimed messages for the universal Church).

APPETITE.

In a mystical sense, the attachment to things that are not strictly spiritual or that do not serve to advance one's state in the spiritual life. Appetites are usually of a sensual or bodily nature, and must be eliminated through the practices of self-denial and mortification. These appetites are desires or thirsts for personal or worldy things, and can come in many forms.

ARIDITY.

A sensation that one undergoes in the spiritual state, whereby one is deprived of the consolations and delights that he once experienced. It is a trial that occurs within the realm of both the physical and the spiritual, resulting in feelings of isolation, abandonment and depression. Aridity serves to detach the soul from pleasures of the world and senses, thereby creating a void that makes one long all the more intensely for God and God alone. It can occur in the dark night of the spiritual state, but is often felt in the ordinary states as well.

ARROW.

A mystical dart or spear that pierces the heart or soul, leaving the victim consumed in the fire of divine love. A seraphim is usually seen as the one who inflicts the soul with this arrow. This can occur in the higher mystical states of ecstasy or rapture, and often is a prelude to the invisible or visible stigmata. Many holy souls, however, receive this wound without receiving the stigmata later. Once received, it is usually a permanent wound of the heart or soul, either invisible or, in some cases, visible as a wound directly in the heart or above it on the exterior body of the victim.

ASCETICISM.

Spiritual exercises designed to help one grow in virtue and perfection. Ascetical practices are in the realm of the ordinary ways of the Christian state, or the first stages of Christian perfection. Practices such as meditation, fasting, penance, and bodily purgations are frequently used to advance in self-control and virtue. Mysticism, on the other hand, goes beyond the personal or self-induced efforts toward perfection through the experimental knowledge of God, whereby the soul more intimately and profoundly experiences the divine love through the direct action of the Spirit. The mystic is involved more directly in the divine relationship, whereas the ascetic experiences Him a bit more from a distance and less impersonally. Asceticism — though a gift in itself — is nevertheless for the most part a human effort; mystical experiences, on the other hand, are strictly supernatural gifts that cannot be gained through one's own efforts, but must be given to the soul from God and God alone.

ASPIRATION.

A short prayer that serves to keep the soul in a spirit of recollection before God. Seldom are the prayers any longer than a dozen words; they are somewhat similar to the prayers of affection, although the latter may use even fewer words or no words at all.

ATONEMENT.

The satisfaction for the offense of sin. In order for the atonement to be meritorious, the atonement must be done voluntarily and in a spirit of reparation. In addition, the atonement is usually made in union with Christ's sufferings or with His Cross. Atonement serves to reconcile the sinner with the Father. If the atonement is done for someone else's sin (as is usually the case with the saints and mystics), it then becomes known as **vicarious atonement**, or **vicarious suffering**. The justification for this vicarious suffering is that the God of mercy is also a God of perfect justice; He has promised to treat all people — the good and the bad — with equality based upon the lives they led while on this earth. Otherwise, there would be no motive to strive for perfection if punishment is not a part of the divine plan.

BEATIFIC VISION.

According to Pope Benedict XII, this is the clear and immediate sight of the divine essence that is God. Only those who have lived a life of sanctity and are now in the state we call heaven enjoy this vision fully. Some pious souls are claimed to have had a partial beatific vision while still on this earth, but these souls are few and far between. Those who have reached the mystical states of divine union and even the spiritual marriage may have reached this partial vision while still in their earthly lives; still, no one has ever enjoyed the complete and perfect beatific vision (to see God as He really is in all His fullness) while still upon this earth. This is reserved for the everlasting blessing of heaven.

BILOCATION.

An extraordinary mystical phenomenon whereby a person is present in two different places at one time. One who sees the bilocation actually experiences a real bodily vision of the person, though sometimes a feeling of that person's presence is all that is experienced. Some souls who have claimed to bilocate actually feel themselves leave their present surroundings and instantly appear in a new location, while realizing that they are still where they were before. The soul who bilocates generally does so because another person is in need of his or her assistance or intercession, usually when there is a serious illness, an extreme danger from a diabolical attack or with the approach of death.

BRIDE.

In the mystical sense, a reference to the Church (2 Cor 11:2), who is the bride of Christ, the heavenly Groom. More specifically, the term used to describe the chosen soul who has reached the heights of perfection, and has become one with Christ in the state of divine union. The words "bride" and "groom" are a part of a figurative mystical language used to describe what is really indescribable, for the intense and intimate love relationship between God and the chosen soul transcends all human understanding.

CHARISM.

A term often used synonymously with the word **gift** or **grace**, although in a technical sense it is really a gift of an extraordinary type given to one for the benefit of others. St. Paul listed several of these extraordinary gifts in his letter to the Corinthians (see 1 Cor 12:4-11). The plural for charism is **charismata**, or **charisms**.

CHURCH MILITANT.

Traditionally used to refer to the pilgrim Church on earth, which strives for perfection and salvation through the virtues of faith, hope and charity toward God and toward neighbor. Although seldom used anymore, this term is as good as any in describing the courage and tenacity a Christian must have in order to follow Christ and His Gospel message, with the hope of obtaining eternal life one day in the world that is still to come.

CHURCH SUFFERING.

A near obsolete term that is sometimes used to refer to the poor souls who are in a state of purgatory. These suffering souls — although not yet enjoying the beatific vision and the union with God in heaven — nevertheless are still saved and are a part of Christ's universal Church. We believe as a matter of faith that these souls will one day be cleansed from their stains of sin and will enter heaven when their time of satisfaction is finished. In the meantime, the Church has always encouraged the faithful to pray, suffer and sacrifice for them, since they can still be helped through the efforts of others (though they cannot help themselves, since the only time for merit is in this earthly life).

CHURCH TRIUMPHANT.

An ancient term used to describe that part of the universal Church that has died and gone to heaven. They have been found worthy to enter the divine presence, and we believe as a matter of faith that they can and do intercede for us before the Father while we are still pilgrims in this earthly life. A soul that had been in purgatory but who now has entered heaven becomes a part of the Church Triumphant.

COHORT.

Cohort literally means "companion" or "a group of warriors and followers." In the area of mystical theology (and specifically in the field of demonology), cohorts refer to the accomplices of the devil in his opposition to and attacks upon the human person who seeks to follow the way of Christ. They are also known as **evil spirits**, **spirits of darkness**, **demons**, or **devils**. The evil spirit seldom acts alone upon a human soul, but rather seeks the aid of these companions who, acting together, are incredibly strong and effective (being that there is always strength in numbers). The only recourse to the onslaught of their attacks is through the power of Christ. No one human — or even many people working together — can ever come close to matching these forces of darkness without the aid of the Cross. Outside of the Father, Son and Holy Spirit, nothing can equal the strength and persistency of these vile creatures (unless, perhaps, we include St. Michael the Archangel in our list of protectors).

CONSOLATION.

A mystical experience that God gives to the soul who is living in spiritual darkness or aridity. This He does in order to renew one's life in the spirit and to give the soul reassurance and confidence in the midst of the trials he is undergoing. Consolations are usually experienced as spiritual delights, sweet impulses or divine touches. In some cases, Christ himself, Mary, or one of the saints might visit the soul to strengthen and to reassure them. Consolations can also be of one's own doing; for example, such as stimulations one can find from the reading of Sacred Scripture or the lives of the saints.

CONTEMPLATION.

A type of affective prayer where the soul experiences God's love and being in a most profound and intimate manner; in a sense, it is a wordless act of love for God, where the mind and will are concentrated on experiencing the presence of God in the reality of the present moment. Although technically anyone has the possibility of experiencing some contemplative moments, the continuous or intensely prolonged states of contemplation are of a mystical and passive nature, whereby God infuses His love and knowledge about himself directly into the soul. In this mystical sense, it is a pure gift from God that one cannot obtain from his efforts alone. One must be called to a state of contemplation although, as was just mentioned, anyone might have many different moments of contemplative experiences throughout their life. If they do, then the moments are usually brief and less intense than the truly mystical contemplative state.

CONTEMPLATIVE LIFE.

A lifestyle dedicated to the pursuit of the union with God, usually found in the religious state or in contemplative orders. The strictly contemplative life (since there are active-contemplatives) seeks God as Love through spiritual encounters with the divine. It involves a life that is really a continuous prayer of seeking and loving the Lord. Even activities within the contemplative life center around the quest for God and the love for neighbor. These actions can take the form of penances, fastings, voluntary reparations for the sinners of the world, etc. This is not to say that true contemplative lives are not found outside the monastery or cloister. Some saintly souls, in fact, have lived their lives in the secular world, though they are very rare, indeed. In most cases, a "secular contemplative" is usually an **active-contemplative**, whereby he or she has degrees of contemplative experiences amidst the activities that are undertaken in the state they find themselves in.

DARK NIGHT OF THE SENSES.

The mystical state whereby one becomes aware of his sins and imperfections, feels an intense sorrow for them, and makes the effort to expiate for the offenses he has committed against God. The best description of this state has come down to us by the spiritual master, St. John of the Cross (1542-91). In this active state, one undergoes severe trials and sufferings in order to pacify the senses through self-denial of all pleasures and consolations they have given. This is extremely painful because the person relies so much on the bodily senses that it becomes difficult to subdue them; the life of the spirit is at continual war with the life of the flesh: the eyes have to be tamed, tastes have to be denied, and old habits and vices must be eliminated in order to progress to a higher, more purely spiritual state (see Col 3:5-10). Yet God is pleased with this dark night, for it purifies the body and helps prepare one for the life that is spirit. When one succeeds in conquering these bodily senses, then God sees fit to further purify the soul of deep-rooted imperfections that only He can purge. This state is called the **dark night of the soul**, and it is much more painful and frightening than the night of the senses.

DARK NIGHT OF THE SOUL.

The passive mystical state whereby God and God alone chooses to purge the soul of the stains of imperfection that hinders one from reaching union with Him. This state normally follows the **dark night of the senses**, and is a much more painful experience. The reason for this is that the person does not have control over the imperfections that God is now purifying. Before, he was aware of what bodily things needed purifying, and was able through his own efforts to partly control them, to dictate what was needed to be done, and to find suitable remedies that he could handle. Not so with this state. God alone knows the deepest and most secretive parts of the soul, all of which need purifying like a crystal in order to be united with the total Purity that is God. Because these frightening purgings are beyond the control and knowledge of the one who undergoes them, the pain experienced has been described like a living flame of fire that consumes the soul but does not destroy. Feelings of abandonment, desolation, fear, and intense sorrow often accompany the soul during this night. Usually the dark night does not last indefinitely, although for some saintly souls called to the very highest degrees of perfection, once started it has lasted for the duration of their lives, simultaneously with the pleasures of the union they have found with the Lord.

DEIFICATION

A mystical state where one has reached such a high level of purity and spiritual perfection that the divine union has been obtained. The soul in this state has acquired such holy virtues and purity of heart that he or she shares in the attributes of the divine nature, by virtue of imitating the divine life and by the extraordinary grace that he has been given from God alone. In a sense, the purified soul becomes a part of God because the Trinity dwells within him, and therefore God chooses to become a part of him. It is in this sense that we speak of the deification of the soul. It does not mean that we become God in the sense of His very essence or being. Rather, we become one with Him and share in His Spirit. It is this sharing in the divine nature that we one day take on a divine image that was ours before the fall and the onset of Original Sin: "God created man in his own image, in the image of God, he created him; male and female he created them" (Gn 1:27).

DELIGHT.

An experience of the awareness of God, a love for Him, or union with the divine that causes the soul to feel a spiritual joy that is inspiring and exuberating, peaceful and delightful. The greatest delight experienced is that of love, for God is Love and all is contained in His love. This joy in the Love that is God causes the soul to love the God that he sees in his neighbor, in all of creation and in himself. These delights of the soul are usually experienced in the heights of prayer, such as the states of rapture or ecstasy. Degrees of spiritual delight are often found in the ordinary states as well, but never quite as intensely as that which is found in the mystical-contemplative experience.

DESERT.
A state or condition in the spiritual life that fills the soul with aridity, desolation and sometimes a feeling of abandonment by God, one's superiors, or even one's family and friends. The height of the desert experience is felt in the dark night of the senses and the soul, although this feeling can come and go throughout one's spiritual journey. Sometimes the soul remains in the desert because of his own doing, such as a falling away from God; at other times, it is God who puts the soul in the desert in order to try and to purify him. No person who advances far spiritually can avoid this desert at one time or another; in fact, he should be concerned if he never sees the desert, for all consolation and delight would not allow the soul to advance, mature or appreciate the joys and delights when they finally arrive. Other names commonly used for the desert are the **dark night**, the **abyss**, the **void**, etc.

DIVINE LOVE.
The most perfect kind of love that is the very essence of God's being, for God is Love (1 Jn 4:8). In the mystical sense, it is that Love which the soul intensely longs for in order to achieve the divine union. When deprived of that Love, the mystic suffers intensely in the spiritual life, because that Love which is God nourishes the soul and sustains its very life. In effect, God's love is the bread of the spiritual life, just as the Body and Blood of our Lord is the Bread of Life (Jn 6:35). For the mystic, one cannot exist without the other because he or she needs both breads to nourish the depths of their being.

DIVINE UNION.
The highest state of the spiritual life, a mystical union whereby the soul is one with the Lord and He with him. This union is rare in this life, and usually only occurs with the holiest of saints who have spent a lifetime perfecting themselves and who have obtained the greatest of virtues. Sometimes the divine union results in the **spiritual marriage**, a state where the Lord as Groom unites himself with His chosen one as Bride, in a spiritual union that is similar to the earthly marriage of two lovers who have become as one. Yet it is incomparably more joyful and perfect than any earthly marriage, for in this state the love of the soul becomes united to the pure Love which is God; one becomes that Love by sharing in the divine nature.

DRYNESS.
A spiritual condition that is void of all delights or consolations. Sometimes God will choose to wean the immature soul from its pleasures and comforts in order to test her soul or to make her long for Him all the more intensely. Dryness can often be caused by one's impatience for favors to be answered by the Lord. In this case, the dryness will apt to be most intense and prolonged in order that the soul will come to learn patience and to seek God for himself alone.

ECSTASY.

A supernatural experience where the senses are suspended and absorbed in God. The soul may experience such phenomena as visions, apparitions, revelations, and even mystical wounds. One in a state of ecstasy is oblivious to the world that surrounds him, and seems to be absorbed in another dimension that is removed from all sense of time and space.

EJACULATORY PRAYER.

An emotional prayer involving one or several words that give praise, adoration or thanksgiving to God. A common ejaculation is a repetition of the word, "Jesus!" These sudden impulses toward the divine are often as beneficial to the soul as the longer, more intense prayer, for with these ejaculations love springs forth from the heart and sighs for the God who in turn loves us. This is really a prayer of the heart, where God alone knows our innermost feelings and desires.

ENEMY.

The primary enemy of the spiritual life is the evil spirit, who incessantly seeks to destroy the workings of God in the soul and to bring him to eternal damnation. This he does through diabolical attacks that serve to frighten, intimidate and frustrate the victim, with the intention of weakening him to the point where he loses faith in the God whom he loves. The enemy has also been called the **devil**, **Satan**, **Lucifer**, and the **evil one**. More than being an enemy to the Christian soul, the devil particularly despises Jesus Christ, who claimed victory over all evil through His death upon the Cross.

ESPOUSAL.

In the supernatural sense, the mystical espousal is a prelude to the spiritual marriage between the Groom (Jesus Christ) and His beloved bride (the soul to whom He is united in love). It is a bond that is built upon the possession of love, whereby the chosen soul is purified, quieted and strengthened in order to prepare it for the complete union of the spiritual marriage, which is the highest state possible in this earthly life.

EUCHARISTIC LIFE.

According to the private revelations from our Lord to Sister Mary of the Holy Trinity, the spiritual state that demands silence, self-renunciation and goods acts to counter the evil sown in the world by means of imitating His life and way of perfection. According to Sister Mary, Jesus welcomes all souls to the imitation of His Eucharistic Life, particularly those souls whom He chooses to be His most intimate friends.

EXCHANGE OF HEARTS.

A mystical phenomenon that is common among many of the saints, whereby the heart of the pious soul becomes one with the divine. This occurs during the state of divine union, particularly within the spiritual marriage. Sometimes this can manifest exteriorly (as in the case with the wound of the heart), or it may be strictly internalized. The exterior exchange is comprehensible from the point of view that the exterior is an expression of the interior. It is the human heart that becomes infused with the Sacred

Heart of our Lord; thus the two unite as one in love, a seal of the divine espousal.

EXPIATION.

The atonement for some wrongdoing. Usually one will offer himself up voluntarily to the Lord in order to satisfy for the punishments due to the transgressions of others (a **vicarious expiation**). This can take the form of penance, suffering or illness for another's sake. If the Lord accepts this voluntary offering, then it becomes meritorious for both himself and the one he suffers for. The prototype for all victims of expiation is Christ himself, who satisfied for our sin through the victory of the Cross.

FIRE OF LOVE.

The mystical expression used by many saints to describe the purifying flame of divine love that wounds and consumes the soul, but does not destroy it. The intensity of God's light and love is so great that it penetrates the person like a dart set afire, permeating every part of his very being. It is in this sense that the saints speak of being "wounded in love," for there is no earthly language that is adequate to explain such a total presence of the divine within the soul.

FLIGHT.

The mystical experience in the ecstatic state whereby the soul takes temporary leave of the body and is "caught up" in the divine presence. This mystical flight is similar to the state of rapture, in that one is so immersed in God that he or she is overcome by His love and His purity. Some pious souls have taken many such mystical flights, which are usually brief but intensely delightful.

GROOM.

The symbolic term used to identify the Spouse of the mystical marriage, Jesus Christ, when the soul has reached the state of complete divine union; forever united to the Spouse of her soul, the Bride becomes, like in an earthly marriage, "one" with her Groom on a totally spiritual and supernatural level.

HIEROGNOSIS.

A gift of discerning holy things from those which are unholy. Many chosen souls have had this gift, which allows them to distinguish between many things: the ability to know when someone is living in mortal sin; knowing whether or not a host has been consecrated; knowing if a person has holy objects — such as a crucifix or rosary beads — in their possession or upon their bodies; etc.

ILLUSION.

In the spiritual realm, a false vision from the evil spirit, who attempts to deceive those who are striving towards perfection. The enemy can appear as an angel of light (2 Cor 11:14), and has often manifested himself as one of the saints, the Virgin Mary and even Jesus Christ. The other way one can experience an illusion is through his or her own preconceived ideas or misconceptions; in a sense, one can see what he wants to see, especially when it comes to supernatural visions or apparitions. The danger of deceiving one's self is always present in the spiritual life, and great caution must be exercised when the supernatural is manifested in the course of one's spiritual journey. A prudent director of the soul is always the best resource for those who feel that they are seeing visions, apparitions or are receiving private revelations which they claim are from God.

IMPULSE.

A sudden emotional inclination to love or praise God. The divine impulse is initiated by the Holy Spirit, who works deep within the soul. Impulses can stimulate or excite one to pray, to contemplate the mysteries of the Faith, or even to shed tears of joy due to the overwhelming sense of the presence of God. Impulses of this kind are normally associated with the more advanced states of spirituality (such as contemplation). More often than not, the divine impulse is usually a spontaneous reaction to the effects of God upon the soul. Impulses differ from inspirations in that the former originate through the workings of the Spirit, whereas the latter can often be self-induced through one's own efforts (although this is not always the case, for the Spirit can "inspire" one to do something, as was the case with the writing of Sacred Scripture).

INEDIA.

In the mystical sense, the lack of nourishment due to the suspension of all eating and/or drinking. Some mystics have survived for years on the Most Holy Eucharist alone, literally fulfilling the promise made by Christ to His chosen ones: "He who eats my flesh and drinks my blood has eternal life and I will raise him up at the last day. For my flesh is food indeed, and my blood is drink indeed" (Jn 6:54-55).

INFESTATION.

A degree of demonic influence that is not as serious as total possession, but which is nevertheless more serious than mere temptation. In the state of infestation, the victim is weighed down by the evil forces to the point where they gain partial control of his or her life. It is at this stage of the diabolical influence that experiences such as nocturnal noises, levitation and breakage of objects, and distortions of the bodily senses can occur. Infestation has often been called the state of **bondage**. This condition is very common among all the mystics, whom the devil loathes with a passion.

INFILTRATION.

A term used to describe the entry of an evil spirit into the sphere of human life; it particularly refers to a specific soul that has become the target for diabolical attack. Infiltration can occur because of many reasons: the sanctity of the victim; dabbling in the occult (such as the Ouija boards, tarrot cards, seances, etc.); a falling away from the faith; a pessimistic and depressive state; living in mortal sin; bondage to a particular vice or habit that leaves the soul susceptible to the enemy's attack; and a pact or allegiance to the devil through ceremonial rituals or through private intentions. Infiltration — the "breaking point" — usually occurs after diabolical temptation has claimed victory over the soul. In some cases, however, such as in the lives of the most holy saints, it can occur precisely because the person has withstood the enemy's attacks. This infuriates the evil one and can cause an all-out attack against the soul who so successfully resists him. As a marked opponent, the victim must struggle all the more against the Spirit of Darkness sometimes for the better part of his life. The soul would quickly be destroyed by this relentless power if it were not for the faith in Jesus Christ that leads him to victory.

INFUSION.

A supernatural act whereby God places in the soul the gift of divine knowledge, an extraordinary virtue, or a special grace needed for an unusual mission. Although technically all supernatural virtues are infused into the soul, some saintly souls are called to a higher and more demanding state than others. Because man cannot rely upon his own intellectual skills, senses or raw talents to fullfill these states, God gives him the necessary graces needed to live in the manner He has called him to and to be able to perform the duties thereof. Most of the saints and mystics have been infused or "injected" with divine knowledge and grace beyond the normal state of life, simply because their role in the kingdom has been more visible and their relationship with the divine more intimately profound.

INTERIOR LIFE.

The total spiritual dimension in the life of the person who strives for perfection and who longs for salvation. It is a part of one's reality that differs from the exterior life, or the **secular life** that is lived out in the world. The "interior way" involves the loving relationship of the soul with the Blessed Trinity; it involves a purity of heart and an openness to the Spirit, who guides and inspires the soul, leading it on the way towards the divine union.

INVISIBLE STIGMATA.

The mystical wounds of Christ that are given to a privileged soul who comes to share in the Passion of our Lord by voluntarily uniting himself with the sufferings of the Cross, thus allowing him to participate as a co-redemptor in the plan of salvation. Some chosen victim souls receive these wounds invisibly with the same intensity of pain as those who have the external stigmata. Many have received these wounds because God has chosen to keep them hidden in order to humble the soul; others who have had these wounds visibly have asked God to remove them exteriorly because of their great humility. Nevertheless, these wounds are very real, corresponding to the five wounds of Christ, with the additional wound of the soul, for one cannot be wounded exteriorly unless he is first crucified interiorly. In fact, the visible stigmata is first and foremost a manifestation of the invisible wound of the soul. When they make their appearance outwardly, these wounds become signs for the faithful of Christ's presence among His people, a suffering Christ who loves the world and continues to save it by the mystery of the Cross.

KARDIOGNOSIS.

The gift of being able to know the secret thoughts and conditions of another's inner being; literally, the "reading of minds." In addition, such a soul can discern if another is living in grace or sin.

LEVITATION.

A mystical state whereby the human body is raised above the ground without the aid of any natural support system. This phenomenon has been experienced by many of the saints, who usually levitate while in the state of rapture or ecstasy. In a sense, this is a prelude to the glory of the resurrection that all believers will experience one day when the body and soul are caught up to be with the Lord forever.

LOCUTION.

A supernatural experience when a heavenly being or the Lord himself communicates something to a person, either to the ears, the imagination or to the intellect. One must exercise great prudence when he claims to experience a locution, for the evil one frequently uses locutions to deceive and to harm the soul. Spiritual direction is needed for one who experiences such supernatural phenomena.

LOVE.

The fundamental reality in the spiritual life; the essential ingredient that brings one to the heights of perfection. Because God is pure Love, in order to attain the divine union the soul must become one with that Love. Human love reflects the divine through charitable acts towards one's family, friends and neighbors — for in serving them, we are serving Christ (Mt 25:40), who gave His entire life as a ransom for others. Above all, the love for God must be the primary concern for all the faithful, because all love has its origin in the Love that is God and Creator; ultimately, all love will find its way back to Him when we share in the eternal glory of our Lord and Savior.

MARTYR.

One who heroically sacrifices his or her life for the faith or out of love for another. In the mystical sense, the voluntary victim of love who offers himself up to God as a just sacrifice for the sins of others. The victim usually suffers a great deal of physical, emotional and spiritual pain in order to satisfy the divine justice due towards the sins of those he atones for. Some victim martyrs known as stigmatists have suffered the Passion and Crucifixion of Jesus Christ in their bodies and souls, imitating and reliving the redemptive life of the Lord who came to sacrifice himself for the sins of the world.

MEDITATION.

A type of prayer that involves reasoning and mental discourse through the intellect and the human will; in effect, it is a "thought prayer," in contrast with contemplation, which is a loving gaze at the divine without the use of discursive reason. Meditation involves the reflection upon the saints, the mysteries of the Faith, or the life and death of Jesus Christ. One meditates in order to understand more about the Faith, or to offer silent praise and adoration to our Lord. Meditation is a stepping stone towards the more advanced stages of the spiritual life, culminating in the contemplative experience, which is the highest state of prayer that one can hope to enter.

MORTIFICATION.

A deliberate attempt at denial or self-renunciation as a sacrifice born out of the love for God. According to the advice given by the Lord, in order to follow Him, one must take up his cross and deny himself (Lk 9:23). Mortification helps to purify the soul from impure and unnecessary attachments to worldly things, as well as to spiritual delights and consolations that hinder the soul from loving God for what He is and not for what He gives us. Many have often performed extreme acts of mortification, causing bodily and mental harm due to an overly scrupulous nature. The need for spiritual guidance in these matters is extremely important.

MYSTIC.

A person who lives the contemplative life and who strives for the divine union. The mystic is involved with many supernatural experiences through his intimate and loving encounter with the divine, and is often the recipient of the most extraordinary graces from God. He lives as if in a heightened state of consciousness, one that is other-worldly and infused with divine knowledge and wisdom. Many mystics, though not all, are eventually elevated to the status of sainthood. Some may not be officially recognized as saints because the process takes so long; some are simply misunderstood, or live hidden lives of obscurity that God alone knows.

MYSTICAL COMMUNION.

The partaking of the Holy Eucharist from a distance or in a state of spiritual ecstasy. Many mystics who have been denied the Sacred Host (or who have been physically unable to attend Mass to receive the Eucharist) have often been given this most Sacred Species directly from the hands of Christ, the Virgin Mary, one of the angels or saints in the mystical state of ecstasy. In other cases, when a priest is about to give the Sacred Host to the one receiving, the Host miraculously jumps or flies into his mouth without the aid of the priest. There have been cases where the host, after having entered the mouth of the communicant, immediately disappears into the body of that soul without having been swallowed. It becomes instantaneously consumed, and does not break down in the body until the need for this Bread of Life arises again the next day. This grace is an extraordinary one, usually reserved for God's most chosen ones who are unable to attend Mass but who need the Lord's Body to survive on a daily basis.

MYSTICAL SLEEP.

A state where the soul is at rest in the divine presence, usually in the realm of higher contemplation. Though seemingly at total rest, God is working on the soul and filling it with the goodness of His love and grace. The mystic may appear to be as if in a trance, because all the human faculties are momentarily suspended during this time of spiritual rest.

MYSTICAL THEOLOGY.

A branch of theology that deals with the extraordinary ways of perfection and the supernatural experiences of the favored soul, in contrast to **ascetical theology**, which takes up the ordinary ways of perfection. The former is concerned with God's intervention upon the soul, unusual charisms that are given for the benefit of others, and the heights of the divine union; the latter is more concerned with ordinary grace and gifts of the Spirit, virtuous practices of self-denial and penance, as well as the lower states of spirituality that involves vocal prayer and meditation. Although many consider mystical theology a branch of ascetical theology, in reality they are two very different studies. More properly, mystical theology is a special type of ascetisicm that is more perfect and of a higher nature. Anyone can practice ascetical exercises, but only God can give the soul a mystical experience or state. One involves human effort along with divine assistance, whereas the other is a pure gift from God.

MYSTICISM.
A supernatural state that cannot be achieved by human effort or will; it is a grace that is given by God alone to those souls whom He chooses to call His own. This unmerited grace involves a personal experience of God that is truly extraordinary, for it calls for the union of the soul with the divine that transcends the normal human condition.

OBSESSION.
In the spiritual sense, any excessive or unnatural preoccupation with a religious practice or thought. Sometimes induced by the devil, one can be obsessed, for example, with the need to perform severe penances or self-disciplinary practices that would only bring harm to the soul. Another tactic used by the enemy is in the area of scruples. Sometimes the enemy suggests obsessive thoughts of unworthiness, past sin and a feeling that God does not love or approve of him. If one feels a tendency towards unusual obsessive behavior in the spiritual realm, he or she ought to seek counsel with a prudent director experienced in such matters. If not, the obsessions could only intensify, bringing the soul to the brink of despair and perhaps to a loss of faith.

OPPRESSION.
In the realm of the spiritual warfare, the partial control or infiltration by the evil spirit who seeks to take over his victim, sometimes even to the point of diabolical possession. Temptations are the normal means the enemy uses to disrupt the progress of one's spiritual life and perfection; however, oppression (also known as **infiltration**) is an advanced stage whereby the evil one pursues the victim more directly through psychological and physical attacks, and sometimes through the manipulation of the natural elements or material things (such as through annoying sounds, the movement or breaking of objects, etc.). If one has encountered oppression, he or she must seek the aid of a spiritual director and/or priest, because this stage in the diabolical attack can be very dangerous to the victim who is pursued. Some have sustained terrible injuries because of these onslaughts, and the deliverance prayer of a priest and his blessing may be needed to stop these actions by the spirits of darkness.

ORDINARY WAY.
The way of the normal progression in the spiritual life, experienced by most of the faithful who seek to improve their ways and who strive for perfection. The ordinary ways of the spiritual life involve vocal prayers, meditations, limited practices of penance and mortification, devotional ex-

ercises, study, and good deeds. The ordinary graces that God gives to these souls are sufficient to live the life He has called them to in their particular states and circumstances. The extraordinary ways involve the mystical experiences of some souls who are called to a higher state, and who need supernatural grace in order to fulfill the divine plan in their lives.

PASSIVE PURGATION.

A spiritual experience whereby God himself acts upon the soul without the effort of the one who is being purified. This usually occurs after the **active purgation**, which involves the personal effort of one to rid himself of all vice, bad habits and imperfections that hinder the progress towards spiritual perfection. The passive state is painful to the soul because he can no longer dictate the ways of his purgation, nor does he always know when it will occur or for how long. Sometimes he doesn't even know what is being purged from his soul, leaving him with feelings of uncertainty and confusion. Yet the Lord must purify the soul to its very core if it ever hopes to achieve the divine union, for the stains of imperfection are unacceptable in the divine realm. In particular, Original Sin leaves the soul with blemishes that one cannot see and purge by himself; rather, he must rely on God to recognize what needs cleansing and to let Him act accordingly.

PENANCE.

Acts of mortification or prayers designed to help one eradicate the effects of his own sin. Penances can be performed in many ways, including acts of self-denial, abstinence, fasting, study, resolutions, and acts of good virtue. The act of **contrition** opens the door to effective penance, for one must start with a true sorrow in his heart for the sins that he commits. Then, through the **Sacrament of Reconciliation**, he cleanses his heart and receives the forgiveness of Christ through His Church, with the understanding that he attempt to sin no more and better his life through actions of good merit.

PERFUME.

In mystical language, the term used to describe the gift that God gives to unusually holy souls who have led exemplary lives of the highest order, and who lived and died in the state of intimate union with the divine. Sometimes referred to as an **odor of sanctity**, the gift of perfume is the heavenly fragrance that emanates from the pious soul, a sign of God's special presence and favor upon him. Many souls have been known to leave this heavenly scent behind, even after they have died. Some, while still living their earthly lives, have had this sweet scent surrounding them, according to many who were in their presence and experienced this sensation. There have even been claims from others who have smelled this perfume in a particular place where the soul had been, as if the scent had remained long after the holy person's disappearance from that location.

PHANTASM.

According to St. John of the Cross, the physical or bodily representations of an object or image, perceived through the human senses and experienced thereof. These forms can occur in the imagination, or they can be induced by the evil spirit who seeks to deceive us. All images presented to our mind or vision must be carefully discerned through a spiritual director or a prudent priest, since our minds can often play tricks on us, and the devil is so clever in deception.

POSSESSION.

In the spiritual life, the term for the total bodily control of a soul by one or many evil spirits. Although recognized throughout the history of the Church, true possession of a person is very rare, and requires a solemn **exorcism** performed by an approved priest in order to expel the demon from one's midst. More common than possession (and often mistaken as such) is the oppression by an evil spirit towards its victim (see **OPPRESSION**). Oppression is much more common and sometimes as equally dangerous. Still, let us not make light of the serious nature of authentic possession; for although it is a rare phenomenon, the Church states unequivocably that possessions can and do occur from time to time, as many a saint will attest. A truly possessed victim will usually show signs of preternatural origin: unusual human strength; foul odors; knowledge of things distant; knowledge of the most intimate details of one's past life; ability to speak in foreign languages normally not known; horrid reactions to religious objects; and an intelligence far superior to the norm. A possessed person is no one to fool around with, and requires the attention of a priest who is commissioned to perform solemn exorcisms.

PRAYER OF QUIET.

A prayerful state of elevated calm whereby the soul rests in the presence of the Lord. This prayer is experienced in the initial stages of contemplation, as the soul begins to taste the sweetness of the divine love. Some have called this experience **affective prayer**, since great consolations and spiritual delights move the person toward a more intimate relationship with the Lord. Even though it may appear that one is doing nothing in this state of quiet, it is really a blessing, for in this state God begins to infuse His love directly into the soul, thus paving the way for the pureness of the contemplative experience.

PRETERNATURAL.

That which is beyond the natural but not totally supernatural. Either God uses natural forces to create something above the norm, or the preternatural involves angelic or demonic forces, which also operate above the natural capacity. Preternatural is most commonly used in the mystical world when referring to the diabolical action in the spiritual realm. **Supernatural**, by contrast, usually refers to the intercessory actions of God himself upon the natural order of man and all creation.

PRIVATE REVELATION.

Messages, signs or impressions that are given to a soul in the state of contemplative rapture or ecstasy, usually from a heavenly apparition such as Christ, the Virgin Mary, angels or saints. Since all **public revelation** concerning the faith ended with the conclusion of the New Testament, private revelations need the discernment of proper Church authorities in order to defend the universal teachings of the Gospel message. Normally, a spiritual director discerns the revelations in question, and the diocesan bishop affirms or denies their credibility in light of the Church's teachings on morals and faith. However, since these revelations are of a private nature, the faithful are free to disbelieve in them if they choose, even if the Church proclaims them to be credible. This is because the nature of all private revelation — even if intended for the universal Church — is based upon **human faith**, and not **divine**. Individual pious souls, though sincere in their intentions, can often err in understanding, hearing or interpreting authentic messages, so great prudence is essential in the discernment process of private revelations. Part of the reason for this caution is because the evil one is often behind some of these revelations and visions, and cleverly works to deceive the minds and hearts of the faithful.

PROFICIENTS.

A term that describes those in the spiritual life who have advanced beyond the **way of beginners**, and who are striving toward the way of the **perfect state**, which is the divine union. Beginners for the most part tend to limit their prayer lives to vocal prayers and discursive meditations, acts of penance and self-denials and pious devotional practices. The proficients have entered the more advanced stages of prayer, including the prayer of quiet and elementary stages of authentic contemplative experience. Often they are purified of their imperfections and vices through a passive state whereby God works in their soul without the active efforts on their own part, thus preparing them for the higher state of divine union.

REPARATION.

It is the act of restoring what has gone wrong, of making up for the distance one has placed between himself and God through his own offenses. When one voluntarily satisfies for the wrongdoings of others in order to appease the divine justice due to them, the reparation is **vicarious**.

SELF-DENIAL.

In the spiritual sense, a sacrificial attitude where one denies all earthly pleasures and pursues the kingdom of God through sacrifice and the submission to the divine will. Self-denial strengthens character, seeks spiritual perfection and imitates the life of Christ, who denied himself in order to serve others.

SPIRITUAL DIRECTION.

The voluntary effort on the part of the soul to seek wisdom and counsel in all things pertaining to the spiritual realm, in order to progress in the spiritual life and to protect himself from error and delusion. The director must be one who is qualified and capable of leading the soul by means of his education, experience and personal sanctity.

SPOUSE.

A figurative term that refers to a beloved soul of Christ, who by way of the divine union becomes one with Him. This union often leads to the mystical marriage of the Groom with the Spouse (also known as the **Bride of Christ**), whereby the two are joined together in the heavenly espousal that seals the soul in the bosom of the divine love.

STIGMATA.
The Sacred Wounds that the Lord imprints interiorly or exteriorly upon a chosen soul who is called to participate in the Passion and Crucifixion of Christ, thus contributing to the plan of redemption and salvation of the world. Stigmata usually refers to the Five Wounds of Christ: the wound of the heart, the two hand wounds and the two wounds of the feet. However, many victim souls have received only one of these wounds (known as a **stigma**), while others have had several wounds that Christ received during the agony of His Passion: a crown of thorns, the marks of the scourging, the shedding of tears of blood, etc. When these wounds are felt but not seen, they are known as the **invisible stigmata**; when they manifest themselves outwardly on the body of the victim, they are called **exterior stigmata** (or just the stigmata, for the exterior wounds are what most associate with this extraordinary grace). Normally the soul must offer himself up voluntarily to God in order to make atonement, reparation or expiation for sinners of the world; furthermore, the stigmata is usually not granted unless the soul has had a profound devotion to the Passion of our Lord, and has led a life of extraordinary piety and holiness. Nevertheless, the stigmata is never a grace attained through the personal efforts or desires of the victim alone; it is a pure gift from God, given to those according to His divine will.

STIGMATIST.
Also known as a **stigmatic**, a chosen soul who bears the Sacred Wounds of our Lord in his body and soul in order to help in the plan of redemption for the world. Exterior wounds of the stigmatist are signs for the world of Christ's presence and mercy among us; if the wounds are invisible, then the victim is called to a silent life of sacrificial reparation for sinners whose transgressions must be atoned for through the trials and sufferings they are called to bear in union with the Crucified Christ. It matters not whether the stigmatist has visible or invisible wounds; the mission and the value of their redemptive suffering is all the same. Some who have received the visible wounds prayed that they might be concealed in order to preserve their humility. Christ has often granted their request with this intention in mind. Let us not assume that the invisible stigmata are any less real or painful than those that are visible! They are just as real and every bit as painful.

SUPERNATURAL.
The order of reality that pertains to the divinity and all that is above the natural order; also, a term referring to the spiritual world, including the angelic and demonic (see **PRETERNATURAL**).

SUPERNATURAL ILLNESS.
In the mystical world, those bodily and spiritual afflictions that come from the hand of the Lord. These illnesses are not of a natural order, as they often baffle the world of science and medicine because they go against the laws of nature and offer no reasonable explanation or cure. In fact, most supernatural illnesses cannot be treated or cured by any known means, and the victim is called to patiently bear whatever the Lord has deemed to send him. Normally, a chosen soul receives these extraordinary illnesses as a type of reparative suffering for the sins of the world, especially if they are called

to a life of a sacrificial victim. Whenever the illness seems certain to cause death to the victim, God intervenes to provide him with the strength necessary to carry his burdens.

SUSPENSION.

In the mystical sense, this term is usually referring to the **suspension of faculties**, whereby the person abandons the use of the five senses in order to allow the Lord to communicate His loving presence to the soul in a total spiritual way. This suspension occurs during the states of ecstasy and rapture, causing the soul to experience God in a way that the normal human faculties cannot comprehend.

TEMPTATION.

A person can be subjected to temptation in three different ways: from the world, the devil or his own human weakness. The spiritual life encounters all three means, although the temptations from the enemy are usually the most pronounced in the soul who has achieved a high state of spiritual perfection.

TRANSPORTATION.

The mystical term that refers to the movement of the soul and/or body to another place as a result of an ecstatic state that carries the person beyond his present location. Similar to **bilocation**, transportation occurs only during the heights of divine rapture.

TRANSVERBERATION.

A type of mystical wound of the soul that pierces the depths of one's being, bringing about a spiritual delight through the experience of God's loving presence. Transverberation of the heart refers to that wound caused by the arrow of the seraphim, a result of the fire of divine love that inflames the soul and unites it to the heavenly Spouse.

UNITIVE WAY.

The highest state of the mystical life where the soul is united with the divine; also known as the **divine union**. This state normally follows that of the way of beginners and the state of proficients.

VICTIM.

A chosen soul who is called to a life of reparative suffering. The victim voluntarily sacrifices himself for the salvation of sinners in an effort to atone for their transgressions against God. Because he has willingly offered himself up for this purpose, God uses this offering to satisfy for the just punishment due the sins of others, sometimes causing him to suffer intensely the pains due to another's transgressions.

VISION.

A revelation of a mystery of God to an individual. Visions can be **imaginative**, **intellectual** or **physical**, and sometimes occur as heavenly apparitions to the one who experiences them. Visions that are claimed must be authenticated by the proper authorities of the Church, for self-delusion and diabolical influence can cause false visions to occur and mislead the faithful.

VOCAL PRAYER.

The prayer of beginners that involves words that are spoken out loud to God, sometimes privately, and oftentimes in a group setting. There are four vocal prayers that have been traditionally used in the Church: adoration, thanksgiving, contrition and petition. All vocal prayers are a result of human effort, and often involve intensive states of meditation. As one advances in the spiritual life and learns to simply gaze at the Divine or rest in His presence, then the stillness can lead to a true contemplative experience that is the way of proficients and those of the unitive way. It is in this still silence that one learns to hear the voice of God and to draw infinitely closer to His loving Word.

WAY OF PERFECTION.

The spiritual course that sets one on the path to a deepened relationship with God. The way of perfection involves the practice of the virtues, elimination of vices and the desire to unite one's self with the divine. The progressive stages along this way involve the state of beginners, followed by the state of proficients and ending in the divine union.

WOUNDS OF LOVE.

Bodily or spiritual wounds that result from the supernatural love that inflicts the soul. Sometimes these wounds are like flames of fire that pierce the victim, leaving a permanent pain which, paradoxically, causes both extreme suffering and ecstatic joy. In some cases, these divine strokes of love will leave a visible wound on the body, but only as a result of the soul being wounded first.

Bibliography

Church Sources: Abbreviations and Bibliography

The Second Vatican Council: Documents of Vatican II

VCII Abbott, Walter M., S.J., gen. ed. *The Documents of Vatican II* (Guild Press, America Press, Association Press, 1966).

VCII Flannery, Austin, O.P., gen. ed. *Vatican Council II: The Vatican Collection*, II Volumes, Revised Edition (Liturgical Press, Collegeville, MN, 1984 reprint).

Abbreviations for **Vatican Council II**:

AA	*Decree on the Apostolate of the Laity*: **Apostolicam actuositatem**.
AGD	*Decree on the Church's Missionary Activity*: **Ad gentes divinitus**.
CD	*Decree on the Bishop's Pastoral Office in the Church*: **Christus Dominus**.
DH	*Declaration of Religious Freedom*: **Dignitatis humanae**.
DV	*Dogmatic Constitution on Divine Revelation*: **Dei verbum**.
GE	*Declaration on Christian Education*: **Gravissimum educationis**.
GS	*Pastoral Constitution on the Church in the Modern World*: **Gaudium et spes**.
IM	*Decree on the Instruments of Social Communication*: **Inter mirifica**.
LG	*Dogmatic Constitution on the Church*: **Lumen gentium**.
NA	*Declaration on the Relationship of the Church to Non-Christian Religious*: **Nostra aetate**.
OE	*Decree on Eastern Catholic Churches*: **Orientalium ecclesiarum**.
OT	*Decree on Priestly Formation*: **Optatum totius**.
PC	*Decree on the Appropriate Renewal of the Religious Life*: **Perfectae caritatis**.
PO	*Decree on the Ministry and Life of Priests*: **Presbyterorum ordinis**.
SC	*Constitution on the Sacred Liturgy*: **Sacrosanctum concilium**.
UR	*Decree on Ecumenism*: **Unitatis redintegratio**.

Sacred Congregations and Departments of the Vatican

PCISC	Pontifical Council for the Instruments of Social Communication.

SCC	Sacred Congregation for the Clergy.
SCCE	Sacred Congregation for Catholic Education.
SCDF	Sacred Congregation for the Doctrine of the Faith.
SCDS	Sacred Congregation for the Discipline of the Sacraments.
SCDW	Sacred Congregation for Divine Worship.
SCEP	Sacred Congregation for the Evangelization of Peoples.
SCR	Sacred Congregation of Rites.
SCRSI	Sacred Congregation for Religious and Secular Institutes.
SCSDW	Sacred Congregation for the Sacraments and Divine Worship.
SPUC	Secretariat for the Promotion of the Unity of Christians.
SU	Secretariat for Unbelievers.

General Bibliography

Alessandro of Ripabottoni and Melchiorre of Pobladura, ed. of Italian version; Fr. Gerardo Di Flumeri, O.F.M. Cap., ed. of English version; Mary F. Ingolsby, transl., *Epistolario: The Letters of Padre Pio, Vol. I* (The Voice of Padre Pio, San Giovanni Rotondo, Italy, 1980).

Alessandro of Ripabottoni and Melchiorre of Pobladura, ed. of English version; Mary F. Ingolsby, transl., *Letters of Padre Pio, Volume II: Correspondence with Raffaelina Cerase, Noblewoman* (Our Lady of Grace Friary, San Giovanni Rotondo, Italy, 1987).

Alessandro of Ripabottoni; Fr. Alessio Parente, O.F.M. Cap., ed., *Padre Pio of Pietrelcina: Everybody's Cyrenean* (Our Lady of Grace Friary, San Giovanni Rotondo, Italy, 1987).

Alphonsus, Sister Mary, O.SS.R., *St. Rose of Lima* (TAN Books and Publishers, Inc., Rockford, Ill., 1982; original copyright by B. Herder Book Co., St. Louis, Mo., 1968).

Anderson, Bernard W., *Understanding the Old Testament* (Prentice-Hall, Inc., Englewood Cliffs, N.J., 1957).

Arintero, Father John G., O.P.; transl. by Fr. Jordan Aumann, O.P., *The Mystical Evolution in the Development and Vitality of the Church: Volumes I and II* (TAN Books and Publishers, Inc. Rockford, Ill., 1978; original copyright by B. Herder Book Co., 1949).

Armstrong, Regis J., O.F.M. Cap. and Ignatius C. Brady, O.F.M., transl., *Francis and Clare: The Complete Works* (Paulist Press, Ramsey, N.J.; copyright by the Society of St. Paul the Apostle, N.Y., 1982).

Arnoudt, Rev. Peter J., S.J., *The Imitation of the Sacred Heart of Jesus* (TAN Books and Publishers, Inc., Rockford, Ill., 1982; original copyright by Benziger Brothers, N.Y., 1904).

Balthasar, Hans Urs Von; transl. by Antje Lawry and Sr. Sergia Englund, O.C.D., *First Glance at Adrienne Von Speyr* (Ignatius Press, San Francisco, Calif., 1981; original copyright by Johannes Verlag, Einsiedeln, 1968).

Barbet, Pierre, M.D.; the Earl of Wicklow, transl., *A Doctor at Calvary* (Image Books, Doubleday & Company, Inc., Garden City, N.Y., 1963; first published by Dillon & Cie, Editeurs, Indre, France, 1950).

Biot, Rene; P.J. Hepburne-Scott, transl., *The Enigma of the Stigmata*

(Twentieth Century Encyclopedia of Catholicism; Hawthorn Books, Inc., N.Y., 1962).

Boyer, Rev. O.A., S.T.L., *She Wears a Crown of Thorns* (Rev. O.A. Boyer, S.T.L., Mendham, N.Y., 1958).

Broderick, Robert C., *The Catholic Encyclopedia* (Thomas Nelson Publishers, Inc., Nashville, Tenn., 1976).

Broek, Rev. Silvere Van Den, O.F.M., ed., *The Spiritual Legacy of Sister Mary of the Holy Trinity* (TAN Books and Publishers, Inc., Rockford, Ill., 1981; original copyright by Impremerie St. Francois, Malines, Belgium, 1950; recopyright, 1981).

Brown, Beverly H., Raphael Brown, transl., *The Little Flowers of St. Francis* (Image Books, Doubleday & Co., Inc., Garden City, N.Y., 1958).

Carty, Fr. Charles M. and Rev. Patrick O'Connell, B.D., *The Holy Shroud and Four Visions* (Radio Replies Press, Inc., St. Paul, Minn.; reprint by TAN Books and Publishers, Inc., Rockford, Ill., 1974).

Carty, Fr. Charles M., *The Stigmata and Modern Science* (Radio Replies Press, Inc., St. Paul, Minn.; reprint by TAN Books and Publishers, Inc., Rockford, Ill., 1974).

Catherine of Genoa, St.; Serge Hughes, transl., *Catherine of Genoa: The Spiritual Dialogue* (Paulist Press, Ramsey, N.J.; copyright by The Missionary Society of St. Paul the Apostle , N.Y., 1979).

Chinigo, Michael, ed. with assistance of the Vatican Archives, *The Pope Speaks* (Pantheon Books, Inc., N.Y., 1957).

Cruz, Joan Carroll, *The Incorruptibles* (TAN Books and Publishers, Inc., Rockford, Ill., 1977).

Cruz, Joan Carroll, *Relics* (Our Sunday Visitor, Inc., Huntington, Ind., 1984).

D'Apolito, Fr. Alberto, *Padre Pio of Pietrelcina: Memories, Experiences, Testimonials* (Our Lady of Grace Friary, San Giovanni Rotondo, Italy, 1978; reprint, 1986).

De Sales, St. Francis; transl. by Rt. Rev. John K. Ryan, *Treatise on the Love of God: Volumes I and II* (TAN Books and Publishers, Inc., Rockford, Ill., 1975; original copyright by Doubleday and Co., Inc., Garden City, N.Y., 1963).

Di Flumeri, Fr. Gerardo, O.F.M. Cap.; transl. by Florence Di Marco, *The Mystery of the Cross in Padre Pio of Pietrelcina* (Our Lady of Grace Friary, San Giovanni Rotondo, Italy, 1983).

Delaporte, Fr., *The Devil: Does He Exist and What Does He Do?* (TAN Books and Publishers, Inc., Rockford, Ill., 1982; originally published in England in 1871; reprinted in 1978 by Marian Publications, South Bend, Ind., and in 1980 by Mater Dei Publications, Inc., Arcadia, CA).

Emmerich, Anne Catherine, *The Dolorous Passion of Our Lord Jesus Christ* (TAN Books and Publishers, Inc., Rockford, Ill., 1983; original publication by The Christian Book Club of America, Hawthorne, Calif., 1968).

Flumeri, Fr. Gerardo Di, O.F.M. Cap., *Padre Pio of Pietrelcina: Acts of the First Congress of Studies on Padre Pio's Spirituality* (San Giovanni Rotondo, Foggia, Italy, 1973; reprint and transl. into English by Miss Mary Brink, 1978).

Gertrude, St., *The Life and Revelations of St. Gertrude* (Christian Classics, Inc., Westminster, Md., 1983; original publication in England, 1862; reprinted by Newman Press, Westminster, Md., 1949).

Glenn, Msgr. Paul, *A Tour of the Summa* (TAN Books and Publishers,

Inc., Rockford, Ill., 1978; original copyright by B. Herder Book Co., 1960).

Groenings, Fr. James, S.J., *The Passion of Jesus and Its Hidden Meaning* (TAN Books and Publishers, Inc., Rockford, Ill., 1987; original copyright by Joseph Gummersbach, 1900).

Heller, Dr. John H., *Report on the Shroud of Turin* (Houghton Mifflin Company, Boston, Mass., 1983).

Herbst, Fr. Clarence A., S.J., transl., *Jesus Reveals His Heart: Letters of Saint Margaret Mary Alacoque* (St. Paul Editions, Boston, Mass.; copyright by the Daughters of St. Paul, 1980).

Huysmans, J.K., transl. by Agnes Hastings, *Saint Lydwine of Schiedam* (TAN Books and Publishers, Inc., Rockford, Ill., 1979; original publication by Kegan Paul, Trench, Trubner & Co., Ltd., London, 1923).

Johnston, William, ed., *The Cloud of Unknowing* (Image Books, Doubleday & Co., Inc., N.Y., 1973).

Jörgensen, Johannes; transl. by T. O'Connor Sloane, Ph.D., LL.D., *St. Francis of Assisi* (Image Books, Doubleday & Co., Inc., Garden City, N.Y., 1955; original copyright by Longmans, Green & Co., Inc., 1912.

Kavanaugh, Kieran, O.C.D. and Otilio Rodriguez, O.C.D., transl., *The Collected Works of St. John of the Cross* (Institute of Carmelite Studies, Washington, D.C., 1979).

Kavanaugh, Kieran, O.C.D. and Otilio Rodriguez, O.C.D., transl., *The Collected Works of St. Teresa of Avila: Volumes One and Two* (Institute of Carmelite Studies, Washington, D.C., 1976 and 1980).

Louis of Granada, Venerable O.P.; transl. by Fr. Jordan Aumann, O.P., *Summa of the Christian Life: Volume 3* (TAN Books and Publishers, Inc., Rockford, Ill., 1979; original copyright by B. Herder Book Co., St. Louis, Mo., 1958).

Liguori, St. Alphonsus; Rev. Eugene Grimm, ed., *The Passion and the Death of Jesus Christ* (Redemptorist Fathers, Brooklyn, N.Y.; copyright by the Very Rev. James Barron, C.SS.R., 1927).

Maloney, Fr. George A., S.J., *Prayer of the Heart* (Ave Maria Press, Notre Dame, Ind., 1981; reprint, 1983).

Manelli, Fr. Stefano , O.F.M. Conv., S.T.D., *Jesus Our Eucharistic Love* (Our Blessed Lady of Victory Mission, Brookings, S.D., 1982).

Menendez, Sister Josefa, *The Way of Divine Love* (TAN Books and Publishers, Inc., Rockford, Ill., 1981; originally copyrighted in 1949 by Sands & Co., Ltd., London, England).

Merton, Thomas, *The Ascent to Truth* (Harvest-HBJ, San Diego, New York, and London, 1981; original copyright by the Abbey of Our Lady of Gesthemani, 1951; renewed copyright by The Trustees of the Merton Legacy Trust, 1979).

Nageleisen, Rev. John A., *Charity for the Suffering Souls: An Explanation of the Catholic Doctrine of Purgatory* (TAN Books and Publishers, Inc., Rockford, Ill., 1982; earlier copyright by Mater Dei Publications, Inc., 1977).

O'Connell, Fr. Patrick, B.D., transl., *The Love and Service of God, Infinite Love* (TAN Books and Publishers, Inc., Rockford, Ill., 1987; original publication by the Irish Members of the Priests' Universal Union of the Friends of the Sacred Heart, John English & Co., Ltd., Wexford, England, 1950).

Parente, Fr. Alessio, O.F.M. Cap., *Send Me Your Guardian Angel: Padre Pio* (Our Lady of Grace Friary, San Giovanni Rotondo, Italy, 1984).

Parente, Fr. Pascal P., S.T.D., Ph.D., J.C.B., *Beyond Space: A Book About the Angels* (TAN Books and Publishers, Inc., Rockford, Ill., 1973; original copyright by the Society of St. Paul, N.Y., 1961).

Peyret, Rev. Raymond, *Marthe Robin: The Cross and the Joy* (Alba House, N.Y.; copyright by the Society of St. Paul, 1983).

Pio, Padre, O.F.M. Cap., *The Agony of Jesus* (TAN Books and Publishers, Inc., Rockford, Ill., 1981; original publication by Radio Reply Press, Inc., St. Paul, Minn.).

Reinhold, H.A., ed.; Pseudo-Dionysius, *Mystical Theology* (Image Books, Doubleday & Co., Inc., N.Y., 1973).

St. Michael and the Angels; compiled from approved sources (TAN Books and Publishers, Inc., Rockford, Ill., 1983; original copyright by Marian Publications, South Bend, Ind., 1977).

Schmöger, Very Rev. Carl E., C.SS.R., *The Life of Anne Catherine Emmerich, Vol. I* (TAN Books and Publishers, Inc., Rockford, Ill., 1976; reprinted from the 1968 edition of Maria Regina Guild, Los Angeles, Calif., itself a reprint of the English edition of 1885).

Schouppe, Fr. F.X., S.J., *Purgatory: Explained by the Lives and Legends of the Saints* (TAN Books and Publishers, Inc., Rockford, Ill., 1986; originally published by Burns & Oates, Ltd., London, England, 1893; reprinted by Burns, Oates, & Washbourne Ltd. in 1926).

Steiner, Johannes, *The Visions of Therese Neumann* (Alba House, N.Y., 1976; copyright by the Society of St. Paul, Staten Island, N.Y., 1976).

Steiner, Johannes, *Therese Neumann: A Portrait* (Alba House, N.Y., 1967; copyright by the Society of St. Paul, Staten Island, N.Y., 1967).

Stevensen, Kenneth E. and Gary R. Habermas, *Verdict on the Shroud* (Servant Books, Ann Arbor, Mich., 1981).

Thorold, Algar, transl., *The Dialogue of Saint Catherine of Siena* (TAN Books and Publishers, Inc., Rockford, Ill., 1974; original copyright by Kegan Paul, Trench, Trubner & Co., Ltd., London, 1907).

Tribbe, Frank C., *Portrait of Jesus?* (Stein and Day, Briar Cliff, N.Y.; copyright by Frank C. Tribbe, 1983).

Trochu, Abbe Francis, *The Cure D'Ars: St. Jean-Marie-Baptiste Vianney* (TAN Books and Publishers, Inc., Rockford, Ill., 1977; originally published by Burns Oates & Washbourne, London, 1927).

Vogl, Albert, *Therese Neumann: Mystic and Stigmatist* (TAN Books and Publishers, Inc., Rockford, Ill., 1987).

Wilson, Ian, *The Shroud of Turin: The Burial Cloth of Jesus Christ?* (Image Books, Doubleday & Company, Inc., 1979).

Topical Index

Abandonment: by God, 108, 117-118, 260, 306-307, self, 109, 133, 302; to divine providence, 126, 178, 203, 260, 285

Abstinence: fasting and, 108, 114, 185, 186, 275, 316

Abyss: 303

Adoration: of God, 96-97, 111, 278, 309, 321

Advocate: devil's, 14, 288

Affection: prayer of, 91, 94, 99, 101-103, 304

Affliction: bodily, 16-17, 151-153, 184, 198, 272, 302; spiritual, 16, 184, 196, 302, 319

Angels: Michael and his, 50, 53, 75, 113, 127, 132, 162, 216; fallen, 39, 127-128, 130-131, 136-137; guardian, 137-138, 161-162, 163-166, 270, 273, 284; heavenly, 127, 136-137, 140, 145, 150, 160, 163, 166, 167, 173, 174, 179, 185, 194-195, 260, 262, 279, 282, 305

Anger: imperfections of, 48, 112

Apophaticism: mystical, 121

Apparitions: visions and, 35, 144-145, 159-160, 167, 281; bodily, 302, 309, 320; phenomena known as, 34-35, 144, 159, 160, 302, 320; diabolical, 159-160, 162-164, 295, 302, 320; heavenly, 160, 258, 320; angelic, 145, 150, 160, 162-164; of the Lord, 145, 164, 167-169; of the Blessed Virgin, 34-35, 145, 164, 295, 302; of the saints, 145, 164, 167, 285, 302; of poor souls, 258

Appetites: sensual, 105, 107, 115-116, 302, 303

Arrow: divine, 16, 154, 194-95, 303, 320

Asceticism: 303-04, 314

Aspiration: 101, 193, 304

Atonement: 9, 12, 29, 58-60, 62, 63, 66, 68-70, 71, 74-75, 161, 176, 208, 262, 264, 270, 272, 289, 304, 310

Attack: psychological, 122, 127, 132-133, 135, 137-138, 140, 284; physical, 87, 122, 132-133, 137-138, 139-140, 171, 195, 284, 296; diabolical, 17, 63, 105, 107, 122, 128, 132-133, 135-141, 161, 166, 171, 260, 267, 273, 279, 284, 295-296

Avarice: spiritual, 111

Beatification: 6, 9, 90, 122, 135, 166, 182, 189, 261, 268, 274, 277, 280-281, 284, 287-288, 290, 291, 292, 300, 301

Beauty: unearthly, 67; heavenly, 104, 127, 155; restored, 188-189

Beginners: way of, 39, 103, 110-113, 117, 159, 318, 320; prayer of, 96-97, 102, 107, 318, 320

Bilocation: as flight phenomenon, 155-157, 188, 266, 304, 320; gift of, 157-158, 199, 216, 281, 284, 295, 304

Body: glorified, 50, 191; resurrected, 62, 180-181, 191; heavenly, 191; spiritual, 119, 155-156; 160, 191; unusual phenomena, 188-191, 212-213, 225-226, 230-231, 259-262, 264, 280, 284

Body of Christ: the faithful as, 40, 54, 69, 72, 79, 83, 175, 201, 203, 288; the mystical, 8, 27, 34, 54, 56, 72, 75, 86, 201, 203, 208; the Eucharist as, 62, 86, 125, 172-173, 174-175; share in the, 12, 25, 39-40, 68-69, 72-73, 74-75, 79, 83, 84, 175, 186

Bondage: spiritual, 45, 133, 182, 311

Bride: of Christ, 61, 71, 96, 102, 195, 206, 304, 310, 318; mystical, 61, 96, 106, 192, 195, 201, 202-206, 304, 310; Groom and the, 61, 104, 106, 192, 195, 202-206, 304, 310

Canonization: 14, 167, 182, 189, 256, 259, 261, 265, 268-269, 273, 280, 288-289

Charity: act of, 25, 30-31, 46-47, 53-54, 56-57, 68, 71, 77, 81, 109, 113, 121, 142, 175, 178, 180, 195, 269, 292

Charism: extraordinary, 13, 89, 106, 145, 157-158, 175-176, 178-179, 181, 208, 305; mystical, 89, 175-176, 189, 203; gifts and, 106, 175-176, 178-179, 189, 305

Charismatic: modern-day, 111; experience, 111-112

Chastisement: the Lord's, 16, 17, 57-58, 69, 70, 74, 114; warning of, 20, 70; the coming of, 70

Christ: as victim, 26, 48-50, 60-62, 71-72, 146, 169-170, 208; sufferings of, 12, 21, 26, 28-29, 39-40, 48-50,

327

330

192-193, 203-204, 309-310, 318
Guardian angels: 160, 163-166, 270, 273, 284

Healing: miraculous, 17, 36, 180-182, 196, 210, 284; gift of, 182, 196, 217
Heart: wound of the, 33, 70, 114, 150, 152, 154-155, 168, 170-171, 183, 188, 190, 193-194, 200, 211, 227, 257, 264, 266, 268, 270, 275, 278, 281, 296, 303, 309; conversion of, 12, 20, 22, 30, 36, 50, 56, 70, 82, 116; Sacred, 30, 50, 51, 57, 70, 71, 75, 100-101, 137, 154, 169, 192, 194, 214, 257, 267-268, 273, 277, 309; exchange of, 106, 214, 309; purity of, 18, 22, 46, 57, 75, 76, 81, 87, 89, 108, 110, 116, 119, 121, 123, 201, 203, 290; humility of the, 18, 25, 31, 44, 46, 55-56, 80, 93, 96, 115, 120, 123, 143-144, 290; prayer of the, 23, 64, 82, 102, 121, 309; reading of the, 80, 101, 175, 178, 217
Heaven: Hell and, 53, 63, 132, 271, 274, 277; Purgatory, 63, 118, 160, 260, 271, 274, 277
Heights: mystical, 89-90, 102-103, 117, 145, 147, 153, 159, 206, 257, 265, 272; spiritual, 89-90, 96, 106, 149, 153, 159, 176, 262
Hell: Purgatory and, 52-53, 63, 114, 116, 135-136, 161, 271, 274, 277
Hierognosis: the gift of, 178, 310; blessed objects and, 178, 310; discernment and, 178, 275, 310
Holy objects: blessed, 136, 178-179, 270
Humility: road to, 13, 15, 16, 18, 22, 27, 30, 46, 49, 55, 71, 106, 109-114, 117, 121, 123, 160, 197, 219-220, 225, 282, 290, 291, 296, 298

Illness: supernatural, 319-320
Illumination: way of, 141-144, 257; the divine will and, 142; divine, 142, 144; experience of, 141, 143-144, 159; knowledge of God and, 141-142,
Illusion: 310-311
Imperfections: sensual, 16, 105, 107, 110-113, 117; bodily, 16, 107, 108; stains of, 16, 18-19, 48, 105, 108, 110, 114, 116, 116-117, 144, 147, 302, 307, 316, 318
Impression: of the stigmata, 167, 169, 172, 193-194, 198, 216, 225
Impulse: divine, 91, 99, 142, 145-146, 154, 196
Impurity: state of, 77, 105, 161

Incorruptibility: 188, 188-190, 259, 261, 262, 263, 265, 268, 291
Indulgence: the Church and, 100, 173
Inedia: 217, 271, 277, 281, 284, 311
Infestation: diabolical operation, 132, 311
Infiltration: diabolical, 311, 315
Infused contemplation: 101, 121, 142, 317
Infused knowledge: 139, 142, 155, 206, 312
Iniquity: mystery of, 127
Interior life: 312
Invisible stigmata: visible stigmata and, 11, 71, 149, 197-198, 312, 319; sufferings of, 32-33, 197-198, 278, 282-283, 312; Catherine of Siena and, 190, 198, 258; Padre Pio and, 148-149, 184, 197-198, 283; Gemma Galgani and, 196, 272; Osanna of Mantua and, 198; Faustina Kowalska and, 276-277; Catherine of Genoa and, 198; Margaret Mary Alacoque and, 267-268; Berthe Petit and, 278; Alexandrina da Costa, 151, 279; St. Mary Francis of the Five Wounds, 174; Anne Catherine Emmerich, 270; Mary Rose Ferron, 275; Adrienne Von Speyr, 282
Invocation: 101

Judgment: divine, 21, 34-35, 47, 53; God's, 13, 48, 52, 54, 113
Justice, divine, 12, 15, 18, 21-22, 32, 36-37, 63, 69-70, 71, 74, 104, 116, 162, 304

Kardiognosis: reading of the heart, 175-176, 271; the gift of, 175-176, 177-178, 312
Kiss: of love, 191-192
Knowledge: human, 13, 76, 118-120, 121, 230-231; speculative, 67, 94; conceptual, 118-120; of God, 22, 57, 91, 93, 118-120, 142, 143-144; supernatural, 67, 91, 94, 121, 129, 142, 146, 176, 206, 273; affective, 121; divine, 13, 92, 121, 142, 206, 312

Levitation: as a flight phenomenon, 155-156, 313; of the body, 155-156, 258, 312-313
Life: mystical, 9, 10, 37, 39, 54, 56, 90-91, 94-96, 102, 106, 107, 125, 145, 147, 156, 159, 207, 265-266, 271, 274-276, 320; contemplative, 91, 95, 101-103, 106, 107; secular, 312

Locutions: visions and, 156, 312; God's, 159

Love: divine, 8,12, 16, 19, 22, 23, 29, 36, 38, 45, 48, 57, 59, 61, 64, 73-74, 76, 78, 80, 83, 87-93, 94-96, 98, 100-102, 118, 121, 124, 126, 133-134, 142, 143-145, 150, 152-153, 154, 167, 190, 191-192, 194, 195, 201, 203-207, 220, 224, 229, 265-266, 270, 273, 274, 276-277, 302, 303, 308, 313, 314, 318, 320, 321; of neighbor, 19, 23, 26,27, 29, 30, 41, 46-47, 49, 56, 68, 71, 73, 77-78, 82, 93, 96, 169, 196, 198, 220, 261, 313; victim of, 26,28, 32, 40-41, 48, 60, 65-66, 70-71, 72-74, 82, 86, 88, 94, 96-98, 124, 144, 168, 171, 187, 196; sacrificial, 17, 18, 22, 26, 54, 62, 65, 68-69, 70-71, 76, 79-80, 84-85, 89, 93, 96, 100, 144, 152, 168, 172, 259; wounds of, 33, 125, 145, 148, 168, 193, 195-196, 197

Lucifer: 309

Lust: 76, 78, 111, 129

Marks: of the stigmata, 11, 41, 93, 147, 150, 171, 188, 195, 198, 199-200, 212, 216, 221, 223, 224, 226, 266, 270, 272, 274, 275, 280-281

Marriage: spiritual, 61, 106, 107, 145, 202-203, 258, 264, 304, 308, 309; mystical; 106, 201, 203, 206-207, 308, 318

Martyr: voluntary, 28, 49, 86-87, 123, 161, 313

Martyrdom: 28, 49, 86-87, 123, 161, 313

Mediatrix: Mary as, 31, 34, 37, 172

Medicine: the stigmata and, 13, 185, 208-220

Meditation: meaning of, 96, 98-99, 101, 102, 303, 313; the basis for, 96, 99, 102, 107, 118, 313; methods of, 98-99, 101, 172, 303, 313, 321; on the Passion, 34, 100-101, 122, 264, 267, 313; discursive, 98-99, 102, 142, 313, 318

Mercy: divine, 31, 58, 69, 71, 88, 96, 178, 276; of God, 8, 11, 12, 16, 17, 18, 21, 25, 36, 39-41, 45, 51-52, 61-62, 69, 80, 86, 88, 97, 101, 105, 107, 196, 273

Metanoia: 36

Miracle: authenticated, 13-14, 181-182, 185, 189, 270

Mortification: bodily, 75, 105, 107, 108, 114, 116-117, 314; of the senses, 105, 107-108, 116, 314; acts of, 75,

105, 107, 111, 114, 116-117, 259, 264, 302; types of, 314; necessity for, 118, 314

Mystic: the Blessed Sacrament and, 125, 172-175, 314-315

Mystical: life, 8, 9, 10, 39, 54, 56, 90-91, 94-96, 102, 106, 107, 125, 145, 147, 156, 159, 207, 265-266, 271, 274-276, 320; prayer, 94-95, 98, 157; contemplation, 91, 95-06, 99, 103, 314; journey, 37, 39, 95-96, 110, 121, 141, 145, 207, 265, 314; illness, 185, 263; communion, 314; sleep, 314

Mystical theology: experience of, 59-60, 91, 92, 106, 118, 314-315; speculative theology and, 94; love and, 94-95; ascetical theology and, 314-315

Mysticism: role of, 37, 54, 59-60, 94, 303, 314; meaning of, 16, 89-91, 92-99

Night: darkness of, 15-17, 37-38, 102, 105, 106-107, 117-118, 120-122, 123, 125-127, 141, 144, 177, 191, 216, 258, 260, 265, 273, 276

Obsession: external, 133, 182, 315

Offerings: sacrificial, 22, 25, 26, 28-29, 40, 57, 59-60, 62-63, 64, 65-66, 68, 72-73, 74, 78, 84, 87, 89, 97, 140, 148, 161, 183, 208, 310

Oppression: diabolical, 126, 133, 141, 182, 216, 315, 317

Order: supernatural, 31, 55, 92, 127, 145, 161, 180, 184, 189, 213; natural, 208, 217; Religious, 200, 256, 258, 261, 262-264, 265-266, 267, 268, 269, 270, 283, 285

Ordinary way: of perfection, 57, 67, 75, 82, 146, 153, 207, 314-315

Original Sin: 18, 30, 32, 44, 52, 108, 130, 316

Passion: our Lord's, 27-28, 29, 31, 41, 59, 61-63, 66-67, 87, 93, 99-101, 126, 198, 227-232, 267; share in Christ's, 11-12, 27-28, 32-34, 37, 39-41, 58, 62, 67, 71-72, 74, 93, 101, 124-126, 150-152, 157, 170-172, 184, 190, 196-197, 198, 208, 215-216, 221, 224, 260-261, 262, 264, 265, 267, 269, 270-271, 274, 276-277, 278-280, 281, 282, 286; devotion to His, 61-63, 99-101, 125, 152, 155, 225, 264, 266, 268-269, 273, 275, 284; visions of, 167, 170, 191, 271, 293

Transport: mystical, 153-154, 156, 161, 173, 174, 193, 320

Transportation: mystical, 156, 320

Transverberation: of the heart, 168, 193-196, 264, 320; and the Seraph's assault, 168, 193-196, 320

Trials: of life, 15-17, 21, 23, 25, 38-40, 45, 48, 50, 54, 57, 69, 72, 75, 78, 80, 86, 88-89, 97, 106, 265, 302, 306; greatest of, 15, 38, 50, 66, 75, 91, 122, 124-127, 133, 135, 144, 166, 184, 276, 280, 306, 307

Tribulations: of life, 17, 18, 23, 48, 54, 57, 72, 86, 89, 91, 97, 122, 144, 183

Union: divine, 16, 19, 29, 37, 38, 49, 56, 57, 60, 67, 75, 76, 84-85, 90-91, 93-95, 104-107, 109, 115, 117-118, 120, 141, 144-145, 148, 150, 168, 172, 177, 191-192, 201-207, 257, 258, 264, 267, 274, 285-286, 289, 304, 308, 314, 318, 321; ecstatic, 145-146, 150, 201-202; transforming, 37, 38, 67, 75, 93-95, 168, 201-203, 204, 206, 258; consummated, 94, 202; rapture and, 145-146, 202; visions and, 145; conforming, 29, 33, 49, 56, 60, 67, 72-73, 206, 264, 266; spiritual, 93-95, 120, 172, 201-202, 203-204, 264, 314; mystical, 37-38, 56, 67, 72-73, 90, 93-95, 97, 141, 145, 192, 202-203, 258, 264, 314

Unitive way: 320

Unknowing: cloud of, 103, 118-122; know God by, 103, 118-122

Victim: sacrificial, 12, 25, 26, 28, 34, 39, 48, 57, 59, 65, 70, 74, 83, 93, 133, 144, 148, 183, 259, 319; of love, 25, 26, 32, 39-40, 48, 59, 65-66, 70, 72, 83, 86, 87, 89, 97-98, 102, 153, 154-155, 157, 167-168, 171-172, 176, 179, 265, 272, 273, 274, 276; vow of, 59, 66, 67, 149; marked, 59, 63, 65, 127, 131-133, 134-140, 161, 182, 260, 309, 311-312, 315; role of, 12, 38, 58-61, 63, 65-66, 69-70, 91, 107, 125, 139, 161, 183; expiatory, 12, 28, 39, 63, 66, 71-74, 176, 182, 188, 310; suffering, 12, 26, 28-29, 36, 41, 58, 62, 67, 68, 72, 87, 91, 94, 96, 107, 114, 124, 144, 148, 150, 151, 157, 161, 168, 182, 184, 195-198, 200, 208, 228, 275, 321; chosen, 55, 59, 62, 65, 67, 69, 74, 83, 85, 89, 129, 139, 183, 203, 264, 270, 272, 275

Vision: beatific, 106, 118, 207, 304

Visions: of the suffering Christ, 70, 145, 150-151, 167-171, 208, 225-226, 226-227, 257-258, 260-261, 274, 281-282, 284; ecstatic, 97, 164, 167, 170, 198, 199, 266, 270, 275, 279, 281, 309; of the Passion, 150-151, 167, 169, 208, 225-228, 279, 281; mystical, 157, 160, 282; corporeal, 160; apparitions and, 34-36, 145, 159-161, 167, 311; interior, 102, 159; imaginative, 159, 320; intellectual, 159, 320; and locutions, 159-160, 265; types of, 145, 159, 167-168, 265, 271, 274, 277; celestial, 152, 159, 160, 167-168, 206, 260, 263, 320; angelic, 146, 160, 167; the devil causes, 9, 159, 160, 295, 310-311, 317-318, 320; authentic, 9, 34-36, 160, 263, 320; supernatural, 159, 160-161, 220, 263; corporal, 159, 160, 161, 304; of incorporeal substances, 160; of Apostles, 258, 282; of saints, 258, 260, 270-271, 281; of Mary, 258, 260-261, 265, 270, 278, 281, 284, 295; of angels; 260, 270, 284; physical, 320

Visit: celestial, 25, 34, 36, 98, 102-103, 104, 150, 162, 165, 166-167, 193-195, 265, 273, 277, 279, 281, 284

Vocation: 26, 41, 58-59, 63, 66, 67, 70, 72, 85, 97, 107, 125, 127, 139, 145, 183, 262, 273-274, 277, 282, 283, 288, 292

Warfare: spiritual, 107, 109, 161, 182, 295-296, 315

Way of perfection: (see Perfection: way of)

World: supernatural, 9, 13, 30, 40, 59, 90, 102, 127, 131, 218-219, 257; temporal, 19, 27, 30-31, 34, 36-37, 42, 45-46, 48-49, 51, 54-55, 57-58, 62, 63-66, 67-70, 73-77, 80, 83, 85-86, 88, 93-94, 97, 104, 106-107, 109, 110, 116, 120-122, 124, 127-128, 130-131, 132-133, 135, 141, 148, 149, 183, 185, 187, 189, 196, 201, 208, 211, 219, 220, 229, 232, 256, 273-274, 276-277, 289

Wounds: sacred, 11, 58, 67, 148, 169, 184, 186, 193-194, 198, 99, 256-257, 258, 260, 262, 264, 280-281, 284, 289; self-inflicted, 124, 217; of the soul, 16, 114, 123-124, 145, 168, 197, 198, 206, 312; mystical, 16, 193-195, 260, 264, 309, 320; exterior, 9, 11, 64, 71, 123, 149, 151, 153, 190-191, 195, 196, 198-200, 210, 258, 278, 281-284, 295,

Name Index

Abraham: 60

Acts, the Book of: Paul and, 37-38; on suffering, 37-38

Adam: Original Sin and, 18, 36; descendants of, 18

Agatha, St.: vision of, 166

Agnes of Jesus, Mother: inedia, 187; stigmata, 199; gift of perfume, 199; visions of, 199; ecstasies of, 199

Agnes of Montepulciano, St.: bodily aroma of, 188

Agnes, St.: Gertrude the Great and, 167; Anne Catherine Emmerich and, 167

Agostino, Padre, O.F.M. Cap. (of San Marco in Lamis, Italy): Padre Pio's letters to, 17, 142, 164-165, 183, 194, 196; Padre Pio and, 163-165, 183, 194, 196, 197, 284

Alacoque, St. Margaret Mary: as victim soul, 96, 267-268; fire of divine love, 96; suffering and, 185, 267; Autobiography, 268; Blessed Eucharist, 154; enraptured state, 154; illnesses of, 185, 267; Letters of, 268; the Passion and, 267-268; crown of thorns, 268; visions of, 267; Blessed Virgin Mary, 267; Ursuline Order, 267; Satan and, 267; Sacred Heart Messages, 267, 273; Pope Clement XIII, 267

Aldegonde, St.: bodily aroma of, 188

Alexandrina da Costa: Evil Spirit and, 135-136; Passion ecstasies of, 136, 151-152, 170, 278-279; the Cross and, 136, 151-152, 170; as victim soul, 136, 279; verbal assaults from the devil, 135-136, 279; diabolical attacks, 135-136, 279; the crucifix and, 135-136; threats from the Evil One, 135, 136; sufferings of, 136, 151-152, 185, 278; invisible stigmata of, 136, 151, 278; Father Pinho and, 170; Dr. Azevedo and, 170; illnesses of, 185, 278; Holy Eucharist, 175, 278-279; heavenly perfume, 279; visions of, 170, 278-279; Fr. Terca and, 170; examinations of, 170; crown of thorns, 278; inedia, 278

Aloysius, St.: visions of, 167-168

Altotting: Bavaria, West Germany: Therese Neumann, 281, 286, 299-300

Alverna, Mt.: Italy, 256

Ambrose, St.: meaning of prayer, 95; temptations of the devil, 134

Amos (the Prophet): love between God and His people, 21

Anderson, Bernard W.: 21

Andriani, Maria Rose: inedia of, 186

Angel, guardian: (see Topical Index)

Angela of Foligno, Blessed: stigmatist, 185; total abstinence of, 185, 187; state of ecstasy, 194; transformation, 206; mystical union, 206; conforming union, 206; the spiritual marriage, 206

Angela of the Cross, Blessed: 173

Angela della Pace: side wound of, 199; stigmata of, 199

Anselm, St.: the Immaculate Heart of Mary and, 33

Anthony of Egypt, St.: vision of, 282

Anthony of Padua, St.: the Cross and, 152; gift of bilocation, 156; vision of, 167; Mary Rose Ferron, 274

Antioch: 38

Apollonia, St.: vision of, 167

Apostles: the Twelve, 86-89, 167

Aquinas, St. Thomas: *Summa Theologica*, 130, 132, 135, 153; the devil, 130, 132; assaults of demons, 130, 135; resisting temptation, 135; on rapture, 153; ecstasy, 153; vision of, 167, 205

Arintero, Father John G., O.P.: mysticism, 90; mystical life, 90, 207; *The Mystical Evolution*; 91, 155, 191-192, 193, 206-207; rapture, 155; transformation, 91, 193; heavenly marriage, 206-207; divine touches, 90, 191-192; espousal, 206-207; divine seal, 193

Athens: St. Paul at, 38

Augustine, St.: *City of God*, 130; the devil, 130, 133; on temptation, 133; vision of, 166, 205, 261

Augustinian: stigmatists, 200

Avignon: Catherine of Siena and, 258-259; the Popes of, 258-259

Azevedo, Dr.: Alexandrina da Costa and, 170

340

189-190, 257; levitation of, 156, 257; St. Paul, 166, 258; St. Peter, 166, 258; St. John the Evangelist, 166, 258; St. Teresa of Avila, 263; Berthe Petit, 278; St. Dominic, 156, 257-258; Holy Eucharist, 174, 185, 258; invisible stigmata of, 191, 198, 258; vision of, 166, 205, 282; visions of, 166, 174, 258; Great Schism, 258; Avignon, 258; as Doctor of the Church, 98, 147, 181, 259, 263; raised the dead, 181; inedia, 187, 258; lack of sleep, 181; mystical ring, 205, 258; wound of the heart, 195; the divine arrow, 195

Cecilia, St.: vision of, 166-167

Cerase, Raffaelina: Padre Pio and, 165; dark night of the soul, 177-178; spiritual direction of, 177-178; spiritual condition of, 165, 177-178; spiritual perfection of, 177-178; guardian angel and, 165

Charney, Geoffrey de: Shroud of Turin, 146

Christ: visions of, 145, 160, 167-169, 226-227, 258, 260-261, 265, 267-268, 272-273, 277, 279, 282, 284, 286, 302-303, 306; apparitions of, 145, 160, 169, 205, 302-303, 317; (also see Topical Index)

Christina Mary of the Cross: stigmatist, 200

Church of San Damiano: St. Francis of Assisi and, 255

Church of Santo Domingo: St. Rose of Lima and, 190

Church of St. Lambert, Cross of: Anne Catherine Emmerich and, 270

Clare, St.: St. Francis of Assisi and, 256; Anne Catherine Emmerich and, 166

Clare of Montefalco, St.: as incorruptible, 190

Claire dei Rimini, St.: bodily aroma of, 188

Claver, Peter: vision of, 282

Clement of Alexandria: meaning of prayer, 95

Clement X, Pope: St. Rose of Lima and, 266

Clement XIII, Pope: St. Margaret Mary Alacoque and, 267

Climatus, St. John: the devil, 134

Colombe dei Rietie, St.: inedia, 187

Congregation, Sacred: the process of canonization, 14; authentication of miracles, 14; Ordinary Process, 14

Constantineau, Dr.: Mary Rose Ferron and, 213

Convent of the Incarnation: St. Teresa of Avila and, 264

Corinth: St. Paul and, 38

Cortona, St. Margaret: Purgatory and, 181; raised the dead, 181; cures of, 181; as stigmatist, 181

Council of Constantinople: *The Decree on Original Sin*, 130; spirits of darkness, 130

Council of Florence: the redemption, 132; dominion of Satan, 132

Council, Fourth Lateran: belief in the devil, 131

Council, Second Vatican: on suffering, 48-50; on expiation, 49-50; on sacrifice, 48-49; on evil, 45; on the devil, 44-45, 131-132; Original Sin, 44; sinful acts, 45-46; acts of charity, 46-47; history of, 42; documents of, 42-43

Council of Trent: on the spirits of darkness, 131-132; St. Paul and the, 131-132

Creator: God as, 14

Creed, Niceno-Constantinopolitan: 181

Cyprian, St., *Mortality*, 130; the devil, 130; vision of, 166

Cyrene: Simon of, 148

Damascene, St. John: on prayer, 95

David, King: the wisdom of, 24; the journey through life, 24

Delaporte, Father: sinners, 130; the Evil One, 130-131

Delicia, Giovanni di: Five Wounds of, 200

Denis, St.: vision of, 166

Deschamps, Cardinal: Louise Lateau and, 215-216

Devil: see Topical Index

Diego, Juan: the Blessed Virgin and, 34

Dodo of Hascha, Blessed: side wound of, 199

Dominic, St.: bodily aroma of, 188; St. Rose of Lima and, 266; St. Catherine of Siena and, 258-259

Dominic dei Paradise: inedia, 187; sweet scented wounds of, 188

Dominicans: as stigmatists, 200

Dorothea, St.: vision of, 166

Donahue, Douglas: Shroud of Turin, 229

343

Innocent III, Pope: warning from, 52; sinful nature, 52; punishment for Original Sin, 52; St. Francis of Assisi and, 256; Osanna of Cascia and, 262

Irenaeus: *Against Heresies*, 130; the devil, 130; worship of Satan, 130

Isaac: 60

Isaiah (the Prophet): the suffering servant, 21, 27-28; punishment of the Lord, 22; patience, 23; consolation to the afflicted, 23-24

Isidore, St.: vision of, 166

Jahenny, Marie-Julie: inedia, 186

James the Apostle: 87-88

James, the Book of: on suffering, 87-88

Jeanne de Chantal: vision of, 282

Jeannie de Jesus-Marie: wounds of, 200

Jeannie Marie de la Croix: sweet scented wounds of, 188

Jeremiah (the Prophet): sinful things, 23

Job: the sufferings of, 15-17; the Evil Spirit and, 15-16

John the Baptist: vision of, 261

John of the Cross, St.: *The Precautions*, 75; dark night of the senses, 106-107, 110, 306-307; dark night of the soul, 105, 120, 192, 218, 307; the devil, 75, 108, 159-160, 316-317; *The Dark Night*, 92, 103, 106, 112-113, 141-142, 144, 192; St. Teresa of Avila and, 91, 156, 263; contemplation and, 92, 103; illumination, 141-142, 144; *The Ascent of Mount Carmel*, 92, 98-99, 110, 115, 120, 141, 142, 159-160; the stigmata, 197; wounds of love, 195, 197; mysticism of, 92; passive states and experiences, 92, 307; active states and experiences, 307; meditation, 98-99; discursive acts, 98-99, 103; mortification, 110; self-denial, 110, 307; on pride, 110-111; on spiritual gluttony, 111, 112; on spiritual avarice, 111; on lust, 111; on anger, 112; imperfections, spiritual, 110, 307; on spiritual envy, 110, 113; on sloth, 110, 113; spiritual exercises, 111-113, 115; appetites, 115; divine light, 142; infused contemplation, 142; visions, 159-160, 316-317; locutions, 159-160; the spiritual marriage, 203-205; the spiritual betroth-

al, 202; odor of sanctity, 187; perfume, 187; discernment, 159-160; visible wounds, 197; invisible wounds, 197; divine union, 204-205, 307; phantasm, 316-317; revelations, 159-160; touch of divine love, 192; Seraph's assault, 195; *The Spiritual Canticle* 187, 204; *The Living Flame of Love*, 197, 204-205

John the Evangelist: vision of, 166, 258, 282

John of St. Samson, Venerable: on God, 93

John Paul II, Pope: new Marian Year, 33; everlasting judgment, 52; on sinners, 52; on Hell, 52; on Purgatory, 52; attitudes towards the Cross, 54; mission of the Church, 54; St. Francis of Assisi and, 256-257; St. Teresa of Avila and, 264

Johnston, William: on The Cloud of Unknowing, 118-119; cloud of forgetting, 118; unknowing, 118-119

Joseph of Copertino, St.: levitations of, 156; bodily aroma of, 188

Justina, St.: vision of, 166

Kaspar, Dr. Karl: Therese Neumann, 218

Kempis, Thomas a: The Imitation of Christ, 133, 259; on temptation, 133; St. Lydwine and, 259

Knock: Mary and, 35

Konnersreuth: Bavaria, West Germany: Therese Neumann, 6, 9, 299-300

Konnersreuth Circle: Therese Neumann and, 299-300

Konrad, St.: 299

Konrad Monastery, St.: 299

Kowalska, Sister Faustina: invisible stigmata, 277; *Diary*, 276; Purgatory, 277; Hell, 277; Infant Jesus and, 277; crown of thorn wounds, 277; visions of, 276-277; victim of love, 276; dark night, 277

Kumi, Josepha: wounds of, 200

Labis, Bishop of Tournai: Louise Lateau and, 215

Lassagne, Catherine: diabolical operations, 132-133; ordinary operations, 132-133; the devil, 132-133; infestation, 133; external possession, 133

Martin V, Pope: Catherine of Siena, 258-259

Mary: her subliminal role, 31, 172; as Mother of God, 31, 32-33, 37, 172; humble of heart, 31; as virgin, 31; trusting, 31; in God's plan of salvation, 31, 36, 172; as Co-Redemptrix, 31-34; suffering of, 31-34, 37; her mission, 31-34, 37; the Passion of Our Lord, 32, 34; Immaculate Heart of, 12; as possible stigmatist, 32; as Mediatrix, 31, 34, 172; Our Lady of Sorrows, 34; vision of, 160, 163, 166, 171, 205, 258, 260-261, 263, 265, 267, 272, 278, 279-280, 282, 284, 302, 306, 317

Mary of the Crown: foot wound of, 199

Mary of the Holy Trinity, Sr.: as victim, 65, 67; revelations of, 65-66, 67, 309; *The Spiritual Legacy*, 65; Eucharistic life, 66, 67, 309; vow of victim, 66, 67; reparation, 71

Mary of the Incarnation, Venerable: mystical marriage, 207

Mary of Jesus Crucified: as Carmelite stigmatist, 124; wounds of, 124, 200

Mary Frances of the Five Wounds, St.: stigmatist, 269; Holy Eucharist, 174; Passion ecstasies of, 270; Franciscan Order, 269; stigmata of, 269; prophecy, 269; trials of, 269; Purgatory, 269

Mary Magdalen dei Pazzi, St.: stigmatist, 199, 265; Passion of Our Lord, 157, 265; Purgatory and, 161, 269; ecstasy of, 161, 206; wounds of, 174, 199, 265; preserved body of, 265; mystical marriage, 206; locutions, 265; illnesses of, 265; visions of, 206, 265; dark night, 265; transformation of, 193, 206; beauty after death, 188; bodily aroma of, 188, 265; St. Catherine dei Ricci and, 157

Mathilda of Hackeborn, St.: 33, 191

Maximus the Confessor, St.: on pure prayer, 95; Centuries on Charity, 95

Mayr, Dr. Franz X.: Therese Neumann, 218-219

Medjugorje: as Marian devotion center, 35-37; the Church and, 35-37

Menard, St.: bodily aroma of, 188

Menendez, Sr. Josefa: as victim soul, 70, 169, 182, 273-274; as stigmatist, 71, 137, 169, 171, 274; *The*

Way of Divine Love and, 102, 137, 169-170, 171, 273; visions of, 169, 171, 273-274; revelations of, 70; words from Our Lord to, 70-71; diabolical attacks, 137, 139-140, 182, 273; Sacred Heart of Jesus and, 70, 169, 273; Crown of Thorns, 169, 274; Blessed Virgin and, 171; as Coadjutrix Sister, 70, 137, 169, 273; Fr. Rubio and, 273; Purgatory and, 274, 278; Pope Pius XII and, 274; St. Margaret Mary Alacoque and, 273; reparation and, 70, 182; on hell, 278

Merton, Thomas: *New Seeds of Contemplation*, 102; on the dark night of the soul, 119; knowledge of God, 119

Micah (the Prophet): Israel's Exile, 18; sins of God's people, 18

Michael the Archangel, St.: prayer to, 132; the devil and, 127, 132, 163; Anne Catherine Emmerich and, 163; bodily vision of, 162

Miraculous Medal: 34

Morice, Madeleine: stigmata of, 199

Moses: burning bush experience, 13

Naber, Father Joseph: on Therese Neumann, 146, 157-158, 174, 211

Neri, St. Philip: levitations of, 156; St. Catherine dei Ricci and, 265

Neumann, Therese: stigmatist, 11, 170-171, 200, 210-213, 280-281, 286-287; sufferings of, 151, 171, 185, 199, 212, 280-281; Passion ecstasies, 150-151, 170-171, 212, 224-225, 226, 299, 300-301; gifts of, 157, 281; as victim soul, 281; Albert Vogl and, 6, 151, 170-171, 299; Johannes Steiner and, 146, 150, 171, 176, 178-179, 211; gift of perfume, 281; bilocation and, 146-281; crown of thorn wounds, 171, 280-281, 287, 300; scourge wounds of, 171, 280-281; inedia of, 186, 213; Konnersreuth, 6, 186, 199, 280-281, 300; Fr. Ulrich Vey, O.F.M. Cap. and, 6, 281, 287, 299-301; Fr. Anton Vogl and, 6, 281, 300; bleeding of, 171, 200, 211, 300; Eucharist and, 174-175, 186; guardian angel of, 166; Therese of Lisieux and, 166, 280-281; visions of, 146, 150-151, 166-167, 171, 224-227, 281; saints and, 166-167; hierognosis, 178, 281; blessed objects and, 179;

physical disorders of, 280; sleep and, 188, 281; Five Sacred Wounds of, 11, 186, 199, 200, 210-213, 227, 280-281, 300; prophecy,281; beatification of, 300; examinations of, 210-213, 218, 281; relics of,300; Eichstatt, 300; cures of illnesses, 166, 280; kardiognosis, 175, 281; Shroud of Turin and, 224-227; St. Francis of Assisi and, 211, 281; Pope Pius XII and, 157-158

Nicodemus, St.: vision of, 166

Nicolas of Flue, Blessed: inedia, 187

Nicolas of Myra: gift of bilocation, 156

Nicholas of Tolentio, St.: Rita of Cascia and, 261

Nierklutsch, Crescentia: wounds of, 200

Ock, Marie: side wound of, 199

Onofrio of Fiamenga: side wound of, 199

Order of Poor Clares: St. Veronica Giuliani and, 268; St. Clare and, 256

Origen: De Principiis, 130; the devil, 130

Osanna of Mantua, Blessed: the invisible stigmata of, 190, 198; Third Order of St. Dominic, 262; Purgatory, 262; Five Sacred Wounds of, 190, 262; Pope Innocent XII, 262; incorruptible body of, 190, 262; trials of, 262; ecstasies of, 262; raptures of, 262; the Blessed Virgin Mary and, 262; mystical ring, 205

Our Lady of Grace Friary: Padre Pio and, 283-284, 290

Pannullo, Salvatore: Padre Pio and, 165

Paray: Visitation convent of, 267

St. Margaret Mary Alacoque and, 267-268

Parente, Father Alessio, O.F.M. Cap.: (Padre Pio's close friend and aide); guardian angels, 163, 165; Padre Pio, 6, 158, 171, 210, 290-292; disappearance of wounds, 210; on charity, 292; interview with, 6, 165, 286, 290-292; St. Francis of Assisi, 292

Parente, Paschal: St. Michael the Archangel, 162; Satan, 162

Paschal, St.: 166

Paul, St.: centrality of the Cross, 29, 38, 39-40; sufferings of, 27, 37-40, 41, 86-87; as possible stigmatist, 41-42; trials of, 37-39; missionary journeys of, 37-38; mystical life of, 40; the devil and, 39-40; vocation of,39, 87; teaching of, 12, 13, 37-41, 112, 153, 156, 181, 186, 190-191, 201; the Cross and, 29, 40; as victim soul, 39-40; the Passion of Christ, 27, 40; on love, 39-40, 68; supernatural states, 38-39, 153, 156; vision of, 166, 258

Paul of the Cross, St.: levitations of, 156

Paul of Moll, Fr.: 100

Paul VI, Pope: Marialus Cultus, 34; helping others who suffer, 54, 68-69; Paenitemini, 68-69, 72, 108; atonement and, 69; expiation and, 72; mortification, 108-109; physical discipline, 108; abstinence, 108; fasting,108; penance, 108-109; on evil, 127-128; General Audience Address, 127-128; on the devil, 127-128; St. Catherine of Siena and, 259; St. Teresa of Avila and,259

Paula, St.: vision of, 166

Perez, Catherine: foot wound of, 199

Perpetua, St.: vision of, 166

Peter, St.: Paul and, 38; sufferings of, 87-88; healings of, 180; vision of,166, 258

Peter of Alcantara, St.: levitations of, 156; inedia, 181; St. Teresa of Avila and, 263

Petit, Berthe: messages about our Lady, 33, 278; The World League of Reparation to the Sorrowful and Immaculate Heart of Mary, 278; invisible stigmata, 278; inedia, 277; visions of, 277-278; illnesses of, 277; crown of thorns, 278; St. Catherine of Siena and, 278

Peyret, Rev. Raymond: Marthe Robin, 170, 219

Philippe, Father Thomas, O.P.: affective knowledge,121

Pia, Secondo: Shroud of Turin, 222-223

Piccirillo, Fr. Giacomo: Padre Pio and, 210

Pietrelcina, Italy: Padre Pio and, 283, 290

Pilate, Pontius: 87

Pinho, Father: Alexandrina da Costa and, 170

Pio, Padre (of Pietrelcina): compared with Job, 17; the Cross and, 64, 148-149, 284; the sufferings of, 17, 64, 122-123, 124, 138-139, 142-143, 148, 167-168, 171, 183-185, 194-195, 197-198, 218, 283-284; the dark night and, 107, 122-123, 202, 218, 294; spiritual directors of, 64-65, 113-114, 123, 142, 148-149, 183, 284; on Purgatory, 65; the wounds of, 11, 148-149, 167-168, 194-197, 200, 209-210, 284, 297-298; on meditation, 99; *The Agony of Jesus*, 99; *The Epistolario*, 64-65, 102, 123-124, 138-139, 196, 284; Fr. Alessio Parente, O.F.M. Cap., 6, 158, 163, 165, 286, 290-292; Fr. Joseph Martin, O.F.M. Cap.,6, 8, 17, 93-94, 117-118, 123, 138, 165, 286, 290-292; Passion of Jesus, 99, 149; his spiritual state, 123, 202, 218; his stigmata, 124, 148-149, 167-168, 194-197, 209-210; temptations of, 284; gift of perfume, 188-189; reading of souls, 176-177, 284; William Carrigan and, 6, 297-298; Mary Pile and, 6; San Giovanni Rotondo and, 6, 8, 17, 158, 283-284; as victim, 147-148, 284; Eucharist, 154; enraptured experience of, 154; guardian angel of, 163-165, 284; Raffaelina Cerase and, 176-178; Mary and, 163, 171, 283-284, 294-295, 296; parents of, 283; the Rosary, 171, 283, 294-295; the devil and, 17, 137-139, 163-164, 171, 183, 284, 295-295; radiance of, 155; inedia, 284; odor of sanctity, 284; as deacon, 283; illnesses of, 283-284; military service, 284; as confessor, 284, 291; prophecy, 284; depression of, 291; beatification of,292; the Mass, 297; Pietrelcina, 283; ordination of, 283; examination by doctors, 209-210, 218; divine union, 202; desire for suffering, 196; transverberation, 194-195; wound of the heart, 194-195, 209-210; bilocation,158, 188, 284, 295; Our Lady of Grace Friary, 158, 171, 283-284, 290; visions of, 163-164, 167-168, 170-171, 284; gift of languages, 176; seraph, 167-168, 194-195, 284; kardiognosis, 176-178; as director, 176-178, 297; as Capuchin,283; raised the dead, 181;

healings of, 182, 284; lack of sleep, 188, 284, 291; high temperatures, 189; St. Francis of Assisi and, 283, 292

Pio X, Father Fernando of Riese, O.F.M. Cap.: Padre Pio and, 122-123; moral sufferings of Padre Pio, 122-123

Pius II, Pope: Catherine of Siena and, 259

Pius XI, Pope: trials and tribulations, 72-73; Christ's expiatory suffering,71-73; *Miserentissimus Redemptor*, 71-72; *Enarrationes in Psalmos*, 72; Catherine of Siena, 259

Pius XII, Pope: the reality of suffering, 51-52; sin, 52; wisdom of, 51-52; evangelical poverty, 55; charity towards our neighbor, 55-56; Mary and, 32; Therese Neumann and, 157-158; St. Catherine of Siena and, 259

Pontmain: Mary and, 35

Portiuncula: St. Francis and, 256

Pseudo-Dionysius: *Mystical Theology*, 121; St. Paul and, 121; darkness, 121; darkness of unknowing, 121

Purgatory: Padre Pio on, 64; the reality of, 18, 160-161, 166; (also see Topical Index)

Quinzani, Blessed Stephana: wounds of, 199-200

Raymond dei Pennafort, St.: bodily aroma of, 188

Religious: stigmatists, 200

Rita of Cascia, St: stigmatist, 190, 260-261; Augustinian Convent, 260-261; penances of, 260-261; crown of thorn wounds, 260-261; St. James of the Marches,260-261; Blessed Mother and, 260-261; Basilica of St. Rita, 190; bees, 261; incorruptibility of, 261; gift of perfume, 260-261

Ritter, Emmeram H.: (Promoter of the Cause for Therese Neumann's Beatification, Regensburg, Bavaria, West Germany), 6

Ritter, Dr. Leo: Therese Neumann, 211

Robin, Marthe: as lay stigmatist, 125, 139, 151, 170, 285-286; aban-

ecstasy and, 145, 201-202; rapture and, 154; levitations of, 156-157; the spiritual marriage, 203-204; the spiritual espousal, 195, 203; Augustinians, 263; Carmelite Order, 263; Fr. Rubeo and, 263; Blessed Virgin and, 263; Pope John Paul II and, 264; transformation, 154, 201-202; transportation, 154, 157; prayer, 157, 160; counseling, 160; confessor, 160; vision of, 166; visions of, 263; raised the dead, 181; transverberation, 263; incorruptible heart of, 190, 263; as Doctor of the Church, 181, 263; gift of perfume, 188, 263; wound of love, 190; divine touch, 192; wound of the heart, 193-194; wound of the soul, 195; divine union of, 201-204; flights of the spirit, 202; ecstatic union, 201-202; St. Peter of Alcantara and, 263; St. Catherine of Siena and, 263; Pope Gregory XIII and, 263; Pope Paul VI and, 263; St. Veronica Giuliani and, 268

Tertullian: on demons, 130; the devil, 130; *Apology*, 130; *The Testimony of the Christian Soul*, 130

Therese of Lisieux, St.: Therese Neumann and, 166, 189, 281

Thessalonica: St. Paul and, 38

Thomas, doubting: 63

Thomas of Celano: St. Francis' stigmata, 214-215

Thomas of Villanova, St.: bodily aroma of, 188

Tribbe, Frank C.: Shroud of Turin, 228-229, 230-231

Turin Commission: 229

Ugolino of Mantua, Blessed: side wound of, 199

Urban VI, Pope: Catherine of Siena and, 258

Urban VII, Pope: Catherine of Siena and, 198

Urban VIII, Pope: decree of, 10

Ursula, St.: vision of, 166

Ursulines, as stigmatists, 200

Valfre, St. Sebastian: the Cross, 152

Vatican II, Council of: Pope John XXIII and, 42; Pope Paul VI and, 42; documents of, 32, 42-50, 61-62, 131-132

Venafro: Padre Pio and, 283

Vey, Father Ulrich, O.F.M. Cap.: (Vice-Postulator for the Cause of Therese Neumann's Beatification); interview with, 6, 286-287, 299-301; meaning of stigmata, 301; Therese Neumann, 6, 281, 286-287, 300-301; Our Lady of Altotting, 286; St. Konrad Monastery, 9, 281, 286; wounds of the stigmata, 300; living stigmatists, 286, 300; Shroud of Turin, 300; beatification, 300; relics of Therese Neumann, 300-301; St. Paul as possible stigmatist, 301; Albert Vogl, 286

West Germany; Postulator for the Cause of Therese Neumann's Beatification), 6, 281, 300; *The Voice of Padre Pio*, 290

Willibrod, St.: bodily aroma of, 188

Willis, Dr. David: Shroud of Turin, 228

Wilson, Ian: Shroud of Turin, 228

Wolfgang, St.: vision of, 166

Xavier, St. Francis: gift of bilocation, 156

Zagnoni, Pudentienne: stigmatist, 140, 200; Satan and, 140; wounds of, 200

Zanic, Bishop Pavao (of Mostar, Yugoslavia): Medjugorje and, 36

Zebedee, son of: 82

Zeuli, Tino: Shroud of Turin, 224

Zophar: Job and, 15